Systems of Production

'Deregulate and be flexible': that has been the message from US and UK governments for the past twenty years. High unemployment in Europe is blamed on inflexible labour markets and the high cost of welfare services. But is social policy a drain on enterprise? Or can it be a productive factor that can underpin economic growth and employment opportunities? That is one of the questions answered in this book, which analyses the role of labour market and employment policies, as well as social policy, as productive factors.

The authors draw on Frank Wilkinson's notion of productive systems. The impressive array of expert contributors include Charles Craypo (University of Notre Dame), Robert Forrant (University of Massachusetts at Lowell) and Jane Humphries (University of Oxford), as well as Frank Wilkinson (University of Cambridge and Birkbeck College, University of London).

This comprehensive yet accessible book will be required reading across a variety of disciplines including labour economics, business and management and political economy. *Systems of Production* will appeal to all those with an interest in economic policy issues, as well as to policy makers themselves.

Brendan Burchell is a Senior Lecturer in the Department of Social and Political Sciences at the University of Cambridge.

Simon Deakin is the Robert Monks Professor of Corporate Governance at the Centre for Business Research and Judge Institute of Management, University of Cambridge.

Jonathan Michie is the Sainsbury Professor of Management at Birkbeck College, University of London.

Jill Rubery is Professor of Comparative Employment Systems and Director of the European Work and Employment Research Centre at the Manchester School of Management, UMIST.

Contemporary political economy series

Edited by Jonathan Michie

Birkbeck College, University of London, UK

This series presents a fresh, broad perspective on the key issues in the modern world economy, drawing in perspectives from management and business, politics and sociology economic history and law.

Written in a lively and accessible style, it will present focused and comprehensive introductions to key topics, demonstrating the relevance of political economy to major debates in economics and to an understanding of the contemporary world.

Global Instability
The political economy of world economic governance
Edited by Jonathan Michie and John Grieve Smith

Reconstructing Political Economy
The great divide in economic thought
William K. Tabb

The Political Economy of Competitiveness
Employment, public policy and corporate performance
Michael Kitson and Jonathan Michie

Global Economy, Global Justice
Theoretical objections and policy alternatives to neoliberalism
George F. DeMartino

Social Capital versus Social Theory
Political economy and social science at the turn of the millennium
Ben Fine

A New Guide to Post Keynesian Economics
Steven Pressman and Richard Holt

Placing the Social Economy
Ash Amin, Angus Cameron and Ray Hudson

Systems of Production
Markets, organisations and performance
Edited by Brendan Burchell, Simon Deakin, Jonathan Michie and Jill Rubery

Systems of Production

Markets, organisations and performance

Edited by
Brendan Burchell, Simon Deakin,
Jonathan Michie and Jill Rubery

Routledge
Taylor & Francis Group

LONDON AND NEW YORK

First published 2003
by Routledge
11 New Fetter Lane, London EC4P 4EE

Simultaneously published in the USA and Canada
by Routledge
29 West 35th Street, New York, NY 10001

Routledge is an imprint of the Taylor & Francis Group

Typeset in Baskerville by
Newgen Imaging Systems (P) Ltd, Chennai, India
Printed and bound in Great Britain by
MPG Books Ltd, Bodmin

British Library Cataloguing in Publication Data
A catalogue record for this book is available from the British Library

Library of Congress Cataloging in Publication Data
Systems of production markets, organisations and performance /
[edited by] Jonathan Michie ... [et al.].
    p. cm. – (Contemporary political economy; 8)
    Includes bibliographical references and index.
    1. Industrial organization (Economic theory) 2. Organizational
effectiveness. 3. Labor economics. 4. Industrial relations. I. Michie,
Jonathan. II. Contemporary political economy series; 8.

HD2326 .S978 2002
338–dc21   2002026931

ISBN 0-415-28283-7

Contents

List of figures   vii
List of tables   ix
List of contributors   xi
Preface   xiii

1 Productive systems: introduction and overview   1
JILL RUBERY, BRENDAN BURCHELL, SIMON DEAKIN,
AND JONATHAN MICHIE

2 Productive systems and the structuring role of   10
economic and social theories
FRANK WILKINSON

3 Productive systems, markets and competition   40
as 'Instituted Economic Process'
MARK HARVEY

4 Inter-organisational trust, boundary spanners   60
and communities of practice
EDWARD LORENZ

5 Social rights and the market: an evolutionary   74
perspective
SIMON DEAKIN

6 Working like a dog, sick as a dog: job   89
intensification in the late twentieth century
DAVID LADIPO, ROY MANKELOW AND BRENDAN BURCHELL

7 **The decline of union bargaining power in the United States: an 'ability to pay, ability to make pay' analysis**   104
CHARLES CRAYPO

8 **Creative work systems in destructive markets**   129
SUZANNE J. KONZELMANN AND ROBERT FORRANT

9 **German industrial relations in a period of transition**   159
ULRICH MÜCKENBERGER

10 **Labour 'flexibility' – securing management's right to manage badly?**   178
JONATHAN MICHIE AND MAURA SHEEHAN

11 **The political economy of the minimum wage**   192
PETER BROSNAN

12 **Economic functioning, self-sufficiency and full employment**   213
ROGER TARLING AND FRANK WILKINSON

13 **Equal opportunities as a productive factor**   236
JILL RUBERY, JANE HUMPHRIES, COLETTE FAGAN, DAMIAN GRIMSHAW AND MARK SMITH

14 **Decent work as a development objective**   263
GERRY RODGERS

Index   279

Figures

4.1	Degrees of inter-personal trust	64
6.1	The percentage of employees experiencing an increase in the speed of work	90
6.2	The percentage of employees experiencing an increase in the effort they put into their jobs	90
6.3	Change in per cent of respondents working at speed and to tight deadlines all or almost all of the time, 1991–96	91
6.4	Mean GHQ scores by how much pressure people felt from work mates or colleagues	93
6.5	Headaches and working at speed	95
6.6	Headaches, working at speed and sector	95
6.7	Scores for job-related tension in the home	96
6.8	The percentage of respondents who agreed with the statement that: 'In this organisation, managers and employees are on the same side'	99
13.1	Percentage change in employees in employment, after redistribution of hours, 1996	248
13.2	Gender wage gap in the European Union, 1995	254

Tables

6.1	Proportion experiencing work-related complaints, by speed of work and tightness of deadlines	94
7.1	The sources of union bargaining power	105
7.2	Change in US private sector employment and employment shares, 1957–99	111
7.3	Hourly earnings of autoworkers and other US production workers, 1950–90	113
7.4	Changes in the number of hourly workers covered by UAW contracts in the motor vehicle industry, 1978–99	113
7.5	Union representation by union, major and selected regional carriers, craft or class and size of representation unit, year 2000	117
7.6	Wal-Mart worldwide operating stores, 2000	119
7.7	Union organizing density, bargaining structure and competitive unionism in three representative industries	123
13.1	Alternative economic analyses of equal opportunity policy	237
13.2	Gender differences in employment intensity for higher educated labour	242
13.3	Estimates of the impact of Working Families Tax Credit on Employment Rates	246
13.4	Effects of bearing two children on employment and earnings	250

Contributors

Peter Brosnan is Professor of Industrial Relations at Griffith University, Australia.

Brendan Burchell is a Senior Lecturer in the Department of Social and Political Sciences at the University of Cambridge.

Charles Craypo is Professor Emeritus, Economics Department, University of Notre Dame.

Simon Deakin is the Robert Monks Professor of Corporate Governance at the Centre for Business Research and Judge Institute of Management, University of Cambridge.

Colette Fagan is Senior Lecturer in Sociology in the Department of Sociology, University of Manchester.

Robert Forrant is Associate Professor in History, Department of Regional Economic and Social Development, University of Massachusetts at Lowell.

Damian Grimshaw is Lecturer in Employment Studies at the Manchester School of Management, UMIST.

Mark Harvey is Senior Research Fellow at the ESRC Centre for Research in Innovation and Competition, University of Manchester.

Jane Humphries is Reader in Economic History, University of Oxford and is a fellow of All Souls. She previously held a readership in the Faculty of Economics and Politics at Cambridge University.

Suzanne J. Konzelmann is Senior Research Fellow, Centre for Business Research, University of Cambridge and Associate Professor in Economics, School of Business and Economics, Indiana University South Bend.

David Ladipo is working for a London consultancy company specialising in corporate governance by the name of 'Institutional Design'. He was previously a lecturer in sociology at the University of Nottingham, and a research associate at the Centre for Business Research, University of Cambridge.

Edward Lorenz is Professor of Economics at the University of Technology of Compiègne, France. He is a Research Associate at both the Centre d'Etudes de l'Emploi, Noisy-le-Grand and Birkbeck, University of London.

Roy Mankelow a Research Associate of the Centre for Business Research at the University of Cambridge.

Jonathan Michie is the Sainsbury Professor of Management at Birkbeck, University of London.

Ulrich Mückenberger is Professor of Labour Law and European Law at the Hamburg University for Economics and Political Science.

Gerry Rodgers is Head of the Policy Integration Department at the International Labour Organisation, Geneva.

Jill Rubery is Professor of Comparative Employment Systems and Director of the European Work and Employment Research Centre at the Manchester School of Management, UMIST.

Maura Sheehan is Associate Professor of Entrepreneurship at the Graduate School of Management, University of Dallas.

Mark Smith is Lecturer in Employment Studies at the Manchester School of Management, UMIST.

Roger Tarling is director of Cambridge Policy Consultants, Cambridge, England.

Frank Wilkinson was previously a Reader in the Department of Applied Economics and is now based at the Centre for Business Research, University of Cambridge. He is also a Visiting Professor at Birkbeck, University of London.

Preface

The idea for this volume arose out of a conference of the International Working Party on Labour Market Segmentation, an informal association of academics and researchers who since the late 1970s have been holding annual conferences to develop an interdisciplinary and institutional approach to the analysis of labour markets and productive systems. In July 2000 the group met at the University of Manchester Institute of Science and Technology (UMIST). The conference took as its theme the application of the notion of productive systems to current academic and policy debates, particularly with respect to the development of the European economy. The title of the conference was 'Towards a productive Europe? Employment and social policy as productive factors?' Deliberate parallels were thereby drawn between the work of the working party, and particularly that of Frank Wilkinson, on the notion of productive systems and the adoption in the late 1990s of the theme 'social policy as a productive factor' as an organizing concept for the work of the Directorate for Employment of the European Commission under the leadership of the then Director-General Allan Larsson.

That conference also marked the retirement of Frank Wilkinson from the Department of Applied Economics at the University of Cambridge in 2001. Frank Wilkinson was one of the founders in 1979 of the International Working Party on Labour Market Segmentation, and has played an active role in the Working Party continuously since then. Frank has since taken up a Visiting Professorship at the School of Management and Organizational Psychology, Birkbeck, University of London, where he is developing a new programme on the Organization of Work, Economics and Labour Law, aimed at trade unionists and others involved in workplace representation.

During a special day long plenary session, papers were presented on the theme of productive systems, out of which have developed many of the chapters included in this volume. The conference was organized by the European Work and Employment Research Centre at UMIST and the editors of this volume would like to thank the Manchester team for their work in organizing the event, namely Jill Rubery, Helen Dean, Mary O'Brien, Mark Smith, Damian Grimshaw, Philip Almond and Rebecca Wilson.

Finally, we are grateful to all at Routledge for their assistance throughout the process of producing this book, and in particular to Terry Clague and Robert Langham.

1 Productive systems

Introduction and overview

Jill Rubery, Brendan Burchell, Simon Deakin and Jonathan Michie

The focus of this book is the concept of 'productive systems' developed by Frank Wilkinson in a paper first published in the *Cambridge Journal of Economics* in 1983. Chapter 2 of the present volume updates and extends the argument made in the original paper. It lays out a distinctive interdisciplinary and institutional approach to the analysis of systems of production. The 1983 paper drew on work carried out by the Labour Studies Group of the Department of Applied Economics at Cambridge in the 1970s and 1980s. Since then, the approach has been widely adopted among a network of researchers meeting annually under the auspices of the International Working Party for Labour Market Segmentation.

The first version of 'Productive Systems' was written at a time when the influence of Keynesian economic thought was clearly on the wane in the face of the revival of neoclassical economic theory. Nearly twenty years on, neoclassical methodology dominates the economics profession, although its influence on other disciplines is limited and there are signs that the wider standing of economics as a subject is suffering as a consequence of its rigid attachment to neoclassical precepts. In terms of policy, it would be premature to assume that the neoliberal agenda which was formed in the early 1980s in Britain and America has necessarily run its course. Adherents of the deregulatory approach regularly call for its extension to continental Europe, Japan and the developing world – all areas which to some degree have so far resisted it. However, in the Anglo-American world, the causal link running from deregulation and market liberalism to greater inequality of income and opportunity, and the growing failure of privatization and marketization to deliver efficient public services, are becoming clearer by the day. This makes it an appropriate time to return to the arguments made in the 1983 paper, and to consider how they may contribute to the kind of refoundation which economics, and economic policy, are so evidently in need of.

Chapter 2 (Wilkinson), in restating the productive systems approach, places at its core the rejection of the claim that there is a set of immutable economic laws, the supposed 'laws of the market', to which institutions must or do conform. The effort of neoclassical economics to deduce the existence of these laws from an arbitrary set of a priori principles is not only fundamentally misguided. It is also highly dangerous from the point of view of policy, since it leads to attempts to force existing institutions into a single, rigid mode. This is what lies behind the rhetoric of 'lifting the burden' of regulation in labour and product markets, and applying market-like mechanisms to the provision of collective goods and services in health and education. Such reforms do not result in perfectly efficient allocations of the kind predicted by the concept of market equilibrium, since that concept is almost completely irrelevant to the real-life conditions under which markets and organizations operate. This is not to say that observed forms of regulation and state provision are always ideal; far from it. However, in order for reforms in these areas to work in the general interest (as opposed to the sectional interests which, in practice, they often end up serving), it is essential for theory to acknowledge that relations between the market, the state, and the forms of production are far more complex and variegated than allowed for in neoclassical economics.

Where neoclassical theory reifies the market and loosens it from its institutional moorings in civil society, the legal system and the organization of the state, the productive systems approach sees these institutions as playing a central role in the constitution and development of productive forces. Systems of production exist at a number of levels: the workplace; the enterprise or firm; the industrial sector or inter-firm network; nation states; and transnational trading blocs. Competition between systems is one of the forces determining their comparative success and survival. However, competition does not work according to the process of linear adjustment implied by the neoclassical model. Rather, systems evolve in a way which is shaped by their history and by the particular institutional environments in which they are located. Productive systems both determine, and are determined by, their institutional settings. Thus competition is not a force of nature; it is structured by institutional forces which determine the direction and pace of change of systems. Hence there is a complex relationship between systems and their environments. Systems evolve just as often in response to an internal dynamic of change, than to shifting external conditions. As a result, the process of change is often unpredictable, and is characterized by sharp discontinuities.

In stressing diversity and the importance of local conditions, the productive systems approach does not neglect certain general conditions which affect all systems operating in a capitalist or market framework. The first and most fundamental of these general conditions is the inequality or asymmetry which exists between capital and labour. This is a function of deeply embedded conventions of property, which allocate residual control and income rights in the assets of most firms to the suppliers of equity capital or, alternatively, but less commonly, to representatives of other external stakeholders such as customers or taxpayers. Most likely through a combination of efficiency (diversification of risk) and historical contingency (absence of general access to finance capital), most workers do not have ownership rights, in this sense, in the organizations for which they work. Hence there is a fundamental and unavoidable separation of interest between capital and labour, and, as a result, the potential for distributional conflict between them. But at the same time, capital and labour are in a relationship of mutual dependence: at a minimum, each needs a certain degree of cooperation from the other if the system of production is to survive and flourish. On this basis, they have the possibility of working together in such a way as to enhance the overall joint product. The central issue for all productive systems, then, is how to achieve and sustain those forms of voluntary cooperation on which the well being of all parties, in the final analysis, depends. This is an issue, at one level, for management theory and practice, and, at another, for the political process.

In the productive systems approach, institutions are thought of as bundles of conventions, norms, laws and practices, some of which are inherited through the force of habit and precedent, and some of which are fashioned to meet particular needs in the manner of legislation. Institutions matter for the process of production, since they shape distributional outcomes, manage risks and set the rules of the game in terms of competition within and between systems. Relevant institutions in this sense include associations in civil society (trade unions, employers' bodies and the professions), the institutions that shape the reproduction of the labour force, including the family and the education and training system, the forms of local, national and transnational government and the legal system. These institutional forces shape the search for conventions of voluntary cooperation in particular contexts, giving rise to particular, local forms of comparative advantage or disadvantage. Efficient productive systems are those in which distributional conflicts are overcome in favour of general agreement on norms of cooperation and cohesion, establishing a virtuous cycle of growth. Inefficient systems, by contrast, are those within which degenerative tendencies towards distributional conflict outweigh efforts at cooperation, thereby engendering a self-reinforcing process of decline.

The evolution of institutional systems and of productive systems is therefore an adaptive process. Distinctive solutions emerge, shaped by local environmental conditions; they may display greater or lesser degrees of efficiency. However, there can be no assumption that the less successful systems will necessarily be 'selected against'. Systems can *survive* even when it is clear to all that there are more successful alternatives; but the costs of institutional change may be so great as to outweigh fundamental reforms. Hence systems may persist, or be destabilized, quite independently of the intensity of external environmental factors. There may well be diffusion of practices through imitation and learning from one system to another, but this inevitably involves an adaptation of general models to local circumstances. In short, what we observe is a non-equilibrium, non-teleological process, in which outcomes are influenced in a non-deterministic way by a variety of internal and external factors.

In this vein, Chapter 3 (Harvey) develops Wilkinson's theoretical framework by arguing that market competition should be understood as an 'instituted' economic process. This means that competition emerges out of historically conditioned forms of production, organization and regulation. Such an approach stands in contrast to neoclassical economics, on the one hand, but also to 'oversociologised' notions of 'embeddedness', on the other, since both reduce economic relations to the micro-level of interpersonal interactions. An institutional focus makes it possible to see, on the contrary, that the form of competition depends on the ways in which the parties to exchange relations are constituted and the relevant property rights and pricing mechanisms are defined. The very formation of separate labour, product and capital markets depends on the 'instituting' of economic processes in this sense. Structural conflict and tension between different forms of instituted processes are a major source of diversity and change within productive systems. This argument is developed by reference to empirical research on the emergence and evolution of retail markets. The effect is to explain more precisely the nature of market competition in particular settings, rather than to see competition itself as an all-embracing explanation for economic and institutional change.

Chapter 4 (Lorenz) offers a further example of empirical work which is informed at a deep level by the productive systems framework. Here the focus is on the conceptualization of relationships between firms. The chapter explores the notion of 'trust' as an influence on the economic relationships between individuals and between firms. The chapter is important at two separate levels. First, it gives an insight into a way in which productive systems might operate well, sympathetic to the discussion of successful and unsuccessful productive systems in Wilkinson's chapter, but going beyond it to explore the roles of key individuals who span boundaries between firms. This understanding is shown to be useful in explaining why some industrial districts perform better than others. It also provides an excellent example of how qualitative empirical work can assist us in understanding the nature of economic relationships between organizations, in the process overturning conventional conceptualizations.

Chapter 5 (Deakin) takes up the theme of the coevolution of productive systems and the institutional environment. It argues that social rights can have a 'central, constitutive role' in shaping labour market relations and are not always, as neoclassical general equilibrium theory suggests, an impediment to efficiency. The chapter first demonstrates the case for social rights using the evolutionary economics perspective developed by Hayek. This perspective focuses on the role of competition in contributing to dynamic efficiency in the sense of acting as a 'process of discovery'. However, these market processes need to be facilitated by 'numerous inter-locking conventions' which act to share information and to underpin mutual expectations of behaviour, thereby saving on transactions costs. Hayek's analysis is shown to provide only a partial fit with the productive systems approach, as it is too narrowly focused on the need for conventions to underpin private property rights. A more general case can be made for social rights once this focus is expanded to include areas where property rights lack relevance. These include goods for which no property rights exist (public goods) and areas of activity where individuals are unable to participate and develop their potential because of social exclusion. Market processes in this context lead to cumulative inequalities. Deakin therefore expands the case for the legitimacy of social rights by utilising Sen's concept of capabilities, that is, the provision of opportunities to individuals to develop their potential contributions to the economic and social order. Social rights and the enhancement of the productive aspect of the economic system are seen as complementary and not conflictual: systems of labour regulation and social rights can contribute towards both dynamic efficiency and the maintenance and advancement of democratic values.

Indeed neoliberalism, in seeking to unravel the welfare state and return western societies to a minimal nineteenth century regime of property and contract rights, can be seen to be aiming to restrict the application of principles of democratic participation within the economic sphere. The apparent success of neoliberalism in stabilizing the economies of Britain and the United States during the long boom of the 1990s needs to be seen as part of a process of adjustment to an earlier period of crisis, in the 1970s. The implications of this process are still not yet completely clear. Neoliberalism was born out of a crisis in productive systems at the start of the 1970s which was most extreme in Britain and the United States since, by contrast with continental Europe and Japan, they were less able to withstand pressures to abandon consensus politics and returned instead to a system of distributional conflict. As the postwar Keynesian consensus was dismantled, established conventions of trust between management and labour were overturned and the terms of trade between social groups were altered. In the process, a new basis for societal cooperation appears to have been established. However, given the weakening of civil society (in particular trade unions and the professions, but also organized capital) which has taken place, together with the diminution in the role of the state as guarantor of social conditions, this new compromise rests on inequality, growing social exclusion and the mobilization of a reserve army of labour. It is a matter of judgment whether cooperation founded on such conditions will prove to be more stable and enduring than the model of social citizenship under the welfare state which it replaced, but there is every reason to think that it may not.

These issues are taken up in Chapter 6 (Ladipo, Mankelow and Burchell) which provides an exploration of the forces leading to and evidence for job intensification over recent decades. For conventional economics the issue of the wage–effort relationship is settled in the marketplace. In contrast a productive systems approach, however, recognises that it is in the workplace that the wage–effort relationship is fully realized. In this context, the chapter provides carefully analyzed and convincing evidence of heightened work intensity over recent decades particularly in the United Kingdom associated with its deregulated productive system. The consequences of these developments for individuals and families are documented, through evidence of raised stress levels, ill-health and family tension. Work intensification has tangible economic costs in its effects on motivation levels, turnover rates and in the risk of compensation claims against employers. However, in keeping with the productive systems approach, it is not assumed that such counterproductive effects will be sufficient to bring about a process of self-correcting change. Without the development of countervailing power, through for example, collective action and trade union organization, employers are unlikely to recognize the destructive impact of work intensification. As Wilkinson argues in Chapter 2, in order for the rhetoric of mutuality of interests, as stressed in the human resource management to hold, the definition of interests needs to be expanded beyond those of management. Otherwise, new forms of human resource management may be little more than a mechanism for promoting self-exploitation of workers.

Chapter 7 (Craypo) provides further consideration of the role of unions within productive systems and in particular within the US productive system. It develops a concept of union bargaining power termed an 'ability to pay, ability to make pay' model. The achievement of reasonable wages is conditional both on employers having the capacity to pay without risking going out of business and on the power of the unions to make the employer pay. The former depends on the system of competition and on opportunities for competitors to pay substandard labour costs. The latter requires not only the organizing of individual workplaces but the development of unionization across the organization and sector, broadly defined, to prevent competitive undercutting by non-union plants or companies. Craypo outlines how the opportunities for negotiating reasonable wages has been undermined, on the one hand, by forces that have reduced the leverage of organizations on prices, and, on the other, by restrictive and outdated regulations which inhibit the ability of unions in the United States to consolidate their organization to prevent destructive competition from non-union firms or competitive unions. Three sector case studies – cars, airlines and the retail trade – provide evidence of the three major contributors to union decline, namely, deindustrialization, deregulation and industrial restructuring. The result has been a vicious cycle which inhibits the development of labour-management cooperation based on trust relations. The new productive system carries with it the seeds of its own destruction; it spreads low prices but brings with it low wages and low living standards and thus cannot sustain in the long term a high value added economy such as the United States.

Chapter 8 (Konzelmann and Forrant) demonstrates the fragility of creative work systems within the context of deregulated and uncoordinated markets, drawing on three contrasting case studies of manufacturing companies in the United States. Creative work systems which involve workers in active problem solving and innovation, do contribute to improvements in productive efficiency, but these systems are expensive to set up and are slow to provide rewards. They are thus vulnerable both to competition from low cost, low road competitors in the same market and to pressures from the financial markets to provide continuous improvement in shareholder value. Of the two case study companies that introduced creative work systems, only one has been able to sustain the strategy protected by a long-term relationship with a major customer. The other experiment proved equally successful in improving productivity and quality but fell victim to takeovers and to changes in management personnel and business strategies. Destructive markets can thus operate to undermine successful systems, viewed from a production rather than a short-term financial value perspective. In the third case, the option of developing creative work systems was eschewed in favour of an explicitly coercive strategy to take costs out, using global relocation as a threat to win concessions both from within the workplace and from its suppliers. Unfortunately it may be the last example which becomes the dominant model if the macro environment and product market structure are not able to protect experiments in new and more productive forms of working.

In the course of the 1990s, the process of market liberalization which began in Britain and North America began to spread to mainland Europe. Chapter 9 (Mückenberger) examines pressures for institutional change in Germany which derive from a combination of forces: the unification of the country in the early 1990s, which drove up unemployment to levels not experienced for several decades; the effort to meet the convergence criteria of European Monetary Union; and the impact of globalization, which led German scholars to speak of the abandonment of the traditional social state by the 'global competition state'. The chapter studies the process of change in relation to six key features of the German system: the 'dual system' of vocational training; the 'standard employment relationship' of permanent, stable work relations; the social insurance system; shop-floor participation through works councils; co-determination at enterprise level; and the framework of collective bargaining. The impact to date of the deregulatory debate is seen to be uneven, in that certain institutional features (such as the vocational training system) remain largely unaffected, while those bearing immediately on wage and indirect labour costs are the focus of discussion. Mückenberger argues that it is inappropriate, under these circumstances, to speak of *de*regulation, and that the modernization of the system is likely to take the form of an adjustment of regulatory mechanisms rather than their complete abandonment.

In the remaining chapters of the book, the contributors take up this theme of looking beyond neoliberalism to the reconstruction of economic and social institutions. Chapter 10 (Michie and Sheehan) takes issue with the free-market dogma that labour market regulation, particularly insofar as it restricts employers' ability to manage their labour markets flexibly, will necessarily lead to inefficiency. Their careful analyses of several surveys of both the demand and supply sides of the UK labour market examine the link between HRM strategies adopted by companies and their record of innovation. Their findings offer no support for the assumptions that flexibility (for instance, willingness to hire-and-fire or use casual and temporary employment contracts) is associated with innovation, product quality or productivity. Rather, the evidence uncovered in Michie and Sheehan's analyses of the data strongly suggests that high-commitment strategies, such as involving employees and trade unions in decisions, lead to more successful productive systems. This chapter thereby bears out Wilkinson's claim, made in the original 'Productive Systems' article, that effective policy is likely to come from careful empirical work, and not from abstract, a priori reasoning.

Chapter 11 (Brosnan) continues the theme of the relationship between a productive systems approach and the regulation of markets, through a study of minimum wages. As well as advocating minimum wages as a tool to combat poverty and inequality, Brosnan makes the case that, from a productive systems perspective, minimum wage legislation can promote good practice by favouring efficient, innovating firms above firms that rely on low paid labour for their competitive advantage. Brosnan argues that, provided that the minimum wage is set at a realistic level and enforced appropriately, the experience of minimum wage legislation is that these benefits can be obtained. Arguments against minimum wage legislation, to the effect that it causes inflation and inefficiency because it acts as an obstruction to market forces, are not borne out by practice. Thus minimum wages provide a further concrete example of the use of a productive systems approach to offer a nuanced understanding of the relationship between economic and institutional phenomena.

Chapter 12 (Tarling and Wilkinson) argues that the key to reform is the problem of the undervaluation of labour. Between the 1930s and the 1970s, there was a consensus on the need for state intervention to counteract inequality. Since then, policy changes have set out to encourage greater inequality on the grounds that this will improve economic performance. However the cumulative impact of neoliberal policies in countries such as Britain has been to spring four 'traps' associated with unemployment, low wages, fiscal disincentives and social exclusion. These are mutually reinforcing and trigger a downward spiral in the resource endowments of individuals. Referring again to the concept of 'capabilities', Tarling and Wilkinson argue for a reversal of policy which would see a return to effective labour standards, the restoration of social insurance and institutional support for full employment. Equalization of pre-tax income is an important precondition for policies which will enhance the economic functioning and hence the self-sufficiency of individuals.

The need for efficient and equitable productive systems to cover the full costs of labour is also taken up in Chapter 13 (Rubery, Humphries, Fagan, Grimshaw and Smith) where the implications of the current system of gender discrimination and family organization are considered. The chapter challenges the orthodox perception of equal opportunities legislation as a cost which introduces market inefficiencies and points instead to the high but often invisible costs of existing arrangements, costs borne primarily by women but also by children. Drawing upon a considerable body of accumulated comparative studies, the chapter argues that such legislation will improve the efficiency of the productive system if it helps to promote the lifetime earnings of individuals and considers the losses to any system which result from employees deciding to underutilize their skills because of inadequate childcare, gender-based occupational segregation or poorly designed tax systems. Taking this wider view, it is argued that inequality, gender discrimination, 'traditional' gender roles and low levels of female labour market participation can all be barriers to the success of productive systems.

Chapter 14 further broadens the productive systems approach to include the need for policy development at the international level. Rodgers uses the 'decent work' framework adopted by the International Labour Organization to make an argument analogous to the productive systems approach for 'a broader framework of the relationship between work, employment and development' within which to debate policy. The argument is made that the promotion of workers' rights, income security and employment opportunities are each valid in their own terms, but pursued together are 'more than the sum of the parts'. Decent work includes four dimensions: access to employment (but without pressure for overwork), rights at work, security in work and for those not able to work, and the right to representation and dialogue. The pursuit of these goals, Rodgers argues, can release synergies between social and economic goals, but in order for this to occur there needs to be a process of institution building. Decent work involves the pursuit of a minimum floor applicable universally, but also allows for moving targets, adjusted to match the capability of the society to provide higher standards. There is no simple relationship between high income and decent work: different productive systems at similar income levels can generate very different combinations of employment, income and security. The decent work agenda also needs to be extended into the informal sector to provide for new forms of agency and voice and to develop productivity through new instruments such as micro-insurance. The formal and informal parts of the productive system are interrelated and the informal sector needs to mobilise resources from within the formal sector to validate the upgrading of informal sector work.

As the chapters in this volume demonstrate, the stability that has apparently resulted from the process of neoliberal restructuring of labour, product and financial markets in the 1980s and 1990s is one based on inequality and social exclusion. It is a fragile compromise which is fundamentally incompatible with policies which aim to build long-term economic prosperity for all. It is important that argument should now be joined over the future direction of change. Part of the globalization debate has been concerned with claims that the triumph of the neoliberal policy agenda represents the 'end of history' for institutional forms, which can now be expected to converge around what are thought to be the essential features of the British and US systems: respect for private property rights, minimal regulatory interference with contracts, marketization of public services and utilities, the marginalization of organized labour, the privatization of responsibilities for the family and for care provision and the pre-eminence of shareholder interests in corporate governance. This point of view replaces the policy prescriptions of the early 1980s with a simple prediction. Institutional economics is called in aid to grant the appearance of inevitability to a process which is, in reality, highly contested.

At this juncture, the overriding virtue of the productive systems approach is to re-emphasize the diversity of institutional forms which are present in capitalist systems and the potential for different solutions to the problem of societal cooperation to coexist. A systems approach cautions against the assumption that changes in national and global trading regimes can in any way be separated from what is happening at the level of the regulatory framework. An emphasis on 'spontaneous' convergence between systems can only obscure the important policy choices to be made in national and global governance.

2 Productive systems and the structuring role of economic and social theories

Frank Wilkinson

Introduction

This chapter represents further development of the ideas presented in 'Productive Systems,' published in 1983, in the *Cambridge Journal of Economics* memorial issue to Joan Robinson. As Joan witnessed her life's work swamped by the resurgence of neo-classical economics, she increasingly turned her back on what she came to regard as the pointless 'logic chopping' of economic theory and advocated a historical and institutionalist approach. It is in this spirit that 'Productive Systems' was written; and it is in this same spirit that it is being revisited.

The ideas embodied in 'Productive Systems' emerged and were developed against the backdrop of the economics profession's mass exodus from Keynesianism. It was a strange time. As economists puzzled over the burgeoning crisis that was wrecking the Golden Age, they abandoned the Keynesian Revolution and returned the conventional wisdom in economics to its pre-Keynesian beliefs that money determines prices and that the market determines everything else. This *neo-liberal* revival rests on the belief in the existence of immutable laws of the market to which organisations and institutions must conform if economic welfare is to be optimised.

The starting point for 'Productive Systems' was that it is a fatal error to believe that institutions must comply with prior laws derived from theoretical constructs because institutions are the central driving force behind productive systems and the way they evolve. This is not to argue that economic theory has no part to play. In fact, the dominant economic beliefs are powerful institutional forces shaping productive systems and determining how they operate. The last sentence in 'Productive Systems' read 'One traditional function of economists has been to provide justification for political answers and the necessary exercise of power that they entail: but that is another story'. One of the purposes for revisiting 'Productive Systems' is to tell that story.

Productive systems

Productive systems are where the forces of production combine in production. Their constituent parts are labour, the means of production, the social system in which production is organised, the structure of ownership and control over productive activity and the social, political and economic framework within which the processes of production operate.

Mutual interests and relative power in productive systems

There are two distinct elements in the organisation and structuring of production: mutual interests and relative power. Labour and the means of production are mutually dependent: the one cannot operate without the other. Therefore, there can be no doubt about the advantage of *cooperation* in production. It allows for the full exploitation of the technical complementarities inherent to production and facilitates the sharing of knowledge necessary for the effectiveness of production and its improvement.[1] Cooperation also fuels the learning processes by which new information and knowledge are created, incorporated and diffused, and by which new products, processes and organisational forms are developed.[2] The resulting *operational and dynamic efficiencies* are crucial determinants of the ability of organisations to compete effectively, and to respond flexibly to changing circumstances and new opportunities. These efficiencies are also important because they generate the value added by the productive system, which forms the basis for the income and employment security of its various stakeholder groups.

In production, relations have both technical and social dimensions. The *technical relations of production* are the functional interlinkages between labour, equipment and materials within and between production processes, the exchange of technical and other information pertaining to production and the development of new products and processes. These relations are objective and impersonal associations, shaped by the technicalities of products and of the methods by which they are produced. By contrast, the *social relations of production* are the subjective and personal associations among the human agents of production. They form the social structure for the technical relations of production by which the production tasks of labour and the means of production are jointly undertaken. By directing, coordinating and controlling the forces of production so as to assure full cooperation, the social relations of production play a central role in determining the effectiveness of technical cooperation and hence operational and dynamic efficiency.

The centrality of cooperation and mutual interest in production, however, does not imply that labour and capital come together on equal terms. Although labour works jointly with capital in production, workers are much more immediately dependent on the relationship. Compared with capital, and with their needs, workers have very limited access to resources except through the market. Moreover, the main asset they have, their labour, cannot be stored so it is difficult for individual workers to stand out for long for a better deal. Labour's inherent economic weakness is fundamental in determining the power of capital relative to labour, but it is not the only factor involved. Although, ultimately, workers can be coerced by need into compliance with employers' demands, they are not powerless because employers are dependent on workers for the use of their capital and for the realisation of its productive potential. This coincidence of mutual dependence and unequal economic power, which can be countervailed to some degree by control in production, is not confined to relations between capital and labour; it is ubiquitous in the network of supplier and customer relationships within which organisations operate.

Generally then, the relationships we are considering are based on mutual dependence so that each party is reliant on others to secure the best from production. But differences in economic power may give one side or the other bargaining advantage over the terms and conditions for cooperation, the exploitation of which could result in a retaliatory withdrawal from full cooperation and a consequent lowering of productive efficiency. In this respect, the social relations of production have a second crucial role to play, that of resolving disputes between the parties to production. Here, the distribution of the value added in production is of crucial importance: for however mutual interests may be in production, they are inevitably conflictual in distribution because what one gets the others cannot have.

Mutual interests, relative power and institutions

Mutuality and power asymmetries are central forces structuring not only the internal social and political framework of productive systems but also the environment in which they operate. This is particularly the case when the role, interaction and evolution of broader institutions representing collective interests of productive system stakeholder groups (i.e. employees, managers, shareholders, customers, suppliers and society) are considered. Trade unions, employers' and trade associations, the state, international organisations and other agencies represent collective interests; but their form, actions and the outcome of negotiations reflect the power differences among their various constituent groups. Thus, trade unions and employers' associations are based on shared objectives of their members, but their internal organisations reflect the balance of power between sectional interests. In their negotiation, trade unions and employers' associations seek to regulate, often jointly, rates of pay and conditions of work, and to provide procedures for resolving disputes. This results from their mutual interest in the firm's and industry's prosperity and the continuity of production from which both profits and wages derive. But the outcome of negotiations also reflects the power balance both within and between the employers' and workers' organisations and the part this plays in the struggle over distributional shares.

Recognition of the coincidence of mutual dependence and power differences is also important for interpreting the activities of the state. The provision of education, health, social welfare, law and order and the regulation of trade unions and business, can be seen as furthering the common interest by increasing production, and by curbing the destructive exercise of sectional interests. Alternatively, state activity can be regarded as serving the particular interest of capital or labour. The state may act on behalf of capital to curb worker organisation, provide services which individual capitalists are incapable of providing and make good the corrosive effect of capitalist rivalry on productive resources, including the workforce. For labour, the welfare state might shift the balance of power in favour of labour by lifting from it the burden of poverty, disease and ignorance. No doubt, all of these elements play some part in the formulation and administration of state policy, and are manifest in the legal and regulatory framework and in the other ways by which the state intervenes in class and sectional divisions.

At the international level, nation states conclude treaties and collaborate in international institutions designed to regulate trade, international payments and capital flows. Many of these institutions – for example the IMF, World Bank, World Trade Organisation and European Union (EU) – originated in the need of nation states to cooperate, to protect themselves from both the unregulated international movements of goods and finance, and the potentially destructive impact of unilateral attempts to control such flows. In this respect, international agencies serve the mutual interests of their member nation states by encouraging trade and financial interaction. However, the form these institutions take, and the way they operate, reflect the relative power of different nation states, trading blocks and economic regions as well as the leverage of interest groups on national governments.

The evolution of productive systems

The concept of productive systems outlined above has general application and provides a basis for analysis at any level – the family, production units, firms, regions and nations. At each level, there is an internal and external network of mutually dependent relationships, the terms and conditions of which are settled by the interplay of the strength each party derives from their position within the relationship, and the strength each brings to the relationship by dint of their wealth, their social, political and legal standing, and other means by which relative power is determined. Essentially, each productive system, its internal relations, those it forms with other productive systems and the terms and conditions for their formation and continuance are the unique outcome of its own history. Moreover, productive systems are subject to continuous change from the interactions among the technical, economic, social and political forces to which they are subject.

The evolution of a productive system is, therefore, a dialectical process in which economic and institutional elements dynamically interact. Change is generated by developments in products and processes, and with changes in productive and power relationships both within and between productive systems. These interact with the broader economic, social and political framework and both are modified in the process. Such forces can lead to the destruction or radical modification of productive systems and to the growth of new forms. This perspective suggests the notion of an economic process radically different from that of 'equilibration' of orthodox theory. What is implied is a *non*-equilibrium evolutionary process determined by the way productive systems, and their relations with other productive systems, mutate in response to innovation in techniques and organisational forms as well as shifting power balances. Such a process cannot be said to be tending to some pre-defined *optimum* because there is no standard of reference for defining what that *optimum* might be and no way of defining how it might be arrived at. The best that can be said is that certain productive systems are relatively successful while others are relatively unsuccessful.

A *relatively successful productive system* is one with comparative advantage in its overall economic, technical, political and social organisation. This does not mean that it is superior in each of these dimensions; rather the system's advantage derives from their combined effects. A successful productive system is likely to be at the forefront of technical and organisational progress and to have evolved social and political structures conducive to effective production. The growth of productivity and the possibility of securing favourable terms from other productive systems with which it has dealings will serve to increase its wealth and help to reduce internal conflicts that could impede cooperation. These benign conditions have the potential to create a virtuous circle of increasing productivity, competitive success, growth in demand and rising prosperity. Examples of successful national productive systems can be found in nineteenth century Britain, in the United States and Germany from the last decades of the nineteenth century and in Japan more recently.

A *relatively unsuccessful productive system* is one where the pace of technical advance is slow, productive forces are ineffectively utilised, and systems of management, control and industrial structure serve to reinforce competitive failure. The slow rate of wealth creation is likely to intensify distributional struggles, hindering cooperation in production and the ability of the socio-political system to find an effective solution through organisational and institutional reform. In this hostile environment, the productive system is under severe pressure but the resulting social, political and economic crisis is unlikely to resolve the underlying causes of degeneration. On the contrary, the struggle over distribution and control will tend to increase the system's inflexibility and hasten its relative decline.

Mutual dependence and relative power in economics

The claim that productive relations are typified by mutual dependence and power, raising issues about coordination and distribution, is uncontroversial. What is perhaps less so is to identify the interaction between mutual dependence and relative power as the major force shaping productive systems and how they evolve. This section examines how the question of power and its possible effects on the cooperation needed for efficient production is handled in mainstream theories of markets and work organisation.

Markets and power

In liberal economics, the theoretical position on power in the market ranges from the static neo-classical view in which it is neutralised by the market or by organisational authority if markets should fail, to the more dynamic notion that the command by entrepreneurs over resources and their deployment in the market empowers entrepreneurial creativity in the interest of economic progress.

Liberal economics rest on the belief in *economic man*, that extreme individualist in whom property rights invest power over the assets he or she owns, and who is inherently driven by self-interest. On the other hand, the division of labour is regarded as the central driving force of economic progress, so that increasingly specialised individuals are more and more inter-dependent (Marshall, 1947). The question then becomes: how can mutual dependence between inherently self-seeking individuals be managed so that the resources they separately own and control can be put to the most effective use in their common interest? Liberal economics offers two alternative solutions: (1) the invisible hand of the market; on, (2) the visible hand of managerial authority.

The invisible hand

The core belief of liberal economics is that, assuming property rights are recognised, freedom of property disposal is guaranteed and contractual promises are honoured, the market coordinates the activities of individuals. Adam Smith's founding contribution to liberal economics was his insistence on the primary role of free exchange, both for driving the division of labour and for coordinating the increasingly specialised parts of the system. He argued that self-interest provides the incentive for specialisation, exchange provides the opportunity and free markets coordinate individual production and consumption decisions.

This idea of the pivotal role of market forces for coordinating productive activity has been handed down to modern neo-classical economists. The *perfect* market based on the freedom of contract provides information and price incentives, ensures contractual compliance by providing opportunities for buyers and sellers to readily switch trading partners among a large number of equally well-qualified alternatives; and determines income distribution. The importance of a freely functioning market in the present context is the role it is given in neutralising individual power, thereby ensuring full cooperation among self-interested individuals.

But this beneficial effect is limited, argue liberal economists, if individuals and groups can marshal the power they have *in restraint of trade*. Trade unions, employers' organisations and other collective monopolies are suspected of restricting supply and fixing prices, and their close regulation is strongly recommended by liberal economists. They have, on the other hand, a much more ambivalent attitude towards dominant firms. As monopolists they are condemned for lowering economic welfare, but as the outcome of successful competition they are applauded for raising it.

The visible hand

The neo-classical case for the beneficial effect of dominant firms was succinctly summarised by Coase (1937) in his seminal paper. He argued that 'an economist thinks of an economic system as co-ordinated by the price mechanism' and posed the question: 'having regard to the fact that if production is regulated by price movements, production would be carried out without any organisation at all, well might we ask why is there any organisation?' His answer was that organisations provide an efficient way of overcoming the market failure which stems from the propensity of trading partners to exploit any monopoly they might secure in supply or demand, control over specific assets, privileged access to information and difficulties in monitoring performance to ensure that it lives up to contractual promise. The proposal is therefore that organisational power evolves reactively to neutralise that of trading partners who, by exploiting their monopoly power, increase transactions costs and lower economic well-being (Williamson, 1985).

Other economists working within the liberal tradition have given the visible hand a more proactive role. Marshall stressed the central role of organisation[3] in the coordination of the increasingly specialised and mutually dependent productive activities. (Marshall, 1947: Book IV, ch. VIII). Thus, whilst Marshall saw freedom of industry and enterprise[4] as a central motivating and integrating force, he also maintained that market success depends on increasingly effective industrial and work organisation, a process driven by the innovating entrepreneur who:

> is the organiser in command of capital, who bears the uninsurable risk. He takes complex decisions with limited information. Superintendence is only a small part of this: co-ordination, imagination and risk bearing are fundamental.
>
> (O'Brien, 1990)

Within this tradition, Chandler (1977) identified superior managerial and production organisation and the economies of their large-scale operation as explaining the emergence of large corporations; Hayek and his followers argued that market success and firm growth were the consequence of entrepreneurial ability in discovering new profit opportunities in a world of uncertainty (Kirzner, 1997); and Schumpeter (1943) theorised that monopoly profits are necessary to encourage innovation. Such theories serve to justify the power exercised by large firms as fostering economic advance. They also extend the disciplinary and creative role of markets for, although large size may be the reward of success, big firms can only survive by generating the operational and dynamic efficiency by which organisations keep their feet in the market driven by 'the process of creative destruction' (Schumpeter, 1943). These market benefits have been extended more recently to include the stock exchange which is assumed to operate as an efficient market for corporate control, the means by which shareholders can punish inefficient and malfeasant managers and reward successful and reliable ones. In this way, hostile takeovers are theorised as serving the public interest (Deakin and Slinger, 1997).

Nevertheless, economists recognise that there are downsides to market dominance. The abuse of power in labour and product markets may have significant distributional effects; mergers and takeovers may be ways of eliminating competition; and corporate actions may threaten the social and natural environment. Regulation is therefore accepted as necessary to counter such *negative externalities* and to contain the destructive capabilities of competition. But, caution liberal economists, the urge to regulate must be tempered by the recognition that in the final analysis the market provides the best opportunity for individuals and society.

And, whilst the market concentrates economic power it also yields important benefits for society in the form of technical progress and economic growth. What is good for business is also good for society, and although the excesses of dominant firms need checking, it would check progress if their market opportunities were unduly restricted.

The theories supporting such argument underpin what Berk (1994) described as *corporate liberalism*. He argued that

> ... corporate liberalism conceived property and economic development prior to the will of collective or democratic choice. 'The laws of trade' its adherents were fond of saying 'are stronger than the laws of men.' Thus, the modern corporation, like the liberal person, owed its existence first and foremost to private purpose. If the result of economic development rooted in such pre-social entitlement was to concentrate the market in huge monopolistic firms, this was deemed inevitable. The only economic role left to the democratic state was to redress the concentration of excessive wealth in the modern corporation through regulated monopoly. The goal of regulation, in other words, was to balance the interests of consumers in redistribution with those of the corporation in accumulation.
>
> (Berk, 1994: 13–14)

Summary

Underlying the theories of markets in liberal economic theory is the concept of *economic* man inherently driven by self-interest. Self-interest provides the driving force for economic activity in which respecting it is creative; but, given the opportunity, its pursuit will become exploitative and destructive of economic well-being. Markets therefore provide the outlet for the creative deployment of self-interest and checks its misuse. They serve to mobilise privately owned resources, provide information, coordinate separate production and consumption decisions and guarantee the competition necessary to counter the exploitation of power for individual or group advantage. However, power also plays a positive role. It counters the negative effects of market failure and, by giving command of resources to innovating entrepreneurs, serves as a vehicle for economic progress. In this process, markets are the selectors of uses of power that enhance economic well-being.

Work organisation and power

The distinguishing feature of work organisation is its positioning *beyond the market*. Labour is inseparable from the worker and although contracted for in the market it is utilised in the workplace under the control of management.

Work organisation and power in economics

The separation of contracting and performance is central to Marxist economics. Marx agreed with orthodox economists that the price of labour is determined by free exchange in the market. However, he argued that away from the market, and in the workplace under the command of the capitalist employers, value additional to that contracted for is extracted from labour and this constitutes profits.[5]

Traditionally, liberal economists ignored the special problems posed by the organisation of work. They supposed that labour markets functioned as any other by assuming that skills were general and abundant. Then, competition fulfils its traditional role and the threat of replacement acts as a powerful inducement on workers and employers to match contractual promise with performance. However, in more recent years, closer attention has been paid to the problem of managing the workplace when markets fail. In these circumstances, as in other branches of transaction cost economics, managerial authority emerges as an efficient alternative to the market. In *efficiency wage* and *insider/outsider* labour market theories, asset specificity, information asymmetry and other ways by which market forces are deflected give the whip hand to incumbent workers, who are then assumed to *soldier* (i.e. to opt for on-the-job leisure rather than work). Management counters labour's exploitation of power by close monitoring and discipline and/or by adding an *efficiency* bonus to the market wage to induce additional effort. This, as in Marxist theory, is made easier when the *reserve army of the unemployed* makes more effective the threat to the worker of being fired.

Labour management and power

Away from economics and in the more practical and dynamic world of production management the problem of securing full cooperation from workers, as measured by productivity and profits, has remained a perennial problem. Addressing this has been the driving force for the evolution of the theories and practice of labour management. These have developed from the idea of *arbitrary* managerial control needed to discipline recalcitrant workers, through the application of engineering science to the *scientific management of work*, to *human relations management* inspired by the socio-psychological redefinition of workers from *economic* to *social* beings, and finally to *human resource management* which combines elements of scientific and human relations management.

Arbitrary management   With the move to factory production, close supervision and stern discipline were the dominant approaches to solving the problem of motivation and discipline (Pollard, 1993). In exceptional cases, notably Robert Owen, factory employers believed that concern for the welfare, education and social development of their workforce offered the best way forward; but the vast majority used close supervision and harsh discipline to 'force human character into a mechanical mode' (Pollard, 1993: 256). This had support from social and economic reformers who argued that workers needed to be poor and exposed to market forces to be driven to productive activity, ideas which also provided the justification for the legislative sweeping away of worker protection and any meaningful social welfare (Wilkinson, 2001). Labour discipline was further tightened by the strengthening of the employers hands by the enactment of the Master and

Servant Laws.[6] These laws built on and extended the employer's disciplinary powers over their workforce entrenched in the Elizabethan, Statute of Artificers. As a consequence,

> Inside the factory … the employer is absolute law-giver; he makes regulations at will, changes and adds to his code at pleasure, and even if he inserts the craziest stuff, the courts say to the working man: "you were your own master; no one forced you to agree to such a contract if you did not want to, but now, when you have freely entered into it, you must be bound to it."
>
> (quoted, with approval, from Engels, by Atiyah, 1979: 275)

The position of workers in the workplace was further weakened as the finer division of labour progressively simplified tasks, with mechanisation and with the growth of the employer's scientific, engineering and managerial knowledge. And, it was from this cumulative process that scientific management evolved (Hollway, 1991).

The scientific management of work   The aim of scientific management was to systematise production. Frederick Taylor, a leading protagonist, was pre-occupied with the problem of worker 'soldiering'. Solving this, he argued, required complete managerial control over the tasks of individual workers and how they were performed. To achieve this, the pioneers of scientific management proposed, managers should acquire workers' craft knowledge, plan production in detail, precisely define each worker's tasks and carefully control every stage of production. The need to achieve these objectives, Taylor claimed, rested on the discovery and development of the scientific laws governing production.

Taylor made far-reaching claims for scientific management. He argued that it provided a rational basis for designing and standardising factory layout, equipment and industrial organisation, and for codifying worker knowledge. It provided the scientific basis for worker selection, vocational guidance, training, planning work to individual capabilities, ensuring workers' physical and psychological well-being and designing wage payment systems to reward efficiency. In doing this, it raised workers' skill levels, stimulated them intellectually, promoted individuality and self-reliance, while at the same time increasing pay, cutting hours of work and improving employment security. Taylor also claimed that his methods improved labour management by creating a cadre of specialists to instruct, train and advise workers and encourage involvement. Of particular importance, was the assertion that replacing a system of arbitrary managerial decisions by one in which managerial control of worker activity was governed by scientific laws would improve management/worker relationships, democratise industry and eliminate the need for trade unions and collective bargaining. Taylor claimed that:

> No such democracy has ever existed in industry before. Every protest of every workman must be handled by those on management's side, and the

right or wrong of the complaint must be settled not by the opinion, either of the management or the workman, but by the great code of laws which has been developed and which must satisfy both sides. It gives the worker in the end equal voice with the employer; both can refer only to the arbitrament of science and fact.

(Hoxie, 1915, quoted in Hollway, 1991: 22)

If his blueprints were followed, Taylor claimed, combining managerial authority with science would remove the conflict resulting from the exercise of, and resistance to, arbitrary managerial power and clear the way for full cooperation.

However, the practice of scientific management proved different from its theory. In his detailed study of the practical application of scientific management, Hoxie (1915) came to quite the opposite view of its effects to those anticipated by Taylor. He found that scientific management mainly served to concentrate into management's hands the power to deskill, control and speed up work and to justify this in the name of science. The main problem, Hoxie argued, was managerial emphasis on short-term increases in production and profit by task and rate setting, without concern for the longer term reform of technical and organisational structures required for full-blown scientific management. As a result, the weight of change fell on workers who experienced it as work degradation, speed up, increased alienation and loss of power.

While recognising this, neither Hoxie, nor the unions he consulted, opposed the principle of the application of science to industry. The problem, as they saw it, was not so much with the *application* of science so much as the way it was applied. On the democratisation of industry, Hoxie wrote:

It is a noble ideal, as old at least as St. Simon, and the time may come when it is capable of realisation. Before this however, the science of psychology must make long strides, industry must attain a much greater degree of regularity and stability than at present exists, and the type of man who is supposed to discover and voice the dictates of science – and stand thus as the just judge between employers and workers – must be very different from the present general run of time study men and task setters.

(Hoxie, 1915, quoted in Hollway, 1991: 103)

Human relations management   The long strides in the application of psychology to industry began at the end of the nineteenth Century when the mass poverty and degradation of work in the Victorian labour market led to a growing emphasis on the *human factor* in industry. In this, Joseph and Seebolm Rowntree, chocolate manufacturers from York, played a leading role (Biggs, 1964). The Rowntrees believed that business efficiency required humane personnel policies and good industrial relations. Concern for the health and well-being of their workers and for their quality, motivation and commitment resulted in the Rowntrees taking a lead in paying wages high enough for an adequate diet,[7] in cutting hours to combat fatigue and encourage leisure time activities, in providing health and welfare services for their employees and in designing workplaces to high environmental standards. They also provided remedial and continuing education, high levels of training; improved communications; and encouraged worker participation, collective bargaining and industrial democracy. The Rowntrees' zeal for reform was driven by their Quaker views regarding the organisation of society. But it was also guided by practical business concerns about the negative impact of poor nutrition and fatigue on worker performance, the advantage of using psychology to improve worker selection and training and the effect on worker motivation and performance of their well-being and job satisfaction (Rowntree, 1938; Biggs, 1964).

The inter-war years were characterised by a rapid growth in employers' interest in the role of human relations in industry and the potential to improve such relations by applying psychological and sociological research findings to work organisation. Increasing attention was paid to matching workers to jobs by means of psychological methods in selection and training, the use of such techniques as ergonomics to fit jobs to workers, and of counselling to improve their mental well-being. Later, after the Hawthorne experiments, even greater emphasis was placed on the importance of human emotions and feelings in determining the effectiveness of group activities and labour–management relations (Hollway, 1991).

These developments in human relations were designed to improve management rather than to challenge its authority or the extent and definition of managerial responsibility. They were largely remedial and targeted at increasing efficiency by making the employment systems more worker-friendly, by fitting workers better into work systems and by providing treatment for their physical and psychological defects. In this process:

> A new conception and practice of the worker emerged. This had as its objective to ensure that the bond linking the individual and the enterprise and also the individual to society would hence forth not be solely economic. The wage relationship and the power of the boss would be supplemented by a personal bond that would attach individuals to the lives they lived in the world of work, to their co-workers and bosses, and to society as a whole. It would be possible to conceive of administering the working environment in such a way as to ensure simultaneously the contentment and health of the worker and the profitability and efficiency of the enterprise.
>
> (Miller and Rose, 1998: 53)

After the Second World War, the importance of the *remedial* benefits of human relations continued to be emphasised as important for operational efficiency. However, the attention of industrial psychologists and sociologists, and the managerial practice they informed, shifted to the idea that human relations was a *productive* factor contributing to dynamic as well as operational efficiency. Wartime experiments at the Tavistock Institute, targeted at the rehabilitation of servicemen suffering psychological disorders, demonstrated the creative possibilities of directly involving individuals in collective activities (Slinger, 2000). After the War, this research was developed collaboratively by an international network of research institutes which fostered its industrial application (Trist and Murray, 1993). In Norway, for example, the Industrial Democracy Project explored the benefits of improved worker/management relations and developed and diffused participatory socio-technical systems, especially in Sweden (Trist and Murray, 1993).

These developments went far beyond the notion that human relations could raise the performance of traditional work systems closer to their real potential. The argument became that greater employee involvement contributes to dynamic efficiency, an important requirement of which was the resolution of the long standing problem of antagonism between workers and managers. To overcome this, emphasis was placed on the benefits of inter-personal skills in labour management, democratic leadership and participative small groups. The reluctance of workers to respond to the new style of management extended the area for reform to include job redesign. The agenda was further broadened by the development of theories of organisational behaviour and organisational change, together with an emphasis on corporate culture as an integrating and motivating force (Hollway, 1991).

Human resource management   Two broad strands in the historical development of work organisation and labour management theories and practices can therefore be identified. The first stems from scientific management and has its roots in engineering science and in the traditional economist's assumption of *economic* man. The second strand developed from the application to the work situation of psychology and sociology, with their emphasis on *social* man. The increasing weight given to this latter strand shifted the focus in labour management from labour as a *factor of production* to be directed and cajoled by hierarchical management, to labour as a *productive resource* with creative capabilities to be developed by interactive management. The expectation was that employers would reap the rewards of greater worker motivation, increased job satisfaction and improved job performance by greater operational and dynamic efficiency and higher profitability. These objectives are seen as requiring the enlarging and enriching of jobs, more challenges and opportunities, new skills and more effective incentives. With this change in management objectives and style came a modification in nomenclature from 'personnel and industrial relations management' to 'human resource management' (HRM).[8]

HRM has been defined 'as a set of policies designed to maximise organisational integration, employee commitment, flexibility and the quality of work' (Guest, 1987); and hard and soft versions have been identified. *Soft HRM* is 'a method of releasing untapped reserves of 'human resourcefulness' by increasing employee commitment, participation and involvement' (Blyton and Turnbull, 1992: 4) and has a greater emphasis on human relations. *Hard HRM* is designed to maximise the economic return from labour resources by integrating HRM into business strategy. Although it usually incorporates *soft* HRM practices, hard HRM has a broader engineering base and is strongly oriented towards meeting market requirements by means of greater production flexibility and product improvement (Appelbaum and Batt, 1994). Key objectives in hard HRM, which have a clear affinity with Taylor's vision of scientific management, include continuous improvement in quality and performance, just-in-time inventory systems, and statistical process control designed to iron out variation in quality, create consistency in meeting standards, locate inventory savings and eliminate waste. Broadly speaking, the purpose of HRM is to foster a pre-emptive rather than reactive approach to operational efficiency, quality control and innovation by shifting responsibility and accountability for decision making towards the shop floor. Its adoption testifies to a shift in labour management practice 'from coercion to the attempted production of self-regulated individuals' (Hollway, 1991: 20).

However, despite recognising the sociological and psychological needs of workers, the importance of democratic management and the central role of worker self-regulation and involvement in management as mechanisms for securing full cooperation, the proponents of human relations have been no more sympathetic to workers' independent representation than liberal economists or the scientific management school. The idea of democratising industry goes no further than Fredrick Taylor's view that this purpose is served by the enlightenment of management by knowledge of scientific laws, except that the science needed extends beyond that of production to include the psychology and sociology of the producers. From this perspective, the power to manage serves as a proxy for representation and a vehicle for efficiency and equity.

Human relations, independent representation, partnership and power

The early case for human relations was that the diagnosis and effective treatment of socio-psychological problems would improve the well-being of group members, the cohesiveness of the group and therefore its productive performance. From this standpoint, conflict was considered dysfunctional. Elton Mayo, of Hawthorne fame, believed that:

> Conflict was neither inevitable nor economic. It was the result of the maladjustment of a few men on the labour side of industry. Even after Hawthorne forced Mayo to grow, he remained firm in his conviction that conflict was an evil, a symptom of the lack of social skills. Cooperation, for him, was symptomatic of health; and, since there was no alternative in the modern world, cooperation must mean obedience to managerial authority. Thus collective bargaining was not really cooperation, but merely a flimsy substitute for the real thing.
>
> (Baritz, 1975: 332–3)

Social scientists have also argued that wage demands mask 'more real and human needs for appreciation, understanding and friendliness'; and they have gone further by identifying the need to join trade unions as a symptom of low intellect and psychological disorders (Baritz, 1975: 332).

More recently, advocates of human resource management have stressed the importance of unity of purpose and values. Total Quality Management (TQM) has been characterised as an organisational form in which 'employees can be trusted and empowered to take on more responsibility in a context of HRM practices which ensure a homogeneity of values' (Sewell and Wilkinson, 1992). Traditional 'pluralistic' industrial relations (where a diversity of interests are recognised) are effectively ruled-out and collective bargaining becomes 'integrative' rather than 'distributive' (Walton and McKersie, 1965). In this context, the role of trade unions is to coordinate the strategic process and facilitate the achievement of managerial objectives, which are assumed to forward the mutual interest of all the firm's stakeholders (Konzelmann Smith, 1996).

Following this trend, the 'New' Labour Government, elected in 1997, endorsed labour–management cooperation and 'partnership' as an effective approach for improving economic performance. In interpreting the Government's position, Wood (2000) identified the requirements of the new system as:

> one of partnership at work ... associated with the kind of model of HRM ... focused on the achievement of a particular role orientation on the part of employees so that they are flexible, expansive in their perceptions and willing contributors to innovation.[9]

He went on to suggest that

> Partnership is a matter of employers having the right to ask employees to develop themselves in order to accept fresh responsibilities whilst they themselves must take responsibility for providing the context in which this can happen.

In this formulation of partnership, the strong emphasis is on the need for workers to make largely unconditional commitments to their employer's business interests and objectives, and to mould themselves to its needs. In this way, workers provide additional and improved resources for the firm's managers to manage more effectively.

This position was neatly summed up by Tony Blair, the New Labour Prime Minister, when he laid out the Labour government's primary industrial relations objectives.[10] They required, Blair argued, 'nothing less than to change the culture of relations in and at work'. He stressed the need for the new culture to be 'one of voluntary understanding and co-operation because it has been recognised that the prosperity of each (employer and employee) is bound up in the prosperity of all'; and he emphasised that 'partnership works best when it is about real goals – part of a strategy for instance for doubling business. Or bringing employee relations in line with market re-positioning. Or ending the often meaningless ritual of annual wage squabbling'. It should be carefully noted that Blair made no reference to the *ritual* of the continuous squabble over the distribution of dividends between managers and shareholders or to the constant insistence on better terms for consumers orchestrated by the government. Rather, what Blair clearly had in mind was the need for workers to recognise the needs of business and their customers by meeting both their production and distributional demands. And, as we have seen, the weight of expert economic and labour management opinion comes down in favour of the government's unitarist line and lends credence to it. However, the validity of this support ultimately depends on the objectivity of the body of knowledge upon which it rests.

The claim of objectivity is important for protecting the expert from responsibility for any negative outcomes from the advice they give and for lending weight to managerial strategies and objectives. But 'knowledge concerned with people at work ... is not objective or true in any simple sense. It is a historical product of the interests and power relations in practice' (Hollway, 1991: 9). This echoes doubts repeatedly expressed about the objectivity of expert knowledge as applied to markets and production.

Marx dated the demise of scientific objectivity in economics as being the accession to power of the middle-classes with the electoral reforms of the 1830s. After that, it was no longer a question of whether 'this or that theorem was true, but whether it was useful to capital or harmful' (Marx, 1976: 97). This view was echoed by Galbraith (1987), when he argued that the supposed subordination of economic agents to the market disguised the central importance of power in economic life. He noted that 'Power is much enjoyed, and its economic and political exercise can also be pleasingly remunerative. Nothing serves it better than a theology that disguises its exercise' (Galbraith, 1987: xiv).

The objectivity of the research underlying scientific management and human relations has also been challenged on the grounds that it has traditionally been undertaken on behalf of employers or strongly relies on their support. Researchers have not been completely free agents; and the employer orientation of the research has determined its scope and focussed its attention on productivity, profitability and employee loyalty. But this is not to imply that researchers have been obliged against their will to accept managerial values. Researchers are commonly of the same mind as managers so that: 'Most managers have had no trouble in getting social scientists to grant managerial premises because such premises have been assumed by the social scientists' (Baritz, 1975: 334). Bearing this in mind, Wilbert E. Moore, in 1947, warned sociologists that the 'persistence of managerial assumptions underlying so much of their work would reduce their profession to a refined type of scientific management dedicated to exploiting labour' (Baritz, 1975: 335).

In this sense, by becoming dependent on the powerful and accepting their premises, and by proposing models of markets and production in which power is assumed to be neutralised or to operate only in the general interest, the scientists and the science they practice become servants of power. As a consequence, by arguing that workers are subject to the laws of the market, production and socio-psychology, as identified respectively by economists, engineers and sociologists/social psychologists, experts could propose that it was to the worker's advantage to go along with management provided they were managed in accordance with those laws. It follows from this that any attempt by workers to organise in their own sectional interests would at best have no beneficial effect and at worst would be counter-productive. But the record does not show unambiguously that what is good for business is necessarily in the best interest of the workers they employ.

Markets and systems of work organisation in operation

There is now a considerable body of literature suggesting a positive link between the use of HRM practices and performance, particularly when such methods as flexible work assignments, work teams, skill training, effective communications and incentive pay schemes are used in combination.[11] The superior performance of close worker involvement and cooperation compared with arms-length market relations and hierarchical management has also been demonstrated by the product market success of what Best (1990) described as the *new competition*. This brought to the market improved design, greater variety, high quality and more rapid product innovation, as well as keener prices.

The *new competition* originated with European and Japanese producers, many of whom combined leading edge HRM and close relations with suppliers and customers.[12] Within these more competitively successful productive systems, work organisation was participatory and non-hierarchical and inter-firm links were close and cooperative rather than hands-off and antagonistic.[13] The result has been a more effective mobilisation of the commitment, skills and knowledge of workers and trading partners, serving to raise efficiency, improve quality and generate a faster rate of product, process and organisational innovation. The effect of the *new competition* has been to create a competitive environment in which top priority is given to the design of organisations such that they can fully exploit the cooperative nature of production.

Such organisational redesign has proved very difficult in Anglo-American productive systems. Rather than radically reforming their work systems, employers in the United States and the United Kingdom have generally attempted to incorporate degrees of worker involvement and other HRM practices into existing managerial structures and forms of corporate governance (Deakin *et al.*, 2001). Moreover, even when these changes have been successfully implemented, they have proven difficult to sustain (Konzelmann and Forrant, ch. 8). Consequently, little has been done to change 'the fundamental nature of the production system or threaten the basic organisation or power structure of the firms' (Applebaum and Batt, 1994: 22). Concurrently, neo-liberal macroeconomic policies, and globalisation have intensified competition in increasingly buyers' markets to the advantage of consumers, whilst deregulation has shifted the balance of power in the labour market in favour of capital and, in the capital market, in favour of shareholders.

Firms have responded to growing product and capital market pressures by passing on costs to suppliers, sub-contracting, cutting jobs and increasing the use of temporary and casual workers. But the main burden of securing higher performance at lower costs has fallen on the core work force. This has been driven by the changing market demands *and* the additional burdens imposed on the survivors by downsizing and the delayering of management. Workers are required to be more responsive and cooperative, to acquire greater skills, to intensify effort, to accept greater responsibilities and become more flexible. But, while employees have generally welcomed opportunities to take more control over the planning and execution of their work, distrust of management is widespread and the perception is that pay levels have failed to adequately compensate for the extra responsibility, accountability, workload, working hours and effort that workers are expected to bear (Burchell *et al.*, 2001).

The logic of the market versus the logic of production

At the heart of the problem is a fundamental contradiction between the logic of markets as an efficient mechanism for allocating resources and distributing income (as conceptualised by liberal economic theory) and the logic of the management of production as a process for effectively combining and exploiting productive forces (as conceptualised by HRM). This contradiction has been wished away by supposition that the market is an efficient coordinating mechanism ruling out the need for human agency. In his book, *The Fatal Conceit: The Errors of Socialism*, Hayek argued that direct cooperation within groups was an instinctual *primitive* trait superseded by individualisation and the ordering principle of the market (Hayek, 1988: ch. 1). What Hayek failed to understand (as no doubt primitive man succeeded in understanding) was that the essence of production is technical cooperation, requiring supportive social relations in order to ensure that those involved in production work effectively together.

The task of recovering the ground lost in understanding between primitive man and Hayek was left to management theorists, who drawing on engineering, psychological and sociological research, concluded that productive efficiency required close cooperation between those involved. What has been rediscovered is that the *primitive traits*, identified by Hayek as a hindrance to the development of markets, is actually essential for production. The human relations school learned that social and psychological well-being are crucial for creating the environment necessary for efficient production. What they failed to sufficiently recognise (or reveal) was that although meeting socio-psychological needs are important, well-being also has a material side. This omission had its advantage because it helped to steer the proponents of human relations away from the thorny question of distribution and towards the pretence of a total singleness of purpose of employers and their employees. However, while it may be true that workers do not live by bread alone, a sufficiency of bread is nevertheless important. And, moreover, it is not unreasonable to suppose that workers might not be content with leaving the determination of that sufficiency solely to the whim of the market or to the unilateral decisions of management.

It cannot therefore be simply assumed that workers are either wholly *economic* (relentlessly pursuing their own interest), or wholly *social* (satisfied if their socio-psychological needs are met). Rather than assuming that workers blindly and relentlessly pursue their own selfish interests or, providing their psyches are appropriately massaged, that they pursue those of their employers, it would seem more reasonable to suppose that workers have a complex set of social, psychological and economic needs. It also seems reasonable to suppose that workers are *reflexive* in attempting to satisfy these diverse needs, and that they respond negatively or positively, in terms of cooperation in production, depending on how they perceive the fairness of the terms and conditions of employment and their treatment by their employers (Sabel, 1992).

It follows from this that there are two stages to determining fairness in employment: the formal contract, which lays out the explicit terms and conditions, and more implicit commitments, which go beyond the formal contract and determine the productive effectiveness of the relationship. These less formal terms have been described as the *psychological* contract, but could perhaps be better described as the *human relations* contract. They capture the commitments made by workers and their employers to work effectively together. The operation of the human relations contract requires workers to be fully committed to their employers' business in exchange for fair pay, job and income security and a good working environment. A breach of this contract risks inciting a retaliatory withdrawal from full cooperation with an adverse effect on productivity and competitive performance. Effective cooperation therefore depends on agreement on both the explicit and implicit terms of the employment relations, together with the expectation by both sides that commitments made will be honoured.

In a complex economic system, however, the ability to honour commitments is not entirely in the hands of those making them. It is necessary therefore to consider the environmental conditions in which relationships are formed as well as the nature of the relationships themselves. To set the scene for this discussion, it is worth re-examining, in somewhat stylised terms, the nature of work systems.

Work systems and the terms and conditions for cooperation

The essence of work systems is that employers and workers have shared and separate interests. Both have a stake in total value added, which is generated by their cooperation in production; but each claims a share which limits what the other can have. The claim to a share that either side makes is likely to be tempered by the necessity of ensuring that the other side continues to cooperate effectively so as to secure the highest level of operational and dynamic efficiency. The important point here is that in production, each party must take into account two different types of incentives: (1) their own; and (2) that needed to get their partner(s) into full cooperation with them. However, the sequence of events is that the decision to cooperate is taken prior to the realisation of the benefits from cooperation. In effect, in deciding the extent of their cooperation, individuals give a hostage to fortune, the outcome of which depends on how their partners respond. The choice being made is therefore between short- and long-term interest: whether to take a larger slice now and risk a smaller pie later or vice versa. What that choice ultimately depends upon is the promises others make and whether or not they can be trusted to keep them.

Cooperation and trust

The essence of trust in production is that it provides a guarantee that the agreed terms will be kept and that what is promised will be carried out to required specifications and quality standards, described by Sako (1992) as *contractual* and *competence* trust. But it goes beyond contract fulfilment to include *goodwill* trust. This includes a willingness to share information and ideas, honouring informal understandings and being ready to renegotiate contracts and, in a more social sense, being willing to give and take, to help in an emergency and to forgive occasional faults (Burchell and Wilkinson, 1997). Goodwill trust gives the assurance that someone is so dependable that they can be trusted to take initiatives without the risk that they will take advantage (Sako, 1992) and is essential for full cooperation within productive systems.

The hallmark of high trust systems is, therefore, that individuals and organisations working together provide open-ended commitments to cooperate, the returns from which are realised over an uncertain, long time period. Mutual trust acts to reduce uncertainty by increasing the confidence in truth, worth and reliability of people required to work together. The greater the trust each side has in the others, the greater will be the certainty that commitments made will not be abused. Trust, therefore, enables individuals to share expectations about the future, reducing uncertainty and allowing them to cooperate more effectively (Luhmann, 1979; Lane and Bachmann, 1996).

Uncertainty, though, is not confined to the unpredictability of the behaviour of those with whom there are close relationships. It extends to the environment in which the relations are formed and maintained. It, therefore, may prove impossible to maintain trust, not so much because of unreliability within the relationship, but also because uncertainty about the environment may make it difficult to make and keep commitments. Environmental uncertainty can be divided into social and economic uncertainty. *Social uncertainty* arises from the social relations which pervade production and exchange, and the social and political environment within which these relations are formed and reformed. *Economic uncertainty* results from economic forces, such as changes in technology, resource availability and consumer tastes. Risk associated with social uncertainty can be moderated by expanding contractual and less formal arrangements to include a wider range of relationships; or by establishing rules, standards and norms that rule out practices which create uncertainty. But economic uncertainty is much more profound because economic change is often difficult to predict and impossible to reverse. Economic change may also be destructive of existing relationships and institutions and the greater certainty they engender. The countering of economic uncertainty may therefore require more radical adjustments and more broadly based institutions.

Institutional foundations for trust

The importance of building trust in a relationship for any individual or group can be expected to be influenced by how dependent they are on the relationship and how long they expect it to last. For casual workers, each employment relationship is transient. As a result, they may believe that putting effort into building trust is not worthwhile. By contrast, establishing trust in an employment relationship may be much more important to a worker with highly specific skills, expectations of long-term employment and whose livelihood is highly dependent on the job. The sharing of such high levels of commitment with employers also contributes to an environment favourable to building trust. However, commitments in employment relations are often asymmetric.

Take for example the employment relationship in one of the plants in a multi-plant corporation. Workers, plant managers, corporate managers and shareholders all have a stake, but the importance of the stake to each of them varies. The well-being and future of workers and, perhaps to a lesser extent, plant managers, are tied up with the particular plant in which they work. On the other hand, the commitment of corporate managers is to the whole corporation. Its future, and that of its managers, may require plant closure in which case the interests of those employed there and the corporate managers are diametrically opposed. The commitment of shareholders is even looser than that of corporate management. Head count has become an important indicator of the value of shares and this puts jobs at risk. Moreover, the ready exit by shareholders via the stockmarket confronts corporate managers with the possibility of a takeover and concentrates their attention on *shareholder* value at the possible expense of other stakeholder interests. In this example, it is the level of the commitment of the least committed stakeholder which determines the level of certainty at the shop floor and hence whether workers can afford to trust. Thus, whilst the performance of an organisation depends on cooperation, which in turn depends on trust, the possibility of generating trust may be determined by those with the smallest commitment. More generally, although the success of productive activity requires all the participants to be trustworthy, the importance of trust, the degree of dependence and their ability to respond to a breach of trust may vary between the participants.

The capability of building trust within an organisation also depends on conditions in its external relationships.[14] The ability to conclude effective internal agreements both influences and is to a degree dependent on relationships within supply chains. Costs, prices, credit terms and speed of payment determine the financial capabilities of firms to meet the competing income claims of managers, workers and shareholders; and the quality and surety of delivery impinges on the firm's ability to meet customer requirements. In turn, the certainty that buyers will take delivery at agreed-upon terms is a major determinant of the supplier's ability to plan production and provide employment guarantees. Long-term trading relationships and the knowledge that customers will not switch suppliers (and vice versa) also make it easier to offer employment guarantees.

The nature of market competition is similarly an important determinant of the quality of productive system relationships, both internally and within supply chains. The use of market power to secure favourable price, credit and delivery terms is not conducive to the establishment of high quality trading relationships, nor is the disruption of supply and demand by unlimited price competition.

In both cases, resultant low trust relationships can be expected to have a cumulative effect as poor standards in employment and business relationships are extended throughout the productive system by protective and retaliatory responses.

This degenerative process, and the uncertainty it engenders, can be countered by the creation of generally applicable behaviour and performance standards to which individuals and groups are expected to subscribe. An example of this, is the effect of the interaction between the legal code and the private ordering of business relations through trade associations in Germany (Lane and Bachmann, 1996). German trade associations regulate against such practices as late payment and unfair pricing. They arbitrate disputes and organise countervailing measures against excessive market power to which members may be collectively subjected. They also establish quality and product standards, and collect and disseminate technical and cost information. Generally, 'by providing a common stock of knowledge and a shared set of norms for production and exchange, they coordinate expectations and remove ambiguity from inter-firm relationships' (Lane and Bachmann, 1996: 18). The workings of trade associations are supplemented and strengthened by the German legal code which requires firms to trade in good faith, to establish just prices and to engage in fair competition. This is further reinforced by the Standard Contract Terms Act, enacted to protect the weaker party to contracts. On the employment front, institutional and legal arrangements establish the rights to representation and collective bargaining, minimum terms and conditions of employment, effective health and safety protection and training; these citizen rights are furthered and protected by Germany's works council system and sector level collective bargaining.

As a consequence, the industrial environment in Germany is characterised by norms, rules and standards which are either legally binding or made *de facto* obligatory by the wide and systematic involvement of the industrial community. These, and the code of business ethics they foster, constitute expected behaviour to which business people conform more as a matter of course than as a matter of business strategy. In turn, this helps to create an environment in which conflict is contained, performance is assured and information is provided; where markets are stabilised by trading standards; and where the ability of smaller and weaker companies to survive and prosper is not unduly threatened by unfair terms and conditions imposed upon them. Such an environment supportive of trust has been created in Japan by closely dependent buyer–customer relations backed up by supportive industrial policies and legislation (Sako, 1992). In Italian industrial districts, a similarly high trust environment has been created by rather more voluntary means (Sengenberger *et al.*, 1990). In each of these cases institutional power contains the abuse of individual power and creates the conditions for trust in business and employment relations (Bachmann, 1999).

In their study of the quality of inter-firm relations, Lane and Bachmann (1996) drew a useful distinction between *systems trust* generated by laws, rules, norms and standards and the more *personal* trust which exists within and between close relationships. Similarly, Dei Otatti (1994) distinguished between *collective* and *personal* trust, treating collective trust as capital in which productive systems invest and which creates an environment in which high standards are expected. Collective trust both enhances and is enhanced by personal investments made by individuals in the building and sustaining of trusting relationships with each other. The importance of these organisational and institutional structures is the social certainty they generate. The more effective they are in this respect, the more successful they will be in improving the availability of resources and information; reducing conflict and the need for monitoring; and increasing the scope for cooperative productive relations. The important point is that an environment is created in which there are mutual obligations to find solutions which take into account the interests of all parties involved and provide incentives for each party to cooperate fully in these objectives.[15]

Nevertheless, periods of fundamental change and growing economic uncertainty can put excessive strains on organisations and institutions and the trust they foster. For example, *collective voice* at the level of the firm or the sector may not be enough in periods of rapid industrial transformation, especially if the changes require radical industrial reorganisation (Dei Ottati, 1997). There can be little doubt that such economic uncertainty is exacerbated by mass lay-offs and bankruptcies, the fears of which can trigger and sustain destructive competition. Breaking such a cycle in order to secure an orderly recovery, replace obsolete technology or restructure industry may require competition-limiting cooperation such as price-fixing, order-sharing and equipment scrapping. In Japan, for example, the consolidation of ownership or the creation of 'crisis cartels' have provided an effective means to these objectives (Best, 1990). Protection of labour standards by industry wide wage agreements has also proved to be an important mechanism for preventing erosion of the skilled labour force and for stabilising markets by taking wages and other employment conditions out of competition.

Effective representation and the related acceptance by unions and their members of responsibility for change played a central part in the evolution of the Swedish *model* and the cooperative environment it engendered. An early settlement between capital and labour at the national level established the rights of managers to manage, the rights of unions to organise and represent their members, and the rights of employees to share in the benefits of technical change. Swedish trade unions combined strong representation, a commitment to technical progress and *wage solidarity* by which wages were fixed by national bargaining so that poor performance by firms could not be compensated for by low pay. The political wing of the Swedish labour movement responded to the high levels of unemployment in the late 1920s by accepting the state's responsibility for joblessness and from this commitment developed the welfare state. The Swedish government also came to accept responsibility for the high rate of job displacement resulting from rapid technical change and developed active labour market policies combining high quality training, job creation and measures to encourage labour mobility.

In the 1960s, the disruptive effects of rapid economic progress and the growing shop floor opposition to Taylorist work organisation led to the enactment of a series of measures designed to limit managerial prerogative. These included the outlawing of unfair dismissal, the protection of the physical and psychological health of employees and the establishment of rights to paid leave for education. New legislation also introduced codetermination which gave unions the right to negotiate local agreements for the joint control of hiring and firing, work assignment and disciplinary matters. Involvement by unions and their members in the introduction of innovations in technology, improvements in work organisation and the work environment contributed significantly to the development of sociotechnical systems in which job satisfaction, responsibility and learning were an integral part of the social relations of production. The beneficial effect of these developments was reflected in growing employer support for them as well as recognition of their positive impact on competitiveness (Persson, 1997).

What the Swedish example demonstrates is that there are points beyond which firm and industry level measures cannot go. Moreover, institutions and organisations themselves may be victims of technical and other forms of economic change. In such cases, what are required are procedural, behavioural and performance standards designed to encourage the development of new industries, new forms of work organisation, training and retraining, industrial and occupational flexibility. But these broader objectives must be cast within the context of policies designed to secure fullemployment and environmental protection, and trade and capital movement regulation aimed at preventing unfair competition, disruptive price fluctuations and global uncertainty. Increasingly, these questions need to be addressed at the international level where as yet the democratic interests of the vast majority of populations are not sufficiently well represented.

Summary and conclusions

The conventional wisdom in economics and other social sciences, the accepted body of knowledge of how economies work, is a powerful force structuring productive systems and how they operate. The conventional wisdom is legitimated by the claims made by its proponents to have discovered scientific laws regulating economic and social activities. These claims rest on the objectivity of the underlying research which is compromised by the power context within which the knowledge is accumulated and the ideas refined and implemented.

Two main streams in the development of conventional economic wisdom have been identified: theories of exchange and theories of the management of production. Liberal economics, which evolved with capitalism, rests on the belief in egocentric *economic* man. Exchange provides the opportunity for self-seeking individuals to develop their capabilities; and competition in free markets both prevents the exploitation of power over resources and optimises economic well-being. With the increasing concentration of economic power, the liberal story has been modified, deployment of that power being justified by the theoretical argument that the markets work to select and foster those forms of power which benefit economic performance. However, any suggestion that such benefits can arise from collective action is denied on the grounds that they restrain the market forces which generate efficient economic outcomes. Liberal economics therefore serves to legitimise the power of large corporations whilst illegitimatising the power that workers and small organisations can mobilise by working together. The incorporation of the logic of the market into law and policy in the Anglo/American system means that there are few intermediating institutions and organisations between large corporations and individuals.

Within liberal economics the immutable laws of the market are assumed to operate in the spheres of both exchange and production. However, from the late nineteenth century onwards the practical need to improve production efficiency led to the development of theories of the management of production which ran counter to liberal economics. The first stage was the elaboration of *scientific management*. This persevered with the notion of *economic man* but claimed to have discovered scientific laws of production, which if properly implemented would provide management with the tools to efficiently organise work, provide incentives for full cooperation and serve as an impartial arbitrator for resolving the conflicting interests of managers and workers. The subsequent incorporation of socio-psychological knowledge into management of production theories by the human relations school challenged the idea of *economic man* and replaced it with the idea of *social* and *sentimental* man. Initially, human relations theory was concerned with identifying the physiological and social needs of workers and using this knowledge to improve the performance of Taylorist forms of work organisation. Further development led to the proposition that the greater involvement of workers in the planning and execution of work as part of a group activity improved their socio-psychological well-being and released their creativity.

Thus, in the development of the theory and practice of work organisation there has been a progressive shift away from the notion of the 'invisible hand of the market', through the idea of the 'visible hand of management' guided by engineering science, to view that hand of management as requiring more covert guiding by psychology and sociology. In this transformation, management's role has been redefined from that of authoritarian, however benevolent, initiator, organiser and director of work to that of a democratic 'facilitator' of a participatory, cooperative and self-regulating system. In this process, workers have been reconceptualised from *factors of production*, compelled when necessary into compliance with contractual promise, though passive participants in centrally planned and regulated work systems, to full partners in cooperative production. This evolution in the roles of management and workers has been accompanied by a redefinition of the workplace from being 'pluralistic', where interests of the two sides are separate and potentially conflictual, to being 'unitary', where their interests are in common. In general, while developments in liberal economics have justified the increasing centralisation of power, developments in theories of production have required an increasing decentralisation of responsibility for production.

These separate developments of the logic of the market and the logic of the management of production have had quite contrary effects. The distributional interests of business prioritise the logic of the market whilst competitiveness in product markets prioritises the logic of production management. Moreover, at the policy level, especially in the Anglo/American system, the distributional interests of business predominate so that the logic of the market dictates labour market, industrial, competition and corporate governance policy. The prioritising of the logic of the market in this way means asymmetry in commitment, for whereas the pre-eminence of the market means that employers can only make conditional commitments to their workers, the efficient management of production requires workers to make unconditional commitment to their employers. The unconditional demands made by management require workers to be totally committed to organisational objectives and to collectivise their effort, while the conditional promises made by managers mean that workers are readily disposable and that risk is individualised. In Wood's words (see above), there is no evidence that workers have failed 'to develop themselves in order to accept fresh responsibilities.' Rather, the evidence is that neither employers nor governments have 'taken the responsibility for providing the context in which this can happen'.

Meanwhile, sandwiched between the needs of the market and the needs of production, the new forms of work organisation have thus become new forms of exploitation, made more sophisticated by worker involvement in the process. But as with more traditional forms of exploitation, the new forms are counter-productive. Increased work intensification and employment uncertainty have served to lower trust, reduce morale and motivation, and turn stress into a major industrial disease. Not surprisingly, the greater involvement of workers has not diminished their sense of need for trade union protection, or the importance of representation, independent of management, in their working lives (Burchell *et al.*, 2001).

The central problem is the clash between the conditions for promoting cooperation and the way markets operate. This is not to suggest that cooperation in production and markets are necessarily incompatible. The problem is that markets, as with other institutions in productive systems, serve two separate and conflicting purposes. First, they serve creativity by providing the opportunity for developing competitive strategies based on improved products, processes and organisational forms so that superior forms of work organisation can better meet consumer needs. In this way, markets provide the means by which the mutual interests of consumers, owners, managers and workers can be realised. But, second, markets also provide the opportunity for the exercise of relative power and the securing of advantage in distribution. In this, the interests of consumers, capitalists and workers are sharply divided and unrestrained rivalry is potentially destructive of the cooperation in production upon which creativity depends.

Expressed in the terms of the productive systems analysis, the mutuality of interest inherent in production has found its expression in theories of production management whereas theories of markets encapsulate the conflict inherent in distribution. However, the relationships of power within which the theories have been formulated have led to a denial of any significant misuse of capitalist power in markets or production, and consequently any need for countervailing forces. Thus, rights of corporations to pursue their interests in markets and managerial prerogative in the management of production are couched in terms of their service to the public interest. Any hindrance to market forces or the exercise of managerial prerogative is then deemed inherently anti-social, effectively ruling out the possible development of institutions and organisations by which the contradictions between mutual and separate interests can be resolved.

In European, Japanese and other productive systems, where the management of production has played a more central role in policy making, the polarisation between corporate interests and those of workers and small organisations is much less than in the Anglo/American system. Rather, institutions and organisations have emerged to mediate these interests and to protect the weaker stakeholders. In this way, *institutional power* (Bachmann, 1999) has been deployed to curb individual power and this has given greater scope for the realisation of mutual interests and for the development of high-road production and marketing strategies. A major threat to this enlightenment is the neo-liberal revival following the inflationary crisis of the 1970s. This has revitalised the logic of the market and strengthened the powers it serves. In the Anglo/American system, this has increasingly polarised income and wealth and added to the difficulties of reforming production. In turn, the pressure for international standards of trade and finance has become increasingly globalised. This has extended the influence of liberal economics, and the threat it poses to the institutional and organisational framework supportive of the realisation of mutual interest in production. As a consequence, despite the superior competitive performance of the countries which took the lead in demonstrating the competitive advantages of cooperative forms of production, they are currently being pressed to deregulate their labour and product markets and scale down welfare provision. This no doubt resonates with the economically powerful in those systems with most to gain from deregulation, and those serving their interests, so that support for neo-liberal solutions is gaining ground. How far the countries which showed the benefits of decency and trust follow the United States and United Kingdom's route will determine whether or not the world progresses further into a new dark age – of extending and deepening inequality, poverty, exploitation and production inefficiency. But that is another and unfolding story.

Notes

1 This is worked out in detail in Wilkinson (1998).
2 O'Sullivan (1998) and Lazonick (1991).
3 Which he considered to be the fourth factor of production together with land, labour and capital.
4 A term Marshall preferred to 'competition' because of the need for a term 'that does not imply any moral quality, whether good or evil, but which indicates the undisputed fact that modern business and industry are characterised by more self-reliant habits, more forethought, more deliberate and free choice' (Marshall, 1947: 9–10).
5 Marx (1976), ch. 25 and, especially, pp. 762–72.
6 Under the Master and Servant Acts the Justices of the Peace were empowered to punish workers for any 'misdemeanour, miscarriage, or ill-behaviour' and quitting employment before the end of the agreed time by abating wages, discharging them from their contracts or by imprisonment. The magistrates sat daily so that the Master and Servant Acts could be speedily enforced. Prosecutions never fell below 7,000 a year between

1854 and the repeal of the Acts in 1875 and peaked at over 17,000 in 1872 (Deakin, ch. 5)

7 'When choosing as the minimum standard of living for his study of poverty in York a physiological minimum based on labour efficiency, Rowntree linked his anti-poverty campaign to industrial performance' (Biggs, 1964).

8 Blyton and Turnbull (1994), Towers (1996) and Appelbaum and Batt (1994) provide surveys of the HRM literature and debates about its deployment. Cully *et al.* (1999) reports on the use of HRM practices in Britain as does Wood and Menezes (1998).

9 Wood (2000: 130).

10 Foreword to the White Paper, *Fairness at Work* Cm 3968 (1998), at p. 3.

11 For a review of the evidence of the effect of clustering HRM strategies on company performance see Slinger (2000) and Ichniowski *et al.* (1997).

12 Applebaum and Batt (1994) in their extremely valuable study identified four main systems of cooperative production: Japanese lean production; Italian flexible specialisation; German diversified quality production; and Swedish sociotechnical systems. The Japanese and Swedish systems are more firmly rooted in Taylorist mass production than the German or, particularly, the Italian. But what the four systems have in common is the importance given to high levels of worker training and the success they have achieved in closely involving workers at all levels in the organisation and management of production, in product and process innovation and in the development of organisations and institutions designed to facilitate cooperative working relationships.

13 Inter-firm relations in Britain have been typified as 'adversarial dealings between short-horizon contractors, each party seeking out its immediate advantage', reflecting the market individualism that has traditionally driven the English law of contract (Brownsword, 1997: 255).

14 For discussion of this see Konzelmann Smith (1996).

15 For the development of these ideas see *International Contributions to Political Economy*, Volume 7 and Wilkinson (1998).

References

Appelbaum, E. and Batt, R. (1994) *The New American Workplace: Transforming Work Systems in the United States*. New York: ILR Press.

Atiyah, P. S. (1979) *The Rise and Fall of the Freedom of Contract*. Oxford: Clarendon Press.

Bachmann, R. (1999) 'Trust, power and control in trans-organisational relations, ESRC Centre for Business Research', Working Papers No. 129.

Baritz, L. (1975) 'The servants of power', in Esland, G., Salaman and Speakman, M.-A. (eds), *People and Work*, Edinburgh: Holmes Macdonald.

Berk, G. (1994) *Alternative Tracks: The Constitution of American Industrial Order*, 1865–1917. Baltimore: The John Hopkins University Press.

Best, M. (1990) *The New Competition: Institutions of Industrial Restructuring*. Cambridge, Massachusetts: Harvard University Press.

Biggs, A. (1964) *A Study of the Work of Seebolm Rowntree, 1871–1954*. London: Longmans.

Blyton, P. and Turnbull, P. (1992) 'Debates, dilemmas and contradictions', in Blyton, P. and Turnbull, P. (eds), *Reassessing Human Resource Management*, London: Sage Publications.

Brownsword, R. (1997) 'Contract Law, co-operation and good faith, the movement from static to market individualism', in Deakin, S. and Michie, J. (eds), *Contract, Co-operation and Competition*, Oxford: Oxford University Press.

Burchell, B., Ladipo, D. and Wilkinson, F. (2001) *Job Insecurity and Work Intensification*. London: Routledge.

Burchell, B. and Wilkinson, F. (1997) 'Trust, business relationships and the contractual environment', *Cambridge Journal of Economics*, 21, 217–37.

Chandler, A. D. (1977) *The Visible Hand: The Managerial Revolution in American Business.* Cambridge: Harvard University Press.

Coase, R. H. (1937) 'The nature of the firm', *Economica*, 4, 386–405.

Cully, M., Woodland, S., O'Reilly, A. and Dix, G. (1999). *Britain at Work.* London: Routledge.

Deakin, S., Hobbs, R., Konzelmann, S. and Wilkinson, F. (2001) 'Partnership, ownership and control', ESRC Centre for Business Research, Working Papers No. 200.

Deakin, S. and Slinger, G. (1997) 'Hostile takeovers, corporate law and the theory of the firm', ESRC Centre for Business Research, Working Papers No. 56.

Dei Ottati, G. (1994) 'Trust, interlinking transactions and credit in industrial districts', *Cambridge Journal of Economics*, 18(6).

Dei Ottati, G. (1997) 'The changing forms of supplier relations in an Italian industrial district: an exit-voice approach', Department of Economics, University of Florence, mimeographed.

Galbraith, J. K. (1987) *The Affluent Society.* Harmondsworth: Penguin.

Guest, D. (1987) 'Human resource management and industrial relations', *Journal of Management Studies*, 24(5), 503–21.

Hayek, F. (1988) *The Fatal Conceit.* London: Routledge.

Hollway, W. (1991) *Work Psychology and Work Organisation.* London: Sage.

Hoxie, R. F. (1915) *Scientific Management and Labour.* New York: D. Appleton and Company.

Ichniowski, C., Shaw, K. and Prennushi, G. (1997) 'The effects of human resource management practices on productivity: a study of steel finishing lines', *American Economic Review*, 87(3), 291–312.

Kirzner, I. (1997) 'How markets work: disequilibrium, entrepreneurship and discovery', IEA, Paper No. 133, London, Institute of Economic Affairs.

Konzelmann Smith, S. (1996) 'Co-operative corporate level strategies', *Journal of Economic Issues*, XXX(3), 797–827.

Konzelmann, S. and Forrant, R. (2001) 'Creative work systems and destructive markets', ESRC Centre for Business Research, Working Papers No. 187.

Lane, C. and Bachmann, R. (1996) 'The social construction of trust: supplier relations in Britain and Germany', *Organisation Studies*, 17(3), 365–95.

Lazonick, W. (1991) *Business Organisation and the Myth of the Market.* Cambridge: Cambridge University Press.

Luhmann, N. (1979) *Trust and Power.* London: Wiley.

Marshall, A. (1947) *Industry and Trade.* London: Macmillan.

Marx, K. (1976) *Capital, Vol. 1.* Harmondsworth: Penguin.

Miller, P. and Rose, N. (1998) 'Governing economic life', in Mabey, C., Salaman, G. and Storey, J. (eds), *Strategic Human Resource Management.*

O'Brien, D. P. (1990) 'Marshall's industrial analysis', *Scottish Journal of Economics*, 61(1), 61–84.

O'Sullivan, M. (1998) 'Sustainable prosperity, corporate governance, and innovation in Europe', in Michie, J. and Grieve Smith, J. (eds), *Globalisation, Growth and Governance*, Oxford: Oxford University Press.

Pollard, S. (1993) *The Genesis of Modern Management.* Aldershot: Greggs Revivals.

Persson, B. (1997) 'Unions, management and the government: the Swedish model', *International Contributions to Labour Studies*, 7, *Special Issue on Co-operative and Antagonistic Work Organisation*: 119–33.

Rowntree, S. (1938) *The Human Factor in Production*, 3rd edition. London: Longmans.

Sabel, C. (1992) 'Building new forms of co-operation in a volatile economy', in Pyke, F. and Sengenberger, W. (eds), *Industrial Districts and Local Economic Generation*, Geneva: International Institute for Labour Studies.

Sako, M. (1992) *Prices, Quality and Trust: Inter-Firm Relations in Britain and Japan*. Cambridge: Cambridge University Press.

Shumpeter, J. (1943) *Capitalism, Socialism and Democracy*, London: George Allen and Unwin Ltd.

Sengenberger, W., Loveman, G. and Piore, M. (1990) *The Re-emergence of Small Enterprises: Industrial Restructuring in Industrialised Countries*. Geneva: IILS.

Sewell, G. and Wilkinson, B. (1992) 'Empowerment or emasculation, shopfloor surveillancs in a total quality organisation', in Blyton, P. and Turnbull, P. (eds), *Reassessing Human Resource Management*, London: Sage Publications.

Slinger, G. (2000). *Essays on Stakeholders and Takeovers*, University of Cambridge PhD. (unpublished).

Towers, B. (ed.) (1996) *The Handbook of Human Resource Management*, 2nd edition. Oxford: Blackwells.

Trist, E. and Murray, H. (1993) 'Historical overview', in Trist, E., Emery, F. and Murray, H. (eds), *The Social Engagement of Social Science: Vol. II, The Socio-Technical Perspective*, Philadelphia: University of Pennsylvania Press.

Walton, R. E. and McKersie, R. B. (1965) *A Behavioural Theory of Labour Negotiations*. New York: McGraw Hill.

White Paper (1998) *Fairness at Work*. Cm 3968.

Wilkinson, F. (1983) 'Productive systems', *Cambridge Journal of Economics*, 7, 413–29.

Wilkinson, F. (1998) 'Co-operation, the organisation of work and competitiveness', ESRC Centre for Business Research, Working Papers No. 85.

Williamson, O. (1985). *The Economic Institutions of Capitalism*. New York: Free Press.

Wood, S. (2000) 'From voluntarism to partnership: a third way overview of the public policy debate in British industrial relations', in collins, Davies, H. P. and Rideout, R. (eds.), *Legal Regulation of the Employment Relationship*, London: Kluwer Law Interntional.

Wood, S. and De Menezes, L. (1998) 'High commitment management in the United Kingdom: evidence from the workplace industrial relations survey and employers', Manpower and Skill Practice Survey, *Human Relations*, 51(4), 485–515.

www.tuc.org.uk/partnership/six_principles.cfm.

3 Productive systems, markets and competition as 'Instituted Economic Process'

Mark Harvey

Introduction

> The central proposition of this paper is that economic, social and political forces combine in determining how economies develop and that the result is a dynamic non-equilibrium process which can only be revealed by empirical observation... There are and can be *no* universal, pre-determined, "true" systems to which underlying economic forces are tending.
>
> ('Productive systems', Wilkinson, 1983: 417)

This synopsis of a 'productive systems' approach contains two key elements which mutually sustain even if they do not imply one another, one epistemological, and the other theoretical. On the one hand, theoretical knowledge of 'how economies actually work' can only be built on the basis of empirical, historical and comparative research which generates new, often messy and discomforting 'facts'. This view places limitations on the role of a priori reasoning in theory building by insisting on maintaining its connection with the grubby practices of generating empirical data[1] (Harvey, 1999). On the other, Wilkinson is arguing for a substantive theory of how economies develop without universal causes or explanations, a theory of historically specific dynamisms located within given productive systems. He is arguing not only that there are no, but that there *can be* no, universal states towards which economies are driven by postulated universal forces.

This chapter explores that idea, theoretically and empirically, with respect to competition. It focuses on competition because, as a 'market force', it is often accorded a role of 'universal equaliser', one of the forces necessary to bring about homogeneity across an economy or economies, and, in the current context, a driver of globalisation. The argument is made, in Wilkinsonian spirit, that competition too forms part of historically specific productive systems, that as a process it changes historically, and that it is hence a different process in different circumstances. As such, both historically and comparatively, forms of competitive process within productive systems underlie the generation of variety of capitalisms, rather than being their exogenous 'equaliser'.

To achieve this goal, an 'Instituted Economic Process' approach is brought together with a productive systems analysis. Originally promulgated by Polanyi,

'Instituted Economic Process' (Polanyi, 1957) is a framework in which specifically *economic* processes can be seen as instituted, in different modes and in different historical configurations, along with other social, legal and political institutions. In this way, it is hoped that a productive systems approach will be both developed and enhanced. In arguing that economies always develop in combination with legal, political and social institutions and norms, there is always a residual possible interpretation that the latter mitigate, modify or regulate otherwise ahistorical, dis-embedded, economic forces. Understanding economic forces as equally instituted as other societal institutions, poses problems for understanding their interaction and articulation. But it is no longer a question of counterposing non-instituted universal economic forces against particular and historically specific social institutions. And to develop this point, some ground-clearing will be necessary to disentangle this Polanyian idea from the much more widespread ideas of 'embeddedness', on the one hand, or his historical see-saw dynamic of societal regulation pitted against economic self-regulation found in *The Great Transformation* (Polanyi, 1944), on the other (Hollingsworth and Boyer, 1997).[2]

The concept of a 'productive system'[3] is itself very much a concept of an *economic* system, and its focus is economic in terms of labour and capital, prices, wages, supply, demand, markets and technology, 'where the forces of production combine in the process of production' (Wilkinson, 1983: 417). It is clear that a productive system has at its core the process of production, which engages labour together with means of production and technologies (soft and hard). But, with firms or individual capitals as key units in capitalist economies, this process of production opens up to the labour market on one side and product markets on the other. A productive system is a historical arrangement which includes production, firm organisation and markets. If much attention has rightly been paid to labour markets (Wilkinson, 1981; Craig *et al.*, 1985) stressing the social and institutional constraints that affect both supply and demand for labour, it is clear that both sectoral business organisation and product markets interact strongly with labour markets, taking the productive system as a whole (Craig *et al.*, 1982).

Thus, as an empirical and historical object, a productive system as a whole is a challengingly complex and interconnected set of relations to investigate. For Wilkinson, markets, whether labour or product, are highly political in the sense that they inherently involve power relations, whether between capital and labour, or between firms with varying degrees of control over prices for production inputs or outputs, depending on levels of concentration, possession of bottleneck technologies, strategic location or other factors from which firms derive such control. In this analysis, competition figures as the exercise of *economic* power between economic rivals. Were such power to be exercised without the restraint of norms of trust and cooperation, as naked economic power, the consequences are generally seen by him as leading to decreased economic efficiency. In combination with cooperation, and in the right balance, competition can stimulate innovation and flexibility (Wilkinson and You, 1992; Deakin and Wilkinson, 1995).[4] But, whether in product or labour markets, excessive competition is seen as 'essentially degenerative', leading to price cutting which may first be expressed in terms of debasement of product quality or the quality and skills of labour, but ultimately destroys the productive capacity of a system which rests upon a level of cooperation, trust, standard setting and information sharing. Thus competition is by no means a universally progressive dynamic force, but critically depends on a countervailing presence of socio-political, and legal frameworks and norms within which it occurs that permit or sustain basic and essential levels of cooperation and trust. Without such frameworks, competition as an economic force always risks running out of control, destroying productive systems.

Finally, perhaps the least developed aspect of the productive systems approach has been in relation to changes in productive systems. Clearly envisaged (Wilkinson, 1983: 421–5) as a historical transformation of the whole set of interconnected relations that make up a productive system, new patterns of demand, alterations in power relations between labour and capital or between firms, changing external economic conditions, and state interventions, are all seen as contributors to such major shifts. Moreover, competitive advantage remains a test of productive systems, in their capacity to sustain productivity growth and create new markets, combined with adaptive socio-political institutions and norms.

Having schematically outlined the 'productive system' as an object of analysis, the following section will undertake a brief ground-clearing necessary to introduce an 'Instituted Economic Process' approach. The third section then sets out the analytical framework for theorising competition as instituted economic process.[5] This is followed by a synthetic empirical analysis of historical changes in competition processes within productive systems, taking the UK food and food-retailing system as an example. It addresses the issue of change from one productive system to another, and the consequently changing *forms* of competition. The chapter concludes by arguing that changes in productive systems, within which competition processes are now fully incorporated, are better explained by contradictions within and between them, than by some external, universal market force.

Towards an 'Instituted Economic Process' approach

The concept of economic processes as instituted was first explicitly formulated by Karl Polanyi, and in order to weigh its full significance, it is first necessary to disentangle it from the concept of embeddedness for which Polanyi is much better known, as well as from its pair 'dis-embeddedness' which equally has found less favour. It should be emphasised that this is an attempt to develop the notion of IEP from the rather confused and tangled usage within Polanyi's own work, on the one hand, and on the other, to suggest that Polanyi had in embryo a much more radical agenda than the notion of embeddedness, as elaborated notably by Granovetter (1985, 1992) and Granovetter and McGuire (1998). The concept of 'embeddedness' carries with it the idea that economic relations are moulded and shaped by the social relations and contexts within which they occur (Polanyi, 1944: 46, 49; 1957: 250).[6] Thus, in the terms of the above discussion on legal and contractual institutions, the concept might be used to say that transactions are 'embedded' in such a societal framework. Granovetter's work, however, appropriated the concept for purposes of developing a more actor-oriented approach, with embeddedness referring to 'dense and stable networks of relations, shared understandings, and political coalitions' (Granovetter, 1985: 501). And he argued that trust and cooperative relations developed through 'concrete personal relations and the obligations inherent in them... quite apart from institutional arrangements' (Granovetter, 1985: 501; 1992: 495).

This notion of 'embeddedness' ultimately entails a double reduction of economic processes, structures and institutions into the 'congealed social networks' from which they ultimately derive, double in the sense of dissolving macro-structural change into micro-interpersonal interaction *and* economic into social processes (Granovetter, 1992). The account of the emergence of the American electrical utilities industry becomes a conspiracy between a handful of interconnected individuals (Granovetter and McGuire, 1998), a view that might be a consoling myth to contemporary inhabitants of California, but has little to do with structures of capital and resource flows necessary to account for bankruptcies and brown-outs.

In tracing this particular appropriation of the concept of embeddedness, its latent potential for sociologising the economy out of existence, and of dissolving institutions of price, capital, competition, industrial division of labour, supply, demand, market etc. into emergent networks of interpersonal relations becomes manifest. This seems quite remote from Polanyi's original intention and usage. Indeed, when analysing the development of the 'self-regulating market' in *The Great Transformation* Polanyi suggested very forcefully that the development of an economy during the industrial revolution involved *all* factors becoming commodities (including notably land, labour and money). Industrial capitalism was a key historical moment when economic institutions became more sharply differentiated from non-economic institutions:

> For once the economic system is organised in separate institutions, based on specific motives and conferring special status, society must be shaped in such a manner as to allow that system to function according to its own laws... A market economy can function only in a market society.
>
> (Polanyi, 1944: 57)

The commodification of labour, in particular its separation from preceding modes of subsistence living, and the development of urbanisation, meant that many more social interactions were mediated by money exchanges and price, and as such became instituted in specifically *economic* institutions. Thus, the institution of the economic in a society was central to Polanyi's later analysis (Polanyi, 1957: 250), and he argues that economic processes then establish their own patterns of regularity, and reproduce themselves through flows of money, capital, production and markets. Moreover, adopting a formula similar to a notion of habitus, Polanyi argues also that 'no individual economic motives need come into play'

(Polanyi, 1944: 49), because social organisation 'runs in its ruts', and the motive for gain, or 'rational economic calculation' also become instituted as distinctively *economic* norms of behaviour (Polanyi, 1944: 41–2). Whether manifest in general characteristics of individual reasoning, calculation or motivation or in major institutions such as markets, currencies or forms of stock-holding, the economic becomes differentiated from the non-economic as an on-going process of institution. *How* the economic is separately instituted – for example in relation to the household – may vary significantly from one epoch of capitalism to another, or from one productive system to another. But *that* the economic is instituted and acquires specific economic dynamisms is central to a concept of 'Instituted Economic Process'. This can be represented diagrammatically.

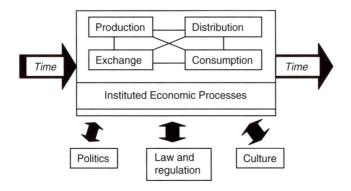

The central consequences that can be drawn out of this approach are three-fold. First, given that economic process is an instituted process – open to de- and re-institution – it is socially, comparatively and historically variable. That applies to capital, labour, price mechanisms, markets – as well as to economic motives, rationales and strategies. It fundamentally underpins a notion of varieties of capitalism. Second, rather than talking of Instituted Economic Processes and their context as socially 'embedding', the specificity of economic instituted processes can be seen to find their 'place' in different articulations with legal, political and civic institutions. So there is no question of the economic being dissolved in the social, or vice versa, as with an oversociologised view of embeddedness. Rather there is mutual conditioning between, for example, competition law and industrial organisation (Best, 1990). Third, and likewise, an IEP approach opens up the possibility of running through from micro- to macro-, from the motive for gain to the Gold Standard, and the articulation between different scales of instituted process. Thus, for Polanyi, both the motive for gain and the Gold Standard are prime examples of 'Instituted Economic Process', the former very likely being articulated with all kinds of networks of interdependencies at the micro-social level; the latter being a transnational, trans-societal instituted economic process, relatively dis-embedded from such micro-social networks.

Competition as 'Instituted Economic Process'

Developing an IEP approach in relation to competition will involve looking at a number of different dimensions, under the basic assumption that competition, far from being a universal or natural law of the market, is instituted differently in different historical and comparative circumstances. The focus becomes to study competition in its varied modes of institution, and, being multi-dimensional, needs to be analysed as a complex phenomenon. Five interrelated aspects of the institutionalisation of competitive processes can be distinguished:

1   The co-institution of markets and competition
2   The institution of classes of economic agent and of competition within but not between such classes
3   The institution of units of competition (e.g. firms, supply chains, clusters and atomistic individuals)
4   The institution of multiple scales of competition (local, regional, global ...)
5   The institution of formal and non-formal norms of competition and their interaction

Here particular attention will be paid to the first three of these aspects.[7]

Markets and forms of competition are mutually instituted

The starting point for an understanding of competition as an 'Instituted Economic process' is that it is manifest in market exchanges, as indeed Weber suggested when schematically characterising a market as comprising social groups of actors, buyers and sellers, between each of which there was competition for opportunities for exchange (Weber [1922], 1968: 635). Beyond arguing that such competition reflected a power struggle based on the relative powers of the actors engaged in exchange, in a 'peaceful conflict' within the 'order governing the market' (Weber [1922], 1968: 38), however, Weber suggests little about how the form that conflict took and the nature of the order of the market might co-vary.

The social organisation of the parties to the exchange, the mode of exchange (e.g. transparency, repeatability integration[8]), the constitution of the 'objects' of exchange (e.g. extent of standardisation, regulation and control of quality), the pricing mechanisms (e.g. centralised auction, bartering, price-taking or price-setting) are each open to variation as a consequence of which *whom* competition is between, *what* competition is about, and *how* competition is pursued will also vary.[9]

Thus, we can take New Covent Garden[10] as a market which conforms to a stereotypic view of markets as a single place where buyers and sellers are gathered together to exchange physical products, as an illustrative example. Throughout many centuries of existence this market underwent many radical and structural changes across all these dimensions of market and competition institution. To become a wholesale market, its current institutional form, wholesale traders as an economic class of agents, had to be distinguished both from direct producer-traders, and from retailer-traders. Only during the nineteenth century did wholesaling, as a distinct economic function, begin to emerge. At its apogee this wholesale market became the dominant price-setting market for the United Kingdom, as the market through which a high percentage of national fruit and vegetable produce was channelled. But it only became such through its strategic metropolitan location at the centre of the rail and road network of distribution. The prices set at New Covent Garden essentially determined the broad parameters of prices arrived at in other primary and secondary wholesale markets across the country.[11] It created the scale of competition by constituting a central point of concentration between highly diffuse, dispersed and often small scale, producers on one side, and 150,000 independently purchasing retail outlets on the other (Runciman Committee, 1957).

Within the market, a characteristic form of trading and spot market pricing developed, with traders obtaining income by charging standard commission rates on traded prices and volumes. Traders acted very much as growers' agents on a regularised 'personal' trust basis,[12] and the market was operated as a daily clearing market, with no floor in quality standards. A 'buyers' walk' displayed unpriced produce, and deals were individually cut between retailers or their agents and wholesale traders. Prices were published at the end of each trading day. Thus a particular institutional form of trading, and a particular form of competitive price adjustment in a clearing spot market, became the dominant institutional form across the country.

But, this form of competition has had its historical day. Supermarkets now no longer source this type of produce from wholesale markets. Competition has both moved elsewhere, and changed form. It is in this sense that market exchanges, market scale and competitive processes are co-instituted. In terms of a 'productive systems' analysis, this particular type of market presupposed an organisation of production, distribution and retail, as well as distinctive forms of product quality, to meet the developing demand in concentrated urban centres.

In a more general but similar way, it can be seen that the formation of the broad categories of labour, product and capital markets, each with their own distinctive competitive processes[13] is itself the outcome of instituted economic process. The institutions of a stock market, for example, involve quite distinct, and historically changing, processes of competition, as can be seen from various developments and possibilities of European or cross-Atlantic merger, alongside distinctive rules for trading, and formal regulation.

In their critique of labour market segmentation theory, the Cambridge Labour Studies Group compared six industries that had been covered by Wage Council agreements for minimum wages, and argued that there was a strong interaction between competition within particular product markets and competition within their respective labour markets (Craig *et al.*, 1982, 1985). The organisation and concentration of employers[14] on one side of the exchange, and of trades unions on the other, were strongly affected by the product markets and the extent to which these were dominated by price-cutting forms of competition, or whether competition was occurring in expanding or contracting markets.

In my own work, comparing different European labour markets, it is clear that different quality and pricing institutions for labour, and different frameworks for regulating long-term, short-term, temporary and part-time contracts fundamentally condition the forms of competition within labour markets (Harvey, 2000; Harvey *et al.*, 2002). A conclusion from this work is that the commodity purchased in the exchange between capital and labour is instituted differently in differing countries: there is not common or comparable commodity, labour, purchasable across all European labour markets. Moreover, such differences have led to major political debates about the competitiveness of 'high social cost' and 'low social cost' labour. However, given the radical incommensurability between what is being purchased in two disparate labour markets; given the 'indirect' competition via product markets; and given exchange rate fluctuations, it is clear that there is an absence of 'normalised' competition at this level. There are no overarching, instituted, measures in the absence of a common currency. So, from an IEP perspective, the *indirect* competition between diverse labour markets via product markets, and institutional forms of fluctuating exchange rates and monetary institutions, exemplify the institutedness of competition. We shall return to this point in considering different instituted scales of competition.

Asymmetric power and mutual dependency

Competition generally takes place *within* the same class of economic agent, but not *between* classes of economic agent, and the formation of such classes is itself a result of instituted economic process. Thus, to continue with labour markets, the focus of competition is *amongst* employers (capital) and *amongst* employees (labour), facing each other across an exchange relationship, as a consequence of the formation of two distinct classes of economic agent performing distinct economic functions.[15] But competition does not occur *between* labour and capital.[16] The exchange relation is characterised by mutual dependency (owners of capital need labour, people are, in varying ways, obliged to sell their labour), and asymmetric power relations. The kind of power wielded by capital (degree of concentration, domination in the market etc.) is different from the kind of power wielded by labour (from individual sale through to various forms of countervailing association). In this exchange relation, the nature of competition as affected by concentration or organisation of capital on one side of this power equation affects the opportunities of exchange, just as the nature of competition on the other side of the equation can be affected by forms of association and by labour market institutions such as the minimum wage or employment contract.

But the more general proposition that competition applies within and not between classes of economic agent is also applicable to exchange relations between retailers and consumers, retailers and manufacturers, manufacturers and primary producers and so on. Each of these pairs can be seen as classes of economic agent, historically instituted, and performing distinct economic functions. New classes, still in the process of institutionalisation (as is the case with the emergence of e-commerce), can fundamentally restructure the configuration of pre-existing exchange relations, thereby instituting new forms of competition. We shall see later how the emergence of powerful supermarkets has affected the structure of exchange relations, and hence forms of competition.

Thus, as with capital and labour, retailers as one class of economic agent can be seen to compete with retailers, but not with farmers or manufacturers or consumers, as other classes of economic agent. Vertical exchange relations along a value chain are significantly affected by the shifts in asymmetric power relations, as we shall see. But these power relations must be distinguished from competitive relations. Consequently, in so far as retailers and manufacturers, for example, are mutually dependent and in asymmetric power relations, it is important to consider that *if competition does not occur across classes of economic agent nor does cooperation in the sense of unconstrained mutual cooperation between similar equals*. It is necessary to distinguish between cooperation between members of the same class of economic agent (trade associations, employers federations, trades unions etc.) and forms of concertation that occur across exchange relations characterised by mutual dependence and power asymmetry, a form of economic constraint (retailers have to acquire goods from manufacturers, manufacturers have to find a way to market). For cooperation between economic agents of the same class, Richardsonian notions of complementarity of dissimilar capabilities (Richardson, 1972) may be appropriate, and Marshallian districts can be taken as empirical examples (Dei Ottati, 1994; Best, 1990).[17]

It should be stressed that there are two aspects to power asymmetry: relative balance or position as a consequence of size and levels of concentration within one of two economic classes party to the exchanges, and the nature of the power wielded. We have already seen how the nature of power exerted by employers' associations differs from that wielded by trades unions, and how that affects both the power asymmetry, and the nature of competition within both product and labour markets. Equally, the type of power exercised by retailers is very different from that wielded by manufacturers. As a result of concentration and organisation of distribution and retail outlets, retailers may control and shape access to market. But this is a very different type of power or capacity to that involved in the productive capacity of manufacturers. In terms of instituted economic process, therefore, one could contrast the power of food retailers in the United Kingdom in relation to food manufacturers with the power of motor manufacturers and franchised retail outlets. These two instituted exchange relations affect fundamentally the nature of the competition, the pricing mechanisms, and also the power of consumers in relation to either of those two arrangements.

The development and differentiation of classes of economic agent can therefore be seen as underlying constitutive aspects of 'productive systems'. By focusing on the different forms of organisation of vertical value chains, and on the institution of new classes of economic agent and hence the changing make-up of value chains, the productive system, as the ensemble of combined inputs and outputs, becomes a central unit of analysis. Organisation within classes of economic agent, forms of competition and cooperation, dynamically affects the power asymmetries and dependency between them in a value chain.

Units of competition and the 'channelling' of competition

If competition is variously instituted by the formation of markets and by the configuration of different classes of economic agent, then a further dimension of the shaping of competition arises from the institution of different units of competition, from individuals, to firms, supply chains or clusters of firms. The formation of different units of competition should be distinguished from formation of different scales of competition, the former concerning primarily the competitive entities *within* markets, the latter the *scale of the markets* themselves, local, regional, national or global.[18] The assumption of much competition regulation is that the firm is the only unit of competition, and the objective of such regulation is to institute norms of competition for firm behaviour, in specified markets. Indeed, in many instituted markets, firms can be the central and dominant units of competition, and there are degrees of 'atomism' in this respect, depending on the levels of repeat trading or formal and informal partenerial relations between firms within different economic classes (Fulconis, 1999).

But, in many contemporary product markets, the competing units are integrated supply chains, networks or clusters, which can be orchestrated by the dominant power within it. The locus of power within the supply chain, and the degree of integration of the supply chain fundamentally affects where the competition is channelled, and, as we shall argue below, what form the competition takes in terms of cost reduction, product differentiation, innovation capability, logistical efficiency or whatever. In their study of the bakery industry, the Labour Study Group argued that price-cutting and discounting in the end market by the three dominant plant bakers was facilitated by their vertical holdings in flour milling, from which they could derive profits not available to traditional small bakers (Craig *et al.*, 1982). More recently, Nike has been seen as exemplifying a 'buyer-driven' supply chain, where the design and marketing node of supply chain, and its associated brand marque is the dominant power. This in turn affects the nature of the competition and its locus and focus in relation to other competitors, such as Raebok and Adidas (Gereffi and Korzenewiecz, 1994). But power can equally be situated upstream, as in the case of Monsanto and biotechnology of seed manufacturing, 'mid-stream' as in the case of motor-manufacturers, or downstream, as in the case of UK food supermarkets or many clothing retailers. Thus, inasmuch as supply chains, or other less linear interfirm entities, produce outputs onto given product markets, they can become in Polanyian terms relatively normal and stabilised forms of industrial organisation, reflecting also a normalisation over periods of time of power asymmetries between them in the markets in which they operate. There is a consequent channelling of competition and also focus of competition on different product aspects (novelty, style, marque, quality, freshness, convenience, price, reliability etc.). Equally, such interfirm organisations create a halo of competition, again at certain loci of the supply chain, between insiders and outsiders.

Scales of competition

From an IEP perspective different scales of markets can be seen to be the results of historical processes of institutions[19] rather than any pre-given frameworks, and as a consequence are intimately connected with the development of sizes of firms, lengths of supply chains, as well as with national and supranational organisations such as NAFTA or the European Union. Moreover, different scales overlay each other, rather than necessarily replacing each other, so that competition, as it were, plays in different registers at the same time. The example given above of whole-sale fruit and vegetable markets in the United Kingdom could equally be read as an instance of scale formation, and of how the national scale came to dominate price setting within that market. The formation of supranational scales, such as NAFTA or the European Union involve distinctive competitive regulatory frame-works which can accentuate market integration over other competitive criteria such as market share, interfirm vertical constraint or cartelisation (Deakin *et al.*, 1997; Anderman, 1997). So the institution of different overlaying scales of mar-kets is a historical process which generates new forms of competition at different registers. To make the musical metaphor, there is no presumption of harmony between scales, and the emergence of new scales can be discordant in relation to 'normal' forms of competition at other scales.

Non-formal norms and formal institutions of competition

The arguments by Best (1990) and Deakin *et al.* (1997) that formal normative insti-tutions regulating competition evolve in relation to organisations of units of com-petition as they in turn evolve,[20] suggest a complex interaction between formal frameworks and informal norms of competitive process. Regulation can thus stim-ulate vertical integration at the expense of interfirm cooperation, but in circum-stances where stock-markets as a main feature of capital markets can also lead to more predatory merger and acquisition processes than in economies where long term banking finance plays a greater role. Particular firm-market structures can become normalised over quite long periods, and thereby establish norms of com-petition. Different and conflicting modes of competition can continue to exist side by side: 'New Competition' is far from having driven out 'Old Competition'. In speaking of 'norms' of competition, therefore, and of the co-evolution of formal regulatory and non-formal norms of competition, there is no presumption of a functionalist process of mutual adaptation. Further, formal norms of competition, which assume the individual firm and the atomistic individual consumers as units of competition, can come into conflict with emergent and distinctive units of com-petition which engage in distinctive forms of competition.[21]

To conclude this section, it is clear that competition is complex, multi-dimensional and variable, both historically and comparatively. Changes in the nature of the competitive process in terms of how 'atomistic' or firm oriented it is co-varies often with changes in the object or focus of competitive process. Under specific, possibly unusual, empirical conditions, purely narrow price competition for homogenous products and high levels of transparency, under conditions of relative equality, may occur. But to do so, infrastructural conditions, and particular market rules, need to be instituted. There is indirect competition between labour markets and product markets, product markets and capital markets, and the relationship between these different markets is open to variable historical process of institution and reconfiguration. Different forms of competition operate at different scales of competition, so that competition is operating in several registers simultaneously. And finally, there is a complex interaction between formal norms of competition enshrined in competition regulation and the non-formal norms of competition occurring in relatively stable, often quite long-term, market formations. To illustrate this multi-dimensionality, and the process of de-institution and re-institution of different forms of competition and their relation to productive systems this chapter will now turn to an empirical example of the historical transformation of food retailing in the United Kingdom.

UK supermarkets and changing forms of competition[22]

In this section the aim is to draw the contrast between two productive systems involved in producing food. The argument will be broad-brush, and involve some considerable stylisation of empirical material, and this picks out one particular aspect of food production and marketing to illustrate the argument made in this chapter. Three economic classes of agent will be considered primarily: food manufacturers, retailers and consumers. The two productive systems can each be seen as outcomes of radical transformations of each of these classes of economic agent and of the relations between them. For shorthand purposes, the first productive system will be called the Manufacturer Brand productive system, and the second the Supermarket Brand productive system.

In terms of the IEP approach developed above, each of these productive systems can be seen as

- Instituting new market forms for consumer products and intermediate markets
- Altering the asymmetric power relations, changing the structure of mutual dependencies
- Creating new units of competition and channelling competition
- Instituting new scales of competition
- Provoking a conflict between an 'old-style' regulatory regime relating to earlier forms of competition with the new norms of competition.

The significance of this change arises from the combination of all of these processes, but, for analytical purposes, each will be briefly separately discussed below.

The Manufacturer Brand productive system

The emergence of the brand food manufacturer began from the 1870s, in the United States with notable names like Heinz and Campbell (Alberts, 1973;

Strasser, 1989; Tedlow, 1990; Collins, 1994) and the Cooperative Wholesale Society in the United Kingdom (Jefferys, 1954). It signalled a revolution in production, distribution and consumption. Standardised food products, of reliable quality and durability, purchasable at any outlet, were a new phenomenon that required a transformation of technologies of food preservation (such as sterilisation and canning) and continuous flow-line methods of production. Unsurprisingly perhaps, this mass production of low cost consumables long preceded mass production of cars, and many of the production and management techniques were pioneered there. 'Upstream' many of these early mass producing food manufacturers developed their own dedicated supply chains for many of the inputs, ingredients, seeds, packaging, bottling or canning. Critically, the manufacturer was the terminal front-end of the supply chain, but the supply chain form existed alongside vertical integration.

Branding and advertising complemented standardisation in production: as a manufactured product, its 'make' became a key identifier of the quality and nature of the product. This too was a revolutionary new development for marketing at the time, with the first six-story neon sign appearing in New York in the shape of a bottle of tomato ketchup in 1906. The manufacturer was the key agent in selling the product to the public. The retailer was no longer assailed by a succession of salesmen, but responded to 'demand' from the 'public' created by advertising and the existence of branded goods. In this sense, the retailer played an exclusively intermediary role between manufacturer and consumer in relation to manufactured foods, with often limited freedom to set prices. Manufacturers could compete with manufacturers in the product market, but for manufactured products, retailers could not compete with retailers.

Production on this scale presupposed a distribution infrastructure capable of reaching all corners of national, and eventually global, markets. Many of the new factory units were strategically placed at railheads and waterways. By the late nineteenth century, both in the United States and the United Kingdom, the first chains of multiple retail outlets had appeared. By the early years of the twentieth century these achieved national scale through processes of expansion, merger and acquisition. Each major retailer acquired many thousands of outlets.

The replacement of street markets or itinerant trading through shops, and then through chains of retail outlets was intimately related both to the manufacturing of new food products and to the new characteristics of demand for food. Increasing urbanisation and total dependence on the wage for purchasing food transformed food from being something consumed by all (to varying degrees) into standardised commodities of mass consumption. Whether as cornflakes or cans of soup, the first 'convenience' foods, pre-prepared, washed and cooked were produced for the new rhythms of urban living, designed for kitchens with gas or electricity. In terms of product market competition, there was hence a process both of new market formation, which no doubt entailed a displacement and decline in old product markets, as well as competition with rival manufacturers. This competition was as much about the shape of the new product market, as about head-to-head price competition in relation to any particular product.

The Manufacturer Brand productive system was therefore the outcome of an institution of new markets with distinctive patterns of product market competition, and new classes of economic agent with new relations between them. Forms of competition emerged with forms of productive system, rather than acting exogenously to drive change as an autonomous market force.

The Supermarket Brand productive system

In the United Kingdom in particular where the phenomenon is now most pronounced, a new productive system based on supermarket branded manufactured goods emerged from the early 1980s to challenge and partially displace the Manufacturer Branded productive system. It can be argued that, as with the system it replaced, this change also entailed the emergence of new classes of economic agent, a transformation of asymmetric power relations between them, new logistical and distribution infrastructure, and new forms and characteristics of demand.

In the United Kingdom, which had earlier established integrated national retail chains, one key to the emergence of supermarket branded goods was the marked increase in relative power of the supermarkets over all upstream suppliers, including manufacturers. This increase was both a result of extensive consolidation with the eventual domination of four major national players, and the centralisation of their purchasing and logistical operations from the mid-1980s. Depending on the measures one takes, these four accounted for upto 80 per cent of the grocery product market.

A major consequence of this combination of concentration and centralisation was a major shift in asymmetric power relations between these major UK retailers and manufacturers. In the UK market, major global manufacturers, such as Campbell's, were obliged to produce soups under supermarket brands and to supermarket recipes. Thus, there was a direct erosion of branded manufacturer market share. The implication should be noted that Campbell's brands and supermarket brands, both produced by Campbell's, would thus appear to 'compete' with each other for both shelf space and consumer market. In addition, however, there emerged a rapidly developing group of supermarket brand food manufacturers, from the beginning of the 1980s.

Whilst at first it could be argued that supermarket brand manufacturers were merely imitating branded manufacturers, producing similar products without the costs of development or marketing, and hence competing by price in a form of 'degenerative competition', very soon they developed quite new product markets especially in the chill and ready made food lines. Within a decade, there emerged major manufacturers (Northern Foods, Hazlewood Foods, Geest, Sun Valley and Hillsdown), each with turnovers of over £1 billion, with a quite unique relationship with retailers. In terms of power and mutual dependency, this relationship cannot be described either in terms of vertical integration (quasi- or otherwise), linear supply chains, or market coordination. The manufacturers are major players in their own right; each produce own-label products for all or most of the major retailers, and so cannot be seen as 'virtually' owned or controlled by any one of them; and there are some product categories for which one manufacturer has a total or near total monopoly of supply to *all* the major retailers, under each of their brands (Hazlewood and lasagna, for example).

There is a set of relations between a small number of manufacturers and a small number of retailers in which the former have production facilities (more often whole factory units, less often production facilities within a factory unit) exclusively dedicated to one of the major retailers, for the production of a particular product line. Three factory units of one manufacturer might produce a specific pizza range (economy, standard quality and high quality) for each of three major retailers, whereas for any one retailer, its whole pizza range might be produced by two or three of the manufacturers. There is thus a 'monopsonistic matrix' between retailers and manufacturers, where products and product ranges are the variables. Moreover, this matrix is relatively stable: a given retailer is unlikely to switch sources for one or a few products when the relationship is based both on sourcing a wide portfolio of products from one manufacturer and, more significantly, on its reliance on the manufacturer's capability to innovate and continuously produce novel products, to the design and style required by that retailer.

A further key distinguishing feature of this relationship is that, unlike the manufacturer branded productive system, access to market is secured within it: the retailer and manufacturer co-plan and design product ranges for shelf-space that the retailer can guarantee. The retailer 'sells' the product to the consumer as one component of an overall shopping basket. This secure access to market permits an entirely different productive and innovation organisation for manufacturers. Time from concept to superstore shelf is reduced from the one to two years for manufacturer brands to as little as four weeks for supermarket brands. Production lines and processes, as well as flexible working hours, are organised to meet these schedules for new product introduction. Products can thus follow current trends and fashions, and can sustain much reduced product life-cycles. Manufacturer brand manufacturers, given the much greater uncertainties of access to market and market presence, launch four to five new products per year, with considerable investment in marketing and advertising. Supermarket brand manufacturers typically launch between over 1,000, of which some will be designed for novelty and short product life and others as variations on 'classics' and core products.

The other major change in relations of asymmetric power and mutual dependency in this productive system is that between retailers and consumers. The Competition Commission deemed the market for groceries to be that in which consumers engage in one-stop shopping. The vast majority (83 per cent) consumers in its survey were found to shop either once a week or less frequently, and a similar percentage always shopped in the same store for their main shopping (Competition Commission, 2001). A store thus creates a 'catchment area', and retailers develop socio-economic profiles of disposable income ranges and social characteristics within it to complement data achieved from Epos and Loyalty Card data in order to match product range to demand. In this respect, this form of retail outlet both aggregated and shaped the pattern of demand in a new and quite distinctive way from the Manufacturer Brand productive system. It could be argued, especially after the entry of Wal-Mart into the UK market through its acquisition of Asda in 2000, that retailers trade in shopping baskets rather than products, and aim to expand their market (into non-food and financial services markets) by increasing their proportion of total spend out of total personal disposable income.

The current Supermarket Brand productive system is the outcome of various processes of institution: centralisation and concentration; the establishment of logistical infrastructures; and the formation of a new class of economic agents (the dedicated supermarket label manufacturers). The new productive system has as one of its constitutive aspects new and 'instituted' forms of competition. The *locus* of competition, the *object* of competition and the *unit* of competition have all changed. The locus of primary competition has shifted to retailers as the dominant class of economic agent, and within them, between a limited number of main players.[23] Although different dedicated production units belonging to a single manufacturer maintain separate resource streams and accounts, operating often as independent profit centres, they do not compete for market share with each other, but aim to maximise their outputs to their respective retailers. The object of competition is no longer the classic product market, but is an aggregated product market (the shopping basket) where the definition of the size and compass of the basket is itself a central aspect of the competition and market creation between retailers. Finally, the unit of competition is the whole ensemble[24] of production–distribution–retail firms as coordinated and assembled by retailers, rather than either manufacturers, or logistics companies, or retailers taken as separate or independent classes of economic agent.

In other words, new processes of competition were formed at the same time and conjointly with the formation of new markets and new economic agents. It is difficult to account for the emergence of these new forms of competition on the basis of 'market forces' and competition that drove the old productive system. Rather, the formation of new economic relations between new classes of economic agent develop *pari passu* with the formation of new markets and instituted processes of competition within them. 'Market forces' are the consequence rather than the cause of such processes of institution, and hence cease to carry the great explanatory weight often attributed to them. They may account for processes and dynamics within a normalised or instituted set of economic processes, but are not explanatory principles independent of the instituted economy of which they form part.

Conclusion

But this interim 'conclusion' raises or leaves open a number of analytical difficulties. And here, to conclude in the epistemological spirit of the opening, I end with some messy questions arising from empirical investigation. In the first place, there is no suggestion that the Manufacturer Branded productive system is being definitively displaced and erased by the emergence of the Supermarket Branded productive system. The norms of competition of the former exist alongside those of the latter. Can there be said to be competition *between* different norms of competition? Is the nature of the conflict between two very differently structured productive systems fully captured by a concept of competition? In terms of narrow definitions of their respective 'market share', or the even narrower terms of a similar product to similar product price competition, it is difficult to deny that there is indeed competition. However, it is clear that both the nature and the consequences of the conflict between the two systems goes much further and deeper. The fact that the two systems are brought into conflict with each other through intersecting but only partially overlapping markets suggests that one system is unlikely to totally eclipse the other. Rather, the continuing tension between the two systems – reflected partly by the battle between the US style of discount retailing of manufacturer branded goods led by Wal-Mart (Ortega, 1999) and the leading UK supermarkets – is likely to generate further change in the nature of perhaps both productive systems.

This leads to a more general question on the dynamics of change from one productive system to another. I have argued elsewhere (Harvey *et al.*, 2002: ch. 11) that this kind of structural conflict and tension between different forms of instituted economic process is one of the major drivers generating both change and diversity within capitalist economic processes. Processes of growth and accumulation within a given productive system – as occurred with retailers – can themselves generate conflicts and tensions in relation to already established classes of economic agent, and consequently induce change. But productive systems are far from being closed systems, and the inter-relatedness and interactions of differently structured productive systems and markets can also be seen as a continuous potential source of tension and change. This explanatory framework of causality by structural conflict requires a great deal more comparative and historical empirical work if it is to be further developed. But as 'market forces', forms of competition will be the explanandum rather than the explanation of such change.

Notes

1 This is a theme which resonates through much of Wilkinson's work, and is one important leg on which he stands his criticism of classical political economy including Marx, and neoclassical and some Keynesian economics: 'the tendency for economists of all persuasions to determine ideal – and idealised – notions of how economies operate from abstract, a priori reasoning' (Wilkinson, 1983: 417).
2 In describing themselves as 'neo-Polanyans', Hollingsworth and Boyer do so precisely in terms of regulating the unregulated, 'taming the market' (Hollingsworth and Boyer, 477).
3 I take the term 'system' used here as being used descriptively rather than as explanatorily.
4 This analysis of competition and cooperation, and the different socio-legal and business environments that affect the balance between them, has recently been substantially enriched by the ESRC Contracts and Competition research programme, in particular the project from the Centre for Business Research at the University of Cambridge (Arighetti *et al.*, 1997; Deakin and Michie, 1997).
5 For a more extended account of these two sections see Harvey, 2002.

6 'The human economy, then, is embedded and enmeshed in institutions economic and non-economic' (Polanyi, 1957: 250). Note here the ambiguity of human economy being embedded in *economic* institutions.

7 See also Harvey, 2002 and Harvey *et al.*, 2002.

8 Boyer has argued that for an 'atomistic' market to function, with multitudes of independent buyers and sellers bidding against each other to arrive at equilibrium and market clearing prices, the exchange process itself has to be highly centralised, almost as though orchestrated by a single auctioneer (Boyer, 1997).

9 Garcia's (1986) strawberry market has been oft-quoted as an example of the highly peculiar and transitory conditions under which a market and competition within it approximates to the ideal-type of neoclassical market as defined by Samuelson, in terms of the relative equality of buyers and sellers, the standardisation of quality, and the transparency of the exchange to all parties.

10 This analysis is based on my research for *Exploring the Tomato* (Harvey *et al.*, 2002), and involved the analysis of primary and secondary historical materials and interviewing in markets at New Covent Garden and Manchester Smithfield.

11 In those days the telephone was used by both sides to the exchange to obtain comparative price information between markets, and was therefore a critical instrument for inter-market integration.

12 It should be emphasised that 'personal trust' of this kind is a macro-social institution, deriving from the societal organisation of growers dependent on wholesalers for their primary opportunities to sell produce. It may have the appearance of personal networking, but personal networking cannot account for its existence.

13 As suggested in a preliminary way by Swedberg (1994: 273–4).

14 'In determining the nature of product market competition, the historically-determined system of organisation among employers is as important as the industry's structure in terms of firm size and market power' (Craig *et al.*, 1982: 68).

15 Most notably analysed by Marx, *Capital*, Volume 1.

16 This is not to say, of course, that capital and labour factor inputs can be substituted for one another, on occasions depending on the relative costs of such factor inputs.

17 Best characterises the Marshallian district as one of static complementarities, as against New Competition dynamic complementarities arising from continuous mutual enhancement of dissimilar but complementary capabilities (1990: 235).

18 To stress the multi-dimensional aspect of such competition, there can be different scales of product, labour and capital market competition at play simultaneously.

19 Braudel's (1982) work exemplifies a long duration approach to the historical formation of different scales of market formation.

20 And indeed as a response to shifts in dominant economic orthodoxies.

21 The legal (and political) tangle between formal and informal norms is well illustrated in the current Microsoft case.

22 This illustrative example is based on research undertaken between 1997 and 2000 which used the tomato as an empirical probe to explore the relationships occurring in supply chains and markets, and the way these shaped innovation processes. Interviews were conducted along the length of the chain, and in the networks surrounding different nodes of the chain. Seed manufacturers, biotechnology companies, scientists, own label and brand manufacturers, supermarkets, wholesale markets, logistics companies, importers and a number of other key players were interviewed during the course of this research.

23 It is interesting that the Competition Commission first defines the market in order to define the agents involved in direct competition. In their case, they restricted the market to one-stop shopping and to stores over a certain size and with a certain product range. For that reason, discount retailers, small independent retailers and convenience stores were *excluded* from consideration, and deemed not to be potential competitors. In this kind of definition of markets, therefore, also excluded is possible competition

between Manufacturer- and Supermarket-branded good manufacturers. This illustrates the difference between establishing formal norms of competition and empirically and theoretically analysing processes of competition.

24 It can be argued that branded manufacturers also bring to bear the ensemble of their supply chains when competing with each other on product markets, rather than the basic unit being the manufacturing firm (Gereffi and Korzenewiecz, 1994).

References

Alberts, R. C. (1973) *The Good Provider: H.J. Heinz and His 57 Varieties*. Boston: Houghton Muffin.

Anderman, S. (1997) 'Commercial cooperation, international competitiveness, and EC competition policy', in Deakin, S. and Michie, J. (eds), *Contracts, Cooperation and Competition. Studies in Economics, Management and Law*. Oxford: Oxford University Press.

Arighetti, A., Bachmann, R. and Deakin, S. (1997) 'Contract law, social norms and inter-firm co-operation', *Cambridge Journal of Economics*, 21(2), 171–96.

Best, M. H. (1990) *The New Competition. Institutions of Industrial Restructuring*. Cambridge, MA: Harvard University Press.

Collins, D. (1994) *America's Favourite Food: The Story of Campbell Soup Company*. New York: Harry Abrams.

Craig, C., Rubery, J., Tarling, R. and Wilkinson, F. (1982) *Labour Market Structure, Industrial Organisation and Low Pay*. Cambridge: Cambridge University Press.

Craig, C., Rubery, J., Tarling, R. and Wilkinson, F. (1985) 'Economic, social and political factors in the operation of the labour market', in Roberts, B., Finnegan, R. and Gallie, D. *New Approaches to Economic Life. Economic Restructuring: Unemployment and the Social Division of Labour*, Manchester: Manchester University Press.

Deakin, S., Goodwin, T. and Hughes, A. (1997) 'Co-operation and trust in inter-firm relations: beyond competition policy?', in Deakin, S. and Michie, J. (eds), *Contracts, Co-operation and Competition. Studies in Economics, Management and Law*, Oxford University Press.

Deakin, S., Lane, C. and Wilkinson, F. (1997) 'Contract law, trust relations, and incentives for co-operation: a comparative study', in Deakin, S. and Michie, J. (eds), *Contracts, Co-operation and Competition. Studies in Economics, Management and Law*. Oxford University Press.

Deakin, S. and Wilkinson, F. (1995) 'Contracts, cooperation and trust: the role of the institutional framework', ESRC Centre for Business Research. Working Paper No. 10, University of Cambridge.

Dei Ottati, G. (1994) 'Co-operation and competition in the industrial district as an organisation model', *European Planning Studies*, 2, 463–83.

Fulconis, F. (1999) 'Les "structures en réseau": nouvelle forme de concurrence', in Krafft, J. (ed.), *Le Processus de Concurrence*, Paris: Economica, pp. 202–19.

Garcia, M.-F. (1986) 'La construction sociale d'un marché parfait: le marché au cadran de Fontaines-en-Sologne', *Actes de Recherche*, 65, 2–13.

Gereffi, G. and Korzenewiecz, M. (1994) *Commodity Chains and Global Capitalism*. Westport Connecticut: Praeger.

Granovetter, M. (1985) 'Economic action and social structure: the problem of embeddedness', *The American Journal of Sociology*, 91(3), 481–510.

Granovetter, M. (1992) 'The sociological and economic approaches to labour market analysis: a social structural view', in Granovetter, M. and Swedberg, R. (eds), *The Sociology of Economic Life*, Boulcler: Westview Press.

Granovetter, M. and McGuire, P. (1998) 'The making of an industry: electricity in the United States', in Callon, M. (ed.), *The Laws of the Markets*, Oxford: Blackwell, 147–73.

Harvey, M. (1999) 'How the object of knowledge constrains knowledge of the object. An epistemological analysis of a social research investigation', *Cambridge Journal of Economics*, 23(4), 485–501.

Harvey, M. (2000) 'Competition as instituted economic process', in Metcalfe, S. and Warde, A. (eds), *Market Relations and the Competitive Process*, Manchester: Manchester University Press.

Harvey, M., Quilley, S. and Beynon, H. (2002) *Exploring the Tomato. Transformations of Nature, Society and Economy*, Cheltenham: Edward Elgar.

Hollingsworth, J. R. and Boyer, R. (1997) *Contemporary Capitalism. The Embeddedness of Institutions*. Cambridge: Cambridge University Press.

Jefferys, J. B. (1954) *Retailing Trading in Britain 1850–1950*. Cambridge: Cambridge University Press.

Ortega, R. (1999) *In Sam We Trust. The Untold Story of Sam Walton and How Wal-Mart is Devouring the World*. London: Kegan Paul.

Polanyi, K. (1944) *The Great Transformation. The Political and Economic Origins of Our Time*. Boston: Beacon.

Polanyi, K. (1957) 'The economy as instituted process' in Polanyi, K., Arensberg, C.M., and Pearson, H. W. (eds), *Trade and Market in the Early Empires*, New York: The Free Press.

Richardson, G. (1972) 'The organization of industry', *Economic Journal*, 82, 883–96.

Runciman Committee (1957) *Report of the Committee on Horticultural Marketing*, HMSO, Parliamentary Papers, Cmnd 61.

Strasser, S. (1989) *Satisfaction Guaranteed. The Making of the American Mass Market*. New York: Pantheon Books.

Swedberg, R. (1994) 'Markets as social structures' in Smelser, N. and Swedberg, R. (eds), *The Handbook of Economic Sociology*, Princeton: Princeton University Press.

Swedberg, R. (1998) *Max Weber and the Idea of Economic Sociology*. Princeton: Princeton University Press.

Tedlow, R. S. (1990) *New and Improved: The Story of Mass Marketing in America*. New York: Basic Books.

Weber, M. [1922] (1968) 'Economy and society. An outline of interpretive sociology', Roth, G. and Wittich, C. (eds), New York: Bedminster Press.

Wilkinson, F. (ed.) (1981) *The Dynamics of Labour Market Segmentation*. London: Academic Press.

Wilkinson, F. (1983) 'Productive Systems', *Cambridge Journal of Economics*, 7, 413–29.

Wilkinson, F. and You, J.-I. (1992) 'Competition and cooperation: towards an understanding of industrial districts', Centre for Business Research Working Papers, 18, University of Cambridge.

4 Inter-organisational trust, boundary spanners and communities of practice

Edward Lorenz

Introduction

The primary objectives of this chapter are to propose a definition of inter-organisational trust and to show how organisational boundary spanners, by virtue of their membership in communities of practice, can play a central role in the emergence of this form of trust. By boundary spanners, I am referring to organisational members who hold responsibility for establishing and maintaining relations of cooperation and exchange with another organisation. Their work requires them to move across the boundaries of a partner organisation in order to become knowledgeable about its personnel and organisational practices.

In order to illustrate the argument I return to my previously reported case study work on subcontracting relations in the Lyon machine building industry (Lorenz, 1988, 1993). I focus on the boundary spanning roles of the purchasing agents within client firms, whose work involves identifying suitable firms for the establishment of long-term subcontracting relations. The case study shows how inter-organisational trust is grounded in inter-personal trust, since its emergence depends in a crucial manner on the relations of trust that buyers establish with their counterparts responsible for sales in the subcontracting firm. However, in the Lyon context, these boundary spanners do not operate as isolated individuals. They are embedded in wider 'communities of practice' or groups of people that are bound together by virtue of a shared practice or activity.[1] The conceptual and empirical work in this chapter is also informed by a conceptualisation of relationships between firms in a productive-systems theoretical framework. I shall argue that such communities of practice provided important institutional support in the Lyon region for the emergence of a new paradigm of subcontracting relations based on the high levels of trust.

This chapter starts with an extended discussion about what it means to say that an individual trusts another individual and how this differs from what it means to say that an organisation trusts another organisation. I find this preamble necessary because of the tendency to treat the two forms of trust as if they were identical in the vast literature on trust and organisations. All too frequently papers on trust in organisational settings start with an analysis of trust in dyadic terms, between two individuals, and then apply the analysis directly to a discussion of organisational relations as if all that has been said about two individuals necessarily applies to two organisations. I would argue that while inter-organisational trust shares certain formal properties with trust between individuals, it is fundamentally different in kind. In this respect, this chapter follows the advice of Hardin (1998) in seeking to unpack the notion of trust at the organisational level.

Defining trust

There is very little agreement in the literature on a definition of trust. Closely related to this, one finds that discussions of trust are riddled with distinctions or qualifying adjectives, such as weak versus strong trust, thin versus thick trust, or personal versus institutional trust. The use of these qualifiers can be explained by the fact that the meaning one attaches to trust in its vernacular use is strongly context dependent. The qualifiers serve to make explicit the distinctions that, in everyday language, are conveyed by the other words and phrases that are used in conjunction with the word trust. For example, if I say that X is not really trustworthy but that X can be trusted to fulfil his side of a contractual agreement, there is no contradiction. There is no difficulty in understanding that a distinction has been drawn between what one can expect from X in general and what one can expect from him in a particular contractual arrangement, given the incentives and constraints that he faces. This is the kind of distinction that is captured by the contrast between contractual and goodwill trust (Sako, 1998) or between weak and strong trust (Livet and Reynaud, 1998).

The multiple ways in which trust is contextualised in the literature raises the question of whether there is a set of properties that are common to the various uses of trust? Or, is it the case that we are dealing with a number of basically different concepts? I would argue that despite important differences, the various contextualised meanings of trust share the following three properties.

1   When we say that an individual trusts (I leave aside for the moment what meaning to attach to the idea that an organisation trusts) we invariably have in mind a tripartite relation of the following form:

X trusts Y to do Z

Y can be another person, an organisation or an institution.

2   X is vulnerable in the sense that Y is a free agent and could conceivably act in ways that harm X. My intuition here is that without such vulnerability we do not consider the relation to involve trust. Of course, in any particular instance it may be that X fully expects Y not to act in ways that cause harm. This expectation could be based on any number of considerations, including what X knows about Y's interests or the constraints Y operates under. What is essential is that Y in his capacity as a free agent could act to cause harm. (see Pettit, 1998).

3   X has reasons for his expectations regarding Y's behaviour. In this sense trust is justified. The idea of routinised trust (Nooteboom, 2001) might seem in contradiction with this property. I do not believe this is necessarily so. If, in

common with a growing body of work, we see tacit knowledge as the foundation for routinised behaviour, then it is quite reasonable to argue that we may only be aware in a subsidiary manner of the reasons for our trust. Much as Polayni (1962: 62–3) argued with respect to 'the huge mental domain of knowledge but also of manners and the many different arts which man knows how to use', we may feel our way forward to trust. And each, 'single step may rely on a act of groping which originally passed the understanding of its agent and of which he has ever since remained only subsidiarily aware'. Thus we cannot preclude that we have reasons for our trust that we do not specify and only become aware of in a focal sense when something happens to upset our expectations.

Can we go farther and say that X trusts Y because X believes that Y has reasons for fulfilling X's trust that are grounded in X. To use the language of Hardin (1998), is X's trust necessarily *encapsulated* in the reasons Y has for fulfilling X's trust? I think not. Consider the following example used by Blackburn (1998) to illustrate what he refers to as the 'austere basis for trust'. The people of Königsberg trust Kant to provide the time of day by taking his afternoon walk at exactly the same hour. This example fulfils the above three conditions, despite the fact that the expectations of the people of Königsberg are grounded in nothing more than a simple extrapolation of Kant's past observed behaviour. The trust they place in Kant is *impersonal* in the sense that it has nothing to with the belief that Kant behaves in the way he does because he understands that the people of Königsberg are relying on him and decides to take his walk at the same hour in order not to disappoint their trust.

Pure cases, where trust is grounded on nothing more than a simple extrapolation of an individual's observed past behaviour, are probably unusual. The encapsulated case, where X trusts Y because of something he believes to be the case about Y's psychological state is no doubt more common. For example, the townspeople of Königsberg may believe that Kant is implicitly committed to taking his walk at an appointed hour each day. Nothing has been spoken, but Kant has observed the townspeople relying on him in this manner, the townspeople have observed Kant observing this, and for this reason they believe that Kant feels committed to taking his walk at the same hour. Or perhaps, more explicitly, Kant has promised the townspeople to take his walk at the same hour and the townspeople's trust in Kant is based on their belief that he recognises that were he to disappoint their expectations their anger and indignation would be justified.

Encapsulated trust

If the encapsulated case is the more common one, do we need to set restrictions on what we mean by saying that X's trust is based on the belief that Y has reasons for fulfilling X's trust that are grounded in X? Let's consider the case of team organisation in a manufacturing enterprise. This form of organisation has increasingly been adopted in substitution for more classic assembly-line methods.

Suppose the division of labour in the team is fluid. All members of the team know how to undertake the full range of tasks necessary to complete the work of the team, and they autonomously set the division of labour independently of upper-level management. For all practical purposes these arrangements preclude monitoring individual performance. Suppose further that compensation is directly tied to group performance. Under such circumstance each team member's earnings will be determined in part by the behaviour of the other members. Why might team member X trust member Y to do his fair share of the work and not to shirk on the efforts of the others?

One reason might be that X perceives Y to be a calculating sort of person. X believes that Y will fulfil X's trust if and only if Y perceives it to be in his or her self-interest to do so. For example, Y's failure to contribute may elicit retaliation from X and the other team members, including the threat of exclusion from the team with a consequent loss of reputation in the enterprise. X may judge that Y's responsiveness to such potential retaliation and it's likely negative impact on his earnings and career opportunities will keep him in line. Or perhaps X judges that Y believes that his shirking will lead X and the other team members to reduce their effort, resulting in a substantial reduction in his earnings. Are we justified in using the word trust to refer to this kind of situation, where X's expectations are based on his assessment of Y's self-interest.

Some economists are clearly not comfortable with the reduction of trust to a calculus of gains and losses as in the above example. Confronted by an argument of this sort, they may assert that we're not talking about trust at all, but rather about decision-making under risk. And since the language and models in economics and operations research for talking about this sort of decision-making are well worked out, there is little need to complicate matters by bringing in the notion of trust. It simply muddies the waters (see, notably, Williamson, 1993).

This in turn can lead to the argument that the notion of trust should be reserved for cases where X perceives that Y will not take advantage of the situation and shirk either because Y is a friend or because Y's behaviour is strongly influenced by certain norms, such as an internalised norm for reciprocity. X's trust is justified and Condition 3 holds, but the justification has nothing to do with beliefs concerning Y's economic interests.

Grounding trust in friendship or internalised norms, however, just amounts to using other sorts of reductions. These kinds of reductions, though, do not seem to bother economists much. And they may be confidently invoked with only the most superficial knowledge of the relevant literature in psychology or sociology. Probably what lies behind this position is a concern not to open up too much what is acceptable as an explanatory concept in an economic model. On this account, it is fine to talk about trust as long as it remains relegated to the domain of sociology or psychology.

In my view there are no good a priori reasons for refusing one kind of reduction and accepting another. Certainly we'll find no comfort for refusing the economic form of reduction in the vernacular use of trust. No one has any problem understanding what is meant when someone says that X trusts Y to fulfil his side

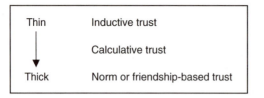

Figure 4.1 Degrees of inter-personal trust.

of a contractual agreement because it's in Y's interest to do so. If we are to accept the sociological reduction while refusing the economic reduction it must be for reasons to do with a logical fallacy or contradiction in the economic argument. Criticisms of the notion of 'calculative trust' (e.g. Williamson, 1993) have not demonstrated any such fallacy or contradiction.[2]

While on my view we cannot exclude the notion of calculative or self-interested trust, the comparison with trust based on friendship or internalised norms nevertheless raises an important qualitative distinction. Calculative trust is relatively thin because of the way it is dependent on external conditions that have little to do with the person who is the object of trust. For example, in the team example I may trust you to do your fair share of the work as long as you are dependent on the enterprise we work in for employment. If alternative employment opportunities become available to you offering higher rates of compensation, the basis for my trust may disappear. Calculative trust is thin in the sense that it is not especially robust to changes in the external circumstances which condition the calculus of economic loss and gain. Friendship or norm-based trust arguably is thicker because it implies a greater willingness to be flexible and adapt to changing circumstances.[3] Friendships presumably do not disappear as the labour market tightens, which is not to say that friendship is unconditional or without limits.[4]

The above discussion suggests a hierarchy of levels or degrees of inter-personal trust, moving relatively thin to thicker forms as in Figure 4.1.

Trust in organisations

Up until now I have been treating the case where the object of an individual's trust is another person. In the tripartite relation set out in Condition 1 above Y may also be an institution or an organisation. Does the hierarchy of degrees of trust presented in Figure 4.1 translate directly onto the organisational case?

Let's take as an example the trust I may hold in a long distance carrier like DHL. I may use it to send an urgent message upon which my well-being or that of a family member depends. I may use it to send a document, fully recognising that if it is lost or misplaced I will suffer a loss. In short, I may put myself into a position of vulnerability. I recognise that it is possible that DHL will not fulfil its commitment to deliver my message or document. If I decide to place my trust in the delivery service, what might be my reasons for doing so?

Firstly, I do not think we are dealing with a case of Luhmann's (1988: 97) notion of 'confidence', where the lack of alternatives gives us little choice but to trust. There are a number of competing companies offering the same services as DHL and I may have reasons for judging one more trustworthy that another. Moreover, it is often possible for me to deliver my message personally, if at greater cost.

Might it be possible, then, that the trust I place in the carrier is similar in nature to what I have referred to above as inductively-based trust? Having never, or only rarely, been disappointed in the past by the service, I take it for granted that my trust will be fulfilled. And, I don't feel any need to delve more deeply into the matter. It seems self-evident that in many cases the trust we place in large organisations doesn't go beyond this extrapolation of past behaviour. We trust them to perform a particular service because that is what they do and our expectations have not been disappointed in the past. However, much as in the case of trust directed at an individual, this form of trust is relatively thin. Are there thicker forms corresponding to the idea of encapsulated inter-personal trust developed above?

My answer to this is a qualified yes. Qualified, because the notion of trust used to characterise my beliefs regarding another individual has to be unpacked before it can be used to characterise my beliefs regarding an organisation. Consider the aspects of the characterisation of my trust for a person that don't readily translate on to the organisational case. First, recall that in the case of the thicker forms of trust, my trust in an individual is based on something I believe to be the case about that person's psychological state and in particular my belief that that person, for one reason or another, is disposed to act in a way that will not cause me harm.

Organisations, however, are not cognitive entities in the same way that individual are and they do not in any obvious sense have reasons for behaving in one way or another. So, as a first approximation, let's say that when I say I trust an organisation I am saying that I trust its employees. I believe that the employees, or at least those whose actions could conceivably have a bearing on the organisational performance characteristics that are of concern to me, have reasons for fulfilling my trust that are grounded in me. This, however, raises an obvious problem. Unless I happen to be an exceptionally large and visible customer, many of the employees whose behaviour could conceivably impact on the organisation's performance will not even be aware of my existence. But even if they were, it is implausible that I could know enough about all of them to believe that each and everyone has reasons for fulfilling my trust that are grounded in me.

How, then, can the notion of encapsulated trust be salvaged in the organisational setting? The answer, I think, is that while I cannot plausibly believe that all the employees are concerned about me, I may reasonably believe that they are concerned about the category of persons I represent, in this case customers or clients. The most plausible reason why they might tie their interests to fulfilling my expectations as a client is because of some aspect of the organisation's administrative policies and in particular the incentives and sanctioning mechanisms it has in place to assure that role holders carry out their assigned tasks in a way that meets the organisation's commitment to its clients. This implies that my trust in an organisation has an impersonal quality relative to my trust in an individual. By and large it is a matter of indifference to me who the organisational role holders are. What concerns me is how the roles are defined and what the mechanisms are that serve to assure quality control and the like.

While the notion of self-interest-based trust in organisations can be salvaged in this manner, it leaves unanswered the question of how an individual client or customer of a firm like DHL might come to acquire the knowledge about its organisational practices that could ground his or her trust? One obvious source is the information that firms make publicly available through advertisements and publicity designed to persuade the pubic at large of their reliability. The large sums of money companies regularly spend in this manner suggests that they believe that such intangible investments have an impact on consumer perceptions. Another possible source is the institutionalised mechanisms that society puts in place for fostering client trust, such as holding a recognised certificate of quality assurance like the ISO 9000 series. As is well-known, these require at a minimum that the enterprise has fully documented and justified its quality control procedures.

Such forms of publicly available, and possibly institutionally-based, information can help ground our trust in an organisation. In particular, by reducing our perceived uncertainty, they can encourage us to take the risk of relying on the services of an organisation in circumstances where we have no personal or direct knowledge of its internal administrative procedures. One can legitimately question, however, whether these forms of information carry much weight when they aren't supported by the sort of knowledge on which simple inductive trust is based. If we place our trust in an organisation and our trust is disappointed, we are not likely to discount this direct evidence because of the fact that the organisation in question is known to hold a certified quality norm. What I am arguing here is that trust based on publicly available information is relatively fragile when it isn't complemented by direct evidence of the sort that grounds inductive trust. Moreover, it can't stand up to countervailing evidence of a direct kind. For this reason, I would argue that in the majority of cases the trust an individual places in a large organisation will be based on little more that an extrapolation of what has been observed of its behaviour in the past.

If this is true for the case of self-interest-based trust in an organisation, it is all the more so in the case of norm-based trust. How might the norm-based argument go? One possibility is that I believe that the employees of the organisation are motivated by concerns of professional pride. For them it is a source of direct satisfaction to accomplish their tasks in a way that satisfies the customer. I trust the employees not because of what I know about the organisation's incentives and sanctioning mechanisms, but rather because what I believe to be the case about the employees' professional standards. Another possibility has been argued by Pettit (1998) and Blackburn (1998) in the case of citizen trust in government. The idea is that those who are the object of our trust will be motivated to act in a trustworthy manner simply by virtue of the fact that they recognise they are being relied upon. They find the state of being relied upon salient and it becomes a concern of theirs.[5]

Leaving aside the question of how plausible these causal chains are, it is implausible that an individual client or customer of a large enterprise might have the sort of detailed information about the psychological state of each and every-one of its employees that would allow him to confirm them empirically. The most plausible source of information for such beliefs is the information that the company makes publicly available its corporate philosophy or culture. If we give any credence to such information, for example, the claim that the company cares, then we may surmise that a screening and recruitment policy has been put in place to assure that only those who are cooperatively disposed are hired. I would contend that such surmises are highly fragile and will not stand up to counter-vailing evidence of the sort that underlies simple inductive trust.

Inter-organisational trust

I have argued that in most cases the trust a client or customer has in a large enter-prise is relatively thin, being based on little more than an extrapolation of past observed behaviour. When an individual's trust in an organisation goes beyond this relatively thin form, it doesn't really correspond to the encapsulated form of inter-personal trust, since it retains an impersonal quality. If an individual trusts an organisation in an encapsulated manner, it tends to be because of what he or she believe to be the case about its operating procedures or its company culture, not because of what he or she knows about the psychological state of each and every member. Having spent some time developing these points, I now can easily develop and illustrate the idea that boundary spanners, who are themselves embedded in communities of practice, can play a key role in developing inter-organisational trust.

First, what can it mean to say that one organisation trusts another organisa-tion? Organisations, as I've observed above, are not cognitive entities in the same sense as individuals and it makes little sense to talk about an organisation's cogni-tive state of mind. Extending the line of argument developed above, let's say that organisation X trusts organisation Y when the members of organisation X believe that the members of organisation Y will act in ways that serve to live up to organ-isation Y's contractual or implicit commitments to X. Thus, if Y happens to be a subcontractor and the Y has a contractual or implicit commitment to deliver certain component parts to X that meet certain recognised quality standards, X trusts Y in so far as the members of X trust that the members of Y will carry out their assigned roles in a manner designed to fulfil that commitment.

Much as in the above discussion of the trust a customer may hold in a large enterprise, this defintion raises an obvious problem. In the case of large organi-sations, at any rate, it is implausible that each and every member of one organi-sation could know this about each and every member of the other organisation. Thus, if they hold this trust for the members of the other organisation it will nec-essarily have an impersonal quality. It might be linked to what they know about the other organisation's internal administrative procedures and practices.

Boundary spanners

One possible source for this latter type of information is a trusted 'boundary spanner'. Consider the case of a purchasing agent working on behalf of a client firm whose job involves identifying and building-up long-term relations of exchange with component supplier firms. The purchasing agent may have the trust of the members of his own organisation. They have been able to observe his behaviour and verify his reliability under a range of circumstances. The purchasing agent in turn, based on his interactions with the people responsible for sales in the subcontractor firm as well as on what he has observed of the operating procedures of the subcontractor, has formed a favourable opinion of its reliability. In particular he has been able to verify the quality of its equipment, to learn about the details of its quality control procedures, and to form a judgement concerning the skills and competencies of its personnel by observing its daily operations. The purchasing agent communicates his trust more widely to his fellow employees and they, as well, come to have trusting expectations regarding the subcontractor.

A mechanism like this was implicit in my previously reported research on partnership relations between client firms and their subcontractors in the machine-building industry of Lyon (Lorenz, 1988, 1993). This study was based on the interviews I conducted with the management personnel of ten machine producers, ranging in size from a low of thirty-nine employees to a high of 500 employees. The firms, which produced sophisticated equipment or machinery, mostly operated in internationally competitive markets, with exports accounting for over half of their annual sales. At the time of my initial interview in 1985–86, the majority of the firms were experimenting with new subcontracting procedures based on the principle of establishing long-term relations with their subcontractors. They described these new relations as a partnership (*partenariat*). When I returned to the region in the early 1990s and extended my interviews to include the representatives of local employers and professional associations, it became apparent that during the interval the partnership system had been widely adopted by metal-working firms in the region.

The importance of trust in the relations these firms maintained with their subcontractors was implicit in their use of what they termed 'moral contracts' (*contrats moraux*) to regulate their relations, rather than detailed written agreement. As a rule, the only written document was the order form, which served as a reference point for on-going discussions between the purchasing agent of the client and the person responsible for sales in the subcontractor. Their reluctance to specify their obligations in formal contracts was a response to the uncertain market conditions they operated in, which precluded specifying in advance exactly what the clients expected of their subcontractors. It was understood that adaptations to unanticipated contingencies might have to be made if the relationship was to continue. This required a foundation of trust as a basis for arriving at acceptable terms.

My interviews revealed that one of the central means by which client firms built-up trust with their subcontractors was through applying what I called the 'step-by-step' rule. This procedure prescribes that the firms should start by making small commitments to each other and then progressively increase their commitments depending on the quality of the exchange. The procedure, though, was not simply a question of registering performance on successive contracts and assigning a probability of trustworthiness on that basis. Invariably the purchasing agents and other management personnel I spoke with stressed the need for personal contacts with their counterparts in the subcontracting firms to facilitate joint problem-solving. A number of them stated that geographical proximity was desirable because it allowed for this. Thus one manager observed, 'It is important to visit and to talk, to know each other. This is partnership. If we know each other it is easier to resolve problems and to adjust. So the closer we are to each other the easier it is'.

Typically, a new relationship would start with an exploratory telephone call. The purchasing agent in the client firm would contact the managing director or the person responsible for sales in the subcontractor and ask for details of the potential partner's capacity, equipment and particular areas of expertise. This would be followed by an initial visit by the purchasing agent to verify the information and, depending on the results, to negotiate a small order. A second visit would be made while the components were being machined in order to assess the subcontractor's methods and to verify its quality control procedures. As a purchasing agent I interviewed put it, 'I look for an enterprising attitude (*esprit d'initiative*) and the ability to anticipate problems.' Successful completion of the first order would typically be followed by a larger second order and contingent on that, a third, after which the subcontractor was considered to be a 'partner'. Most of my interviewees stated that this process required a considerable amount of personal contact over a minimum time span of a year.

In short trust was built up through a learning process. Small risks were followed by larger ones, contingent on the quality of the on-going relationship. The Lyon machine building case points to the way the trust that boundary spanners may develop for the members of another organisation can serve as the departure point for cementing more general relations of trust between organisations.

Communities of practice

One of the most intriguing features of the partnership system I observed in Lyon was the uniformity of the subcontracting procedures used by client firms in the region despite the absence of formal or contractual relations among them. Managing directors and buyers of independent client firms, often separated geographically by as much as 40–50 kilometres, described quite similar procedures and objectives. There clearly was a macro-dimension to the partnership system, in the sense that it involved multiple actors.

The importance of this macro-dimension can be seen in the way the system at a collective level served to balance flexibility and security. Client firms were interested in providing longer-term guarantees to their trusted subcontractors in part to encourage them to invest in up-to-date equipment and new skills. Being able to rely on subcontractors operating at the cutting edge of technical change contributed in an important way to the ability of the client firms to maintain their capacity for high quality machine production. Given that many of the client firms were relatively small operators, operating in uncertain international markets, they were reluctant to offer full guarantees to their subcontractors. The rule generally applied by the client firms was to set the value of their orders at between 10 and 15 per cent of a subcontractor's total sales. According to my interviewees, the purpose of this was to limit the degree of dependency of a subcontractor in order to avoid the possibility that the market difficulties faced by the client might have a crippling effect on the subcontractor. Nonetheless, because subcontractors operated within a context where multiple clients offered comparable guarantees, the system as a whole provided them with a high degree of market security. For this reason, the trust that any one client firm managed to build-up with its subcontractors was dependent of the trust that other client firms were simultaneously building-up with those same subcontractors.

My interview evidence suggested that the diffusion of the partnership system was closely tied to the way key boundary spanners – buyers and sellers, managing directors, and owners – were embedded within wider 'communities of practice' that transcended the boundaries of any single firm. By communities of practice I am referring to the forms of identification that emerge amongst people engaged in the same type of activity or practice. What links them is not their position within the firm's occupation hierarchy or their mutual assignment to a particular project, but rather their shared practice. Around this practice they create resources in the form of a shared language, routines and artefactual meanings. These resources may be transmitted from 'old timers' to 'newcomers' via the latter's participation in the practices of the community.

Recent work on communities of practice, notably by Wenger (1998) and Snyder (1997) has been concerned to situate the concept relative to research in the field of strategy on organisational competences and organisational learning. This accounts, perhaps, for their emphasis on the often unrecognised and informal communities that emerge spontaneously within organisations and how they differ from such formally administered structures as teams and project organisation. Earlier work, notably by Lave and Wenger (1991), emphasised the way the members of such communities were embedded in wider forms of formal association, possibly involving well established and codified rules of apprenticeship.[6]

My research in the Lyon area showed that formal organisation can play an important role in creating the common language and worldviews that facilitate communication and joint problem-solving activity by the members of a community of practice. The boundary spanners in the Lyon machine building industry benefited from the existence of two well-established regional associations: the Chambre Syndicale des Industries Métallurgiques du Rhône (CSMIR), and the departmental branch of the Compagnie des Dirigeants d'Approvisonnement et Acheteurs de France (CDAF), a professional organisation of buyers and suppliers. These organisations, like most professional associations, provide a variety of benefits and services to their members. They also contributed to the diffusion of the partnership system of subcontracting in two ways. First, they popularised the idea of long-term subcontracting by holding seminars on the Japanese *Kanban* system. Second, and of greater importance, they provided forums for the boundary spanners to exchange personal histories about the typical problems they encountered in their daily practice, and more generally for exchanging information about the subcontracting practices used in the more successful firms in the region. In this way, formal organisation contributed to the diffusion of knowledge and the generalisation of the routinised practices underlying the trust-building partnership system.

In order to avoid possible misunderstanding, my argument does not depend on the proposition that boundary spanners in Lyon, by virtue of their common membership in a community of practice, automatically trusted one another. Rather, I am arguing that the shared language and understandings that defined the local communities of practice formed a social context favourable to the build-up of trust over time. Thus buyers and suppliers in Lyon region came to share a new language of partnership and they came to share a vision of what this new form of subcontracting involved in terms of risks and mutual obligations. On this basis they could easily signal to their counterparts in other organisations their understanding of the rules of the game and their willingness to undertake the risky investments needed to forge these new forms of cooperation.

Conclusion

A number of contributors to the vast literature on trust and organisational behaviour have argued that society's institutional arrangements may contribute to consolidating trusting relations between organisations.[7] The basic idea is that institutions, by reducing the degree of uncertainty that agents face in their contractual relations, provide a foundation for establishing trusting expectations regarding each other's behaviour.

This chapter provides support for this view in pointing to the way local professional associations in the Lyon region served to stabilise the expectations of client firms and their subcontractors regarding the rules and obligations inherent in a new system of subcontracting relations. This chapter has also argued that there is a need to unpack this kind of argument. Organisations, as such, do not in any obvious sense have expectations regarding each other's cognitive state.

In unpacking the language of inter-organisational trust, a role has been identified for an individual actor, the boundary spanner, who enjoys the trust of the members of his own organisation. I have argued that the first step in establishing inter-organisational trust is establishing inter-personal trust between a boundary spanner and his counterpart in the other organisation. This inter-personal trust is the foundation for the development of a more generalised trust on the part of the boundary spanner for the members of the other organisation. This relatively impersonal form of trust can then be communicated and transferred to the members of the boundary spanner's own organisation.

Seen from this perspective, inter-organisational trust exists at the interface of institutional and inter-personal relations. It depends on the beliefs and actions of an individual, the boundary spanner, who himself is embedded in wider forms of formal association that serve to forge the common language and shared understandings characteristic of a community of practice. Such bonds of trust are essential to the success of productive systems.

Notes

1 The term 'community of practice' was coined by Lave and Wenger (1991). Also see Brown and Duguid (1991). The idea grew out prior to ethnographic work by these researchers and others at the Palo Alto Institute for Research on Learning on the situated nature of learning and knowledge in the 1980s. It finds its intellectual roots in a strong tradition of American sociology on the situated nature of practice and action, including Chicago school symbolic interactionism, associated notably with Herbert Blumer (1969). For a fuller discussion, see Lorenz (2001).
2 See, however, Nooteboom (2001). Starting out from the assumption that trust implies risk (Condition 2) he observes that if we treat trust as a subjective expected probability, with higher probabilities corresponding to higher levels of trust, we end up in the contradictory position of arguing that the highest level of trust corresponds to a probability of one in which case there would be an absence of risk. One possible response to this is to argue with Pettit (1998) that although X may be absolutely certain of Y's behaviour in a particular instance, in so far as X treats Y as a free agent there is nonetheless a risk in the sense that Y could conceivably act in ways that disappoint X's expectations.
3 The distinction I am making here corresponds closely to that made by Sako (1998) between 'goodwill' trust and 'contractual' trust.
4 As Nooteboom (2001) has observed, we probably would not consider as a condition for our friendship that an individual should guard a personal secret when subjected to torture.
5 The argument of Pettit intertwines this induced trustworthiness with an argument about trust responsiveness based on self-interest. Thus, even if the fact of being relied on doesn't induce my trustworthiness it may lead me to act as if I am trustworthy because I seek the admiration and approval of others. Acting as if I am trustworthy may in turn foster real trustworthiness, since it gives me reasons, 'to let impulses of trustworthiness have their way and indeed to try to drum up such impulses' (Pettit, 1998: 308).
6 Thus many of the examples of communities of practice in Lave and Wenger (1991), including tailors and quartermasters, correspond to craft or occupational communities with well defined rules for entry to the trade based on regulated forms of apprenticeship.
7 See, for example, Deakin and Wilkinson, 1998; Coriat and Guennif, 1998.

References

Blackburn, S. (1998) 'Trust, cooperation and human psychology', in Braithwaite, V. and Levi, M. (eds), *Trust and Governance*, New York: Russel Sage Foundation.
Blumer, H. (1969) *Symbolic Interactionism: Perpsective and Method*. Berkeley: University of California Press.
Brown, J. S. and Duguid, P. (1991) 'Organisational learning and communities of practice: toward a unified view of working, learning and innovation', *Organization Science*, 2(1), 40–57.
Coriat, B. and Guennif, S. (1998) 'Self-interest, trust and institutions', in Lazarick, N. and Lorenz, E. (eds), *Trust and Economic Learning*, Cheltenham, UK: Edward Elgar.
Deakin, S. and Wilkinson, F. (1998) 'Contract law and the economics of interorganizational trust', in Lane, C. and Bachmann, R. (eds), *Trust Within and Between Organizations*, Oxford: Oxford University Press.

Hardin, R. (1998) 'Trust in government', in Braithwaite, V. and Levi, M. (eds), *Trust and Governance*, New York: Russel Sage Foundation.

Lave, J. and Wenger, E. (1991) *Situated Learning: Legitimate Peripheral Participation*. Cambridge: Cambridge University Press.

Livet, P. and Reynaud, B. (1998) 'Organisational trust, learning and implicit commitments', in Lazarick, N. and Lorenz, E. (eds), *Trust and Economic Learning*, Cheltenham, UK: Edward Elgar.

Lorenz, E. (1988) 'Neither friends nor strangers: informal relations of subcontracting in French industry', in Gambetta, D. (ed.), *Trust: Making and Breaking Cooperative Relations*, Oxford: Basil Blackwell.

Lorenz, E. (1993) 'Flexible production systems and the construction of trust', *Politics and Society*, 21(3), 307–24.

Lorenz, E. (2001) 'Models of cognition, the contextualisation of knowledge and evolutionary approaches to the firm', Paper presented at the DRUID Nelson and Winter Conference, Aalborg, 12–15 June.

Luhmann, N. (1988) 'Familiarity, confidence and trust: problems and alternatives', in Gambetta, D. (ed.), *Trust: Making and Breaking Cooperative Relations*, Oxford: Basil Blackwell.

Nooteboom (2001) 'How to combine calculative and non-calculative trust', Paper presented at the Symposium, *Trust and Trouble in Organizations*, Erasmus University, Rotterdam, May.

Pettit, P. (1998) 'Republican theory and political trust', in Braithwaite, V. and Levi, M. (eds), *Trust and Governance*, New York: Russel Sage Foundation.

Polayni, M. (1962) *Personal Knowledge: Towards a Post-Critical Philosophy*. Chicago: University of Chicago Press.

Sako, M. (1998) 'The information requirement of trust in supplier relations: evidence from Japan, Europe and the United States', in Lazarick, N. and Lorenz, E. (eds), *Trust and Economic Learning*, Cheltenham, UK: Edward Elgar.

Snyder, W. (1997) 'Communities of practice: combining organizational learning and strategy insights to create a bridge to the 21st century', Document, Cambridge, MA: Social Capital Group.

Wenger, E. (1998) 'Communities of practice; learning as a social system', *Systems Thinker*, June.

Williamson, O. E. (1993) 'Calculativeness, trust and economic organization', *Journal of Law and Economics*, XXXVI, April, 453–87.

5 Social rights and the market

An evolutionary perspective

Simon Deakin

Introduction

Social rights, including rights to fair treatment and collective representation at work, are usually seen as opposed to market or economic rights, such as property and contract rights and rights of access to the market. This is because the regulation of contracts is seen as limiting or constraining market forces, thereby causing inefficiency and diminishing the wealth or (in some versions) the well being of society. Alternatively, social rights are viewed not as regulating but as redistributing the results of economic activity. They enter the picture after the process of exchange has been completed, in order to reverse or modify distributional outcomes which are seen as unjust. However, for critics, these interventions may also have anti-efficiency effects, by blunting incentives. Opponents of labour regulation therefore argue that these so-called market-correcting rules (i.e. rules which correct for the undesirable effects of markets) end up undermining the market no less than rules which act directly on contractual relationships.

A different perspective suggests that certain social rights may be understood to have a role in offsetting market failures which arise from high transaction costs. Regulation of the employment relationship may be needed to overcome asymmetries of information between employer and employee, and the obstacles faced by both parties to making credible commitments to the maintenance of a long-term economic relationship. These rules are sometimes thought of as 'perfecting the market'. This is a useful perspective, and a valuable corrective to arguments which invariably portray regulation in anti-efficiency terms. There is nevertheless some uncertainty as to how far such rules truly perform the function ascribed to them of reproducing hypothetically 'efficient' resource allocations (for discussion, see Deakin and Wilkinson, 1999).

This chapter will seek to outline a third role for social rights, one which sees them as having a central, constitutive role with regard to labour market relations. This idea will be explored using an evolutionary economic framework, which seeks to locate the emergence and operation of conventions, norms and legal rules in a dynamic perspective. Within this framework, the chapter will explore links between the economic notion of 'capabilities', which was developed first by Sen (1985, 1999) and was recently adopted by the Supiot report on the transformation of work (Salais, 1999; Supiot, 1999) and the juridical concept of social rights.

It might seem odd to seek to construct the case for social rights using the conceptual tools of economic theory. It is certainly true that to see social rights not as separate from, and imposed on, the labour market, but at the very core of labour market relationships, is strongly counter-intuitive from the vantage point of the contemporary debate about labour market 'flexibility'. Most of those who write about flexibility, whether they do so in the context of globalisation or the 'new knowledge economy', assume that labour regulations impose costs on employers and that they engender rigidities which prevent the market from functioning. For many labour lawyers, perhaps, the whole point of employment rights is precisely that they do constrain the forces of competition in this way. For others, the growing use of labour law regulation as a mode of market governance implies the opposite, namely a downgrading of labour law's traditional, redistributive functions in favour of a process of market steering.

Nevertheless, the argument presented here returns to an important but somewhat submerged tradition within labour law, which denies that the two spheres of the 'economic' and the 'social' are irredeemably divided. The use of labour law techniques to reconcile social protection with considerations of economic efficiency has a significant history. It was in a time similar to our own, when a new century witnessed global markets and rapid technological change, that arguments were first made for the 'paramount necessity of so fixing and gradually raising the National Minimum as progressively to increase the efficiency of the community as a whole' (Webb and Webb [1896], 1920: 788–9). The renewal of this agenda of social and economic reconstruction is arguably no less a priority now than it was in the different conditions of a hundred years ago.

Part of the work involved in this reconstruction involves a close consideration of the methods and applications of the economic analysis of labour law. The present chapter carries on work begun elsewhere with this end in view (Deakin and Wilkinson, 1991, 1992, 1994, 1999). The section on 'The market as a spontaneous order' outlines the evolutionary view of the market as a form of 'spontaneous order'. The section on 'Regulation and efficiency in a spontaneous order' considers how issues of regulation and efficiency fit into this conception of the market, and the section on 'Inequality and endowments: why redistribution matters' questions whether it is compatible with the persistence of deep inequalities. Section on 'Social rights as institutionalised capabilities' introduces the concept of 'capabilities' and aims to show how it can be used to understand certain forms of labour law regulation. Section on 'Social rights, regulatory competition and the "rules of the game"' completes the movement from economics to law by outlining a role for social rights in terms of setting the 'rules of the game' for regulatory competition in an increasingly global economic and legal order.

The market as a spontaneous order

For many critics of regulation, the search for labour market efficiency involves an attempt to recreate the general equilibrium framework of neoclassical labour economics. Under conditions of perfect competition, the fundamental theorems of welfare economics tell us that resources will gravitate, through voluntary exchange, to their most efficient use. Specifying the role of law in the general equilibrium model, however, is inherently problematic. In a world of zero transaction costs, there would be no need for either norms or law, as new institutional economics recognises (Coase, 1988). This makes conventional neoclassical theory singularly unhelpful for telling us about the relationship between law and the market system.

Some progress is made by approaches which accept the existence, in the real world, of positive transaction costs, and see a role for the law in seeking to reproduce the outcomes which a competitive market would have achieved, had it been able to operate as the model predicts. This 'market perfecting' agenda is superficially attractive since it holds out the promise that the legal system can enhance efficiency by selective interventions which address particular issues of market failure. However, it faces the formidable theoretical objection made by Hayek, namely that courts and legislators alike are unlikely to have the information which they require to make these interventions effective. Economic systems are too complex to be easily amenable to centralised legal direction (Hayek, 1973, 1976). The power of this critique, and the problem which it poses for those who wish to defend market regulation, are now widely recognised (see Hodgson, 1998).

The theory of the market as a spontaneous order seeks to address this central issue of complexity. It is assumed that information and knowledge (or applied information) are privately held and cannot be mobilised through centralised direction or command. Under these circumstances, the contribution of the market is to operate as a mode of coordination which enables each individual to benefit from the possession and use of information *by others* (Hayek, 1973: 10–17). Competition operates as *a process of discovery*, generating information which is transmitted through the price mechanism. By mobilising the resources available to a society in this way, the market enhances the total wealth (or well being) of its members.

The market is one form of spontaneous order or self-organising system. Hayek defines a system as 'a state of affairs in which a multiplicity of elements of various kinds are so related to each other that we may learn from our acquaintance with some spatial or temporal part of the whole to form correct expectations concerning the rest, or at least expectations which have a good chance of proving correct' (Hayek, 1973: 36). This definition, then, implies a certain type of relationship between the overall properties of the system and its constituent parts. Sugden (1998: 487) spells out the implications of this as follows:

> [a]n order is a regularity among a set of elements. To say that the order is spontaneous is to say that in some sense the elements have *arranged themselves* into that order ... For the elements to be able to arrange themselves, each must act on its own principles of behaviour or laws of motion; the regularity among the set of elements must be capable of being explained by the individual actions of the elements. This requires that each element results from, and operates through, the *particular mechanism* of the self-interested behaviour of each actor.

The price mechanism is just one of the means by which coordination problems are overcome through the market. The market rests on numerous interlocking *conventions* which guarantee the conditions under which it operates. Conventions or social norms can be thought of as forms of shared information which enable parties to coordinate their behaviour on the basis of mutual expectations of each other's conduct (Lewis, 1969). Another way of putting this is to say that the value of the information contained in conventions and norms is equivalent to the sum total of the transaction costs which prevent actors from knowing what the strategies of others are going to be (Warneryd, 1998). The price mechanism, for example, encodes knowledge about scarcity in a way that saves on transaction costs, in the sense that consumers do not need to know the reason for a particular shift in prices (such as a disruption to supply); the price signal is enough for them to adjust their behaviour. One of the features of norms, both social and legal, is that they too operate as 'information transmission systems' to overcome coordination problems.

The existence of norms is in a general sense, a source of efficiency, since it enables those who follow the norm to save on the transaction costs of endlessly searching for the solution to commonly recurring coordination problems. The returns to following a particular norm increase, the larger the number of people who can be expected to adhere to it. The institution of money is an example of this: its use enhances efficiency by saving on the transaction costs which would otherwise arise in a system reliant on barter. Its effectiveness rests on a widely-shared convention to the effect that coins or notes, which may have little or no inherent worth, have value when used as a medium of exchange in the context of commercial transactions (see Agliétta and Orléan, 1998).

Other norms which operate to sustain market activity include property rules which serve to identify the subject-matter of exchange. Property rules can be thought of as conventions which, in the terminology of evolutionary game theory, solve coordination failures which would otherwise arise from individually self-interested behaviour (Sugden, 1989; Hargreaves Heap and Varoufakis, 1995; Costabile, 1998: 12–14, 24–7). Repeated disputes over ownership result in socially-wasteful conflicts. The emergence of rules for settling these disputes is therefore a precondition of an extended system of exchange. Norms favouring the enforcement of contracts and respect for the security of commercial undertakings can be seen in the same light. In Hayek's terms, the function of these 'abstract rules of just conduct' is that 'by defining a protected domain of each [individual] [they] enable an order of actions to form itself wherein the individuals can make feasible plans' (Hayek, 1973: 85–6). In other words, these norms supply institutional support for the 'motive power' of individual economic actors, without which there would be no basis for the decentralised action upon which the spontaneous order depends for its effectiveness.

Recent evolutionary accounts of norms have placed most of their emphasis upon self-enforcing conventions which appear to operate independently of any centralised enforcement mechanism. Sugden (1989: 86) suggests that '[m]any of the institutions of a market economy are conventions that no one has designed, but that have simply evolved', and that '[a]lthough markets may work more smoothly when property rights are defined by formal laws and enforced by the state, they can come into existence and persist without any such external support'.

The basis for this claim is the argument that self-enforcing conventions emerge through an evolutionary process of social learning. In a world characterised by complexity and 'bounded rationality', actors have an interest in following those strategies which have proved to be successful in overcoming coordination problems. Norms, in the sense of regularities, can therefore emerge on the basis of repeated interactions between individuals (Ullmann-Margalit, 1977; Schotter, 1981; Sugden, 1986; Young, 1996; Costabile, 1998).

However, those who argue for the spontaneous character of many of the conventions which are characteristic of market exchange do not seek to deny that, in a wide range of contexts, these norms are supported by legal mechanisms of various kinds. In suggesting that markets may work 'more smoothly' when legal enforcement is present, Sugden echoes Hayek, who argues that social norms are not sufficient for the preservation of the spontaneous order of the market: 'in most circumstances the organisation which we call government becomes indispensable to assure that those rules are obeyed' (Hayek, 1973: 47). Hence, for Hayek, the exercise of 'coercion' or legal enforcement of norms is justified within a spontaneous order 'where this is necessary to secure the private domain of the individual against interference by others' (Hayek, 1973: 57). While a given rule of just conduct may have had a spontaneous origin, in the sense that 'individuals followed rules which had not been deliberately made but had arisen spontaneously' (Hayek, 1973: 45), such rules do not lose their essential character merely by virtue of being put into legal form: '[t]he spontaneous character of the resulting order must therefore be distinguished from the spontaneous origin of the rules on which it rests, and it is possible that an order which would still have to be described as spontaneous rests on rules which are entirely the result of deliberate design' (Hayek, 1973: 45–6). In this perspective, it is the particular function of private law – what Hayek quoting Hume, refers to as 'the three fundamental laws of nature', *that of stability of possession, of its transference by consent*, and *of the performance of promises*' (Hayek, 1976: 140) – to underpin the spontaneous order of the market.

Regulation and efficiency in a spontaneous order

Legal norms may therefore have a role to play in establishing the conditions for the effective operation of the market. Neither Hayek nor Sugden go into much detail on why this might be so. One reason could be the fragility of many social norms, that is to say, their tendency to be destabilised by changing environmental conditions. Legal enforcement of social norms could provide some degree of protection against this kind of effect. If this were the case, legal enforcement would have the important but somewhat limited role of crystallising in juridical form practices which were widely followed in practice.

A much broader role for law as an instrument for changing, rather than confirming, norms arises from the tendency for spontaneously-emerging norms to give rise to inefficient solutions over time through lock-in effects and other features of *path dependence* (Roe, 1996). Although, as we have seen, a normative foundation of some kind is arguably essential if a market order is to operate at all, it does not follow that norms evolve and adapt over time in such a way as to supply solutions which are *optimal*. In the case of conventions which emerge on the basis of social learning, the usefulness of a particular norm is a function of its adaptiveness in the *past*; hence 'evolution will tend to favour versatile but inefficient conventions relative to ones that are less versatile but more efficient' (Sugden, 1989: 94). The adaptation of existing concepts and ideas to new ends means that 'features of existing conventions and institutions may often have arisen for one reason, but now serve very different functions and purposes' (Balkin, 1998: 72).

The notion of efficiency in a spontaneous order is therefore a highly qualified one. Norms which emerge spontaneously are unlikely to be optimal in the Paretian sense of producing situations in which no further gains from trade can be made except by making at least one party worse off (see Costabile, 1998: 27–30). However, the configuration of incentives which emerges from the accumulation of conventions may be the best that is available. The costs of attempting to shift the system to a notional optimum through 'market perfecting' laws may outweigh the resulting gains (the so-called 'irremediability' principle; Williamson, 1996: ch. 9).

The use of intervention to achieve Pareto improvements may be undesirable for other reasons. This is because spontaneous orders may be *self-correcting*. According to the Hayekian or neo-Austrian school, it is precisely because of so-called imperfections – such as imperfect transmission of information – that opportunities for profit from entrepreneurial activity or, more generally, from innovation in organisation and design of goods and services, exist. In the general-equilibrium world of pure competition, in which information and resources moved perfectly freely in response to the price mechanism, such opportunities would be instantly competed away. In the real world of positive transaction costs, by contrast, it is the possibility of capturing 'supra-competitive rents' or surpluses representing a competitive advantage over their rivals which motivates potential entrepreneurs or innovators and which, as a result, ensures long-run technological and organisational progress (Kirzner, 1997).

In this account, the appropriate role for the law, then, is to support private property rights, ensure that returns accrue to those who make investments in the process of discovery, and guarantee freedom of access to markets. The inequalities and concentrations of power and wealth which arise from the unbridled operation of market forces produce their own solution by incentivising those who, by misfortune or otherwise, fail to profit from the system. Even if certain gains and losses accrue by chance, leaving some with 'undeserved disappointments' (Hayek, 1976: 1127), *ex post* redistribution of resources blunts incentives for individuals to invest in their own skills and efforts. This and similar interventions which might be justified from a 'market perfecting' point of view merely block the *process* of competition as discovery which provides the means by which dispersed knowledge and information are put to use: hence, 'attempts to "correct" the market order lead to its destruction' (Hayek, 1976: 142).

The precise claim being made here needs to be carefully identified, and distinguished from those made by neoclassical economists who see regulation as giving rise to 'rigidities' which impede market equilibrium. From the evolutionary perspective, it is not being suggested that markets, if left to their own devices, will tend towards an optimally efficient state. The market never 'clears' in the sense used by neoclassical economic theory. Rather, the market is a beneficial institution because it generates a process of discovery which makes the best available use of society's resources. It is accepted that the process of economic change which this account implies is one which is dynamic and non-linear, in contrast to the linear reallocation of resources to their most efficient use which is imagined by the theory of general equilibrium. It is therefore the *dynamic efficiency* of the market system – in other words, its capacity to generate new knowledge and information in a way which will ensure the system's long run survival in a changing environment – which justifies institutional support for individual property and contract rights, but which, at the same time, allows for only a very limited degree of market regulation, and rules out redistribution carried out in the name of 'social justice' (Hayek, 1973: 140–2).

Inequality and endowments: why redistribution matters

One of the virtues of the theory of spontaneous order is that, in addition to explaining the many benefits of markets, it also helps us to understand their limits. Sugden (1998) acknowledges the limits of market ordering when he accepts that the market is good at meeting one particular type of objective, namely satisfying those wants or preferences which can be encapsulated in property rights. The market will not provide well in relation to those wants or preferences for goods for which no property rights exist. It therefore fails to work well in relation to non-excludable public goods or indivisible commodities (see also Sen, 1999: 127–9).

The spontaneous order argument for markets is based on the power of individuals to make mutually-agreed exchanges with others; but this only satisfies wants *in general* if each transaction affects only those who are party to it. If there are externalities, then transactions between some parties affect the opportunities of others to satisfy their wants. As the Coase theorem recognises (Coase, 1988) the state has a role in dealing with externalities in situations where negotiation is unduly costly. But this opens up another arena for policy intervention in an area where the market is not self-correcting. Nor is this point simply related to limits to the spillover effects of exchange. Sugden argues that for the market to operate effectively, it is necessary not simply to have a system of property rights, but for individuals to have *endowments* in the sense of items of value which are tradable – 'the market has a strong tendency to supply each person with those things he wants, *provided that he owns things that other people want, and provided that the things he wants are things that other people own*' (Sugden, 1998: 492, emphasis added). Another way of putting this is to say that the market has no inbuilt tendency to satisfy the wants of those who do not have things that other people want.

This leads us to pose the central question in understanding the role of labour law in relation to the present process of global economic change: can a market order function effectively in a situation in which there are large and enduring disparities in the wealth and resources of market participants? For neoclassical economic theory, the answer is clearly that it can; supply and demand can still be brought into equilibrium and resources will flow to their most highly valued use, value simply being measured by willingness to pay (Posner, 1998).

From the point of view of the theory of spontaneous order, however, the answer is not so clear. Extremes of inequality have the effect of excluding certain groups from the market altogether. The result is not just that these individuals no longer have access to the goods which the market can supply; the rest of society also suffers a loss from their inability to take part in the system of exchange. Resources which could have been mobilised for the benefit of society as whole will, instead, remain unutilised. The logic of this position, as Sugden makes clear (Sugden, 1998: 493), is that redistribution is needed not to reverse the unpleasant results of the market, but rather to provide the preconditions for the market working in the first place. Although Sugden does not put in such terms, one implication of his approach is that many of the redistributive and protective rules of labour law have a market-creating function.

The argument for redistribution, and for regulation, can be taken a step further. The market itself may be a cause of inequality; inequality, in other words, may be *endogenous*. Neoclassical theory simply denies this on a priori grounds; the causes of inequality are assumed to be *exogenous*, in the sense that different individuals have different capacities and propensities to work. The market itself tends towards proportionality of effort and reward, by setting wages in proportion to the contribution which particular individuals bring to the employment relationship.

However, an implication of the path dependent nature of norms and conventions within labour markets is that forces are at work which disrupt this assumed correspondence of efforts and rewards. Notwithstanding Hayek's suggestion that, at the end of the day, it is imperfections which drive the process of competitive market discovery, markets which are completely unregulated contain within them the seeds of their own destruction. This is because, in the terms used by spontaneous order theory, the symbiotic relationship between the general and particular mechanisms can break down. When this occurs, the market loses its capacity for self-correction. Persistent inequalities mean that groups and individuals may lack the resource endowments to enter the market in a meaningful way. In an extreme case, the market will destroy itself unless these negative effects are counteracted by non-market institutions in the form of regulation and redistribution. In a less extreme case, the market order will continue to function, but will fail to provide adequate economic opportunities for an increasingly large segment of the population.

In this context, it is important to remind ourselves that one of the principal findings of theories of labour market segmentation has been that, in so-called 'unregulated' markets, cumulative processes are at work which reinforce the effects of disadvantage and exclusion from participation (Craig *et al.*, 1982, 1985; Tarling and Wilkinson, ch. 12). The suggestion that labour markets tend towards a fundamental lack of correspondence between endowments and efforts, on the one hand, and rewards on the other, can be understood by considering the role of norms and conventions which structure both the demand-side and supply-sides of the exchange. Norms operate, first, to structure the conditions under which labour is supplied. The traditional household division of labour, is one example of this (Humphries, 1977), as are notions of what constitutes a minimum 'fair wage' for which the non-employed are prepared to work (Solow, 1992). Second, at the level of the organisation of production, what might be termed the 'managerial prerogative' norm expresses the practice of allowing to management an area of discretion within which to direct the pace and nature of production. Norms about fair treatment and equity in the treatment of employees also undoubtedly affect the practice of many organisations. The form and content of these norms may be (and very often will be) highly contested. Moreover, the degree to which their contractual form is given legal support may differ considerably between otherwise similar systems, such as those of the United States and Britain (compare Rock and Wachter, 1996 and Deakin, 1999, on the degree to which the terms of the contract of employment reflect social norms).

To sum up this part of the argument: the operation of spontaneous order within labour markets is a complex process, involving the interaction of a number of forces on the supply-side and demand-sides of the exchange. Conventions structure both the demand and supply for labour in such a way as to produce persistent inefficiencies, or structural inequalities. Because of the path-dependent nature of conventions, these effects may become locked in, with the result that they influence the direction of economic change independently of the forces of supply and demand. The trajectory of economic development is determined by cumulative, feedback effects, which can produce a 'pathology of the labour market' in which inefficiencies, and hence inequalities, become endogenous.

Under these circumstances, there can be no assumption that a self-correcting mechanism will undo these effects. A role for policy is opened up, in terms of redressing what may be seen as effects which are undesirable not just for particular groups, but for society as a whole, given the waste and underutilisation of resources which they produce. We now turn to consider the nature of the policy responses which this perspective implies.

Social rights as institutionalised capabilities

In Hayek's account of the role of law in market ordering, it is the institutions of private law – in particular, property and contract – which guarantee to individuals the conditions for their effective participation in the market. The inadequacy of this conception in the context of the labour market is what inspires the idea of social rights. Social rights can be seen as the institutional form of those capabilities which Sen argues are the conditions for the effective mobilisation by individuals of the resources at their disposal as the means of becoming and remaining self sufficient.

According to Sen (1999: 75),

> the concept of 'functionings'... reflects the various things a person may value doing or being. The valued functionings may vary from elementary ones,

such as being adequately nourished and being free from avoidable disease, to very complex activities or personal states, such as being able to take part in the life of the community and having self-respect.

Within this context, a 'capability' is 'a kind of freedom: the substantive freedom to achieve alternative functioning combinations' (Sen, 1999: 75).

Capabilities are a consequence not simply of the endowments and motivations of individuals but also of the access they have to the processes of socialisation, education and training which enable them to exploit their resource endowments. By providing the conditions under which access to these processes is made generally available, mechanisms of redistribution may not just be compatible with, but become a precondition to, the operation of the labour market. Some specific examples may help to illustrate this point.

A conventional economic view of laws which protect women against dismissal on the grounds of pregnancy would be as follows (see Gruber, 1994). From the viewpoint of enterprises which would otherwise dismiss pregnant employees once they become unable to carry on working as normally, such laws impose a private cost. These enterprises may respond by declining to hire women of child-bearing age who will, as a result, find it more difficult to get jobs. If this happens, there may be an overall loss to society in terms of efficiency, because resources are misallocated and underutilised, as well as a disadvantage to the women who are unemployed as a result.

An alternative way of thinking about discrimination against pregnant workers is as follows. In the absence of legal protection against this type of discrimination, women of child-bearing age will not expect to continue in employment once (or shortly after) they become pregnant. It is not necessary for all market participants to make a precise calculation along these lines; rather, a norm or convention will emerge, according to which pregnant women expect to lose their jobs and their employers expect to be able to dismiss them without any harm attaching to their reputation. The overall effect is that investments in skills and training are not undertaken, making society worse off as a result. Women workers will have an incentive not to make relation-specific investments in the jobs which they undertake. In an extreme situation, they may withdraw from active participation from the labour market altogether, and norms may encourage this too – as in the case of the 'marriage bar' norm, according to which any woman who married was expected thereupon to resign her position. This norm was widely observed in the British public sector up to the 1950s and, in the case of some local authorities, was actually enshrined in regulations.

What is the effect of the introduction of a prohibition on the dismissal of pregnant women under these circumstances? In addition to remedying the injustice which would otherwise affect individuals who are dismissed for this reason, a law of this kind has the potential to alter incentive structures in such a way as to encourage women employees to seek out, and employer to provide training for, jobs involving relation-specific skills. The demonstration effect of damages awards against employers may over time lead to a situation in which the norm of automatic dismissal is replaced by its opposite. Stigma attaches to those employers who flout the law. As more employers observe the new norm as a matter of course, it will tend to become self-enforcing, in a way which is independent of the law itself. Conversely, more women will expect, as a matter of course, to carry on working while raising families, in a way which may have a wider destabilising effect on the set of conventions which together make up the 'traditional' household division of labour between men and women.

Pregnancy protection laws, therefore, can be seen as a form of institutional capability. In other words, they provide the conditions under which, for women workers, the freedom to enter the labour market becomes more than merely formal; it becomes a substantive freedom. This effect is not confined to laws in the area of equality of treatment. Consider laws which set minimum wages or which otherwise establish legally-binding wage floors (such as the principle known as 'inderogability' in Italian labour law and observed in some form in most continental labour law systems, although not well represented in the British labour law tradition (see Wedderburn, 1992)). These laws have been the subject of severe criticisms from economic and legal commentators (Ichino and Ichino, 1998). The objection made against them is that they artificially raise wages above the market clearing level, thereby reducing demand for labour and excluding the less able from access to the labour market. By doing so, they potentially infringe the basic constitutional right to work in systems which recognise that concept.

This argument assumes that a 'free' labour market more or less accurately allocates wages to workers according to their relative productivity. As explained above, there are spontaneous forces at work in the labour market which make this unlikely. In an unregulated or 'free' labour market without effective labour standards, wage rates are only weakly linked, at best, to the comparative productivity of workers (Craig *et al.*, 1985). By removing protective legislation which has a general or 'universal' effect, protecting all labour market entrants, deregulation directly undermines the capabilities of those individuals who are at most risk of social exclusion through discrimination and the undervaluation of their labour. The demotivation of those who find themselves excluded from access to productive employment is met by ever-increasing pressure on them to take jobs at any cost. This takes the form of measures within social security law which discipline the 'voluntarily' unemployed by, for example, withdrawing benefits from individuals who refuse to accept jobs offering low-standard terms and conditions of employment. On the demand side, employers are encouraged to take on the unemployed by subsidy schemes which top up low wages. This exacerbates the effect of removing the incentives for training and investment in human capital which flow from a legal requirement for employers to pay a minimum wage. All these developments are well documented in the case of the British experience of deregulation which reached its high point in the early 1990s (Deakin and Wilkinson, 1991).

By contrast, legislation setting a floor to wages and terms and conditions of employment in effect requires firms to adopt strategies based on enhancing the quality of labour inputs through improvements to health and safety protection, training and skills development. This form of labour regulation may therefore be expected to have a positive impact on incentives for training. Minimum wage laws are therefore another form of institutional capability, improving the substantive labour market freedoms of workers.

Social rights, regulatory competition and the 'rules of the game'

The previous section gave examples of the way in which certain instances of labour law regulation can be seen to operate as capabilities. The idea of social *rights* refers to a more specific category or subset of legal relations within labour (or, more generally, social) law. However, the particular juridical form of social rights is difficult to define precisely. Lo Faro (2000: 152) helpfully suggests that 'the notion of social rights can refer to a series of predominantly, but not exclusively, financial benefits bestowed by the public machinery within the context of social policies of the redistributive type'. The problem with this idea, as he notes, is that many of the 'rights' in question depend, for their realisation, on certain economic and political conditions which are independent of the legal form of the benefits or claims in question. The idea of the 'right to work' can be cited as one example of this problem; its effective realisation appears to depend upon external economic conditions or, according to taste, on various kinds of government action, which the legal system is more or less powerless to affect. The 'substantive' version of social rights may be contrasted, Lo Faro suggests, with a 'procedural' version which has the twofold merit of avoiding the straightforward association of social rights with economic 'costs', and stressing the links between social rights and participative democracy. This version takes, as its concrete form, constitutional guarantees of freedom of association and collective representation.

There is no doubt that the idea of reflexive or 'proceduralised' labour law (Rogowski and Wilthagen, 1994) has done much to help operationalise the otherwise inchoate idea of fundamental social rights. At the same time, a close study of proceduralised forms of labour law regulation suggests that there is a close relationship, in practice, between 'procedural' and 'substantive' rights.

This point may be illustrated through an example. The 1989 EC Framework Directive on Health and Safety refers to a number of 'general principles of prevention' in the operation by employers of health and safety standards, including the principle of 'adapting the work to the individual, especially as regards the design of work places, the choice of work equipment and the choice of working time and production methods, with a view, in particular, to alleviating monotonous work and work at a predetermined work rate and to reducing their effect on health'. The origins of this idea may be found in German labour law, where it is referred to as the principle of the 'humanisation of work'. The same general principle reappears in the Directive on Working Time, which provides that member states are required to take the steps necessary to ensure that an employer 'who intends to organise work according to a certain pattern' takes account of the principle, 'especially as regards breaks during working time'. Through the Working Time Directive, the substantive social right which is embodied in the concept of the 'humanisation of work' finds concrete form in a set of essentially procedural provisions. This is because, thanks to the numerous derogations contained in the

Directive, the implementation of the standards it lays down in relation to working time limits, breaks and shift patterns is left to collective bargaining (or some other form of joint decision making) at various levels. It seems unlikely that the reference to the humanisation of work in the Directive would be regarded by the courts as a completely empty formula. Although the fate of this provision remains to be seen, it seems more likely that it would be called in aid in construing the legitimacy of derogations made from the standards contained in the Directive.

At the micro level of collective bargaining (or its equivalent) over working time, then, the thrust of the Directive is that the principle of the humanisation of work should be a reference point which is capable of 'steering' or 'channelling' the process of negotiation between the social partners. Very much the same process may be observed at the macro level of regulatory competition between different legal orders within the parameters of the single market. Here, too, the role of social rights is to set the parameters within which procedural solutions are sought. This can be seen from a consideration of decisions in which the Court of Justice has attempted to resolve potential conflicts between the social policy provisions of the EC Treaty, and those parts of the Treaty which are concerned with free movement of economic resources and the removal of restrictions and distortions of competition. In *United Kingdom* versus *Council (Working Time)*, the Court gave a broad reading to the term 'working environment' in Article 118a of EC Treaty (now in Article 137), holding that 'a broad interpretation of the powers which Article 118a confers upon the Council for the protection of the health and safety of workers' was appropriate (see Barnard and Deakin, 1999). In *Albany International*, the Court's decision that collective agreements were not, as such, subject to review under the competition policy provisions of the Treaty, was based on an analysis which recognised the strong encouragement given by the Treaty itself to collective bargaining, in the form of Article 118 (now Article 138) and the provisions of the Maastricht Agreement on Social Policy (now part of Article 137) (see Barnard and Deakin, 2000). What the Court was doing, in each case, was to use the social policy provisions of the Treaty to guide the process of regulatory competition; in the one case, the Council itself, and, in the other, the social partners, could legitimately act to regulate terms and conditions of employment, without infringing the economic freedoms which the Treaty also guarantees.

The search for a system of labour regulation which enhances dynamic efficiency while also reflecting other, widely-held democratic values is one which must respond to a variety of diverse local conditions. Path dependence implies that solutions which work well in one context may not be readily supplanted into others. Finding the 'right' form of regulation is therefore a process of discovery, in the case of the labour market as elsewhere. However, it is precisely in this context that fundamental social rights have a vital role to play. The role of social rights is to set the 'rules of the game', or the architectural framework, within which the evolution of welfare states and labour law systems in an increasingly globalised economy takes place.

The recognition of fundamental social rights within the legal framework of the European Union would have an important bearing on the debate over the changing nature of work and the response of labour law to these changes. In the words of the

Supiot report (1999: 271), the increasing flexibilisation and individualisation of work necessitates the establishment of a 'convention of trust' as the basis for the governance of the employment relationship. The importance of trust in this context lies precisely in the growing importance of flexibility both in production and in the movement of individuals between jobs and careers across the life cycle. Radical uncertainty creates a set of conditions in which the effectiveness of the employment relationship depends upon the presence of goodwill trust, in the sense of both parties being willing to perform over and above the express terms of their contract (Marsden, 1996). At the same time, this is a high-risk strategy which exposes each side to the risk of exploitation or 'opportunism'. The question is, given the high-risk strategy which is implicit in the pursuit of goodwill trust, how is it achieved? The role of goodwill trust extends, in Fox's terms (Fox, 1974), 'beyond contract', to encompass a degree of open-ended cooperation with expected returns only being realised over a long period. As a result, 'in the context of flexibility, the governance of employment amounts to more than just the management of opportunism; it must provide room for creative action on the part of the social partners, a space for the exercise of freedom' (Supiot, 1999: 270–1). It is for social rights to create this space.

References

Agliétta, M. and Orléan, A. (eds) (1998) *La monnaie souveraine*. Paris: PUF.

Balkin, J. (1998) *Cultural Software: A Theory of Ideology*. New Haven, CT: Yale University Press.

Barnard, C. and Deakin, S. (1999) 'A year of living dangerously? EC social rights, employment policy, and EMU', *Industrial Relations Journal*, 30, 355–72.

Barnard, C. and Deakin, S. (2000) 'In search of coherence: social policy, the single market and fundamental rights', *Industrial Relations Journal*, 31, 331–45.

Coase, R. H. (1988) *The Firm, the Market and the Law*. Chicago: University of Chicago Press.

Costabile, L. (1998) 'Ordine spontaneo o ordine negoziato? Conflitti e resoluzione dei onflitti nella nuova teoria economica delle istituzione', in Amendola, A. (ed.), *Istituzione e mercato del lavoro*, Rome: Edizione Scientifiche Italiane.

Craig, C., Rubery, J., Tarling, R. and Wilkinson, F. (1982) *Labour Market Structure, Industrial Organisation and Low Pay*. Cambridge: Cambridge University Press.

Craig, C., Rubery, J., Tarling, R. R. and Wilkinson, F. (1985) 'Economic, social and political factors in the operation of the labour market', in Roberts, B., Finnegan, R. and Gallie, D. (eds), *New Approaches to Economic Life*, Manchester: Manchester University Press.

Deakin, S. (1999) 'Organisational change, labour flexibility and the contract of employment in Great Britain', in Deery, S. and Mitchell, R. (eds), *Employment Relations, Individualisation and Union Exclusion*, Annandale, NSW: Federation Press.

Deakin, S. and Wilkinson, F. (1991) 'Labour law, social security and economic inequality', *Cambridge Journal of Economics*, 15, 125–48.

Deakin, S. and Wilkinson, F. (1992) 'The law and economics of the minimum wage', *Journal of Law and Society*, 19, 379–92.

Deakin, S. and Wilkinson, F. (1994) 'Rights versus efficiency? The economic case for transnational labour standards', *Industrial Law Journal*, 23, 289.

Deakin, S. and Wilkinson, F. (1999) 'Labour law and economic theory: a reappraisal', in De Geest, G., Seegers, J. and Van den Bergh, R. (eds), *Law and Economics and the Labour Market*, Aldershot: Elgar.

Fox, A. (1974) *Beyond Contract*. London: Allen & Unwin.

Gruber, J. (1994) 'The incidence of mandated maternity benefits', *American Economic Review*, 84, 622–41.

Hargreaves Heap, S. and Varoufakis, Y. (1995) *Game Theory: A Critical Introduction*. London: Routledge.

Hayek, F. (1973) *Rules and Order*. London: Routledge.

Hayek, F. (1976) *The Mirage of Social Justice*. London: Routledge.

Hayek, F. (1979) *The Political Order of a Free People*. London: Routledge.

Hodgson, G. (1998) *Economics and Utopia*. London: Routledge.

Humphries, J. (1977) 'Class struggle and the persistence of the working class family', *Cambridge Journal of Economics*, 1, 241.

Ichino, A. and Ichino, P. (1998) 'A chi serve il diritto del lavoro? Riflessioni interdisciplinari sulla funzione economica e la giustificazione costitutizionale dell'inderogabilitá delle norme giuslavoristiche', in Amendola, A. (ed.), *Istituzione e mercato del lavoro*, Rome: Edizione Scientifiche Italiane.

Kirzner, I. (1997) *How Markets Work: Disequilibrium, Entrepreneurship and Discovery*, IEA Paper No. 133. London: Institute of Economic Affairs.

Lewis, D. (1969) *Convention: A Philosophical Study*. Cambridge, MA: Harvard University Press.

Lo Faro, A. (2000) *Regulating Social Europe. Reality and Myth of Collective Bargaining in the EC Legal Order*. Oxford: Hart.

Marsden, D. (1996) 'Employment policy implications of new management systems', *Labour*, 9, 17.

Posner, R. (1998) *Economic Analysis of Law*, 5th edition. New York: Aspen Law and Business.

Rock, E. and Wachter, M. (1996) 'The enforceability of norms and the employment relationship', *University of Pennsylvania Law Review*, 144, 1913.

Rogowski, R. and Wilthagen, T. (eds) (1994) *Reflexive Labour Law*. Deventer: Kluwer.

Roe, M. (1996) 'Chaos and evolution in law and economics', *Harvard Law Review*, 109, 641.

Salais, R. (1999) 'Libertés du travail et capacités: une perspective pour une construction européenne?', *Droit Social*, 471, 467–71.

Schotter, A. (1981) *The Economic Theory of Social Institutions*. Cambridge: Cambridge University Press.

Sen, A. (1985) *Commodities and Capabilities*. Deventer: North-Holland.

Sen, A. (1999) *Development as Freedom*. Oxford: OUP.

Solow, R. (1992) *The Labour Market as a Social Institution*. Oxford: Blackwell.

Sugden, R. (1986) *The Economics of Rights, Co-operation and Welfare*. Oxford: Basil Blackwell.

Sugden, R. (1989) 'Spontaneous order', *Journal of Economic Perspectives*, 3, 85–97.

Sugden, R. (1998) 'Spontaneous order', in Newman, P. (ed.), *The New Palgrave Dictionary of Economics and the Law*, London: Macmillan.

Supiot, A. (ed.) (1999) *Au delà de l'emploi. Transformations du travail et devenir du droit du travail en Europe*. Paris: Flammarion.

Ullmann-Margalit, E. (1977) *The Emergence of Norms*. Oxford: Clarendon Press.

Warneryd, K. (1998) 'Conventions and transaction costs', in Newman, P. (ed.), *The New Palgrave Dictionary of Economics and the Law*, London: Macmillan.

Webb, S. and Webb, B. [1896] (1920) *Industrial Democracy*. London: RKP.

Wedderburn, L. (1992) 'Inderogability, collective agreements and community law', *Industrial Law Journal*, 21, 245–64.

Williamson, O. (1996), *The Mechanisms of Governance*. Oxford: OUP.

Young, H. P. (1996) 'The economics of convention', *Journal of Economic Perspectives*, 10, 105–22.

6 Working like a dog, sick as a dog

Job intensification in the late twentieth century

David Ladipo, Roy Mankelow and Brendan Burchell

This chapter draws upon data from the *Job Insecurity and Work Intensification Survey* (JIWIS).[1] Although the project started with a narrower focus on job insecurity, the interviews and early analyses of the data quickly brought us to realise that there was another recent change in the United Kingdom workplaces that might be even more important than job insecurity – work intensification. There has been a lot written recently about the longer hours of work in the United Kingdom and the United States than in Continental European countries. While this is an important phenomenon in its own right, work intensification, or the effort that employees put into their jobs while they are at work, has received less attention. But, as the data we will be presenting in this chapter show, the intensification of work may be a far greater problem in terms of stress, psychological health and family tension, the quality of working life and the functioning of establishments.

The approach to studying employment in this chapter is grounded in a *productive systems* approach at a number of levels. In personal terms, the author of the original *productive systems* article in 1983, Frank Wilkinson, was one of the principle investigators of the project, funded by the Joseph Rowntree foundation, which brought together the authors of this paper to investigate job insecurity and work intensification (Burchell *et al.*, 1999, 2001). And at a methodological and theoretical level, there are a number of themes that are raised in that 1983 article, and the chapter by Frank Wilkinson in this book, which influenced this research project and this chapter. Methodologically, this chapter is based on the sort of genuine enquiry into systems of production advocated by Wilkinson, taking very seriously the nature of the social and political forces that impinge on economic phenomena, rather than attempting to reduce the observations to a model which simplifies them out of consideration.

Theoretically, this chapter addresses one of the issues which is raised in the 1983 paper, the intensity of work. On page 422, Wilkinson stated 'The cost of production of a productive system are determined by ... the effectiveness of management in ... extracting labour power'. The results that we present here suggest not only that managers have become more effective in this respect than they were in the 1980s, but also that the forces beyond the control of managers have been even more effective in extracting the labour power of the managers themselves!

Measuring the intensity of work

As Green (2001) argues, the United Kingdom experienced a real intensification of work in the 1990s. This evidence will only be considered briefly here, because Green's analysis is both comprehensive and compelling.

In his review of the literature on work intensification, Green (2001) suggests a number of ways in which effort might be measured. Apart from self-report, the other possibilities he considers are by quantifiable proxy (for instance, industrial accidents), case studies, productivity and a measure called 'Percentage Utilisation of Labour' based on work study. Unfortunately, he concludes, none of these measures is reliable or valid enough to be useful. There are too many other variables, apart from effort, which influence them. For instance, industrial accidents are also strongly influenced by health and safety regulation and enforcement, and productivity is also a function of skill, managerial efficiency and reliability of machinery, as well as effort.

This leaves only self-report measures as a reliable indicator of work intensification. Surveys have typically asked questions in two forms. First, respondents can be asked how their effort, or pace of work, has changed over the past, say, five years. This was done in the JIWIS survey, and Figures 6.1 and 6.2 show the results. Taking the responses at face value, the results are quite remarkable. In both cases over 60 per cent of respondents have reported an intensification of their work, compared to only 4 and 5 per cent, respectively, who reported a reduction in effort.

Other surveys have also found very high levels of reported work intensification. For instance, in 1986 the SCELI survey asked a question about increased effort and pace of work in the past five years, and 55.6 and 38.1 per cent of the 3,000 employees reported increases respectively, compared to only 8.1 and 7.8 per cent who reported a decrease. A 1999 UK survey of the members of the Institute of Management revealed that 69 per cent of the respondents reported experiencing an increase in workload in the past twelve months (Wheatley, 2000).

But this survey question has its problems. The net increases may, at least in part, be attributable to either life-cycle effects (i.e. employees having to work harder as

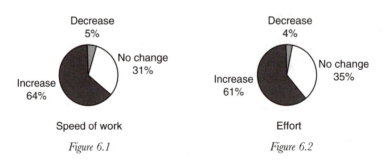

Figure 6.1   *Figure 6.2*

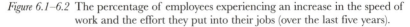

Figure 6.1–6.2 The percentage of employees experiencing an increase in the speed of work and the effort they put into their jobs (over the last five years).

Source: Burchell *et al.* (2001, figure 3.4).

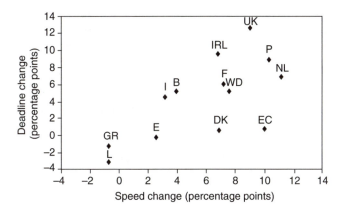

Figure 6.3 Change in per cent of respondents working at speed and to tight deadlines all or
almost all of the time, 1991–96.

Source: European Working Conditions Surveys.

they get promoted into positions of greater responsibility), or to distortions in
recall (perhaps painting the past with rose-tinted spectacles). Luckily, there now
exists a repeated cross-sectional measure, which overcomes this problem.

The European Surveys of Working Conditions in 1991 and 1996 asked 1,000
respondents in each of the EU countries how much of the time in their jobs they
had to work at speed or to tight deadlines. One could argue that, as 'tight deadlines' and 'working at speed' are somewhat subjective constructs, it is not valid to
compare workers from very different cultures – a Mediterranean worker used to
a more relaxed working day may have very different normative templates to a
more disciplined northern European worker! But, when we compare each country with its own data from five years before, we can more safely chart the relative
changes in work intensification between countries.

Figure 6.3 does this, showing, on the vertical and horizontal dimensions respectively the changes in the proportion of workers in each country working at speed
and to tight deadlines most or all of the time. The general trend in all European
countries has been up, but one country stands out as having experienced work
intensification more than any other country – the United Kingdom. This suggests
that, indeed, our JIWIS data are grounded in reality when the employees report
that their jobs require more effort and speed than before.

The distribution of job intensification

Like making comparisons between countries, it is difficult (if not impossible) to
make direct comparisons of effort between very different jobs. How might it be
possible to objectively compare the effort expended by, say, a busy labourer on
a building site and a busy midwife? The former uses his muscles more, and
expends more calories each hour, but the latter might feel more 'drained' by her

work and feel that the job is more relentless. But we can explore the ways in which the effort required of different occupations has changed over time.

In the SCELI data, where employees were invited to compare their effort at the time of the survey in 1986 with their jobs in 1981, there was a clear social class effect. Sixty-four per cent of professional and intermediate white-collar workers reported having to increase effort, compared to only 45 per cent of semi-skilled manual workers and 39 per cent of 'unskilled' manual workers. This effect was more marked among female workers; female manual workers reported the lowest levels of work intensification. This greatest intensification for the most skilled workers is consistent with the findings of the Institute of Management survey; it only surveyed managers, but found higher levels of reported intensification than other surveys.

Reasons for the intensification of work

Like many changes in the labour market, there has probably been more than one force driving the increase in work effort in the United Kingdom. It could be the reduction in trade union powers; strict demarcations between workers were one (albeit crude) way in which employees could guard against relentless work. It could be that management are now much better trained and highly skilled at managing the flow of work; previously one heard of employees having to spend much of their working days waiting for plant, materials or supervisors to arrive. Or it could be simply that jobs are more engaging or rewarding now than in the past, and so employees are more self-motivated than they used to be. Green's analyses also suggest that the reduction in trade union power and the use of computers are two further culprits.

But, in the eyes of the JIWIS employers and employees, the clear culprits were increased competition and shareholder influence in the private sector, and reduced treasury funding in the public sector, leading to downsizing. Yet, there was a clear expectation that the reduced number of employees would still achieve the same quantity and quality of work.

Job insecurity and pressure: the effect on health and well-being

Our main measure of psychological well-being in the JIWIS study was the 'General Health Questionnaire' (GHQ), a measure of mild symptoms of anxiety and depression. It is used widely in organisational psychology, having been shown, in a wide variety of studies, to be a valid method of detecting harmful levels of stress and a good predictor, not only of a wide range of physical illnesses, but also of rates of premature mortality.[2]

As shown in Figure 6.4, there is a clear relationship between poor psychological health and pressure at work. Although the graph refers to the extent to which employees feel under pressure from work mates or colleagues, similar findings

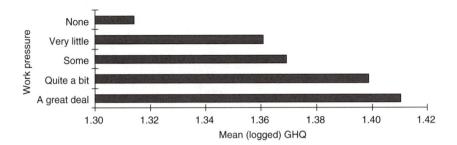

Figure 6.4 Mean GHQ scores by how much pressure people felt from work mates or colleagues. High scores indicate poor health.

Source: Burchell *et al.* (1999).

were found when we looked at pressures from managers, from the sheer volume of work and from inadequate staffing levels. We also found that pressure from managers and inadequate staffing levels were both associated with fewer hours of sleep. Once again, these findings are consistent with the literature as well as with many of the statements made in the open-ended interviews, such as this comment from an agency worker:

> I think the stress at the moment is the fact that every day we go into work in the morning, and when we finish work at night, I always tend to draw up a list of what to do tomorrow, jobs which if 50% get done you've achieved something.

A demanding job can be seen as challenging and can often increase job satisfaction. But when jobs become too demanding, leading to pressure and work overload, they have been found to lead to a variety of forms of low well-being including low life satisfaction, psychosomatic complaints, generalised anxiety, exhaustion, cardiovascular illness and depression (Karasek, 1979; Warr, 1987).

New analyses of data from the European Survey on Working Conditions suggest that the physical health of employees is suffering too. The survey, of 1,000 employees in each of the EU countries, asked them whether their work affected their health. Analyses of the different patterns of health-related illnesses for those who work at speed all of the time or almost all of the time, compared with those who only have to work at speed about a quarter of their time or less, showed that pressure to work at speed increased employees susceptibility to every single illness recorded from backaches to heart problems. As Table 6.1 shows, many illnesses and complaints were more than twice as common amongst those working at continuous high speed, including headaches, stomach aches, muscular pains in limbs, skin problems, stress, fatigue, insomnia, anxiety and personal problems. Similarly, those working to tight deadlines all or most of the time were more than twice as

Table 6.1 Proportion experiencing work-related complaints, by speed of work and tightness of deadlines (**bold** indicates doubling of rate)

Nature of problem caused by work	Working at very high speed		Working to tight deadlines	
	All or almost all of time	25% of time or less	All or almost all of time	25% of time or less
Ear problems	9.5	4.9	9.4	5.0
Eye problems	12.6	6.8	12.6	6.8
Skin problems	**8.7**	**4.2**	8.1	4.6
Backache	40.0	22.9	36.8	24.6
Headaches	**21.3**	**9.6**	19.0	11.0
Stomach ache	**7.3**	**3.1**	**6.9**	**3.2**
Muscular pains in arms or legs	**27.2**	**13.5**	23.4	15.5
Respiratory difficulties	5.6	3.1	5.2	3.6
Stress	**41.2**	**20.5**	39.8	21.6
Overall fatigue	28.4	14.3	23.4	16.9
Sleeping problems	**10.0**	**4.9**	**10.1**	**5.0**
Allergies	5.1	3.0	5.1	3.1
Heart disease	1.7	0.9	**1.9**	**0.8**
Anxiety	**10.4**	**5.1**	9.9	5.3
Irritability	15.4	7.8	**15.8**	**7.8**
Personal problems	**5.1**	**2.2**	4.7	2.4
Others (spontaneously)	1.5	1.3	1.5	1.4
None	31.1	51.6	34.6	49.5

Source: European Workings Conditions Surveys.

likely to experience stomach aches, insomnia, heart disease and irritability from their jobs when compared to those working to deadlines less than 25 per cent of the time.

As noted above, the British workforce also reported experiencing a massive increase in having to work to tight deadlines, and British workers now top the European Union in the proportion having to work to tight deadlines all or most of the time. Again, the reported health effects were pervasive; those working to tight deadlines all or most of the time were more than twice as likely to experience stomach aches, insomnia, heart disease and irritability from their jobs when compared to those working to deadlines less than 25 per cent of the time.

There was some evidence to suggest that pressure of work had a more powerful effect on women's health than men's health, perhaps due to the fact that women have more additional sources of pressure from their domestic lives than men do: the 'double shift' of employment and domestic responsibilities. As Figure 6.5 shows, working at speed approximately doubles the rate of headaches for men, but triples it for women.

There was also some evidence that pressure of work has a greater impact on health for those in the public sector than those in the private sector, as shown in Figure 6.6.

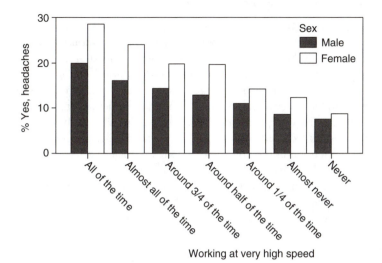

Figure 6.5 Headaches and working at speed.
Source: European Working Conditions Survey 1996.

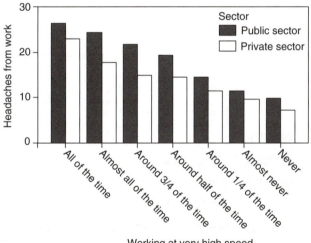

Figure 6.6 Headaches, working at speed and sector.
Source: European Working Conditions Survey 1996.

Workplace pressures and tension at home

To examine the degree to which workplace pressures spilled over into people's family lives, we used the JIWIS data to investigate the relationship between the amount of tension they experienced at home and the questions: '*How much pressure do you feel from the following sources: managers, colleagues and sheer quantity of work?*' to which they were asked to respond using a 5 point scale running from: 'a great deal of pressure' to 'none at all'. In addition, we also asked them to rate the adequacy of the staffing levels within the work area (on a 4 point scale running from: 'more than adequate' to 'very inadequate'). While we found highly significant associations between tension in the home and all four workplace pressures, it was 'sheer quantity of work' which seemed to have the greatest impact (see Figure 6.7). Interestingly, we found no significant differences between men and women or between full-time and part-time workers when we compared the various sources of stress with tension in the home. In our sample, neither sex seems able to claim immunity from the negative spillovers of understaffed and over-pressurised work environments.[3]

So, while increasing individual workloads may be beneficial to the organisation, it certainly seems to be associated with increased tension in people's family relationships. A few quotes from our respondents may help to illustrate this from their point of view:

> The big thing is going home at night time and not being able to relax properly because you've got work spinning round in your head and you're thinking 'God, I'll never get it all ready'.
>
> (lecturer in an FE college)

> When we've got a big job on, I get niggly with the wife … I've got no patience with the kids.
>
> (manual worker, construction industry)

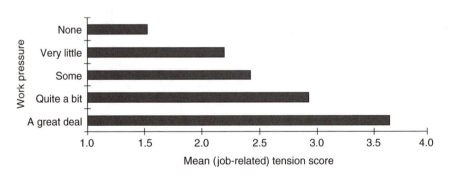

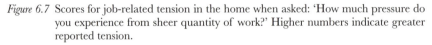

Figure 6.7 Scores for job-related tension in the home when asked: 'How much pressure do you experience from sheer quantity of work?' Higher numbers indicate greater reported tension.

Source: Burchell *et al.* (2002, figure 6.3).

On a more positive note, however, 46 per cent of our sample claimed that job-related stress caused either 'none' or 'only a little' tension within the home. This may be because they simply did not experience any tension at work or because they made deliberate efforts to stop it influencing their family. Again, some quotes may help to clarify this point.

> A thing blew up … and my manager said to me, 'Oh well, that appears to be your weekend gone'. In other words, 'take this home and do this mate'. I took it home but I didn't do it mate! I wasn't going to prejudice my weekend, which involved going out with the children and watching my boy playing football – that's more important to me.
>
> (white-collar worker, financial services sector)

> I work to live, not live to work, it's as simple as that. My family life comes first.
>
> (engineer, manufacturing industry)

So, while workplace pressures *do* have a negative influence on the family lives of many, it needn't apply in every single case (only 8 per cent of our sample claimed they were concerned about the very *stability* of their relationships because of job-related stress). Certain people seem to have access to resources (both personal as well as economic) which may enable them to resist these pressures to some degree.

Stress and lost productivity

We have already presented evidence on the effects of work intensification on individual employees and their families. Nonetheless, the 'knock-on' effects that are of most concern to senior management are not those which impact upon their employees' family life but those that damage the health and efficiency of the organisations for which they work. And recent decades have seen a plethora of studies seeking to estimate the 'true' costs of workplace stress (and suggesting ways of controlling these through closer involvement with and by the workforce). Moreover, as emphasised by the government's Health and Safety Commission, work stress gives rise not just to demoralisation and disaffection but also to increased rates of absenteeism and other manifestations of work-related illness.[4] Included among the work-related 'stressors' cited by the Commission are: the working environment and working conditions, new technology and other forms of change in the way work is performed, work overload (and underload), lack of control over how the work is done and the pace at which the worker is forced to operate, poor communications and involvement in decision-making, as well as issues such as performance appraisal, job insecurity and organisational style (e.g. whether it is participative or authoritarian).[5] Each of these stressors can act to 'reduce work performance and productivity, increase absenteeism and employee turnover' and, in some instances, they can also 'increase the likelihood of accidents' (HSC, 1999: 3).

In their assessment of the 'costs and benefits' of 'stress prevention', Cooper *et al.* (1996) cite a study by Harris (1985) purporting to show that by 1985, US industry was losing as many as 350 million working days per annum as a result of absenteeism. Using estimates supplied by Elkin and Rosch (1990), they then suggest that 54 per cent of these absences 'were in some way stress related'. They also point to evidence suggesting that stress was a 'contributory factor' in 60–80 per cent of all accidents at work. Another calculation of the costs imposed by workplace stress has been published by Greenberg *et al.* (1999), who estimate the total cost of anxiety disorder in the United States at approximately $42 billion per annum.[6] In Canada, meanwhile, the figures published by the insurance company, Sun Life, show that during the 1990s claims related to stress rose from 10 per cent of total disability claims to more than 30 per cent.[7]

Within the European Union, Cooper *et al.* (1996: 3) estimate the death toll from occupational accidents and disease at 8,000 per annum and claim that 'a further 10 million people suffer from some form of work-related accident or disease', the cost of which – in terms of annual compensation payments runs to more than ECU20 billion (£12 billion). In the United Kingdom alone, according to a recent report by the Confederation of British Industry (1999), sickness absence amounts to some 200 million days per annum, representing 3.7 per cent of total working time, at a total cost to employers of £10.2 billion.[8] The report also notes that among non-manual workers workplace stress is now the second highest cause of absence, behind 'minor illnesses' such as the common cold.

Nonetheless, amongst many of the people who were interviewed for the JIWIS survey, there was a deep frustration at their managers' failure to recognise the inefficiencies created by work-related stress. This frustration is well illustrated in the comments made by an education service provider when she told us that:

> We have somebody off at the moment. A diabetic, but a lot of stress has built up and he is now off for some time. Not only the union but also the management should take that on board and recognise what's happening. It's ignored because I think they don't want to deal with it. But it should be recognised because I can see, again it's back to the selfish attitude of companies, that actually if they are aware of employee welfare and will try to do something about it, they will actually get something back [from the staff].... What is happening here is management aren't responding and unions aren't responding and *stress is building up and you can see the absenteeism, the result of that. People looking elsewhere.* They're all the results of management digging their heads in the sand and not wanting to deal with the issue, which is stress building up.

Frustration at the productivity lost as a result of workplace stress was also evident in the comments made to us by a manager in the utilities sector when he suggested that the best way for any manager to improve the performance of his or her staff would be through:

> ... taking more account of what I call the human factor, and not trying to put on your employees all of the tasks in the world that you know they're not

going to complete. It must be known what a person can do reasonably within a day, and give them a little bit less than that and then maybe they'll be a bit creative as well. Rather than if you're overloading people, I'm sure that's what causes most of the stress.[9]

Other respondents reminded us that the costs of workplace stress are not restricted to sickness and absenteeism. Excessive work pressures (as with job insecurity) can also damage the goodwill and morale of the workforce. Thus, it was hardly surprising that, of the respondents we spoke to in the JIWIS fieldwork, those who described themselves as feeling very pressured at work exhibited the lowest morale and the strongest feelings of alienation (see Figure 6.8). As a lecturer at a college of further education commented:

> I'm sure they're fully aware we work excessive hours, but, at the same time, they're looking to increase those hours and the workloads. So what they say in terms of feeling compassion towards the number of hours that we actually work, doesn't match up with the number of hours they want us to work. So in terms of loyalty towards them, I don't have a great deal of loyalty towards the management team.

Some of the employees we spoke to also stressed the demoralising effect of feeling 'that you cannot make a mistake'. And their comments support the observations of Ridderstråle and Nordström (1999) when they argue that the innovative organisation needs to have a high tolerance of mistakes and that the failure to adopt this tolerance as part of the organisational culture inhibits creativity – one of the most valued qualities in any successful business. As one worker in the electrical engineering sector put it:

> Things will go wrong in manufacturing, but when you know that your immediate boss is a listener and he's a good administrator who can make his own mind up whether you've done something wrong or the guy on the floor has

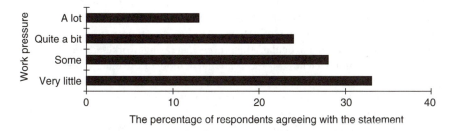

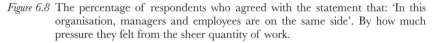

Figure 6.8 The percentage of respondents who agreed with the statement that: 'In this organisation, managers and employees are on the same side'. By how much pressure they felt from the sheer quantity of work.

Source: Burchell *et al.* (2001, figure 7.4).

done something wrong, or you've done right and recognise what is going on. Not only do you feel confident, you feel comfortable that I could work in this environment.

Moreover, in addition to the costs imposed by absenteeism, workforce turnover and production difficulties, there are also the insurance and litigation costs generated by the growing number of court cases brought by workers seeking compensation for work-related illness. For example, with much of the UK's employment law now being driven by the European Union, British firms are being progressively required to introduce measures to protect workers from unreasonable exploitation. Meanwhile, the size of court settlements for work-induced stress has grown sharply in the past few years and employees are now more willing to sue their employers, partly because of the growing pressure under which they are working, but also because of the publicity given to the large sums being awarded in compensation.[10]

In July 1996, a senior social worker with Northumberland County Council became the first person to succeed in arguing at the High Court (with the aid of his trade union, Unison) that his employers were liable for the nervous breakdown he had suffered as a result of an impossible workload.[11] He was awarded damages of £175,000. Another well-publicised case was that brought by Beverley Lancaster, (who was also supported by Unison) who, in July 1999, won damages of £67,000 from Birmingham City Council, in compensation for the work-related stress which had forced her to change her job from senior draughtsperson to housing officer. Six months later, an even more spectacular settlement was achieved by Randy Ingram who accepted a record £203,000 out-of-court settlement for the stress caused by the physical and verbal violence to which he was subjected as an employee of Hereford and Worcester County Council. Other, less publicised claims, were being pursued in other parts of the country to the extent, that, by the end of 1998, the TUC reported that the number of stress-related compensation cases handled by the trade unions[12] had soared to 783 in that one year alone, an increase of 70 per cent over 1997.[13]

For the employers, the problem they now face is that each successful prosecution increases the likelihood that more will follow. When a school teacher won £47,000 in October 1999 because she had been made ill by the excessive amount of work she had to complete, the door was opened to a flood of new cases from a profession that has been increasingly vocal in its protestations about the stresses of their work and, in particular, their ever increasing workload. As Graham Clayton, the senior solicitor of the National Union of Teachers, pointed out, 'a teacher forced into retirement in her mid-30s could expect a settlement of up to £250,000' reflecting the years she would normally have expected to have continued teaching.[14] Indeed, so serious is the risk of large sums of compensation for stress, and other industrial illnesses, that insurance companies are now asking many employers to document the measures they have introduced (or plan to introduce) to alleviate workplace stress. And it is likely that those firms that fail to take appropriate action will, in future, be required to face higher insurance premia (Unison, 1999).

Nonetheless, there is no shortage of advice as to the steps necessary to improve the working environment. The employers' associations, such as the CBI and the Institute of Directors have published material discussing health at work matters, and suggesting some of the actions employers should consider taking in order to reduce levels of stress. Unison, like many other trade unions, has issued guidelines to its branches to tackle the problems of stress in the workplace that, perhaps understandably, highlight the need for management to work in partnership with the trade unions in this area (Unison, 1999). The Health and Safety Commission produced a discussion document in 1999 in which the outline of a possible draft Approved Code of Practice and Guidance on work-related stress was set out. It remains to be seen what success this initiative will have with employers, and whether a voluntary code of practice will be sufficient to ensure worker protection.

Conclusions

The increase in the intensity of work across Europe may well have brought about productivity gains and economic growth. But, as we have argued here, the economic benefits may have been brought about at the cost of impaired individual health, family function and workplace cohesion. While we might expect rational employers to be interested in the health and profitability of the workplace, it is naïve in the extreme to expect that employers will demonstrate the same level of concern when it comes to social costs experienced outside of the establishment. The individual cases where work intensification has led to legal battles and compensation payments may be one way to make employers consider these externalities non-trivial, but it is highly unlikely that they will have an impact large enough to offset the forces that have brought about such high levels of work intensification.

However, in the absence of effective trade unions, it is not clear what forms of labour market regulation might be effective to prevent employers increasing the intensity of work to unhealthy levels. Low pay can be tackled with minimum wage legislation. Job insecurity can be reduced by a variety of measures such as protection against unfair dismissal and statutory compensation rates. It is not clear, however, what types of regulation might be effective in combating this more insidious form of over-exploitation in the labour market. But like many other less tangible forms of workplace disadvantage or discrimination, as the phenomena become more measurable and better understood through research, new possibilities for intervention, persuasion and legislation emerge.

Notes

1 The authors of this chapter would like to acknowledge the other researchers involved in the project for their contributions to data and the ideas expressed in this chapter. They were Maria Hudson, Jane Nolan, Hannah Reed, Ines Wichert and, last but not necessarily least, Frank Wilkinson.

   The paper has also been revised in light of a very useful discussion at the 2000 IWPLMS conference.

2 We also examined other outcome measures such as positive and negative feelings about work. These other measures tended to show the same patterns of responses, so will be omitted here for the sake of brevity.

3 A more detailed consideration of the relationship between work and family, using the JIWIS data, is the central concern of Jane Nolan's PhD thesis (see also Nolan, 2001).

4 The Health and Safety Commission describe stress as 'the reaction people have to excessive pressures or other types of demand placed on them' (HSC, 1999: 2).

5 Although the British Institute of Directors prefers to understate the health costs derived from stress at work, it acknowledges the link between stress and coronary heart disease (and other illnesses caused by high blood pressure including strokes). But, as with the Health and Safety Commission, it also emphasises that stress at work is caused by a variety of factors including, but not restricted to, long working hours. It suggests that although illnesses resulting from long working hours are undesirable, they are 'unlikely to be one of the major causes of public ill-health' (Day, 1998: 2). And it emphasises that 'there are likely to be other work-related factors that may well have larger influences'. Nonetheless, whether or not long hours or other work-related factors have the greater influence on health, there is a growing recognition (not just in Britain but across the industrialised world) that the absences and poor performance caused by work-related illnesses represent a considerable cost to the employer, in lost production, replacement staff, sick-pay and/or sick-leave and disruption of operations.

6 Of which, 88 per cent is attributed not to absenteeism but to 'lost productivity whilst at work'.

7 The figures are quoted by Felix (1998) who also cites other estimates putting the cost of workplace stress in the United States at more than $65 billion per annum.

8 According to the UK Health and Safety Executive at least half of these days can be attributed to workplace stress (HSC, 1999).

9 Complementing the issue of work overload, our respondents found the lack of adequate staffing critical as a cause of stress in the workplace. An employee in the financial services industry made a typical comment: 'Stress in general I think could be sorted out a lot by having the right number of people to do the work. That's the main thing – we've had meetings of the employee groups in the last three or four months and that's the one thing that always comes out, the fact that if we had enough bodies in the right places, then a lot of stress would disappear'.

10 'Work-related stress cases hit all-time high' (*The Independent*, 7 December 1999).

11 The three cases discussed here have been taken from the following newspaper article: Jill Papworth, 'Pioneers who broke new legal ground' (*The Guardian*, 22 January 2000).

12 Indeed, this is one of the few areas where the trade union movement has been able to demonstrate its continuing relevance following the sharp decline in membership numbers since the early 1980s. The trade unions have long warned industry of the dangers inherent in ignoring work-related health problems and they have been at the forefront of the campaign – through the courts and industrial tribunals – to gain recognition of the employers' responsibilities, and to win compensation where employers have been negligent. By contrast, the British government has long appeared reluctant to strengthen employment protection legislation, preferring to leave employers a relatively free hand in order not to increase their costs and competitiveness. However, EU directives on working conditions are increasingly being introduced and enforced, with consequences which will inevitably be reflected in penalties and compensation claims if regulations are ignored.

13 'Work-related stress claims soar' (*The Guardian*, 6 December 1999).

14 'Payouts predicted for stressed teachers' (*The Guardian*, 5 October 1999).

References

Burchell, B., Day, D., Hudson, M., Ladipo, D., Mankelow, R., Nolan, J., Reed, H., Wichert, I. and Wilkinson, F. (1999) *Job Insecurity and Work Intensification: Flexibility and the Changing Boundaries of Work*. York: York Publishing.

Burchell, B. J., Ladipo, D. and Wilkinson, F. (eds) (2001) *Job Insecurity and Work Intensification*. London: Routledge.

CBI (Confederation of British Industry) (1999) *Focus on Absence*. London: Confederation of British Industry.

Cooper, C. L., Liukkonen, P. and Cartwright, S. (1996) *Stress Prevention in the Workplace: Assessing the Costs and Benefits to Organisations*. Loughinstown, Ireland: European Foundation for the Improvement of Living and Working Conditions.

Day, G. (1998) *Health Matters in Business – Health at Work*. London: Institute of Directors.

Elkin, A. J. and Rosch, P. J. (1990) 'Promoting mental health at the workplace: the prevention side of stress management', *Occupational Medicine: State of the Art Review*, 5(4), 739–54.

Felix, S. (1998) 'Taking the sting out of stress', *Benefits Canada*, November.

Green, F. (2001) 'Its been a hard day's night: the concentration and intensification of work in late 20th century Britain', *British Journal of Industrial Relations*, 39(1), 53–80.

Greenberg, O. E. *et al.* (1999) 'The economic burden of anxiety disorders in the 1990s', *Journal of Clinical Psychiatry*, 60(7), 427–35.

Harris, L. (1985) Poll conducted for the Metropolitan Life Foundation.

HSC (Health and Safety Commission) (1999) *Managing Stress at Work*. London: Health and Safety Commission.

Karasek, R. A. (1979) 'Job demands, job decision latitude and mental strain: implications for job redesign', *Administrative Science Quarterly*, 24, 285–308.

Nolan, J. (2001) 'The intensification of everyday life: workplace stress and family life', in Burchell, B. J., Ladipo, D. and Wilkinson, F. (eds), *Job Insecurity and Work Intensification*, London: Routledge.

Ridderstråle, J. and Nordström, K. (1999) *Funky Business: Talent Makes Capital Dance*. Stockholm: Bookhouse Publishing AB.

Unison (1999) *Stress at Work* (Unison Health and Safety Information Sheet). London: Unison.

Warr, P. (1987) *Work, Unemployment and Mental Health*. Oxford: Oxford University Press.

Wheatley, R. (2000) *Taking the Strain: A Survey of Managers and Workplace Stress*. London: Institute of Management Research Report.

Wilkinson, F. (1983) 'Productive systems', *Cambridge Journal of Economics*, 7, 413–29.

7 The decline of union bargaining power in the United States

An 'ability to pay, ability to make pay' analysis

Charles Craypo

Introduction

American unions currently represent fewer than one-in-ten eligible workers in the private sector, in contrast to one-in-three in the 1950s. They also are not able to negotiate the kinds of wage and benefit improvements and income and job security they could in the past.

This chapter examines the forces behind organized labor's decline. Using an ability to pay, ability to make pay model of relative union–management bargaining power, it contends that union decline is largely the product of three major trends in American productive systems. First, deindustrialization has decimated jobs in high-wage, highly unionized durable manufacturing industries including cars, steel, and electrical products. Second, government deregulation has eroded labor standards by destabilizing established bargaining structures and procedures, especially in transportation and communications. Third, rapid expansion of jobs in the low-wage, essentially nonunion service providing industries forces unions to go into unfamiliar, hard-to-organize productive systems in search of new members and bargaining structures.

Together these trends have created a vicious cycle of declining union membership and bargaining power. This will be difficult to reverse barring a repeat of the economic crisis of the 1930s that fostered industrial unionism or of the kind of determined worker demands for organizing and bargaining rights that preceded massive unionization of government employees in the 1960s and 1970s.

The section on 'The ability to pay and make pay model of union bargaining power' of the chapter defines and describes the ability to pay and make pay model. The section on on 'Union ability to make pay' uses the model to describe the impact of structural and behavioral changes on union organization and bargaining power in three representative industries. The section on 'Summary and conclusion' summarizes the interaction between declining union power and adverse market and institutional changes in the US productive system.

The ability to pay and make pay model of union bargaining power

The ability to pay model identifies and applies those factors that determine union organizing and bargaining effectiveness (Craypo, 1986; Craypo and Nissen, 1993;

Cormier, 2000) It uses social science case study methods to analyze the ability of industries and firms to pay negotiated wage and benefit increases and the corresponding ability of unions to make employers pay (Kitay and Callus, 1998).

The model defines employers as business enterprises that combine capital, labor and management to produce wealth and unions as institutions that represent labor in the creation and distribution of that wealth. Interaction between the technical and social aspects of production determines the extent and pace of wealth creation. The amount of wealth a firm or nation produces determines the potential living standards of its employees or population. Relative bargaining power determines how it is distributed, that is, actual worker livings standards (Biricree *et al.*, 1997). For the union to have bargaining power and carry out its role within productive systems, the employer must have the ability to pay higher direct labor costs and still stay in business and the union must be able to make the employer provide good jobs and still be competitive.

Employer ability to pay

Table 7.1 summarizes the sources of union power. Employer ability to pay depends mainly on the nature and extent of competition in the product market and the firm's productive efficiency. Industrial organization analysis of product competition involves industry structure, behavior and performance. Structure refers to the degree to which product sales are concentrated among the largest firms. Behavior defines the way individual firms design, produce and market products, the prices they charge, their labor relations and other relevant aspects of doing business in today's geographically expanding and increasingly competitive environments. Performance refers to operating results including market share, operating profit and productivity (Caves, 1977).

Table 7.1 The sources of union bargaining power

Wealth creation	*Wealth distribution*
Employer ability-to-pay	Union ability-to-make-pay
Industrial organization	*Union density*
1. Industry market power	1. Organize the relevant work force
2. Spatial limitation of production	2. Maintain high union density
3. Government regulation	3. Establish informal representation
4. Cost-plus contract work	4. Informed/mobilized membership
Productive efficiency	*Bargaining structure*
1. Mass production capacity	1. Establish appropriate units
2. Technology advances	2. Ensure comparable authority
3. Improved labor processes	3. Establish strong settlement patterns: intra- and inter-industry patterns
	Union structure and behavior
	1. Non-competitive unionism
	2. Merger and consolidation
	3. Allocation of resources
	4. Informed/mobilized membership

Employers typically have the ability to pay higher labor costs when one or more of the following conditions prevail. Product market competition gives way to oligopolistic control by the largest firms. Geographic spatial restrictions protect existing firms against low-cost competitors. Government regulation also protects existing firms by restricting low-wage entrants; government cost-plus supply contracts do so by allowing vendors to pass on higher labor costs without reducing profits. Consistent productivity gains enable employers to offset increases in direct labor costs with decreases in unit labor cost. Whether union employers can pay high wages without losing market shares depends in part on the ability of competitors to find ways to pay substandard labor costs and still get the same output in the short run. Should that occur, employers inevitably demand union concessions under the threat of job loss (Craypo, 1986: ch. 2).

Industrial oligopoly and spatial limitation

A few large firms dominated American basic industry before and after the postwar decades. In cars, for example, there was the Big Three – General Motors (GM), Ford and Chrysler. Natural and institutional barriers effectively precluded new firm entry despite sustained high profits. Capital intensity also assured high production output and productivity levels. Under these conditions negotiated labor cost increases could be passed on as higher product prices, offset through productivity gains or absorbed in lower profits.

Manufacturing oligopolists had, since the turn of the century, sought to avoid mutually harmful price competition and allocate relatively stable market shares in order to achieve target rates of return on shareholder equity. They routinely reduced industry output to accommodate stair–step price increases – as opposed to lowering prices in response to declining product demand. This meant administered product prices and wages under the leadership of the largest firms. Then, after the rise of the industrial unions in the 1930s, labor standards were administered bilaterally through national bargaining patterns within and among industries.

The result was a period of industrial dominance, stability and high labor standards. Ford and Chrysler, for example, consistently met or exceeded their target profit rate of 15 percent of equity after taxes, as did GM its 20 percent rate, throughout the 1950s and 1960s (Blair, 1972: 482–3). At the same time, negotiated wage and benefit gains made American autoworkers the world's highest paid. But by the 1970s concentrated productive systems in basic manufacturing were beginning to unravel. Foreign imports and new firms with new products and production methods combined with novel marketing strategies and the rise of low-wage competition to undermine traditional oligopolistic ability to pay (Adams, 1992).

Spatial limitation, for its part, occurs when either nature or social institutions restrict the geographic area within which products can be made or services provided. There are, for example, only so many sites upon which a building can be built or a public project constructed; it cannot be done in one place and then transported to another. Similarly, an ocean freighter cannot unload cargo without an ocean port. Thus, if the sheet metal craft union organizes and brings under common terms all the sheet metal contractors in a given labor market, it should have make-pay ability.

Government regulation

Before the advent of widespread government deregulation in the late 1960s, the spatial limitation rule applied to industrial support industries – rails, trucking, airlines, telecommunications and power plants. State and federal agencies licensed firms, allocated markets, set user fees and imposed rates of return for suppliers. They routinely let firms pass on higher labor costs as higher fees. Employers, whether oligopolists or not, thus had the ability to pay. Moreover, given the economies of large-scale production that had motivated state regulation in the first place, productivity gains tended to be both sizable and predictable. Under these conditions unions had bargaining leverage and wages and labor standards were high. Inter-city truck drivers, airline pilots and mechanics, and telephone and electrical company linemen, to mention a few, were better paid, better treated and accorded greater occupational esteem and security than were comparable workers elsewhere.

Another form of government regulation that gives affected employers ability to pay is cost-plus contracting. Here, the industry provides products or services to government departments and offices on negotiated terms and conditions including provision of guaranteed profit margins over and above the total cost of production, usually stipulated as a percentage of total cost. Prominent in this regard are military weaponry contracts. Cost, in effect, determines price and negotiated labor standards become one of several determinants. Consequently, military vendors may prefer unions because they get the best workers and pocket a premium in the bargain (Erickson, 1994).

Productive efficiency

Productivity is crucial to understanding the ability to pay and make pay. It drives long-term wealth creation and, therefore, wage gains over time. Yet, when it comes to wage negotiations productivity is more a concept than a formula. It cannot normally be calculated with accuracy. Labor productivity is defined as the change in output per worker or hour of labor during a specified time period, usually a year. The formula itself is uncomplicated. Divide the change in output (units of product) over time by the change in input (hours of labor) during the same time. But these variables are in constant flux and in practice difficult to estimate, even more so when trying to determine the monetary value of labor productivity gains, where product mix and prices as well as wages and job classifications, are all changing. As a result, the parties haggle over rather than try to calculate the precise amount of wage increase to be attributed to increased productivity.[1]

Union ability to make pay

In order for a union to establish and maintain bargaining power it must, as shown in Table 7.1, do three things. It must organize and keep organized the relevant work force. It must establish and maintain an appropriate bargaining structure. Finally, it must avoid having its membership base and bargaining structures undermined by the actions of competitive unions.

Organize the relevant work force

The relevant work force is defined as those workers a union or unions need to organize in order to take wages out of competition. It can be identified within productive systems at all levels: the firm, the industry, the industrial sector or the national economy. In the single firm it consists of those groups of hourly or salaried workers that are essential to continued production and profit perform-ance. Unions must, for instance, organize production and maintenance workers in all the plants of a multi-plant manufacturing company in order to prevent or at least discourage the firm from shifting production to low-wage, nonunion plants.

At the industry level unions must organize all the lead firms in order to prevent nonunion producers from gaining competitive wage advantages over unionized firms. At the sectoral level unions must organize all the industries whose products substitute with others in that sector in order to prevent similar competitive wage advantages and disadvantages in product markets. At the national level unions must organize every major sector of the national productive system, given the interactive nature of wealth creation and distribution, if they are to maintain high labor standards. Implicit in this analysis is the inability of unions to organize rel-evant work forces in the face of unregulated international trade systems – the final phase of corporate consolidation.

Union ability to organize relevant work forces within industries depends on a number of interactive variables. Foremost are existing union density and organ-izing resources; differences between union and nonunion labor standards; the extent to which competition in product markets encourages short-run cost-cutting in labor markets and, hence, resistance to unionization; employer ability and will-ingness to threaten workers with job and benefit losses in the event of unioniza-tion; and hostile geographic, community and worker attitudes toward unions.

Density levels within most manufacturing and support industries were high before deindustrialization and deregulation, typically greater than half and often approaching unity within the core operating areas of manufacturing oligopolies and regulated support providers. Current density ratios in the private sector stand at postwar lows: an estimated 37 percent in motor vehicles and equipment, 41 percent in basic steel, 46 percent in tires, 10 percent in household appliances and 19 percent in meatpacking. The picture is no more encouraging in the sup-port industries: 21 percent in all of trucking, 37 percent in airlines, 27 percent in telecommunications and 24–37 percent in gas and electric utilities. Construction density is down to 20 percent, although, as indicated above, bargaining power is local and regional in nature. Coal mining, once the domain of fiercely militant miners, is now just 29 percent. Bad as these numbers are, they appear robust when compared to union density in the service providing sectors: 6 percent in personal services, 5 percent in retail trade and 3 percent in business services and in finance, insurance and real estate. Hospitals, one of the more active union sectors, is still only 13 percent organized (Hirsch and Macpherson, 2000: 48–51).

Such low-density figures are not the result of workers leaving their unions but of their jobs leaving them. Manufacturing plants were closed in the unionized north and Pacific Coast and relocated in southern and mountain states and overseas. In the generally immobile support industries, by contrast, nonunion firms came in and lowered labor standards following deregulation and existing firms responded by setting up nonunion subsidiaries, eliminating traditional union jobs, shifting into unorganized product lines, and downsizing employment following corporate mergers and acquisitions.

Unions try to compensate for ongoing membership losses in their core industries by organizing workers in new, unrelated sectors, in the process coming to resemble European general unions, but without the advantages of European wage solidarity policies and practices. US unions today are fewer in number than in the past but broader in their range of industrial representation. This centralizes individual unions administratively but decentralizes the larger union movement functionally. It fragments union efforts to organize and bargain for new relevant work forces in an effectively systemic way. Rather than single unions for particular skilled occupations (the old AFL craft union approach) or for single manufactured products (the old CIO industrial approach) two or more unions typically represent workers in particular industries, with no coordinating or integrating organization.

Establish appropriate bargaining structures

Organizing the relevant work force involves both density and strategy. The two interact to enhance union power from different perspectives, density based on sheer numbers and strategy on favorable bargaining structures. The last concerns the coverage of negotiated contracts. A favorable structure is one that enables the union to confront those making employer decisions and, if necessary, to stop production effectively or take other suitable job actions. Where goods are produced and services provided nationally, it usually requires company- or industry-wide bargaining structures or, if that is not possible, then strong contract settlement patterns within and among firms in the same industries. The object is to extend the same terms and conditions of employment to firms or industries in competition in product markets and, hence, to take wages out of competition. Where product markets are local or regional, favorable bargaining structures are more decentralized in keeping with the level of product competition and of real or potential wage competition. These are precisely the kinds of bargaining structures and patterns that American craft and industrial unions established after the Second World War.

Steel-making illustrates the ideal union structure in national product markets and, as described above, sheet metal and longshoring in local and regional markets. The Steelworkers union organized production workers in all the vertically integrated steel mills in the country and brought them into an industrywide bargaining structure in which companies controlling more than 80 percent of national steel production negotiated a single contract that the independent producers then adopted. This structure survived until the 1980s. By then foreign steel imports and mini-mill output, mainly nonunion, flooded domestic steel markets, which changed the composition of the relevant work force and caused most integrated steel producers to abandon industrywide bargaining.

Historic organizing and bargaining successes of US unions have been confined to the firm and industry levels. Legal and institutional factors explain such 'American exceptionalism' among the labor movements of industrialized countries. These include federal labor law restrictions on the scope of election and negotiating units; traditional craft and industrial union structures that preserve existing units; the absence of any centralized organizational authority to direct and coordinate organizing and bargaining activities among US unions. The National Labor Relations Act forces unions to organize employers in bits and pieces, workplace by workplace, unit by unit. It then prohibits the union from consolidating election units into companywide bargaining structures unless the employer agrees to do so – an unlikely response. National union theory and practice compound the problem by pursuing opportunist, often competitive, organizing activities that create fragmented, unproductive bargaining structures. Affiliated national unions then limit the role of the AFL–CIO or any other union federation in organizing and bargaining from a coordinated, strategic perspective. Consequently, union bargaining effectiveness is precluded at the industry, sectoral and national levels. This at a time when rampant corporate merger and acquisition activity further consolidates most industries in the private sector and globalization rapidly displaces national structures and markets.

Further worsening the outlook for unionization of relevant sectoral and national work forces is the changing structure of employment. Current expansion is out of areas of traditional union strength and into traditionally hostile areas. As Table 7.2 shows, the American economy created more than 68 million jobs during 1957–99. But fewer than 1.5 million of those were in manufacturing, which dropped from one-third to one-fifth of total employment. Nor did construction, mining and support industries – the other high-wage, unionized sectors – fare well in this regard, together losing nearly 5 percent percentage points of employment share. By contrast, two-of-every-three new jobs were in the low-wage service-providing sectors.

Avoid competitive unionism

A third condition for union bargaining power is the absence of competition among labor organizations to represent and negotiate contracts for the same groups of workers. Recent membership losses and the rapid growth of unorganized

Table 7.2 Change in US private sector employment and employment shares, 1957–99

	Increase in the number of employed workers (000)	Share of total employment (%)		Average weekly earnings $	Earnings ratio[a]
	1957–99	1957	1999	1999	
Total	68,316	100	100		
Private sector	55,772	87	84	457 (35)[b]	1.00
Goods producing	4,516	34	20		
Manufacturing	1,367	28	14	580 (42)	1.27
Construction	3,033	6	5	668 (—)	1.46
Mining	−253	2	<1	742 (44)	1.62
Support industries[c]	2,308	8	5	606 (39)	1.33
Service providing	51,256	53	64		
Retail trade	14,940	13	18	263 (29)	0.58
Services	32,292	11	30	436 (—)	0.95
Government	12,544	13	16		

Source: Bureau of Labor Statistics, *Earnings and Employment*, May 1996, table B-1, 39; *Monthly Labor Review*, July 2000, table 12, 69–70; 'Earnings and Hours Data,' *Monthly Labor Review*, 123(3), tables 13 and 16, March 2000.

Notes
a Ratio = industry sector weekly earnings ÷ private sector weekly earnings.
b Average hours worked per week.
c Transportation, communications, and energy utilities.

industries compound the danger of national unions competing against one another to their mutual detriment. Where this happens management can play off one union against another, thus jeopardizing labor standards for everyone. Individual unions can be willing or unwilling parties.

Competitive unionism in the private sector presently affects organizing and, in many instances, bargaining effectiveness in railroads, airlines, meatpacking, public employment, construction and health care. Some competitive situations involve AFL–CIO affiliates and some both independents and affiliates. In rails, for example, four crafts combined in 1969 to form the United Transportation Union (UTU) with the stated purpose of putting an end to competitive unionism in that industry. Soon, however, UTU got into disputes with the remaining crafts, including the charge that it settled for inferior industry contracts, which government regulators then forced upon the other rail unions. The controversy intensified until 2000 when the AFL–CIO censured UTU, which then left the federation altogether. Regardless of the relative merits in the dispute, the effect has been to diminish potential union power in rails.

Yet, the classic case of competitive unionism was both union and industry inspired. As the Cold War intensified in the 1940s, with Senator McCarthy's congressional hearings and passage of the Taft-Hartley loyalty oaths for union officers, CIO leaders began expelling their left-wing affiliates. Among them was the United Electrical (UE) workers, the dominant union in that industry. UE officers refused to sign the loyalty oath, thus depriving the union of its legal bargaining status. Both CIO and AFL unions rushed in to replace ousted UE locals. General Electric (GE) and other large appliance makers soon found themselves negotiating separate contracts with at least a dozen national unions.

Seizing the opportunity, GE devised an effective anti-union strategy. It offered to what it perceived to be the weakest union at the time an economic package that was slightly better than its current offer to the others. GE then informed negotiators from the targeted union that if they called a strike they would lose it because the other unions would eventually accept the same offer they had refused. That union's officers would be left to explain to their members why they had lost weeks or months of wages for a settlement that could have been gotten without striking. So successful were GE and the others that within a decade wages and working conditions in electrical products had fallen far behind those in other basic manufacturing industries. But by then the unions had set aside their differences and agreed to establish common bargaining goals, to present them simultaneously at each bargaining table and then to hold out until GE accepted – rather than dictated – identical terms for each union. Coordinated bargaining, as they called it, was challenged in federal court and found legal. No sooner had coordination begun to make up for previous union losses, however, then the industry began closing plants and relocating work in places hostile to union organization (Chamberlain *et al.*, 1980: 248–9).

Bargaining experiences in representative industries

Three industry case studies follow: cars, airlines and discount retail trade. Together they describe the impact of the major contributors to current union decline: deindustrialization, deregulation and industrial restructuring.

The car industry

Bargaining experiences in the domestic car industry typify those in oligopolistic manufacturing. Until recently, the Big Three dominated domestic and global production and the United Auto Workers (UAW) had formidable bargaining power. As Table 7.3 shows, average auto wages and fringe benefits exceeded those in manufacturing generally. But the industry is not what it once was. Poor product quality, lagging innovation and resistance to small car production, cost it significant market share to foreign imports and transplants. Each company has closed or phased down some assembly plants and divested its parts divisions, yet each is still burdened with excess plant capacity.

Auto bargaining once set the pace for much of American labor relations. In 1948 GM and the UAW negotiated a path-breaking productivity agreement that soon spread to the rest of basic manufacturing and eventually into other unionized sectors. Using 'formula bargaining,' the parties agreed that future pay raises would be calculated on the basis of cost of living increases and unspecified but anticipated productivity gains. Proposed by GM to avoid future work stoppages,

Table 7.3 Hourly earnings of autoworkers and other US production workers, 1950–90

	Ratio of auto assemblers to all production workers in the private sector[a]	Ratio of all autoworkers to all non-supervisory workers in the private sector[b]
1950	1.18[c]	—
1960	1.18	1.39[d]
1970	1.32	1.37
1980	1.55	1.62
1990	—	1.78

Notes
a Katz (1985), p. 22.
b Milkman (1997), p. 189.
c Current dollars.
d Constant 1973 dollars.

Table 7.4 Changes in the number of hourly workers covered by UAW contracts in the motor vehicle industry, 1978–99

	1978	1988	1999	% change 1978–88	% change 1978–99
General Motors	390,000	335,000	227,000	14	42
Ford	170,000	104,000	97,000	39	43
Chrysler	115,000	69,000	55,000	40	52
Total	675,000	508,000	379,000	25	44

Source: *Monthly Labor Review*, August, various years.

the objectives were to maintain real living standards by indexing hourly earnings and then to raise standards through additional regular wage increases. Formula bargaining eventually characterized wage determination in the United States until being replaced by 'performance bargaining,' during the 1980s.

Plant shutdowns, discontinued product lines, job consolidations and production relocations were decimating UAW ranks. By the end of the 1980s, as Table 7.4 shows, Big Three contracts covered 167,000 fewer workers (25 percent) than they had in 1978. Then, in 1979, in return for the federal government's financial rescue of Chrysler the union had to make substantial concessions in wages and benefits. Chrysler contracts meanwhile had fallen out of sync with those at GM and Ford, so when their contracts expired the other two companies demanded and got comparable union concessions. In that and subsequent rounds of bargaining, prior profit and productivity performance replaced productivity, cost of living and profitability in determining negotiated wage changes; and lump-sum payments replaced regular increases in base wages. In addition, the UAW could no longer extend what little it got from the Big Three in economic gains to its second-tier contracts with independent parts suppliers. Nor could it organize most of the new domestic and foreign parts plants that were coming on line.

These losses convinced the union to shift its bargaining objectives from maximizing economic gains and holiday time in the 1970s to negotiating job losses through attrition and early retirement plans giving veteran workers a degree of income security and extended health care benefits in the 1980s. It also tried unsuccessfully to negotiate contract language forcing the companies to maintain existing job levels despite continued overcapacity. As one industry analyst put it, commenting on a precedent-setting arbitration ruling that managerial responsibility to shareholders supercedes ambiguous labor contract language: 'Nobody is going to order a company to operate a plant to produce something that nobody is buying' (Patterson, 1990).

Even so, during the 1990s the UAW effectively restored pattern settlements and formula bargaining among the Big Three. This was partly because it was in the interest of the companies to minimize labor cost differentials in view of increased foreign competition and partly because they had made themselves vulnerable to work stoppages by adopting cost-saving, Japanese-style, just-in-time assembly methods. Under its contracts the UAW can strike individual plants at selected times and places over accumulated production standards and safety grievances. In today's no-inventory production system, a work stoppage in one or more strategic car plants quickly shuts down affected assembly plants, making small stoppages extremely costly for management. The union of course can also strike company-wide during regular contract renegotiations, an especially damaging or threatening action for the target carmaker at a time of skyrocketing vehicle sales during the 1992–9 expansion.

But the strike weapon is double edged. The UAW can win job-related skirmishes in specific plants and force substantial wage and benefit gains in national bargaining, but it cannot force the companies to make permanent job guarantees. Nor can it put an end completely to troubling work practices such as forced overtime, intensified work paces and recurring safety issues. This presents a bargaining irony – the more the union raises direct labor costs and improves working conditions the more it encourages carmakers to eliminate domestic jobs. It can make already good jobs even better but it cannot then save them. By the end of the 1990s, as Table 7.4 shows, the union had lost nearly 300,000 jobs since 1978, or 44 percent of its industry coverage. Meanwhile, German and Japanese carmakers had built or were building nine assembly operations employing 29,200 workers – all in the South and all nonunion (*Wall Street Journal*, 2000a, b).

Passenger airlines

Government regulation of passenger flight was until recently the institutional basis of industry ability to pay. Deregulation was critical to airline labor relations because regulation had kept wages out of competition by allowing carriers to pass on negotiated labor cost increases as higher fares. This was in addition to the cost-saving productivity gains carriers obtained with every new fleet of faster, bigger aircraft. In order to keep their planes fully loaded and in the absence of price differentials, airlines competed through non-price inducements – red-carpet waiting rooms, courteous service, on-time departures and arrivals, in-flight meals and leg-room.[2]

Airline deregulation began in the early 1970s when President Nixon appointed an antiregulation lawyer to head the federal regulatory board. Subsequent board rulings opened previously closed routes to small, typically nonunion carriers, allowing them to pick and choose which markets they wanted to enter and which fares they wanted to cut. Travelers historically excluded by high fares and willing to trade care and comfort for rock bottom prices flocked to the new carriers. A 'no-frills, economy flight' industry sprang up. Inspired by reports of the change going on in air travel, urged on by free market advocates, and buttressed by the support of industry leader United Airlines, Congress and President Carter essentially deregulated airline travel in 1978. The result was lower ticket prices between metropolitan centers but higher ones practically everywhere else. Competition for customers also prompted trunk and feeder carriers to construct hub-and-spoke connecting systems in which passengers stayed with one carrier but seldom flew directly to their destinations, instead being shuffled in and out of hub airports.[3] What followed amounts to the most intense customer dissatisfaction in airline history by the 1990s: crowded hubs, delayed and canceled flights, misinformed ticket holders, progressively smaller seats and tons of lost baggage.

Meanwhile, the major carriers eliminated most of their no-frills competitors using both price and non-price tactics, forcing them either to become subordinate feeder lines, to remain independent but confined to short-haul flights or to disappear altogether. By now there were fewer carriers than before deregulation and the industry resembled an unregulated oligopoly, except for continued price competition on selected routes and widely uneven profit performance.

Airlines is one of the last industries the government should have deregulated if it wanted to maintain stable labor relations. Labor attorney Martin Seham (1988: 87) aptly described why.

> During the days of regulation, limited competition, and limited entry, the labor market in the airline industry reflected the commercial stability of the industry itself. Labor supply was only one component of the bargaining process. Foremost among the other components was the capital-intensive nature of the industry. The high cost of capital and the relatively low ratio of labor costs to capital investment encouraged companies to avoid confrontation whenever peace could be bought with a relatively small increase in labor costs.

The Railway Labor Act (RLA), which applies to airlines, mandates systemwide, craft-exclusive bargaining units. This gives individual crafts the ability to strike systemwide and thus impose maximum economic cost, especially those unions representing licensed ground mechanics and flight crews, employees not easily replaced in the event of a work stoppage but without which the plane is prohibited from flying. Yet, the law also hinders union strike power by, among other things, specifying amendable rather than expiration contract dates. In practice it means that airline contracts do not expire and become moot like those under the National Labor Relations Act, but instead continue in force pending negotiated amendments at some future, unspecified time. It is not uncommon for airline negotiations to continue months and years without settlement and thus without pay raises and other contract improvements. Before the union can strike, however, the National Mediation Board (NMB), the controlling agency under the RLA, must find that a negotiating impasse exists, offer to have the dispute arbitrated and, failing that, impose a 30-day waiting period before any strike or lockout. The President can then order another 60-day wait before any union job action. Finally, Congress can and has ended airline disputes with legislated, binding settlements.

Table 7.5 shows the effects of RLA mandates and fragmented structures – a patchwork of bargaining units and patterns among separate unions, crafts and carriers. Between January 1999 and April 2000, nine unions, which together represented all four crafts, negotiated twenty-one contracts with fourteen airlines, including seven of the eight major carriers. This precludes emergence of clear settlement patterns. It is not surprising then that significant differentials exist within crafts, among major carriers, and between major and regional lines. A 1998 report of the Association of Flight Attendants (AFA), for example, identifies negotiated monthly compensation rates for flight attendants at eight major and eighteen regional carriers. Fourteen of the twenty-six carriers were paying wages under contracts that had been amendable but unchanged for three or more years, thus contributing to the differentiated pay scales in effect. Except for comparable rates negotiated by the AFA, an AFL–CIO affiliate, at United and US Airways, monthly earnings throughout the industry generally were within a range of several percentage points but never identical (Association of Flight Attendants, 1998, 2000).

Differences among carriers in their organizational structure and operating behavior also affect airline labor relations. Most major carriers had established labor policies and practices before they were unionized; labor relations therefore evolved within a particular corporate environment and philosophy and with union demands and strategies fashioned accordingly. By contrast, the newer trunk lines and regional carriers were created through mergers and acquisitions involving two or more lines, some unionized and some not. Labor relations in them thus reflects the melding of multiple systems, particularly with respect to pay structures within and among crafts and key working conditions such as crew scheduling.

Fragmented labor relations under government regulation probably enhanced union bargaining power during that time. But it also gave the industry the stability essential to licensed public utilities. By taking wages out of competition it facilitated contracts that recognized and rewarded the contributions of skilled, experienced labor. Airline unions could demand and usually get the same increases that had been negotiated by the same craft at another carrier or, perhaps, by another craft at the same carrier, and then add something to that – a type of pattern bargaining somewhat unique to the industry and referred to as 'leap-frogging.'

Table 7.5 Union representation by union, major and selected regional carriers, craft or class and size of representation unit, year 2000

Union	Carrier	Craft or Class
AFL–CIO affiliates		
AFA	Alaska Airlines	Flight attendants (2,000)
	America West	Flight attendants (2,300)
	American Eagle	Flight attendants (1,170)
	American Trans Air	Flight attendants (1,400)
	Mesaba Airlines	Flight attendants (500)[a]
	United Airlines	Flight attendants
	US Airways	Flight attendants (9,000)
ALPA	American Eagle	Pilots
	American West	Pilots (1,500)
	Delta	Pilots (9,200)
	Frontier	Pilots (228)
	Midwest Express	Pilots (330)
	US Airways	Pilots (5,500)
CWA	US Airways	Passenger service (10,600)[b]
IAM	Alaska Airlines	Passenger service (3,270)
	Continental	Flight attendants (8,500)
	Northwest	Passenger service
	Southwest	Passenger service
	TWA	Mechanics (7,500)
	TWA	Passenger service (4,500)
	TWA	Flight attendants (4,100)
	United Airlines	Mechanics and related (30,000)
	US Airways	Mechanics and related (7,500)
	US Airways	Ramp workers (6,000)
IBT	Northwest	Flight attendants (11,000)
TWA	American	Mechanics[c]
	America West	Baggage handlers (2,000)[a]
	Delta	Ground training instructors (110)[a]
Independent unions		
AMFA	Alaska Airlines	Machinists and related (1,100)[d]
	Northwest	Mechanics and related (9,500)[b]
APA	American	Pilots
APFA	American	Flight attendants

Sources: Various issues of: BNA, *Daily Labor Report*; *The Wall Street Journal*; *The New York Times*; union publications and interviews.

Notes
a 1999.
b 1997.
c 1995.
d 1998.

Code: (AFA) Association of Flight Attendants; (ALPA) Airline Pilots Association; (CWA) Communication Workers Association; (IAM) International Association of Machinists; (IBT) International Brotherhood of Teamsters; (TWA) Transport Workers of America; (AMFA) Aircraft Mechanics Fraternal Organization; (APA) Airline Pilots Association; (PFA) Professional Flight Attendants.

Now, in the face of deregulation and industry adversity, unions began making short-term economic give-backs to ailing carriers and long-term work rule concessions to healthy ones.[4] American Airlines initiated the most pervasive roll-back when it negotiated a systemwide, two-tiered wage structure – called the 'b-scale' by unions and the 'market rate' by management – on the strength of company promises to use the lower costs to expand operations, which in fact it did. Other carriers demanded and got b-scale wage structures, making this the nearest thing to an airline industry wage pattern at the time.

Then, with at least partial industry recovery in the 1990s, carriers adopted an 'economic parity' bargaining strategy in sharp contrast to that pursued under regulation. Long-standing wage disputes at one carrier were resolved by linking future increases there to changes in average wages among several carriers. It represented, in effect, reverse 'leap-frogging.' Carriers with the greatest ability to pay were instead allowed to negotiate wage increases at or slightly above a composite of wages accepted by unions at carriers having less ability to pay. Low-wage carriers thus were holding down average wage gains instead of high-wage carriers pulling them up.

This bargaining pattern in turn was abandoned in early 2001, beginning with the flight attendants' settlement at US Airways. After obtaining NMB strike release, AFA threatened to conduct brief, previously unannounced strikes at hub locations, thus creating havoc throughout the system. Horrified at the prospect, US Airways agreed to a 'parity plus' settlement that raised flight attendant wages much above industry averages. Settlement of longstanding craft disputes between other licensed crafts and carriers soon followed. Airline wages and benefits rose but company negotiators steadfastly refused to make long-term job security and other commitments. Nor would they agree to equalize wages at their regional feeder lines and their major trunk lines. Delta, for example, threatened to break-up or even divest entirely its Comair (Delta Connection) subsidiary rather than eliminate wide earnings differentials between Delta and Comair pilots, or to allow Comair pilots to bid on job openings at Delta (Swoboda, 2001a). Like the UAW, the airline crafts can negotiate real wage gains now but cannot fully protect jobs against the vagaries of deregulated transportation – mergers and acquisitions, substitution of lower- for higher-paid employees, and elimination of routes.

Expanding service and retail sectors

Hourly service and retail jobs are, as shown in Table 7.2, the lowest paying but fastest growing employment sectors in the United States. Hourly and salaried jobs in service providing industries increased by 51 million during 1957–99, which raised their share by 11 percentage points. Growth in the service industries was especially strong: 33 million new jobs, nearly tripling its share. Less dramatic but also significant was retail trade. Writing in 1993, a labor reporter took note of the changing face of employment. 'Almost unnoticed,' he wrote, 'discount retailers like Wal-Mart and Home Depot are becoming a huge source of new employment in America' (Uchitele, 1993: sec. 3, p. 6).

Table 7.6 Wal-Mart worldwide operating stores, 2000

Location	Number
Worldwide	4,093
US	3,055
Wal-Mart discount merchandise stores	1,749
Supercenters	825
Sam's Clubs	469
Neighborhood Markets	12
Foreign countries	1,038
Mexico	478
UK	240
Canada	168
Germany	95
Brazil	18
Puerto Rico	15
Argentina	11
China	8
Korea	5

Source: Wal-Mart Stores, Inc., http://www.walmart.com, February, 2001.

Wal-Mart is the largest and most successful of the new breed retail giants. Started in 1962 with a single store and twenty-five employees, by 2000 it surpassed GM as the largest US employer with about a million workers and more than 1.25 million worldwide. (Ortega, 1998: 55; Wal-Mart Stores Web Page, February, 2001) As Table 7.6 shows, it operates more than four thousand stores in ten countries. It reached this pinnacle by offering one-stop, low-price shopping to American families increasingly stressed for time and money. It also used state-of-the-art communication and transportation systems to make its warehouse-to-store supply operations as efficient as possible. It also forced vendors to agree to minimal supply prices, give heavy discounts, and accept other terms and conditions favorable to Wal-Mart as the cost of doing business with retail's largest buyer. It meanwhile expanded aggressively into new product lines and geographic areas in order to increase economies of scale and market share (*Harvard Business Review*, 1993; Vance and Scott, 1994: 43–8, 70; Kaufman, 2000: 1,10).

The final ingredient in Wal-Mart's commitment to offer customers 'Always low prices' was and is its ability to maximize labor value while minimizing its cost. From the beginning the company has pursued a low-cost labor philosophy and strategy. Its workers tend to be either young, inexperienced labor force entrants or hard-luck veterans. What they have in common is lack of better job options. Prominent among them are married mothers whose part-time earnings supplement family incomes; single mothers who are sole income providers; experienced workers displaced from higher-paying jobs; older workers and retirees who need the money or, rarely, want to keep busy. For most hourly workers and low-level supervisors these are dead-end jobs. High school graduates do not last long in them and store managers burn out and leave. Annual labor turnover reportedly exceeds two-thirds of store employees (*National Public Radio*, 2001). It is not a matter of concern, however, because Wal-Mart prospers on volume sales, not informed hourly worker.[5]

Exactly how much hourly store employees are paid is confidential, but hourly wages in most stores hover near the legal minimum, which in 1999 was $5.15, considerably less than the $13 average in the US private sector at that time.[6] Retailing is, however, a low-wage industry and Wal-Mart stores are competitive in that regard. After interviewing Wal-Mart workers and managers across the country in 1993, the first full year of US economic expansion following back-to-back recessions during 1990–2, Uchitele (1993: sec. 3, p. 1) concluded that jobs at Wal-Mart were 'mostly at $5 to $9 an hour ... unappealing in another era [but] one of the best deals that corporate America is offering to the mass of Americans looking for "good" jobs.' Fringe benefits in the industry at the time were optional, expensive and largely unsubscribed. Wal-Mart workers could buy company-sponsored health care insurance if they worked 20 or more hours a week and were both able and willing to pay the bulk of the premium. Most did not participate (Vance and Scott, 1994: 53, 73–4).

Sam Walton had a talent for making others subsidize Wal-Mart's operating costs. One way was to substitute rising share values in the company for higher pay. In 1970 he established a stock option plan for Wal-Mart executives. The following year he expanded it to include store managers and hourly employees, having been convinced that 'worker stakeholders' make committed, loyal employees. Subsequent stock splits and rising share prices enabled full-time employees who were both in at the beginning and had heavy investments to retire with small fortunes. Buyers of Wal-Mart shares thus subsidized Wal-Mart wages. 'It's the single best thing we ever did,' Walton later boasted (Walton and Huey, 1992: 315). But no pot of gold awaited either part-time employees, many of whom did not work enough hours to be eligible or able to purchase even subsidized shares, or the countless full-time employees not earning enough to buy stock. The program may have achieved Walton's performance objectives, but not in the long run. As Wal-Mart share prices leveled off, regular employees could no longer get rich quick through stock ownership.

Sam Walton opposed unions in theory and in practice, on grounds they prevent labor–management cooperation, which makes them unacceptable in an industry that depends on direct communication between store managers and employees and between them and the customer. Workers did not need unions and employers did not want them, he insisted (Walton and Huey, 1992: 166). From the beginning Walton did what was necessary to see that his workers did not have unions and his managers did not have to suffer them. But he did so in a non-threatening, soothing manner, one that promised to correct bad management practices.

His response to a 1976 labor dispute at a Wal-Mart distribution center illustrates his method. Alerted to rising discontent among hourly workers and a Teamsters organizing drive underway, he met face-to-face with the dissatisfied workers. Walton knew the origin of the dispute was his refusal to expand the center fast enough to handle the volume of merchandise needed by the increasing number of stores the center supplied. It was, as a result, operating at twice its designed capacity and employees were working under crowded, unsafe and stressful conditions. 'I don't know how I could have been so stupid,' Walton conceded. But he promised that if they gave him time to correct the situation he would do so without a union. 'Can you imagine having some Teamster in here saying you can't talk to me, that you have to go to the union and make them talk to me?' Walton asked. He then intimated that if they rejected the union their wages might be raised. Sure enough, they abandoned the union and their wages rose. But Wal-Mart's labor practices did not change. 'Walton doesn't seem to have taken much to heart from this episode;' a Walton biographer later observed, 'within a few years, disgruntled workers at another Wal-Mart distribution center would call in the Teamsters again, under nearly identical circumstances' (Ortega, 1998: 93).

After Walton's death in 1992 new management began intimidating and punishing workers involved in unionizing rather than reassuring and cajoling them as Walton had. Working conditions also deteriorated as industry overcapacity and deeper price discounts made managers even more cost conscious. By 1994 hourly workers in four Wal-Mart stores were talking union. After a brief but unsuccessful effort to dissuade them, store managers fired the leaders. This apparently illegal retaliation led to several National Labor Relations Board and federal court cases. The company prevented them from coming to judgment by making private settlements, in one instance for $15,000, roughly $1\frac{1}{2}$ times the amount the plaintiff was likely to have received in back pay and then only after lengthy proceedings. Wal-Mart was thus able to stymie organizing efforts without having to admit guilt. Employees at several other stores tried to unionize over the next few years, with generally the same company responses and results (Ortega, 1998: 354–9).

Unions in general have not effectively organized the retail sector. The United Food and Commercial Workers (UFCW), the largest union that claims jurisdiction, has had considerable success with retail food chains, but not with department stores, specialty chain outlets, and large discount merchandisers like Wal-Mart. But as the latter move into the retail food business by opening combination merchandise/food stores called 'supercenters,' they take markets away from unionized national and regional food store chains, threaten UFCW's organizational base in the industry, and leave the union little choice but to do whatever it must to organize them.

Wal-Mart expanded into food retailing in 1987. By the end of the 1990s it was 'closing in on a stunning 10 percent share of grocery-chain sales' and had become the nation's second largest food retailer. Since food sales increase proportionately with population, Wal-Mart's entry and growth create industry overcapacity and drive out existing chains and independents. More than a dozen regional chains were bankrupted or acquired during the late 1990s alone. Supercenter discount retailing has given rise to a kind of Gresham's Law in which low-wage stores are driving out high-wage ones. Direct labor costs in grocery stores account for about 60 percent of overall operating costs, giving nonunion Wal-Mart a decided advantage (Kaufman, 2000: 24).

Moreover, retail workers are exceedingly difficult to organize. Given the way the industry uses labor and the high turnover it seems to encourage, employers do not value the acquired skills and experiences of clerks and cashiers, who in turn conclude that one retail job is as good as another.[7] Wal-Mart's response to organizing is thus swift, unforgiving, and overwhelming. When meat cutters in its Jacksonville, Texas supercenter voted 7–3 for UFCW representation, it was the first such US union win in a Wal-Mart store. In addition, according to union officials meat cutters at two other Texas stores were petitioning for elections. Rather than accept the result and negotiate terms and conditions with dissatisfied employees, Wal-Mart chose to close its meat-cutting operations in that and 180 additional stores in Texas and five surrounding states. A company spokeswoman insisted that the new policy was part of an industry move toward pre-cut, pre-wrapped meat. It 'was in no way related to the Jacksonville situation,' she insisted. 'To role out a program of this magnitude takes months of preparation' (Swoboda, 2000b).

Summary and conclusion

The American productive system has been deindustrialized, deregulated, and reindustrialized in ways that minimize union bargaining power. Moreover, as Table 7.7 indicates, intense product market competition characterizes each of the representative industries discussed above. Under these conditions, relevant work forces within these and other industries will, sooner or later, be made to compete with one another in ways that unions cannot stop. In addition, federal labor relations law hinders union organization and effectively prohibits unions from establishing appropriate bargaining structures in newly organized firms and industries (Gross, 1997).

Trends in organizational density summarized in Table 7.7 vary considerably, which reflects the uneven success unions have in trying to keep traditionally unionized industries organized while at the same time organizing expanding but nonunion ones. Meanwhile, established bargaining structures reflect earlier productive systems and product markets now made obsolete by industrial and institutional evolution. Competitive unionism also seems to be on the rise. Environmental change makes previously uncontested union jurisdictions contestable and rapid expansion of nonunion sectors invites competitive organizing efforts. Fragmented bargaining structures increase the likelihood that the weakest union will accept inferior labor standards in order to survive or will exploit perceived organizational opportunity. Meanwhile, market and institutional barriers to union power intensify in the new economy, making it generally more difficult to achieve in the private sector.

Core manufacturing, for example, has been in steady decline for three decades. The effect is to reduce the size and bargaining power of the industrial unions whose negotiated terms and conditions fueled organized labor's postwar prosperity; it also lowers significantly the ratio of good to bad jobs in the economy. Experiences in the car industry typify the bargaining dilemma facing industrial unions. Revival of

Table 7.7 Union organizing density, bargaining structure and competitive unionism in three representative industries

Industry	Organizational density	Bargaining structure	Competitive unionism	Market and institutional barriers
Car	Declining. Unable to organize foreign assembly transplants and sufficient numbers of independent, multi-plant parts suppliers, foreign- and domestic-owned.	Companywide pattern settlements confined to Big Three assembly plants and former parts divisions. Sharply reduced ability to extend Big Three patterns to organized parts supply plants. Inability to organize foreign transplants and parts suppliers undermines union job security.	None among Big Three assembly plants and former parts divisions. Some multi-union representation among independent supply plants.	Intense product market price competition; industry production overcapacity. Big Three global uncompetitiveness.
Airline	Relatively high. Likely to increase with favorable work forces and legal environment. Increased union organizing activity.	Fragmented among carriers and crafts. Uneven contract amendment and negotiation settlement dates. No clear settlement patterns.	Mandated multi-craft representation within carriers. Competitive organizing among unions; may result in increased union bargaining demands. No coordinating authority among affiliated unions; results in erratic bargaining cooperation.	Intense product market price competition. Deregulation of product market; continued regulation of labor market in ways that restrict exercise of natural union bargaining power. Unions are vulnerable to industry reorganization and consolidation and to unfavorable regulatory policy and administration.
Discount retail	Virtually none.	Single store.	Not a factor.	Intense product market price competition. Temporary, part-time and devalued work forces.

traditional companywide, pattern settlements covering Big Three assembly plants gives the UAW leverage in that part of the industry. But its inability to organize the rest of the industry – the fastest growing portions – jeopardizes union jobs by exposing them to low-wage competition. The union can once again negotiate better jobs but in the face of production overcapacity and Big Three uncompetitiveness cannot prevent them from being eliminated or de-unionized.

Union density in airlines is now relatively high and likely to increase in the future. As Table 7.7 indicates, however, deregulation has enabled a few large carriers to gain effective control over the most lucrative routes via multiple hub-and-spoke systems. At the same time it retains regulatory constraints on union power. Such restraint may have been justified under regulatory fare and route controls but less so under the privatized oligopoly that is rapidly emerging. It is hard to imagine how more union power could produce greater industry chaos and passenger dissatisfaction than is presently the case. As it stands, the combination of fragmented bargaining structures on the one hand and unending merger and acquisition activity on the other contributes to the poor state of airline labor relations. Major problem areas include the increasingly adversarial relationship between the parties, the erratic and uneven pattern of contract amendments, the unduly long delays between wage increases, and the loss of job and income security.

Finally, much if not most of new hourly job creation has been in persistently low-wage, nonunion service and trade sectors. Organizational density is nil and bargaining structures, to the extent they exist, typically involve single store units. This is at a time when national and regional discount chains completely dominate retail shopping. The inadequate labor standards that prevail and the devalued, transient labor force that results interact to compound the barriers confronting unionization efforts. Not only does this hostile environment make improbable any imminent organization of discount trade, but currently threatens union power among retail food chains, the only area of extensive union representation and regional bargaining strength. Unionists in other countries should be forewarned that as Wal-Mart and other mass merchandisers expand globally, they bring with them their anti-union, low-cost labor philosophy and practice.

In addition to the structural changes occurring in US productive systems, a number of social, political and legal factors over and above those in Table 7.7 contribute to union decline. Most important among them are managerial beliefs hostile to unions and collective bargaining, cultural individualism, obsolete labor relations laws, large and increasing numbers of immigrant labor, and an ideological shift in political power.

During the high-wage postwar decades, American managers accepted – however reluctantly – unions, collective bargaining and the strong wage patterns that prevailed. Today they are more likely to accept union avoidance and wage competition as industrial norms. American individualism has been on the rise again along with financial share prices; voters appear to have forgotten why markets were regulated in the first place. As Veblen (1961/1899) saw it, 'self help' defines life in America, especially the desire to 'emulate' rather than displace the rich. Meanwhile, US labor law is stuck in time. The RLA was enacted in 1913 and the

NLRA in 1935, the latter when business operated largely within single product lines and in one country and American workers were, for once, thinking and acting along group and class lines rather than as diverse individuals, ethnicities and geographic interests. Court and administrative labor law subsequently froze the legal rules within which unions grew powerful. Now, after six-and a-half decades of industrial and institutional evolution, labor relations law denies unions the flexibility and opportunity needed to adapt to current employer structures, attitudes and practices. The political environment is also now hostile to unions. As in Britain, previous heads of state governed as if 'there is no society, only individuals and their families.' When that proved too harsh, US voters chose Bill Clinton. Although dedicated to the 'third way,' he did little to harm unions, with the notable exception of free trade agreements, but also little to support them. Now they confront a uniformly hostile White House, Congress and Supreme Court.

All things considered, a vicious cycle has emerged in America regarding the interaction between union bargaining power and productive systems. Among other things, it inhibits short-term labor–management cooperation and long-term productive effectiveness. Resurgent wage competition depresses living standards of the most vulnerable segments of the labor force while undermining trust between workers and employers at all levels.

Postwar collective bargaining is criticized as adversarial and therefore detrimental to productive labor–management relationships, notwithstanding the high growth rates and general prosperity that were achieved. But, as the three case studies show, the new productive systems are themselves essentially adversarial, seemingly less efficient in productivity and market performance and – judging from America's large and persistent merchandise trade deficits – uncompetitive in global markets. They prompt managers to view workers as inadequate and disposable and workers to view managers increasingly as exploitative and duplicitous. The king of workplace that results must eventually undermine the production effort.

Conditions in US retailing make the point. The anti-union urgency of Wal-Mart and other large retail discounters is the unavoidable result of the productive system they have created. Each is driven to increase market share in order to increase economies of scale–scale production in order to expand and generate greater economies of scale. But in order to gain market share when direct labor costs account for more than half of all operating costs it is necessary to curb wage and benefit increases. And the way to do that is to keep out unions. Thus, they have a productive system that delivers 'Always low prices' but in the long run at the expense of the system itself. The danger is not just with retailing but the fact that retail labor relations are becoming the norm. At this juncture it is imperative to ask what the world would be like if we all worked and shopped at Wal-Mart.

Acknowledgment

The author wishes to acknowledge the generous research support of the George Meany Center for Labor Studies/National Labor College, Silver Spring, Maryland, US, where he is a Research Fellow.

Notes

1 In 1959 the chief negotiator for the Pacific Maritime Association offered the dock workers union a million dollars in wage increases for anticipated productivity gains if the union agreed to give up certain restrictive work practices. 'Where did you get the million?' the union president wanted to know. 'It's a nice round figure and I didn't want to insult you with anything less than a nice round figure,' the chief management negotiator answered. The next day the union countered with a million-and-a-half dollars. 'Where did you get the million and a half?' asked management. 'From the same place you got the million,' replied the union. The parties settled for $1.5 million (Larrowe, 1972: 353).

2 Although it is a highly concentrated industry with fares no longer subject to federal regulation, the major carriers have not been able to stabilize prices on historically lucrative routes. Attempts by one or more industry leaders to raise prices during economic downturns or in the face of rising costs have been thwarted by the refusal of other carriers to go along for strategic reasons of their own. It is an abiding problem for the industry. Eastern's attempt to raise prices after the 1980–1 recession failed when low-cost Florida Air refused to raise theirs. Then, when American CEO Robert Crandall considered initiating an industrywide fare increases, he was secretly recorded while trying to persuade another CEO to follow his lead and, as a result, found himself answering to Justice Department officials. By contrast, attempts to raise fares in response to increased oil prices in 2000 did succeed no doubt because they appeared entirely defensive (Petzinger, 1995: 149–51).

3 As United and other major airlines built their hub systems, the new entrants pilfered historically lucrative direct routes. They operated partially or entirely nonunion, they negotiated substandard contracts with certified but weaker independent unions, they were newer and therefore had greater operating flexibility under deregulation, they flew cheaper, older (and often more fuel efficient) aircraft than did the majors, and they cut customer services drastically.

4 These and other strategies characterized airline bargaining in the 1980s and early 1990s. In academic work that was supported by and sympathetic to airline unions, Cremieux (1996) calculated the effects of deregulation on industry earnings. He found that in the face of industry overcapacity, low-cost, low-price competition, unilateral pay cuts and union concessions, union workers fared better than did nonunion workers, and pilots and mechanics better than flight attendants, in terms of pay and benefits. He attributed this to the industry-specific nature of pilot and flight attendant occupations, which gives them little alternative but to stay, compared to the occupational options of airline mechanics.

5 Like many employers, founder Sam Walton referred to hourly workers as 'associates' to imply that they shared proportionately in the proceeds of the business and had something to do with running it, although they did not (Walton and Huey, 1992: ch. 9).

6 A Canadian citizens group reported in 1994 that Wal-Mart, which employed about 540,000 at the time, seldom paid much above minimum wages and employed mostly part-time workers. The average full-time Wal-Mart employee made about $12,000(US) a year including profit-sharing, at that time an income below the official poverty line for a family of four (Council of Canadians Analyst, 1994).

7 Asked whether she feared being disciplined, a Wal-Mart clerk active in union organizing replied, 'If they fire me, I don't care. They only pay me $6.00 an hour. I can get a job anywhere for that money.' She was fired (Ortega, 1998: 355).

References

Adams, Walter (1992) *The Structure of American Industry*, 8th edition. New York: Macmillan.
Association of Flight Attendants, Communications and Research Department (1998) *Summary of Flight Attendants Agreements*. Washington, DC (April).

Association of Flight Attendants, Communications and Research Department (2000) *Flight Attendant Negotiations and Contract Status Report*. Washington, DC (10 May).

Birecree, Adrienne, Suzanne Konzelmann and Frank Wilkinson (1997) 'Productive systems, competitive pressures, strategic choices and work organization: an introduction,' *International Contributions to Labour Studies*, 7, 3–17.

Blair, J. (1972) *Economic Concentration: Structure, Behavior and Public Policy*. New York: Harcourt Brace Jovanovich.

Caves, Richard (1977) *American Industry: Structure, Conduct, and Performance*, 4th edition. Englewood Cliffs, NJ: Prentice-Hall.

Chamberlain, N. W., Cullen, D. E. and David Lewin (1980) *The Labor Sector*, 3rd edition. New York: McGraw-Hill.

Cormier, David (1997) 'Industrial restructuring implications for collective bargaining,' in *Proceedings of the (1997) Spring IRRA Meeting*. Madison, WI: Industrial Relations Research Association, pp. 498–503.

Council of Canadian Analysts (1984) 'Attention shoppers: can you afford the Wal-Mart price?' *SCN Community Links Database* (May).

Craypo, Charles (1986) *The Economics of Collective Bargaining: Case Studies in the Private Sector*. Washington, DC: Bureau of National Affairs.

Craypo, Charles and Bruce Nissen (1993) *Grand Designs: The Impact of Corporate Strategies on Workers, Unions, and Communities*. Ithaca, NY: Cornell ILR Press.

Cremieux, Pierre-Yves (1996) 'The effect of deregulation on earnings: pilots, flight attendants, and mechanics, 1959–92,' *Industrial and Labor Relations Review*, 49, 223–42.

Erickson, Christopher, L. (1994) 'Collective bargaining in the aerospace industry in the 1980s,' in Paula Voos (ed.), *Contemporary Collective Bargaining in the Private Sector*, Madison, WI: Industrial Relations Research Association, 97–133.

Gross, James A. (1997) *Broken Promises: The Subversion of US Labor relations Policy, 1947–1994*. Philadelphia: Temple University Press.

Harvard Business Review (1993) 'The ecology of competition: The evolution of Wal-Mart: Savvy expansion and leadership' (May–June), 82–3.

Hirsch, Barry T. and David A. Macpherson (2000) *Union Membership and Earnings Data Book: Compilations from the Current Population Survey*. Washington, DC: Bureau of National Affairs.

Kaufman, Leslie (2000) 'Wal-Mart casts eye Northward,' *New York Times*, 16 February, 1, 10.

Kitay, Jim and Ron Callus (1998) 'The role and challenge of case study design in industral relations research,' in Keith Whitfield and George Strauss (eds), *Researching the World of Work: Strategies and Methods in Studying Industrial Relations*, Ithaca, NY: Cornell ILR Press, pp. 101–12.

Larrowe, Charles (1972) *Harry Bridges: The Rise and Fall of Radical Labor in the US*. Westport, CN: Lawrence Hill Publishers.

National Public Radio (2001) 'Morning Edition,' 26 March.

Patterson, Gregory A. (1990) 'GM wins arbitration in UAW dispute over firms closing of Michigan Plant,' *Washington Post*, 30 March, A3.

Petzinger, Thomas, Jr. (1995) *Hard Landing: The Epic Contest for Power and Profits that Plunged the Airlines into Chaos*. New York: Random House.

Seham, Martin C. (1988) 'From Jerusalem to Dallas: the impact of labor markets on airline negotiations,' in Jean T. McKelvey (ed.), *Cleared Fro Takeoff: Airline Labor Relations Since Deregulation*, Ithaca, NY: Cornell ILR Press.

Swoboda, Frank (2001a) Frank Swoboda, 'Delta pilots reject arbitration,' *Washington Post*, 29 March.

Swoboda, Frank (2001b) 'Airline reaches accord,' *Washington Post*, 9 April.

Uchitelle, Louis (1993) ' "Good jobs in hard times",' *New York Times*, 3 October, 1, 6.

Vance, Sandra S. and Roy V. Scott (1994) *Wal-Mart: A History of Sam Walton's Retail Phenomenon*. New York: Twayne Publishers.

Veblen, Thorstein (1961) *Theory of the Leisure Class* [first published in 1899]. New York: Modern Library.

Wall Street Journal (2000a) 'Daimler Chrysler plans big expansion of Mercedes-Benz output in Alabama,' 28 August, B2.

Wall Street Journal (2000b) 'UAW's reception in Alabama Mercedes Plant is sour,' 31 January, A15.

Wal-Mart Stores Web Page (2001) 'In Sam we trust: The untold story of Sam Walton and how Wal Mart is devouring America.' New York: Times Business, Random House.

Walton, Sam and John Huey (1992) *Sam Walton: Made in America: My Story*. New York: Bantam.

8 Creative work systems in destructive markets

Suzanne J. Konzelmann and Robert Forrant

Introduction

During the past two decades, inspired by the apparent success of Japanese work and production systems, many US firms have been experimenting with new forms of work organization, often referred to as 'high performance' or 'co-operative' work practices. These work system experiments push decision-making responsibility to the lowest appropriate level in the organization. They also typically involve some combination of hierarchy compression, team-working, continuous improvement and training. In exchange for accepting greater responsibility for production and output, employees are often given employment security, and a proportion of their income is linked to performance through such arrangements as bonus, gain or profit sharing schemes. Although most studies find that these new workplace techniques generate substantive productivity and quality gains for manufacturers implementing them and financial results that are at least equal if not superior to those associated with more traditional work systems, in the United States, they have proven difficult to maintain (Appelbaum and Batt, 1994; Huselid, 1995; Ichniowski *et al.*, 1996, 1997; Black and Lynch, 1997; Pfeffer, 1998; Baker, 1999). Diffusion is relatively slow and not extensive and the medium and long-run survival of even the most promising new workplace techniques is far from guaranteed (Osterman, 1994; Pfeffer, 1996; Doeringer *et al.*, 1998). Using case studies of three American manufacturing firms, our study examines this issue and its implications for firms attempting to implement and maintain cooperative work systems in unregulated markets.

The fragility of these 'creative' work systems is due in part to the fact that what constitutes a truly cooperative system has yet to be developed in the United States. It is also due to pressures from the external environment that must be resolved within the productive system. These include stresses from 'destructive' financial and product market requirements as well as internal institutional vulnerabilities and weaknesses in the work system experiments themselves. Because creative work systems are expensive to implement and maintain, they require a long-term commitment to production relationships in order to ensure sufficient time to recover short-run costs and to generate long-term performance benefits. They are thus particularly vulnerable to competition from low-road firms that focus on cutting short-run costs. They are also vulnerable to financial and stock market pressures to generate continuous share value appreciation. These, and the shift in focus to share value performance over product market performance often have unanticipated adverse effects on the firm's work system.

Mainstream economic theory provides little help in understanding these trends or the process and outcomes associated with corporate restructuring of which they are a part. This is in large part due to its overwhelming concern with developing a theory of value and exchange rather than a theory of production (by which value is created) and distribution. The neoclassical theory of production views labour and capital as substitutes in production, ignoring the inherently cooperative nature of production relationships. The overwhelming popularity of the theory of shareholder value in debates about corporate governance reinforces the problem. This theory asserts that the stock market operates as an efficient market for managerial control and that the firm's value is most accurately measured by its stock market share price. Because workers and managers are assumed to receive incomes based on the value of their respective contributions to firm performance, shareholders are the 'residual claimants' with a right to the residual income generated by the firm. Increases in shareholder value thus represent increases in efficiency. Because both the firm and the economic system as a whole are assumed to benefit when shareholders' interests are pursued, this theory argues that corporations should be run in the interests of their shareholders.[1]

Despite these assumptions and claims, neoclassical economic theory fails to shed light on the process and outcomes associated with corporate restructuring and the development of modern capitalism. In contrast, Frank Wilkinson's *Productive Systems* framework[2] makes an important contribution to our ability to analyze and understand these developments. His model focuses on the dynamic process by which productive resources are developed and utilized to create value and to innovate. Because labor and capital are complements in production and because the economy as a whole benefits when its constituent firms are healthy and productive, *cooperation*, both within and among productive systems, is the key to effective performance at both the micro- and macro-levels of analysis. Institutions play a critical role in shaping both productive system relationships (technical and social) and distribution; and interactions among productive systems and productive agents in this context are important because their strategic choices, responses and counter-responses help to shape behavior and outcomes as the system evolves over time. Using the productive systems approach, our study examines the inter-relationship between cooperative or 'creative' work systems, and unregulated or 'destructive' markets using a sample of US manufacturing firms in the metalworking, jet engine production and steel processing industries.

The section on 'The firm, work systems and corporate restructuring' reviews theories of the firm, work systems and corporate restructuring. It examines the respective roles of and relationships among product markets, financial and stock markets, and work systems; the effect of creative work systems on performance; and the difficulties experienced by these work systems in the context of the unregulated American economic and industrial system. It also demonstrates the inability of neoclassical economic theory to explain these developments, highlighting the important contribution of the productive systems approach in this context. The section on 'Destructive market pressures, responses and macro-level outcomes' describes the destructive market pressures, industry responses and macroeconomic outcomes characterizing the American economic system. The section on 'Work systems in destructive markets' presents and analyses the firm-level case evidence, in light of received theory and current practice. In this, special attention is focused on the sources of performance effectiveness and the contribution of the work system to this process; the sources of both strength and vulnerability in the work system; and the firm's approaches to maintaining the work system in the face of intensifying competitive and technological pressures. The section on 'Conclusions and policy implications' draws conclusions from the previous discussion and highlights the policy implications that emerge from the analysis.

The firm, work systems and corporate restructuring

In the United States, the past twenty years have been marked by significant restructuring of both physical and financial corporate assets. In the face of intensifying domestic and international competition, firms have restructured work systems in an effort to improve production efficiency, product quality and flexibility. They have also engaged in financial and stock market restructuring designed to strengthen their relative position in these markets either voluntarily or in response to the threat of take-over. Both areas of restructuring have generated changes in corporate governance, or the system determining 'who has what control rights under what circumstances, who receives what share of the value created, and who bears what associated risks' (Blair, 1995a).

Production system restructuring

For the past two decades, management and industrial relations researchers and practitioners have debated and analyzed the relative contribution of cooperative or 'high performance' work systems (from here-on referred to as 'creative' work systems) as an effective approach for strengthening productive efficiency and competitiveness at the level of the production system. In this literature, creative work systems typically involve flattening managerial hierarchies and assigning responsibility for the production process and output to front-line workers. Continuous training, involvement in decision-making (both on- and off-line), teamwork and continuous improvement efforts are characteristics of these work systems; and in exchange for accepting greater responsibility for production efficiency and product quality, workers are usually guaranteed employment security and a share in the value they are contributing through participation in bonus, gain or profit sharing schemes.

Most studies find that creative work systems improve production efficiency, productivity and quality and that their financial returns are equal or superior to those associated with more traditional work systems (Appelbaum and Batt, 1994; Huselid, 1995; Ichniowski *et al.*, 1996, 1997; Black and Lynch, 1997; Pfeffer, 1998; Baker, 1999). However, despite this evidence of their effectiveness, most firms have struggled to maintain these work systems in the US context. Even those firms that have successfully implemented and maintained creative systems over the short and even medium term, find that sustaining them over the long term is difficult if not impossible (Osterman, 1994; Pfeffer, 1996; Doeringer *et al.*, 1998).

The fragility of creative work systems often stems from characteristics of the work system experiments themselves in combination with broader pressures from the American institutional and economic environment. Although the best performance outcomes are associated with creative work systems that form a coherent whole, most American work system innovations tend to be imposed from above, experimental in nature and adopted in a piecemeal fashion (Lawler *et al.*, 1992; Appelbaum and Batt, 1994; Osterman, 1994; Kling, 1995). Efforts to impose workplace changes from above generate opposition from middle managers, union representatives and workers, undermining their effectiveness (Hill, 1991). The relative instability in American top management is also a problem. Because of the importance of stable and supportive commitment from top management, creative work systems are particularly vulnerable to resulting changes in management policy that accompany changes in management personnel and company circumstances (Appelbaum and Batt, 1994). The relatively low and declining union presence in American workplaces is another impediment to the likelihood that work system changes will endure. Many studies find that union involvement has a strong positive influence on the sustainability of work system innovations; further, the greater the union's involvement, the more cooperative its stance (Eaton and Voos, 1992; Kochan and Osterman, 1994; Turner and Auer, 1994).

The institutional context in which a firm attempts restructuring is also important because work system restructuring does not take place in a vacuum: the firm's broader institutional environment profoundly affects the process (Levine and Tyson, 1990; Brown and Reich, 1997). In this context, financial, product and labor markets play a significant role in either shaping and encouraging or discouraging reform internal to the firm. Further, the absence of an external institutional imperative that socializes some of the costs of creative work systems means that it may not be profitable in the short run for firms to introduce and/or to maintain these more efficient modes of work. The weak US institutional environment means that firms must independently implement and sustain work system innovations. Because creative work systems involve high short-run costs, they are difficult for many firms to afford, particularly in the face of competition from cost minimizing firms pursuing a low-road strategy of competition. This is reinforced by the pressure to focus on short-term measures of performance and cost. The long lead times before investments in work system innovations are realized increases their vulnerability to competition from traditionally organized low-road firms.

The work system is also affected by the ability of the dominant form of corporate governance to support investments in human resources and trust, which appear as costs while their returns are not separately recorded. Because the firm's corporate governance system often shapes choices regarding employment relationships, in shareholder-based systems, like that in the United States, the high costs associated with creative work practices are difficult to justify. The US financial environment is thus an impediment to the implementation and long-run viability of cooperative work systems. American managers and strategic decision-makers are under intense pressure to cut costs in the short run for the benefit of largely absentee shareholders. Therefore, instead of encouraging or being indifferent to the nature of the firm's work system, the US financial system operates as a *constraint* on the diffusion and maintenance of creative work practices. By rewarding short-run profitability, it undermines the ability of shareholders to act as long-term investors, willing to see expensive projects through. It reduces the ability of managers to invest in research and development, new process technology, and training required for new work practices to be effective; and it can undermine the ability of firms to undertake long-term employment contracts with hourly and managerial employees (Lazonick, 1992). It also facilitates rapid, often unexpected changes in ownership without concern for other stakeholders' approval, leading to erosion of trust and morale among employees. Faced with these kinds of pressures, it is easy to understand why firms find it extremely difficult to implement and sustain creative work systems in the US context.

Financial and stock market restructuring

In the financial economics literature, the corporate restructuring debate is currently dominated by the *theory of shareholder value* that argues firms are 'bundles of assets' that belong to shareholders. Essentially indifferent to production, this theory assumes that the firm's stock price accurately reflects its value. Hence, anything that contributes to stock price appreciation by definition creates value, not only for shareholders but also for the economy as a whole. Using this theory, financial economists justify the rights of shareholders to control corporate decision-making and to lay claim to the income generated therein by identifying them as 'residual claimants' to the firm's income. They are 'residual claimants' because all other stakeholders receive a share of income based on mutually agreed upon contractual arrangements: creditors and suppliers have fixed claims and employees negotiate compensation arrangements in advance of performance. Shareholders as residual claimants thus bear the risk of fluctuations in firm performance in exchange for which they are assigned ownership rights and rewards.

Based on these assumptions, maximizing shareholder value is synonymous to maximizing efficiency. The more efficient the firm is, the greater the wealth created net of costs, the larger the residual income accruing to shareholders and the higher the value of the firm's shares. Managers are employed to manage the firm with the objective of maximizing efficiency, measured by shareholder value. The principal–agent problem between shareholders (principals) and managers (agents) is also solved by the stock market which operates as an efficient 'market for corporate control,' assumed to generate efficiencies in the form of superior management. Managers are forced to pursue shareholder interests by the threat of take-over because a firm can only be taken-over if other potential shareholders believe that they can buy the firm's shares at the current market price and bring in managers who will manage it more efficiently than the incumbent managers.

Critics of shareholder theory focus on the existence of firm specific skills that provide control rights and income claims to other stakeholders besides shareholders and on the failure of shareholder theory to explain the relationship between the production and distribution of value created by the firm. According to Margaret Blair, 'anytime there are parties other than shareholders who make investments specific to a given corporation – employees with specialized knowledge and skills, to cite probably the most prominent example – shareholders are no longer the residual claimants in that corporation' (Blair, 1995b). Although her critique is interesting and persuasive, it does not put forth an explanation of the corporate restructuring process or the role of work systems within it. Mary O'Sullivan's work addresses this problem by highlighting the failure of shareholder theory to address the important role of innovation and its implications for resource allocation and income distribution. She argues that it is impossible to explain how the return to investment is generated and how it should be distributed without first analyzing the process through which productive resources are developed and utilized to create that value.

> Since it has no theory of the business enterprise that generates returns that are not market determined, nor a theory of the distribution of these returns, it provides no direct guidance on the generation or allocation of the persistent profits of dominant enterprises with which the contemporary discussion of corporate governance is centrally concerned.
>
> (O'Sullivan, 2000: 29)

The nature of the firm and production systems

Although mainstream conclusions in both the production and financial restructuring literature are widely embraced from within, the prescribed corporate governance outcomes, or the stakeholder groups assigned responsibility and control in the production and financial market arenas vary considerably. Focusing on restructuring of physical corporate assets, management and industrial relations experts widely agree that in production, responsibility and control should be pushed downward in the system. In contrast, financial economists and financial market experts, focusing on restructuring of corporate financial assets, argue that pulling control upward in the organization and assigning it to shareholders benefits both firm and macroeconomic performance.

In these debates, the absence of a widely accepted framework for analyzing corporate restructuring that links component parts of the productive system (financial and productive) within its market and institutional context is problematic. Research on corporate restructuring tends to be segmented into studies focusing on either production or financial performance, by researchers in separate disciplines, using different methodologies and coming to divergent conclusions about appropriate responses. The implicit assumption of mainstream theory is that the firm's market performance is accurately measured and reflected in the value of its stock market shares. However, as evident in the cases below, production efficiency is often *not* reflected in corporate share values; and efforts to generate share value growth can involve approaches that undermine long-term performance viability in production. For example, short-run cost cutting risks stripping the productive system of assets and skills required for long-term success; and mergers and acquisitions aimed at boosting share values generate managerial changes that can be very destabilizing to production system relationships. Although short-run cost cutting does generate short-run profits by increasing the difference between revenues and costs, it damages the institutional framework upon which trust and cooperation are dependent and often strips the productive system of physical and human assets necessary for long-run performance viability. A firm will not remain viable on the stock market if it fails in its product market; and long-run product market viability depends on a long-term strategy aimed at achieving operational and technical efficiencies, rather than a short-term strategy aimed at short-run cost cutting.

In short, neoclassical economic theory fails to provide a theory of value rooted in production and an explanation of the relationship between the stock market and the production system. It therefore provides little help in understanding the contribution of cooperative work systems to performance, their fragility in the context of unregulated markets and the corporate restructuring process of which they are a part.

Recent debates about the nature of the firm do little to fill the gap. Emphasizing opportunism-based theories or resource-based theories, the firm is viewed as the result of transactions costs and the need to control opportunism (Coase, 1937; Williamson, 1975) or a 'bundle of resources,' among the most important of which are the skills and knowledge of their workers and what Chandler calls 'organizational competencies' (Penrose, 1959; Odagiri, 1984; Chandler, 1990). More recently, some researchers have attempted to identify the linkages that help to synthesize the two (Connor and Prahalad, 1996; Kogut and Zander, 1996; Marsden, 1999). However, in all of these cases, production is essentially a 'black box,' where the factors of production (labor and capital) are considered to be substitutes in production. Given the unit cost and relative productivity of each, subject to a given technological and market constraint, profits are maximized, costs are minimized and production efficiency is achieved by choosing the level of output that equates the additional revenue (marginal revenue) and additional cost (marginal cost) associated with the last unit produced. Each factor of production receives a payment equal to the value of its relative contribution to output. There is thus a technical trade-off between the quantity of labour and quantity of capital (and other productive resources) employed that ultimately determines the financial return to each factor of production and hence the distribution of income.

Productive systems and creative work systems

According to Pasinetti (1977)

> in dealing with production, whenever anything came to light that was not quite consistent with the [neoclassical] model of pure exchange, the typical reaction has been to modify the production side of the picture, i.e. to introduce into the theory of production all the assumptions that are necessary to restore its consistency with the preconceived model of pure exchange.
>
> (Pasinetti, 1997: 26)

The narrow mainstream view of the firm and of production is based on simplifying assumptions about production relationships that ignore the essentially cooperative and complementary nature of these associations in production and their competitiveness in distribution. The *productive systems approach* takes this as its starting point, arguing that rather than being substitutes, the factors of production are complements. Effective production requires that productive agents work together; and the failure of any to satisfactorily perform its productive role lowers the joint product of the whole. In distribution, productive agents are competitors because what one receives, the others cannot have.

In this context, production relationships have both a technical and social dimension that together and independently impact performance and distributional shares. The *technical relations* of production are the functional inter-linkages between labor, equipment and materials in the production process and between stages of production. They are objective and impersonal relationships, determined by the nature of products and the methods by which they are produced. In contrast, the *social relations* of production are the subjective and personal relationships between the various human agents of production which form the social network within which the technical relations are formed and productive tasks jointly undertaken.

While all parties to productive relationships benefit from cooperation in production, from which their incomes are ultimately derived, they compete over distribution of the proceeds divided among them. In this context, the social relations of production have the dual role of securing cooperation in production and agreement over distribution of the outcome from production. This is important for performance and efficiency because failure to secure agreement over distribution has the potential to set off a retaliatory withdrawal of productive cooperation, which serves to reduce both efficiency and the 'size of the pie' created. The trade-off is essentially one of short-term individual interests in relative shares versus longer term shared interests in the size of the pie.

In neither the short or long term, however, is the size of the pie likely to be exclusively determined within the productive system. Each productive system is subject to continuous pressures from the technological, market and social, legal and political environment within which it operates. In turn, similar processes within productive systems, both independent of and in response to external pressures, initiate changes that also help mold its environment.

Within the productive system, *operational efficiency* is to an important degree dependent upon how well products and processes are designed, labor is trained, materials and components are prepared and productive tasks are performed. It is also critically dependent on cooperation because, as discussed above, to maximize efficiency, labor and the means of production must work effectively together within each stage of production and the stages of production must mesh seamlessly together. In relations with its broader system context, a productive system's *dynamic efficiency* depends on its ability to respond to changes in market requirements, as well as on its capacity for organizational transformation and innovation, both of which are enhanced by the system's ability to motivate organizational learning (O'Sullivan, 1998; Lazonick, 1992). Both operational and dynamic efficiency are critically dependent on cooperation. They are also important in determining the competitiveness of productive systems. Competitive success generates additional resources for distribution and increases the prospects for increased cooperation and operational and dynamic efficiencies. Competitive failure risks the opposite, setting off a degenerative cycle of conflict over distribution, withdrawal from cooperation in production and declining economic performance.

In this context, a work system is 'creative' when it promotes operational and dynamic efficiency, which together rely on a high degree of both technical and social cooperation. In general, creative work systems feature innovative forms of work organization and management methods, in particular flatter, less hierarchical employment structures with fewer middle managers and greater worker participation in decision-making, often in the context of self-directed teams and greater flexibility in job definitions and organizational structure; enlightened human resource policies featuring increased emphasis on workforce training, greater employment security and incentive pay systems such as profit sharing; and cooperative industrial relations reinforced by a relative balance in power between workers and managers. In contrast, destructive systems feature traditional forms of work organization, management methods and human resource policies, and relatively adversarial approaches to industrial relations.

Based on a system of cooperation among productive agents and resources, creative work systems are efficient in helping the firm to meet and even exceed the demands of its product markets. Further, the long-term nature of production relationships within these systems provides a context in which the firm can focus on continually improving product and process quality and efficiency for long-run productive system success rather than on cost cutting and other strategies designed to maintain short-run profit margins. Creative work systems provide stable employment, relatively high and stable incomes, high levels of training and skill development, good working conditions, employee autonomy and participation in the productive process. As a result, they lay a foundation for high and rising living standards. Creative work systems provide sufficient compensation to support living standards required for a healthy and growing labor force. Continuous training is also a component of these work systems, contributing positively to the reproduction of a highly skilled labor force and hence to the quality of the labor supply in the external labor market and the long-run strength of the broader productive system. In contrast, destructive work systems, if allowed to reach their logical conclusion result in impoverishment of the labor force. They also economize on training, undermining reproduction of labor force skills.

The important question is then: how can a 'creative' work system be sustained over the long term and how can the common interests in production and divergent interests in distribution be reconciled? This depends to an important degree upon the nature of the social relations of production and the context in which they are conducted. The establishment of a base secure enough to create and maintain the requisite long-term commitments for establishing and sustaining trust and cooperation requires overcoming the effects of both social and economic uncertainty. Social uncertainty arises from the social relations that pervade production and exchange, and the social and political environment within which these relations are formed and reformed. Economic uncertainty results from economic forces, such as changes in technology, resource availability, and market pressures (financial and product).

In short, the quality of the productive system's relational network, the prosperity and dynamism of the economy within which it trades, and the supportiveness of the social and political environment within which it operates are instrumental in creating the necessary conditions for 'creative' work systems and cooperative long-term employment relationships. In the next section, developments in the market and institutional environment within which American firms and workers interact are examined. These provide the context for analyzing the cases of Ferodyn, Smithfield Tool and General Electric (GE), in which the focus is the interrelationship between creative work systems and destructive market pressures. Our objective is to understand the pressures generated by product and financial markets and regulation, firm responses to those pressures and resulting work system and performance outcomes.

Destructive market pressures, responses and macro-level outcomes

At the turn of the new millennium, global market pressures and short product life-cycles have forced the corporate officers of many firms to consider worker intellect an asset, not a liability. But, as the evidence in this section demonstrates, in the drive to maximize production and increase shareholder value, worker empowerment and team-building still play second violin to the first chair occupied by output demand and 'line speed-up.' The delicate underpinnings of plant-level trust are threatened by the wherewithal of owners to arbitrarily shift production to gain even the slightest competitive advantages. Workers and their unions are thus squeezed between a rock and a hard place: They are condemned as backward thinkers should they refuse to consider management-proposed work changes that might give their plant a chance to prosper, yet they are equally doomed when they accede only to have managers 'pick their brains' and transfer the work to plants in less expensive parts of the world.

Less than fifty years ago, the United States accounted for close to half of global manufacturing output. High and increasing productivity coupled with the benefits of Keynesian fiscal and monetary policies contributed to high and rising living standards for American workers. However, this premier position was eroded during the 1960s, 1970s and 1980s as Japan, continental Europe, and developing Asian nations emerged to challenge US pre-eminence in autos, steel, major household appliances and consumer electronics. Between 1979 and 1983 employment in the highly unionized durable goods sector declined by 15.9 percent, representing slightly over two million jobs, as American corporations shifted large segments of their manufacturing activities overseas and the nation de-industrialized (Shaiken, 1987; Bluestone and Harrison, 1988; United Nations, 1995; Kochan *et al.*, 1997; Kohler and Woodward, 1997; Meredith, 1997). Between 1980 and 1990, one in five American workers saw their job disappear, with thousands more being made redundant since that time. This corporate and labor market restructuring has been catastrophic for US industrial unions; the percentage of unionized manufacturing jobs declined from almost 50 percent in 1970 to approximately 10 percent in the 1990s.[3] In the mid 1950s, 1 in 3 American workers belonged to a union, compared with 1 in 5 in the 1980s and 1 in 7 in 1999 (Belsey, 2000: 1).

A consequence of these developments and the disappearance of well-paying manufacturing jobs in the United States has been wage depression, declining household wealth and increasing income inequality. Between 1987 and 1996, average compensation grew only 1.1 percent, compared with 4 percent between 1977 and 1986 (including the 1983 recession) (Hansen, 1998). For most workers, real wages are below their 1973 levels; and adjusted for inflation, the median income of American employees in the mid-1990s was approximately 5 percent below that in the late 1970s (Hansen, 1998). In aggregate terms, labor's share of the national income has dropped from 66.2 percent in 1970 to 62.6 percent in 1980 to 59 percent in 1995 and continues to decline (Hansen, 1998). Declining household wealth is evident in the fact that for nearly 20 percent of American households, debts exceed assets, meaning that net worth is zero or negative. US household income is now more concentrated than ever before, with the top 5 percent of households (those making $133,000 (83,125 pounds) or more) controlling 21.4 percent of all income while the bottom 60 percent control 27.6 percent.

On the surface, these current developments seem inconsistent with US macroeconomic and stock market conditions during the 1990s because they coincide with one of the longest macroeconomic expansions in US postwar history, with unemployment and inflation at record low levels. In 1999, unemployment was 4.2 percent while inflation was 2.2 percent (US Department of Commerce, Bureau of Labor Statistics, 2000). They also coincide with the longest US stock market boom in history, with yields on corporate stock significantly above their depressed 1970s levels (O'Sullivan, 2000: 6). Since 1990, productivity has risen 7 percent, due to enormous gains in certain sectors (Hansen, 1998). By the mid 1990s, corporate profit rates were back to the level they had reached at the peak of the post Second World War boom; in 1997, corporate profits rose to 11.8 percent of revenues, up from 11.5 percent in 1996, representing their highest level since 1959, when the Commerce Department first began tracking this data (Hansen, 1998).

Globalization is also playing a role by increasing the labour pool and making both capital and work more mobile, as corporations move jobs to low cost locations around the world. During the 1990s, US firms rapidly globalized corporate assets and expanded corporate direct foreign investment in factories, office buildings, office equipment and machine tools. Whereas in 1965 this amounted to less than $50 billion (31 billion pounds), it reached $124 billion (77.5 billion pounds) in 1975, surpassed $213 billion (133 billion pounds) in 1980 and climbed to $610.1 billion (381 billion pounds) in 1994. At the same time, global over-capacity in steel, autos, computer chip fabrication and aircraft production will only serve to reinforce these negative trends well into the future (Collins *et al.*, 1999).

Even in those industries where US-based producers have been successful at maintaining market share in international competition, enterprise success has not necessarily served to insulate workers in the United States from the effects of corporate restructurings and the job losses they entail (Almeida, 2000). It is commonplace for corporations to interject the possibility of work removal from their US plants during union organizing campaigns and contract negotiations, while the surge in global mergers in the automobile, banking, telecommunications and pharmaceuticals sectors has put 'bite into the bark' of such intimidation. This has come about in large measure as a result of corporate direct investment abroad. General Motors and its major suppliers, for example, are investing over $1.3 billion (8 million pounds) in seven new plants in two Mexican cities to produce transmissions, chassis, axles and drive trains. Simultaneously, the auto giant is engaged in the largest American corporate investment in China, spending over $2 billion (1.25 billion pounds) in the construction of sixteen assembly and components plants there (Kapstein, 1996; Cappelli *et al.*, 1997; Greider, 1997; Mitchner, 1997; Smith and Blumenstein, 1998).

It is in this context that corporations are experimenting with new forms of in-plant work organization designed to reduce direct and indirect labor costs, improve productivity and quality, and achieve greater control over the daily deployment of labor. Whether called 'high performance practices,' 'employee involvement,' 'mutual gains enterprises' or 'flexible work organizations,' these efforts are intended to gain functional flexibility on the shop floor, rather than to share control. Functional flexibility refers to the efforts of managers to redefine work tasks, re-deploy resources, and reconfigure relationships with suppliers to achieve rapid product development and faster changeovers from one product to another (Harrison, 1994: 129; Kochan and Osterman, 1994). Corporations are also investing in computer-controlled machinery that eliminate large numbers of skilled blue-collar workers, decrease reliance on workers' tacit knowledge and ease the relocation of work to other regions of the world. A 1998 report by the International Labour Organization summarizes these trends:

> Recently, while many trade unions have been pressing for reduced work time, guarantees of employment security and measures to combat unemployment, some employers have been seeking to modify many of the hard-won social protection measures in an effort to make labour markets less rigid.
>
> (International Labour Organization, 1998: 1)

Work systems in destructive markets

Smithfield Tool, Ferodyn and GE represent cases where in response to potentially destructive market pressures, the work system has figured prominently in the company's overall business strategy. In a brownfield site, Smithfield's creative work system emerged from the rubble of earlier failures to effectively compete using a Taylorist approach to work organization and adversarial relationships between labor and management. At Ferodyn, a creative work system was established in a greenfield site, as an integral component of a high-road strategy to compete on the basis of exceptionally high quality and responsiveness to market requirements. In sharp contrast to the other two, GE's work system demonstrates the devastating effects of a global manufacturing strategy on local work systems, workers and managers, and communities. Together, these cases demonstrate the contribution of the work system to performance and the fragility of creative work systems in unregulated and destructive markets.

Smithfield Tool

Smithfield Tool[4] is one of the few surviving union metalworking plants in Springfield Massachusetts,[5] and a producer of hand-tools. Like most other metalworking firms, its performance deteriorated in the 1970s and 1980s as foreign competition in several of its key product lines combined with earlier failures to invest in new technologies throughout the 1960s and 1970s. During this period, numerous changes in corporate ownership and a high turnover in the management team generated instability in strategic approaches. In the early 1980s, for example, Smithfield invested $15.8 million (9.9 million pounds) in a program designed to improve manufacturing processes and cut costs. However, when the sought after savings remained elusive, 150 workers, all members of the International Union of Electrical Workers (IUE), lost their jobs. As workers and production lines permanently exited the plant, strains between managers and workers intensified.[6] A series of lengthy strikes ensued as high seniority workers fought to preserve the job classification and seniority provisions of their contract, arguing that it was these measures that kept them employed. By the late 1980s, the workforce dropped to around 100 workers, no investments were made in new technology and a contingency plan to close the plant was drawn up.[7] According to one union officer, the plant was 'at death's door.'

Although marked by persistently adversarial labor relations as the unionized workforce scrapped for survival, there were perceptible changes in 1986 with the arrival of a new production manager. Addressing a regional gathering of trade union leaders, plant managers and academics, the new manager announced:

> Frederick Taylor is dead. Today, management needs an entirely different system. Cooperation and integration between labour and management ... is the key to success in today's marketplace ... To solve its problems, Smithfield had to radically change the way it operated and the way its employees – both union workers and managers – worked together.

Soon after the public meeting, Smithfield's ownership agreed to keep the plant open, in part because its principal customer wanted their product manufactured in the United States.

The company next began to attack production inefficiencies in earnest with the invited participation of production workers. Although union leaders were skeptical, they urged their members to participate in the work teams. Soon afterward, a new company purchased the facility and Smithfield became a subsidiary of a publicly traded global manufacturing corporation with a commitment to continue production a bit longer in Springfield. A visual manifestation of this commitment was the expenditure of $4 million (2.5 million pounds) on new machine tools. A Joint Productivity Council (JPC), comprised of four unionists and four members of management, was also established, charged with seven objectives including: the elimination of a specialized inspection function by building quality in at the source; the establishment of hands-on and classroom training; and training for all workers in continuous improvement techniques.[8] Teams of machine operators, engineers and managers began to meet regularly to tackle production and quality problems.

In the 1994 contract, management gained the right to eliminate most labor grades and job classifications and was thus able to establish and eliminate work cells and create, combine and eliminate skill levels and job classifications without negotiating changes with the IUE. In return for this shopfloor flexibility, workers were guaranteed employment security and a share in productivity gains through monthly bonuses. Union officials participated in meetings to determine the bonuses and the company was required to share financial information with the union. Smithfield's compensation system was based on knowledge and skill, with equally shared quarterly bonuses, contingent on the plant's achievement of defined output and quality goals. Smithfield workers were trained in systematic problem-solving techniques. In addition, they completed a 42-week course in mathematics and technical report writing, taught in the plant three hours a week by instructors from near-by universities.

Committees were set up, charged with the development of shopfloor improvement projects; and each team received a budget for project implementation. 'Idea Boards' were located throughout the shop and workers were encouraged to write down daily production problems as they occurred.[9] The 'idea boards' provided everyone with visible proof that ideas were responded to and that changes were being made. Explicit employment security language took effect when improvement activities eliminated particular jobs. New jobs were to be found for any worker whose job was eliminated through a kaizen project and the worker's rate of pay would be protected until he or she learned how to perform the new job. In addition, management agreed that no product lines would be moved out of Springfield as long as markets were maintained and productivity in the plant continued to improve. To make certain that productivity objectives were met hundreds of kaizen projects were completed since 1996.[10]

In May 1994, Smithfield Tool received a top vendor award for superb quality and on-time deliveries from its largest customer; it was ranked in the top 1 percent of the customer's 10,000 world-wide suppliers. The union workforce has climbed to 240 from 160 in the late 1980s, the parent corporation has shifted work to Smithfield from non-union southern affiliates and new product lines were introduced in 1993 and 1999.

Ferodyn

Ferodyn[11] is a greenfield steel processing plant located in a rural Midwestern community. In response to serious industry difficulties during the 1970s and 1980s, Ferodyn was built as a joint venture between American-owned Landis Steel Company[12] and a large Japanese-owned steel company. The plant produces high quality finished steel coils using a computerized, state-of-the-art continuous production process for customers in the automobile, appliance and office furniture industries. Its internal labor market strategy and work system were designed to accommodate both the technology employed and consumer demand for steel of consistently and exceptionally high quality. Teamwork, shared responsibility and broadly defined jobs characterized the organization of work. Job ladders were flat, with promotion lines based on training, knowledge and skill and the expectation that all employees would advance to fully qualified status. Self-directed autonomous teams were assigned control over the entire process, with authority to make on-the-line decisions regarding production, product quality and purchasing. Instead of supervisors, engineers and other management resources were available as needed. However, during the second and third shifts each day and on weekends, there were no managerial or white-collar personnel in the plant. Thus, 16 out of the 21 shifts per week were managed by the workforce without managerial supervision. Information about team and plant performance was shared and major plant- and production-related decisions were made by consensus.

Although the core workforce was recruited from Landis's main plant, Ferodyn's local autonomy and its location away from the parent plant, provided opportunities to divorce itself from the traditional labor market system in steel and to pursue a radically different system in the new facility. Employees were carefully selected based on cooperative-ness and capacity for working in groups, flexibility, motivation and trainability. They were then trained in both technical and social skills for a year prior to start-up, part of which included training in Japan to gain experience and insight into the effective operation of a plant like Ferodyn.

To promote employee commitment to the Ferodyn work system and its objectives, bargaining unit employees were guaranteed employment security; and a bonus system based on team performance was designed such that all employees would share equally in the system. On a regular basis, employees received work-related technical training; training in math, chemistry and computer programming; and training in social skills including teamwork, team building and communication skills. Ferodyn's compensation system was a pay for knowledge system where workers' pay reflected their skill classification level. All workers were guaranteed a 40-hour week generating relatively high annual incomes by local and industry standards ($60,000 (40,000 pounds) in 1998 (including bonuses)). Labour relations were amicable and characterized by a high degree of trust and mutual respect, based on learning through experience that parties could be depended on to keep their promises and commitments.

After reaching steady-state operating levels, the Ferodyn productive system was highly effective, reinforcing plant-level strategies and behaviors. It set world records for efficiency and product quality. Employee performance bonuses were high, averaging approximately $4,000 (2,500 pounds) per quarter ($16,000 (10,000 pounds) per year). The Ferodyn work system was also exemplary, attracting the attention of more than one team of researchers who identified it as a surprisingly creative work system. Employee turnover and grievances were virtually non-existent and Ferodyn employees overwhelmingly agreed that it was a good place to work. According to one bargaining unit employee, 'It felt like a career, not a job. For me, it was always what I thought work should be.' Similarly, a top Ferodyn manager said, 'It was exciting to have the opportunity to take this ride of a lifetime where our instructions were to go out there and run this company.'

Despite these successes and Ferodyn's obvious profitability, intense competition from global low cost producers and pressure from customers to sell high quality steel at a competitive price, prevented Ferodyn from extracting a premium for its high quality products. According to the local union president, 'when we started, our product was going to be so much better than the competition that it would command a premium. But that never happened. Market pressures never allowed us to extract the expected premium.' Thus, since Ferodyn operated in an industry populated by low-road competition; and it was a supplier firm to customers who, too, were under pressure to compete on the basis of cost and price, it was vulnerable to pressure from low-road firms in both its own and its customers' markets.

During the implementation and development stages of operation, visionary corporate management and international union support were important in shaping the new company. Landis's CEO and the president of the United Steelworkers of America (USWA) were avid supporters of the Ferodyn productive system. It also had the support of top plant management and union leadership. In this context, plant level employees bought-into the system and it thrived, despite shifting pressures from Landis Steel Company with changes in its CEO, company president and management philosophy during the 1990s. According to a top managerial representative at Ferodyn, the changes in management were the greatest stresses operating on the subsidiary because 'it pulled us in all different directions.'

Despite outward appearances, however, there was evidence that Ferodyn's creative work system was never effectively institutionalized, making it vulnerable to changes in and pressures from its environment, both internal and external. A subsidiary of Landis Steel Company, Ferodyn was never a legally or institutionally independent entity. This meant that it was subject to decisions made at the corporate level that may or may not be in the best interest of the plant. Failure to train new managers in the technical and social requirements of the work system served to slowly but steadily erode the Ferodyn work culture. Although the initial employee base at Ferodyn (management and labor) received such training, in-coming managers did not. As a result, they had difficulty identifying with the Ferodyn work culture and they lacked the desire to make it succeed.

The structure of Ferodyn's top leadership system and its effectiveness in protecting the plant from pressures from Landis corporate and the union were also unstable in that they were dependent on personalities. Ferodyn's first plant president was an officer of Landis Steel Company with a direct reporting relationship to Landis's president. Under his leadership, lines of authority were direct: Ferodyn managers reported to Ferodyn's president who in turn reported to Landis's president. Ferodyn's local union also had strong support from the international USWA as they forged a more cooperative relationship with the company, despite persistent tensions between the Ferodyn local and the local at Landis's main plant. The retirement of the USWA president in 1994 and Ferodyn's plant president in 1998 left the plant without strong leadership protection and support, making it vulnerable to opposing managerial paradigms and an unsympathetic union position regarding the type of work system it embodied. With the retirement of Ferodyn's first president, reporting relationships within Ferodyn and between Ferodyn and Landis were also unilaterally changed. Ferodyn's Human Resources manager, for example, now reports to a manager at Landis's main plant while its new president reports to a vice president at Landis Steel Company, much like a plant manager would. This change has substantially reduced the plant's relative position and security within the corporate productive system.

The Ferodyn work system was also vulnerable to the impact of decisions made by Landis Steel Company that would affect its ownership structure and management. Although clearly profitable, and one of the largest American steel producers, Landis was a relatively small player in an increasingly global marketplace. On top of this, global market pressures steadily pushed steel prices down, giving rise to widely publicized complaints of dumping. As a result, despite its relative efficiency and the fact that it had recorded profits for four straight years, steel stock prices in general (and Landis's in particular) were accorded a low valuation by Wall Street. This was a continual frustration to Landis's top managers, many of whom were terminated during the 1990s for failure to generate share value appreciation. By the late 1990s, under pressure from a group of institutional investors, Landis's top managers decided it needed 'to find a buyer' as pressures from shareholders to boost share prices by selling to a larger global player grew more intense. In 1998, in a quickly negotiated buyout, Maximetal,[13] a global steel holding company took advantage of the structural weakness in steel stock values and Landis's anxiousness to improve them. It purchased Landis (and Landis's share in Ferodyn), which by now was a restructured and efficient integrated steel company, at a relatively low price. The resulting change in management and uncertainty about Maximetal's long-term business plan added to the pressures already operating on Ferodyn. According to Ferodyn's local union president, 'It's really rough to be left in a vacuum to try and figure out Maximetal's business model because we don't know what they want. All we know is the cost cutting part and that Maximetal wants to become the biggest and richest steel company in the world.'

Maximetal's low cost strategy is in many ways incompatible with the requirements of a creative work system and the customer mix Landis chose to pursue in building the Ferodyn facility. Maximetal's first action following the take-over was to reduce managerial employment by 17 percent in Landis Steel Company, which included a reduction of one-third at Ferodyn. It restructured lines of authority such that control is now centralized in Landis Steel Company. Additionally, many Ferodyn employee rights and responsibilities relating to production have been removed. Ferodyn bargaining unit employees no longer choose and order from vendors. Regular training has ceased; scheduled maintenance has been suspended and the flow of information has stopped.

As a result of these developments and expectations about the future, Ferodyn managerial and bargaining unit employees are increasingly demoralized and fearful of the next stage in the process. Perhaps most concerned are remaining plant management personnel who do not have employment security or contractual protection. According to a high level manager at Ferodyn, 'almost everyone is now counting those inches of paycheck until retirement.'

Despite these concerns, or perhaps because of them, Ferodyn continues to perform effectively and its bonus system still pays. However, its ability to do so over the long term is uncertain. According to the local union president,

> I'm worried about Maximetal's approach and our current customer base. The long-term question is whether we will be able to maintain the type of customer base we were built to have. They have the highest quality standards in the industry.

Already, there is evidence of deteriorating quality which if continues will jeopardize Ferodyn's ability to maintain its current customer base. According to the local union president, during the first quarter of 2000, Ferodyn used up more than half of its annual reject allotment for several of its major customers because of inferior quality steel inputs. He likened Ferodyn's situation to a car whose hood is welded shut. 'If it is a well-built car, it can go a good long time before the engine blows out. But the question is *when*, not if, that will happen.' Employee morale has also deteriorated, as evident in a sharp drop in employee suggestions for process and product improvements and innovation, recent problems associated with absenteeism[14] and a dramatic increase in the rate of grievances.[15] In 1999, at the union's insistence, the collective bargaining agreements between Landis Steel Company and its five union locals were negotiated at the same time to prevent the possibility of whipsawing one local against the other. In this agreement, major gains were made by the union. Among these, the pension provision was increased as part of the steel industry pattern. Ferodyn's employment security clause was strengthened to include entry-level bargaining unit employees; and the union won the right to first refusal should Maximetal decide to sell Ferodyn off.

General Electric

GE[16] is the global market leader in supplying engines to power aircraft of all types. In jet engine manufacturing (as in machine tools and steel), the employment picture has been gloomy for most of the 1990s. Both the blue-collar and the white-collar workforces have shrunk by about 35 percent since 1988. While much of the downsizing in the early part of the decade could be attributed to declining defense orders, the recovery of the aircraft market by the mid 1990s did little to restore employment levels in the jet engine sector. Employment in the industry remains stuck at a level fully one-third below 1990 employment levels while inflation-adjusted average hourly earnings have remained flat throughout the 1990s (Almeida, 2000).

In 1998, GE registered $1.7 billion (1.1 billion pounds) operating profits on $10 billion (6.25 billion pounds) in sales, translating into an operating margin of 17 percent. However, this market strength and bright profit picture failed to provide good things for GE's American workforce. GE's jet engine manufacturing complex in Lynn, Massachusetts employs over 2,000 members of the IUE and is extremely important to the economy of Eastern Massachusetts. In this facility, GE has implemented numerous shopfloor programs designed to boost productivity, improve quality, and capture production cost advantages through continuous improvement on the shop floor. But unlike Smithfield and Ferodyn, job security has not been linked to these efforts. In fact, GE workers more often have been used as pawns in GE's global manufacturing strategy.[17] Starting in the late 1950s GE moved to parallel production, the practice of building several production facilities capable of handling the same work. By so doing, it could extract union concessions under the very real threat of work removal. Thus, parallel production served as a means to reassert workplace control, first by minimizing the potential damage strikes could cause, and by providing the leverage needed to compel changes in work organization (Almeida, 2000; interview with Jeff Crosby, President, IUE Local 201 at GE Aircraft Engines, Lynn).

This occurred in the late 1980s when GE began to implement continuous improvement strategies, called the 'GE Workout,' in its aircraft engine plants. This program was designed to accomplish four things: establish trust on the factory floor between workers and managers; empower employees to make production improvement suggestions; eliminate unnecessary work; and establish a new shopfloor paradigm of boundary-less work. As part of this strategy, GE sought to change the union labor agreement to eliminate job classifications and broaden the tasks workers were expected to perform (Harry and Schroeder, 2000; Tichy, 1997). Employees were told to welcome the freedom that boundaryless work offered and 'to take advantage of it by using their minds creatively to figure out how to improve the company's operations.' (Slater, 2000: 50). GE's Evendale, Ohio, aircraft engine facility was the first to respond. When workers there refused to ratify contract changes, the company shifted work to other facilities. Forty percent of all parts made at Evendale were removed and 3,900 workers lost their jobs.[18] GE then turned to its workforce in Lynn, seeking the same contract concessions, only to be similarly rebuffed. Chastened, but moving straight ahead, managers shifted work from Lynn and offered it to Evendale if they would accept GE's work reorganization demands. Some changes were accepted there, and jobs were relocated to Ohio. Eventually the Lynn local agreed to modification as well to introduce GE's multi-skilling program. However, unlike the reorganization at Smithfield and Ferodyn, the changes at Lynn came from coercion.

In 1995, GE introduced its 'Six Sigma' program, the company's latest improvement program. Six Sigma aimed at establishing a virtually defect-free company. Millions of dollars were spent training top managers in the techniques needed to implement the program, but no production workers were trained. Unlike Smithfield and Ferodyn, where unionists knew that production improvements would translate to wage bonuses, at Lynn 'Incentive bonuses are reserved for management. The threat of job loss due to shifts of work is the only incentive held out for production workers' (Crosby, 2000a).

In late 1999 GE flexed its global muscles to move well beyond parallel domestic plants and workforce dislocation in its own ranks to focus on their large supplier base. GE hosted a series of conferences where it introduced 'Globalization and Supplier Migration', a 70-page report describing its cost-cutting strategy to suppliers (Bernstein, 1999: 74). In what *Business Week* described as a 'super-aggressive round of cost-cutting,' suppliers were pressured to achieve 10–14 percent cost reductions, savings that could be realized only by shifting work to countries with lower cost structures. The report stated: 'Migrate or be out of business; not a matter of if, just when. We expect you to move and move quickly.' (Bernstein, 1999: 78). A carrot was offered: 'We sincerely want you to participate and will help, but if you don't we will move on without you.' The benefits for such a move to Mexico, according to GE, included average daily wage rates of $6 (3.75 pounds), friendly unions, and the promise of long-term low labor costs. The *Wall Street Journal* indicated that several hundred additional American jobs would be lost in the shift of appliance production from Indiana to a 48 percent GE-owned Mexican factory (Millman, 2000: 8).

This program is likely to cost thousands of skilled machinists their jobs in the next two to three years, while it 'chills' efforts to extend labor – management cooperation in hundreds of independently owned mid-size metalworking firms and destroys creative work systems that might exist in these companies. One supplier already affected is Ametek Aerospace, a unionized plant in Wilmington, Massachusetts. Scores of Ametek's IUE workers have been notified that they will lose their jobs when work is transferred to an aerospace industrial park under construction in Monterrey, Mexico. At the Ametek plant managers and union workers had together implemented a creative work system. According to the local union president, 'We had multi-skilled the workforce in a union negotiation and had brought state training money to increase the workforce's skill level. We had thought we were doing everything right, and so had Ametek' (Crosby, 2000b: 35). The work transfer also comes despite union and worker involvement in numerous manufacturing improvement programs at Ametek. According to the local union president, until Ametek was pressured by GE, it was 'a textbook example of a high-road, high value-added, high tech company. The Massachusetts plant took good care of its employees, brought work in from other locations, and even won GE's Supplier of the Year award' (Bass, 2000). Now,

> What you have is a third party (GE) ordering a profitable and top quality company (AMETEK) to export its jobs and technology to Mexico in order to increase the profit margin of the prime contractor which is GE, and which already made $10 billion (6.25 billion pounds) in profits last year, of which $1.7 billion (1.1 billion pounds) came from the Aircraft Engine division.
>
> (Crosby, 2000a: 1)

The 'supplier migration program' fits well with GE CEO Jack Welch's figurative vision for the corporation. 'Ideally you'd have every plant you own on a barge,' he recently stated, ready to move if any national government tried to impose restraints on the factories' operations, or if workers demanded better wages and working conditions. Just as it shifted work between its US plants in the 1980s and 1990s, GE now moves work between low-wage countries. GE recently shuttered a factory in Turkey to move it to lower wage Hungary, and it has threatened to close a factory in Hungary and move it to India. Union officials in Malaysia say they fear GE 'putting our plant on a barge and moving to Vietnam,' according to Inter-Press Service. GE's approach to labor relations is clearly the opposite of what is being attempted at Ferodyn and Smithfield (Mokhiber and Weissman, 2000). However, it demonstrates the pressure of a low-road approach on both competing firms and supplier firms attempting to maintain creative work systems.

Conclusions and policy implications

Throughout the 1950s and 1960s a bureaucratic industrial relations system came to narrowly define jobs and the skills required to complete them. Workers were paid to perform precise functions by rote; and a rules-bound set of relationships negated the possibility for labor–management collaborative problem-solving on American shopfloors. This approach to work organization and relationships was inconsistent with a strategy of innovation and quality production, which are the essential ingredients of long-term productive system viability and hence employment security. However, in an era of US economic dominance, this approach did not deter the generation of substantial profits for stockholders and wage increases and job security for many industrial workers. The intensification of global competition during the 1970s in such industries as automobiles, steel, machine tools and consumer electronics, exposed the flaws in this approach to production.[19] By the late 1970s, most American manufacturers found themselves in an increasingly difficult economic and financial position, reflected in low operating rates, large financial losses, bankruptcies, plant closures and massive employment reductions. In response, they were forced to restructure productive operations and focus on meeting if not exceeding the demands of their product markets in an effort to survive. An important part of this restructuring involved the work system because of its direct impact on product quality, responsiveness and cost.

In this context, Smithfield Tool, Ferodyn and GE provide examples of firms in which the work system has figured prominently in the company's broader strategic approach. Each of these companies faced serious economic and industry difficulties during the 1970s and 1980s; and each is currently owned by a publicly traded global parent. All three are now highly efficient and profitable in a competitive environment of unprecedented technological and market opportunities, where customers demand high quality products that are responsive to changes in their needs, competitively priced and delivered in a timely fashion. In each case, the work system was developed to accommodate the requirements of production technologies as well as increasingly competitive product market conditions.

At Smithfield, Ferodyn and GE, the work system approach was borne out of difficult industry conditions and a recognition by management that the work system could provide a powerful basis for competitive advantage. At Smithfield and Ferodyn, employee involvement was seen to be an effective means of achieving high quality output and production efficiency objectives. This gave rise to the establishment of creative work systems in both facilities, despite a historical legacy of rigid job structures and adversarial labor–management relationships. The Smithfield work system was transformed when workers and managers recognized that the plant's production and performance viability depended on it. Despite initial skepticism, good faith bargaining, joint participation in the transformation process, tangible performance results and a sharing of the benefits from cooperation, combined with a realization by both sides that they could rely on the other to deliver on promises and agreements. This provided an important foundation upon which the new work system and relationship could develop and flourish within the context of a brownfield production site. At Ferodyn, the creative work system was carefully designed and implemented in the context of a greenfield production facility with imported industrial relationships from a traditional American steel-making plant. Although its core employee base was transferred to the new facility from its American parent's main plant, careful selection and Ferodyn's location away from Landis's main plant made it possible to divorce from tradition. Ferodyn's strong and committed top management then provided the buffer from both external pressures and pressures from within the corporation that might threaten the work system at Ferodyn. Despite their differences, at both Smithfield and Ferodyn, the new work system was founded on an institutional framework that supported the trust and cooperation required for its success.

In both the Smithfield and Ferodyn cases, there was a turn for the better production-wise when workers got involved in the shopfloor transformation process. Workers were not being deskilled, nor were they being directly threatened with job loss. On the contrary, investments in education and training were made, equipment was maintained and workers were assigned responsibility for the production process and output. Compensation was linked to the achievement of measurable performance goals and employment security was provided in exchange for worker commitment to the production and work system. These changes increased production flexibility and efficiency, helped to achieve exceptionally high product quality standards and led to significant cost improvements and market growth.

In contrast, GE focused on achieving its performance objectives through unilateral control over the organization of work and production relationships and the threat of plant closure and layoff should its demands not be met. Using this approach in relations with its suppliers, it also destroyed the foundation for creative work systems in their plants by exerting extreme pressure to minimize costs to the lowest possible level by global standards or lose business from GE. Despite prior quality recognition awards and production efficiency, many of its suppliers were unable to maintain their creative work systems in the face of these pressures.

Although the Smithfield and Ferodyn cases show that it is possible to buffer the productive system from the damaging effects of destructive market pressures, in a capitalist institutional framework that drives firms to compete on the basis of low-road strategies,[20] competitive pressures make it difficult to maintain a creative work system over the long run. Such 'destructive' market pressures can originate in both product markets and financial markets. Destructive product market pressures can originate in competitive relationships with low-road firms as well as in supply relationships with customers who are either low-road firms themselves or in competition with them. GE represents a classic example of this dynamic, achieving its cost objectives through coercion and control over the work process and by putting the squeeze on its suppliers to deliver low cost, low price inputs. Evidence of the threat of this approach to firms attempting to maintain creative work systems can be found in the impact of GE's 'supplier migration' program on suppliers like Ametek.

At Ferodyn, competition from cost minimizing foreign and domestic steel producers coupled with pressure from customers who were forced to compete on the basis of low cost and low price made it difficult to extract a premium for high quality steel products. For a time, Ferodyn was protected by strong plant management, a nominally committed corporate parent and customers who were willing to pay a reasonable premium for exceptionally high quality products. However, this evaporated with the retirement of the plant president, the take-over of Landis by Maximetal and the dumping of cheap, 'good enough' quality steel into the American market. Following the Maximetal take-over, the elimination of employee authority in many areas of production-related decision-making, the removal of key plant management personnel who had been leaders under the earlier regime, and drastic and immediate cost-cutting efforts severely damaged the institutional framework upon which the creative work system was built. As a result, the work system is rapidly deteriorating into a more traditional form and performance is suffering. In contrast, Smithfield continues to maintain its creative work system, to an important degree because it is protected by a main customer that is willing to commit to a long-term supply relationship with Smithfield and to pay a premium for high quality products that are produced in the United States.

Stock markets have also exerted important destructive pressures on firms and their work systems. Especially during the 1990s, pressures on publicly traded firms to maintain high and appreciating short run share values have been intense, resulting in efforts to continually reduce costs and/or to expand market share and global reach. However, in mature manufacturing industries, production efficiencies may not be reflected in share value performance, especially in the face of recent speculative activity relating to 'new economy' stocks.[21] Speculation on these stocks is currently drawing capital away from the stocks of traditional manufacturing firms, depressing their share values and making these firms targets for take-over by global corporations intent on market expansion. This has increased the vulnerability of subsidiaries in these firms to resulting shifts in top leadership and management philosophy as well as to strategic decisions of new owners that may not be in the best interest of the subsidiary. Ferodyn is a good example because despite continual efforts to interest Wall Street in Landis's stock through information sharing about Ferodyn's unique work system and performance achievements, and the linking of top management compensation to share value appreciation, Landis was never able to generate the share value appreciation its shareholders demanded. Many top managers consequently lost their jobs throughout the 1990s; and eventually, under pressure from a group of institutional investors, the top management team sold the company to Maximetal, a global low road firm. Maximetal's cost cutting approach has already destroyed many of the key bases for Ferodyn's creative work system; and although output targets continue to be met, there has been a deterioration in product quality and employee morale that threatens to jeopardize the plant's long-run productive viability.

Together, Smithfield, Ferodyn and GE demonstrate the contribution of the work system to performance effectiveness and the difficulty of maintaining creative work systems in unregulated and destructive markets. As evident in all three cases, labor–management relations have a strong impact on the industrial development process and performance at the firm; they also effect on the economy as a whole. While a high-road strategy of investments in human and physical assets benefits firm performance, it also strengthens macroeconomic productive capabilities and living standards. A wage cutting strategy, on the other hand, can be employed to generate higher returns to the firm; however, should this be the dominant strategy employed by a nation's corporations, the failure to invest in more efficient technologies and skills that such a strategy entails, will eventually lead to a sharp decline in national productive capabilities.

For high wage firms in a region to sustain themselves, there must be a capacity to be innovative. Workers must be able to contribute freely to the cumulative learning process inside the firm based on a realistic expectation that their jobs are secure. Firms have to invest in skills to create an atmosphere where workers are able to provide their input, and managers must be committed to a style that solicits and uses the input. Increased supervision, a heightened work-pace, and employment insecurity are not likely to foster this kind of environment. In the Smithfield and Ferodyn cases, the firm's innovative capabilities depended on the integration of front-line workers into at least some aspects of the decision-making process. In both cases, workers were educated in problem-solving techniques and encouraged to use these skills to continuously improve plant efficiencies, knowing that they would share in any increased profits resulted from their involvement. This served to strengthen not only the firm's productive capability but set into motion a virtuous cycle of innovation, continuous improvement, improved labor and living standards and macroeconomic growth. At GE, the opposite dynamic was set into motion as GE pressured both its own workforce and those of its suppliers to accept steadily deteriorating employment terms and conditions, with damaging effects on the broader productive system.

As evident in these cases, in an effort to extend their global reach and achieve incomparable shopfloor control, managers have sought to capitalize on two conflicting predilections among workers: the first is the deep-seated fear of the loss of one's job; the second is the desire to contribute one's knowledge and skills in the work environment. In the absence of a consistent, concerted and collective international labor voice, global production giants like the GE, Maximetal and Smithfield's global parent have the ability to exercise significant bargaining leverage over their worldwide workforce, as well as the power to worsen wages and working conditions for growing numbers of manufacturing workers (ILO, 1997; Zuckerman, 1997). The question is whether and how they choose to exercise that power and what form of regulation might prevent the sort of global race to the bottom of the nature of GE's strategic approach.

At the end of the day, however, a simple truth remains: regardless of the level of trust between local managers and workers, should there be a substantial lessening of demand for the products being produced, or some sort of 'iron law of diminishing improvement gains' that blocks the ability to reduce costs, it is likely that the factory will close. Because of the direct relation between work systems (i.e. earnings, especially) and demand, a strategy of continual cost cutting will ultimately erode a nation's demand base. Failure to train and involve employees in the productive process and innovation will erode the requirements for productivity and quality improvement that together make long-run per unit cost reductions possible. As a result, low-road approaches inevitably undermine the ability of productive systems to survive over the long-run in markets where such approaches are a basis for competition. Intrinsic to success at plants like Smithfield and Ferodyn is an accretion of production and organizational improvements that contribute to exceptional firm performance. Yet, it still remains the case that the exigencies of global capitalism foster and impose destructive market pressures and decision-making that is far removed from individual production floors and void of a collective workers' voice. As a result, creative work systems are extremely fragile in the context of unregulated and destructive markets.

Notes

1 For reviews of this literature see Hart (1995) and Morck *et al.* (1989).
2 For further discussion, see Wilkinson (1983) and Birecree *et al.* (1997).
3 Among the Fortune 500's largest manufacturers, employment dropped to 12.4 million from 15.9 million between 1980 and 1990. General Motors, Ford, Boeing and GE collectively eliminated 208,500 jobs from 1990 and 1995. By 1996 about three-quarters of all employed Americans worked in service industries, up from two-thirds in 1979

(Herzenberg *et al.*, 1998: 21). Giant retailer Wal-Mart, the fourth-largest US corporation in 1998 measured by revenues, has created over 500,000 jobs since the late 1980s. (What's good for America is no longer what's good for General Motors but what is good for Sam Walton and Wal-Mart.) At century's end GE generates more than half its revenues from financial and other business services, while pharmaceutical companies making pain-killing drugs, ulcer medications and anti-depressants comprise four of the ten largest corporations in the United States (Cappelli *et al.*, 1997: 33, 68; Greider, 1997, especially chs 5 and 7; ILO, 1997; Lazonick and O'Sullivan, 1997; Tagliabue, 1997; Uchitelle, 1997).

4 Smithfield is not the real name of the company. It was changed at the request of management there. The case study benefited from numerous interviews with workers and managers at the facilities in 1997. I also spent a good deal of time observing the way work is performed there and took part in a one-week continuous improvement training workshop at Smithfield in 1995.

5 There were over a dozen machine tool and metal working plant closing in greater-Springfield in less than 10 years in the late 1970s and 1980s that cost the region thousands of well paying, skilled jobs. They were each plagued by the same organizational failures as Smithfield, but none attempted to reorganize for survival as Smithfield has (Forrant, 2001, 2002).

6 Throughout the Second World War, Smithfield Tool's employment averaged 5,000; but at the war's end, employment dropped to approximately 1,500. It fluctuated between 1,000 and 2,000 into the 1960s before falling to under 500 by the early 1970s.

7 Smithfield Tool's history in Massachusetts dates back to 1845 when it built wooden carriages. After 1900 the company began to forge bicycle frames and forge and perform secondary machining operations on a variety of hand tools and automotive parts. Henry Ford's burgeoning River Rouge Model T plant was one of Smithfield's top customer.

8 Unions members are the president, vice-president, recording secretary, and chief steward; company representatives are the director of operations, the Human Resources manager, and two operations managers.

9 In the two-week period that I observed the plant one team had come up with fourteen issues that became the basis for team meetings.

10 Many of these are aimed specifically at improving the flow of production in the plant. Smithfield's operating philosophy is based on the notion of 'one piece flow.' Parts are no longer machined and placed in inventory, instead completed parts move from operation to operation in the smallest quantity possible to satisfy a particular customer order. Hourly and salaried employees are responsible for keeping orderly things like tools, fixtures, furniture and break areas and there is a systematic approach to maintenance and machine repair to avoid costly down time.

11 Ferodyn is a fictitious name.

12 Landis Steel Company is a fictitious name.

13 Maximetal is a fictitious name.

14 According to the local union president, 'absenteeism has started to be a problem. In the old system, this was an empowering place to work. You were glad to be here and to work hard. Now, people are feeling burned out, tired, over-worked and emotionally drained.'

15 According to the local union president, whereas fewer than five grievances were filed during Ferodyn's first 6 years of operation, more than 30 have been filed during the most recent two years. Almost all relate to grievances over unilateral change.

16 Our analysis borrows heavily from the work of Beth Almeida.

17 For example, former GE engineer Oswald Jones (1997) cites GE manager Charles Pieper, who supervised several plant reorganizations in Europe, as he describes how workers relate to participation programs: 'I have never see a group of people who are not interested. Never. Never. Never. Whether you are Chinese, Hungarian, Japanese, Swedish, people love to go and make their workplace better...' While Pieper was

president of GE Lighting Europe, passionately committed workers saw factories drop from 24 to 12 and employment from 24,000 to 13,000. Jones concludes: 'it is hardly surprising that workers regard GE managerial initiatives to make the workplace better with considerable skepticism' (Jones, O., 1997: 20–2).

18 Employment at Evendale was close to 20,000 in 1988; at the end of 1994 only 8,000 remained (Almeida, 2000).

19 For a more detailed case study see Forrant, 1998.

20 Low-road strategies involve aggressive cost cutting, managerial control over the production process and output, and competition on the basis of low price and minimal quality standards.

21 New economy stocks are those of companies operating in high technology industries such as the internet, electronic commerce, computer hardware and software and satellite and telecommunications. Many of these companies are realizing high share values and enormous share price appreciation, despite the fact that they may not yet be producing anything for market. This is because of speculation about the future value of their stock.

References

Almeida, B. (1997) 'Are good jobs flying away? U.S. aircraft engine manufacturing and sustainable prosperity,' Working Paper No. 206, Annandale-on-Hudson, New York: Jerome Levy Economics Institute.

Almeida, B. (2000) 'Linking institutions of governance and industrial outcomes: the case of global aircraft engine manufacturing,' Industrial Relations and Research Association.

Appelbaum, E. and Batt, R. (1994) *The New American Workplace: Transforming Work Systems in the United States*. New York: ILR Press.

Baker, T. (1999) *Doing Well By Doing Good: The Bottom Line on Workplace Practices*. Washington, DC: EPI.

Bass, C. (2000) 'Neutron Jack strikes again: GE to suppliers – move to Mexico,' *New Haven Advocate*, 20 January, p. 1.

Belsey, L. (2000) 'Labor's place in the new economy,' *Christian Science Monitor*, 92(86), 1.

Bernstein, A. (1999) 'Welch's march to the South,' *Business Week*, 6 December, 74.

Birecree, A. Konzelmann, S. and Wilkinson, F. (1997) 'Productive systems, competitive pressures, strategic choices and work organization: an introduction,' *International Contributions to Labour Studies*, 7(1), 3–17.

Black, S. and Lynch, L. (1997) 'How to Compete: The Impact of Workplace Practices and Information Technology on Productivity,' *NBER Working Paper Series*, Working Paper No 6120.

Blair, M. (1995a) 'Rethinking assumptions behind corporate governance,' *Challenge* 38(6), 12–18.

Blair, M. (1995b) *Ownership and Control: Rethinking Corporate Governance for the Twenty-first Century*. Washington, DC: Brookings Institution.

Bluestone, B. and Harrison, B. (1988) *The Great U-Turn: Corporate Restructuring and the Polarizing of America*. New York: Basic Books.

Brown, C. and Reich, M. (1997) 'Micromacro Linkages in high performance employment systems,' *Organization Studies*, 18(5), 765–83.

Cappelli, P., Bassi, L., Katz, H., Knoke, D., Osterman, P. and Useem, M. (1997) *Change at Work*. New York: Oxford University Press.

Chandler, A. (1990) *Scale and Scope: The Dynamics of Industrial Capitalism*. Cambridge, MA: Harvard University Press.

Coase, R. H. (1937) 'The nature of the firm,' *Economica*, November, 386–405.

Collins, C., Leondar-Wright, B. and Sklar, H. (1999) *Shifting Fortunes: The Perils of the Growing American Wealth Gap*. Boston: United for a Fair Economy.

Connor, K. and Prahalad, C. (1996) 'A resource-based theory of the firm: knowledge versus opportunism,' *Organization Science*, 7(5), 477–501.

Crosby, J. (2000a). 'AMETEK buckles to severe GE pressure,' *Local 201 Electrical Union News*, 25 January, p. 1.

Crosby, J. (2000b) 'The kids are all right,' *New Labor Forum*, Spring–Summer, 35–9.

Doeringer, P., EvansKlock, C. and Terkla, D. (1998) 'Hybrids or Hodgepodges? Workplace Practices of Japanese and Domestic Start-ups in the United States,' *Industrial and Labour Relations Review*, 51(2), 171–86.

Eaton, A. and Voos, P. (1992) 'Unions and contemporary innovations in work organization, compensation and employee participation,' in Mishel, L. and Voos, P. (eds), *Unions and Economic Competitiveness*, New York: ME Sharpe.

Forrant, R. (2001) 'Neither a sleepy village nor a coarse factory town: skill in the greater Springfield Massachusetts industrial economy, 1800–1990,' *Journal of Industrial History*, 4, 24–47.

Forrant, R. (2002) 'Good jobs and the cutting edge: the US metalworking industry and sustainable prosperity,' in William Lazonick and Mary O'Sullivan (eds), *Corporate Governance and Sustainable Prosperity: Industrial Innovation, International Competition and Intergenerational Dependence*, New York: Palgrave, pp. 78–103.

Forrant, R. (1998) *Restructuring For Flexibility and Survival: A Comparison of Two Metal Engineering Plants in Massachusetts*, Geneva: International Labour Organization.

Greider, W. (1997) *One World Ready or Not: The Manic Logic of Global Capitalism*. New York: Simon & Schuster.

Hansen, F. (1998) 'Compensation in the New Economy,' *Compensation an Benefits Review*, 30(1), 7–15.

Harrison, B. (1994) *Lean and Mean: The Changing Landscape of Corporate Power in the Age of Flexibility*. New York: Basic Books.

Harry, M. and Schroeder, R. (2000) *Six Sigma: The Breakthrough Management Strategy Revolutionizing the World's Top Corporations*. New York: Currency Books.

Hart, O. (1995) 'Corporate governance: some theory and implications,' *Economic Journal*, 105, 678–98.

Herzenberg, S., Alic, J. and Howard Wial, H. (1998) *New Rules for a New Economy: Employment and Opportunity in Postindustral America*. Ithaca (New York) & London: Cornell University Press.

Hill, S. (1991) 'Why quality circles failed but total quality management might succeed,' *British Journal of Industrial Relations*, 29(4), 541–68.

Huselid, M. (1995) 'The impact of human resource management practices on turnover, productivity and corporate financial performance,' *Academy of Management Journal*, 38(3), 635–72.

Ichniowski, C., Kochan, T., Levine, D., Olson, C. and Straus, G. (1996) 'What works at work: overview and assessment,' *Industrial Relations*, 35(3), 299–333.

Ichniowski, C., Shaw, K. and Prennushi, G. (1997) 'The effects of human resource management practices on productivity: a study of steel finishing lines,' *American Economic Review*, 87(3), 291–313.

International Labour Organization (ILO). (1998) *World Labour Report: Industrial Relations, Democracy and Social Stability, 1997–1998*. Geneva: International Labour Office.

Jones, O. (1997) 'Changing the balance? Taylorism, TQM, and work organisation,' *New Technology, Work and Employment*, 12, 13–24.

Kapstein, E. (1996) 'Workers and the world economy,' *Foreign Affairs*, 75, 16–37.

Kling, J. (1995) 'High performance work systems and firm performance,' *Monthly Labour Review*, May, 29–36.

Kochan, T., Lansbury, R. and MacDuffie, J. P. (1997) *After Lean Production: Evolving Employment Practices in the World Auto Industry*. Ithaca: Cornell University Press.

Kochan, T. and Osterman, P. (1994) *The Mutual Gains Enterprise*. Boston: Harvard Business School Press.

Kogut, B. and Zander, U. (1996) 'What do firms do? Coordination, identity and learning,' *Organization Science*, 7, 502–18.

Kohler, C. and Woodward, J. (1997) 'Systems of work and socio-economic structures: a comparison of Germany, Spain, France and Japan,' *European Journal of Industrial Relations*, 3(1), 59–82.

Lawler, E., Mohrman, S. and Ledford, G. (1992) *Employee Involvement in Total Quality Management: Practices and Results in Fortune 1000 Companies*. San Fransisco: Jossey-Bass.

Lazonick, W. (1992) 'Controlling the market for corporate control: the historical significance of managerial capitalism,' *Industrial and Corporate Change*, 1(3), 445–88.

Lazonick, W. and O'Sullivan, M. (1997) *Corporate Governance and Employment: Is Prosperity Sustainable in the United States?* Annandale-on-Hudson, NY: The Jerome Levy Economics Institute.

Levine, D. and Tyson, L. (1990) 'Participation, productivity and the firm's environment,' in Blinder, A. (ed.), *Paying for Productivity*, Washington, DC: Brookings Institution.

Marsden, D. (1999) *A Theory of Employment Systems*. Oxford: Oxford University Press.

Meredith, R. (1997) 'The brave new world of general motors,' *The New York Times*, 26 October, section 3, 1.

Millman, J. (2000) 'GE boosts Mexican output as labor talks in US near,' *The Wall Street Journal*, 5 January, 8.

Mitchner, B. (1997) 'Europe looks askance at auto subsidies as overproduction looms as a problem,' *The Wall Street Journal*, 14 December, 8.

Mokhiber, R. and Weissman, R. (2000) 'GE: every plant on a barge,' http://www. corporatepredators.org.

Morck, R., Shleifer, A. and Vishny, R. (1989) 'Alternative mechanisms of corporate control' *American Economic Review*, 79, 842–52.

Odagiri, H. (1984) 'The firm as a collection of human resources,' in Wiles, P. and Routh, G. (eds), *Economics in Disarray*, Oxford: Blackwell.

Osterman, P. (1994) 'How common is workplace transformation and who adopts it?' *Industrial and Labour Relations Review*, 47(2), 173–88.

O'Sullivan, M. (2000) 'Shareholder value, financial theory and economic performance,' Presented at the 52nd Annual Meeting of the Industrial Relations Research Association. Boston, MA, January.

O'Sullivan, M. (1998). 'Sustainable prosperity, corporate governance and innovation in Europe,' in Michie, J. and Grieve Smith, J. (eds), *Globalization, Growth and Governance*, Oxford: Oxford University press.

Pasinetti, L. (1977) *Lectures on the Theory of Production*. London: Macmillan.

Penrose, E. (1959) *The Theory of the Growth of the Firm*. Oxford: Blackwell.

Pfeffer, J. (1996) 'When it comes to best practices, why do smart organizations occasionally do dumb things?' *Organizational Dynamics*, 25(1), 33–45.

Pfeffer, J. (1998) 'Seven practices of successful organizations,' *California Management Review*, 40(2), 96–124.

Shaiken, H. (1987) *Automation and Global Production: Automobile Engine Production in Mexico, the United States, and Canada.* San Diego: University of California, Center for US Mexican Studies.

Slater, R. (2000) *The GE Way Handbook.* New York: McGraw-Hill.

Smith, C. and Blumenstein, R. (1998) 'In China, GM bets billions on a market strewn with casualties,' *The Wall Street Journal*, 11 February, 1.

Tagliabue, J. (1997) 'Buona note, guten tag: Europe's new workdays,' *The New York Times*, 20 October, D1.

Tichy, N. (1997) *The Leadership Engine: How Winning Companies Build Leaders at Every Level.* New York: Harper Business.

Turner, L. and Auer, P. (1994) 'A diversity of new work organization: human-centred, lean and in-between,' *Industrielle Bezeinhungen*, 1, 38–60.

Uchitelle, L. (1997) 'Global good times meet the global glut,' *The New York Times*, 16 November, D1.

United States Department of Commerce (2000) Bureau of Labour Statistics.

United Nations (1995) *World Investment Report: Transnational Corporations and Integrated International Production.* New York: United Nations.

Wilkinson, F. (1983) 'Productive systems,' *Cambridge Journal of Economics*, (7), 413–29.

Williamson, O. (1975) *Markets and Hierarchies: Analysis and Anti-trust Implications.* New York: Free Press.

Zuckerman, L. (1997) 'Boeing startles market with delays costing $2.6 billion,' *The New York Times*, 23 October, D1.

9 German industrial relations in a period of transition

Ulrich Mückenberger

Germany, like many other European societies, is being seriously challenged by current domestic, European, and worldwide upheavals. The domestic challenge is due to the fact that the costs of unification have exacerbated the existing effects of economic rationalisation and tertiarisation in the German labour market, with the result that unemployment has risen to a level not seen for decades. The European challenge is a result of the imminent European Monetary Union (EMU) forcing the Member States to combat both inflation and budget deficits via rigid cuts in public expenditure, in order to meet the Maastricht monetary convergence criteria (see Bercusson *et al.*, 1996, chs 2 and 3). Lastly, the challenge is worldwide in that what is commonly called 'globalisation' (that is commodities and services, manpower and capital, above all speculative capital surmounting national and continental boundaries) tends to universalise productivity and price competition leading towards regime competition among developed states, between developed and less developed states, and among the less developed.

With reference to the ensemble of these challenges, social state[1] scholars start to speak of the replacement of the traditional social state by the global competition state (Streeck, 1995). By that, they mean that the 'social' is no longer perceived as a means of solidaric assistance and social cohesion; more and more it is being interpreted and remodelled as a means of economic efficiency and global competitiveness.

Germany is a highly regulated, 'juridified', nation – in their social and industrial relations, as elsewhere (such as in the spheres of consumer protection, company and trade law, ecology, taxation etc.). I shall try to show that this high degree of regulation has hitherto largely contributed to the German success story. Nowadays however, under the challenges mentioned before, the deregulation and privatisation discourse is increasingly gaining ground. Germany is still a social state – a 'social market economy' as Ludwig Erhard called it; critics even state that the Kohl administration is rather more Social Democratic than Conservative (Frankfurter Allgemeine Zeitung, 1997). There are severe cuts in social benefits, there are substantial privatisations in the transportation and communication industries, employment protection is being restricted. But the neoclassical hardliners do not rest to grieve that the radical systemic reform they desire is not met by these measures.

It is not by chance that those who plea for radical reforms in Germany nowadays often refer to countries where such a high degree of social regulation never existed (like the United States or Japan) or where such radical reforms have been implemented within a relatively short period of time (like New Zealand or the United Kingdom). For example, the Kiel Institute of World Economics,[2] well-known partisans of neoclassical reforms, has vociferously promoted Wolfgang Kaspar's analysis of the New Zealand Employment Contracts Act 1991 (Nr. 22) (Kaspar, 1995 and 1996). The President of the Institute, Horst Siebert, is one of the five members of the German government's 'Economic Experts' Committee'.[3] The recently published annual Opinion of the Committee contains a chapter on New Zealand as 'a case study for supply-oriented economic policy' (Sachverständigenrat, 1996: pp. 44 ff.). The chapter contains, without qualification and without comment, Kaspar's thesis suggesting that this might be a paradigmatic example. What is omitted with this type of un-analysed allusion is a scholarly comparison. I have the impression that such a comparison should be made in a very careful manner. For example, it seems that the way that collective bargaining is being reshaped by the 1991 Act leads it more in the direction of the autonomous German collective bargaining system (so one wonders why a German scholar should take this example as a proposal for Germany). Similar cases of ecclectic misuse of foreign experience to support internal claims could easily be demonstrated with respect to the United Kingdom and to Japan, within the current German debate.

I am not here to assess those approaches, but to avoid traps which are inherent in allegedly comparative findings and which stem from the fact that comparison is used as a weapon rather than a matter of experience. This is why I shall confine myself to describing and analysing the evolution of the German system of industrial relations, the crucial challenges to the system in its present form, and what might be the future prospects for the German system. I shall concentrate on some 'pillars' of the system, the importance of which I shall try to demonstrate.

The German system of labour law and industrial relations seems to be based mainly upon the following characteristics:

1   The system focuses upon skilled labour (craft). Within the regulatory framework this is expressed by: (i) the so-called 'dual system' of vocational training (apprenticeship); (ii) the 'standard employment relationship' which shapes individual labour law (that is the law concerning the employment relationship between the single employer and the single employee); and (iii) a system of social insurance which establishes firm links between the extra-work legal status of employees (particularly wage substituting benefits in the cases of sickness, professional injuries and diseases, unemployment, invalidity, and old age) and their legal status within employment.

2   The system implies strong, if precisely differentiated, collective representation of labour's interests within the spheres of establishment, enterprise, and labour market. From the point of view of regulation this implies: (iv) an effective

system of shop floor participation; (v) a nearly paritarian co-determination at the level of the supervisory council of large enterprises; and (vi) a system of collective bargaining which, as a rule, mediates workers' and employers' interests on a sectorial level (as opposed to firm level, craft level, and general level) and on a regional level (as opposed to national level).

With respect to all these six items the German system does not only differ from many other systems in the world, but also from other systems within the EU. This is why I would like to discuss more in detail both on how they have contributed to the success of the West German postwar society and in what way, and from what perspectives, they are being challenged at the present time.

Remarkably, these six characteristics are not being challenged equally by the present proposals for deregulation. For example, the element with the strongest regulation – the dual system of vocational training – is hardly mentioned during the current discourse. This is also true of the qualitative components of the standard employment relationship, the social insurance, and the participation systems. Rather, it is those components which, due to their quantitative character, bear implications for labour costs (such as wage and hours agreements, redundancy payments, qualifications for and amounts of insurance and other social benefits, etc.) that are under consideration for change (either reduced or cut). This has an important implication for the deregulation debate: at least for Germany 'deregulation', in the general and comprehensive sense of the concept, is the wrong label for what is being discussed. Regulation, on the contrary, is an integrative element of the functioning of the German system. The only question is whether this or that regulation is correct, that is, is capable of coping with the challenges of the future, and hence can be maintained, or whether it is wrong, and hence has to be amended or abolished (see Mückenberger/Deakin, 1989; Bercusson *et al.*, 1996).

Let me elaborate on these six themes in the following sections.

Vocational training

One element of German industrial relations which is very important is the so-called 'dual system' of vocational training (apprenticeship). The importance stems from two sources. First, the dual system provides producers with a continuous source of craft-based manpower as a result of which German industry is, to a large extent, equipped with skilled labour. Secondly, more than 60 per cent of the school-leavers of every age cohort – a level rarely found elsewhere in the world, with perhaps the exception of Denmark and Switzerland – are integrated into the dual system, which comprises a highly regulated curriculum of between 2 and 3½ years of vocational training. The system provides for cooperation between firms and the state – hence the label 'dual system'. The state, with a large degree of participation on the part of social partners, elaborates strict rules for recognised craft profiles ('Berufsbilder' – the number of which is now around 310), a time-scheduled syllabus over the years of apprenticeship which has to be implemented by firms and professional schools, skill requirements for vocational trainers, procedures for examinations of apprentices, and a monitoring system by public-law chambers of industry, artisans and commerce for the proper application of the rules mentioned. As a rule, apprentices receive their vocational training in a private or public enterprise on the basis of a private-law full time apprenticeship contract; during the period of apprenticeship they have to attend (normally one day a week) professional schools which teach theoretical subjects connected with the chosen skill (2/3), and civic education (1/3).

It is true that the dual system of vocational training is not unchallenged at present. However, the structure of the training as such, or the degree of regulation inhrent to it, is not in question. It is mainly two other issues which are under debate. First, is the question of how to achieve modernisation of the dual system under conditions of globalisation and tertiarisation of the post-Fordist economy. The roots of the apprenticeship system lie in the medieval guild system. It was easy to transform it according to the needs of the industrial society. It is much more difficult to adapt it to the needs of a service and information society. The way the state and firms have tried to tackle this challenge is to establish broader (and less numerous) areas of skilled work (in fact the number of crafts has been reduced from more than 900 to 310 within about two decades), and to integrate more abstract and information-technology based skills. But whether – in which form, and to what extent – the dual system can survive is subject to further assessment. Second, the number of apprenticeship posts provided by the firms is in decline (70 per cent in the glorious 1970s, now 63 per cent and possibly 50 per cent in the foreseeable future).

Vocational training expenses for firms are substantial (around DM28 billion per year against around 8 billion provided by the state). These expenses used to be regarded and accepted by firms as a human capital investment, with an amortisation period of say three or four years. At present, however, firms tend to take a short-term shareholder value perspective and regard vocational training as a 'cost' rather than an 'investment' factor. In fact, there are unsolved problems inherent to the system (for example the free-rider problem between firms which train and those which do not) which will have to be adjusted in the future: what might be necessary is some sort of inter-firm redistribution of training costs or the provision of other incentives to train (see Mückenberger, 1986).

The Standard Employment Relationship

A leading paradigm within German individual labour law is what I called the 'Standard Employment Relationship' (SER). As developed elsewhere (Mückenberger, 1988; Mückenberger/Deakin, 1989), the rules of the individual employment relationship (via statutory law, collective agreements, and plant agreements) follow a 'hidden regulatory programme' which protects certain employment relationships (that is the 'standard') more effectively than others (that is 'atypical' or 'non-standard' or 'marginal' word). When trying to sort out which type of employment is most protected under German industrial relations one discovers seven criteria according to which social protection is provided or 'distributed':

- seniority within the firm (long-term employment as opposed to short-term, 'casual', 'occasional' employment),
- a 'work biography' based upon lifelong gainful employment (continuous work biographies versus 'puzzle' biographies),
- age (the older the employee, the better he or she is protected),
- in-plant employment on the basis of the legal status of an 'employee' (as opposed to freelance occupation),
- amount of weekly working hours (fulltime as opposed to part-time),
- status within the plant hierarchy (skilled labour as opposed to unskilled),
- size of the firm (larger firms more readily meet the legal threshold requirements for the application of laws).

The 'ideal-type' of employment which can be extrapolated out of these criteria (hence the SER) is as follows: long-lasting fulltime employment within a medium-sized or big firm on a skilled basis. One will immediately recognise the linkage between the SER and the system of vocational training as described earlier. The well-trained performance-oriented craftsman is the point of reference upon which the social protection system is based.

To turn to the present challenges again, I would like to mention three of them, all of which have to do with the fact that the social protection system is linked to craft work. Firstly, it is true that the German employment system relies to a large extent on skilled labour (20 per cent unskilled, 60 per cent skilled within the dual system and 20 per cent extraordinarily skilled [including academic freelance], when compared to the United States with a 40 : 20 : 40 ratio according to Kern, 1996). However, under conditions of decentralisation of production, tertiarisation of the economy, and fragmentation of the workforce, 'atypical employment' is increasingly gaining ground among the three groups of employees. This enhances friction and segmentation within the effective shelter provided by the system of social protection as a result of which social exclusion becomes more and more prevalent (witness the formation of the 'two thirds-society'). Secondly, the SER obviously has a gender bias. The biography associated with it is the one of the craft*man*. Women with higher orientation toward non-gainful work and with 'scattered' rather than continuous work biographies often fail to meet the requirements for social protection. With the increasing entry of women into the labour market, with the increasing amount of households living without a 'male family-wage earner', the SER-oriented system of social protection is being more and more assesed and questioned as a system of structural (that is, indirectly built-in) discrimination against women. Don't forget that female workers represent large parts of the service sector labour markets, and that atypical work is substantially more widespread in the service sector than it is in the secondary sector. Thirdly, there is an increasing awareness of the fact that there are economic rationales for better protection of the so-called atypical work. Kern (1995 and 1996) has pointed out that the German craft-based system is enormously efficient with respect to what he calls 'incremental innovation' (that is, a type of in-plant innovation constantly improving production methods and products within the given basic structures of work organisation and product selection). However, the German economy nowadays needs 'radical innovations' with regard to production organisation and product mixes. Kern argues that the initiative for such radical innovations does not stem from the skilled core workforce but rather from highly qualified mobile, often freelance, individuals. If this is true, one can ask whether it is wise for a social regime to discriminate against these innovative actors as 'atypical workers' instead of providing them with incentives to develop their innovative power as much as possible.

These challenges lead towards new debates on how to reshape the individual employment regime in a way that weakens, if not altogether breaks, the link with the traditional SER. Here again, a mere deregulatory formula is much too simplistic in order to cope with the problem. What is paramount here is to adapt in a knowledgeable and intelligent way the existing model of regulation to modern conditions, in essence to re-regulate the developing variety of employment relationships. The basic idea which we have developed toward such a plan (Mückenberger *et al.*, 1989; Matthies *et al.*, 1994) is to 'decouple' a large amount of legal protection (labour law as well as social security protection) from the SER, even from gainful employment itself, in order to give more space of 'optionality' for employees, both men and women, to freely choose their duties and responsibilities within society and the economy, to be able to reconcile their working biography with their extra-work life (without the danger of enduring lifelong discrimination or being trapped in social deadlocks), and to be protected against social exclusion as citizens in the Marshallian sense (Marshall, 1949).

System of social insurance

It is well known that the German social state provides for a well-developed system of social security which is mainly based upon the social insurance principle. But, it is also guided by the principles of social promotion and, subsidiarily, the principle of social assistance. Social insurance is organised on the basis of risks typically linked to working life and on compulsory membership in public–legal insurance associations which cover the risks on a contribution-financed, and only very rarely on a tax-financed, basis (Bismarckian system).

The risks so covered are: illness, old age and invalidity, industrial injuries and professional diseases (since the 1880s), unemployment (since the 1920s), and need for care of elderly people (since the 1990s). As a rule, membership in the public-law insurance associations covering these risks is mandatory, within the framework of certain minimum and ceiling income thresholds. Employers and employees pay equal contributions which are income-related (injuries' association employers only). Benefits in cash ('wage replacement payments') follow the 'principle of equivalence' – that is their level corresponds to the contributions paid by the insured person and his/her employer. Alternatively, benefits in kind follow the 'principle of need' – that is there is no linkage between the benefit (e.g. medical treatment) and the income/contributions or with actuarial risk. The coexistence of equivalence and need principles constitutes what we call 'social insurance'.

Here again, I dare not go into detail. I just give two examples which show how the system works, how it is linked to the SER as a paradigm, how, via a high degree of regulation, it creates incentives, and how it is challenged now.

The first example is the *old age pension system* – one heavily debated element of the social insurance. Let us just look at the so called '*old age pension formula*' (§ 64 Sozialgesetzbuch, 6. Buch). The monthly old age pension is determined by multiplying your personal credits with a factor which characterizes old age with respect to other pensions (we leave it aside in the further description because old age pension has the factor, 1, 0) and the current old age pension's value. Most important is the first multiplicator: the amount of personal credits. Personal credits have two components – a time component and an income component.

- The biography of the employee qualifying for old age pension is calculated in *time periods* which are recognised as either normal insurance times (for example years of gainful employment) or as fictitious insurance times (for example three years of child care during which the employee was on parental leave). As a result of this calculation the insured person has a certain amount of insurance time periods which play a role in calculating personal credits.
- However, these insurance time periods do not count equally. On the contrary, each of the periods is counted subject to a certain *weight factor*. As a rule, (there are exceptions for fictitious insurance periods) the weight factor expresses the relationship between the individual wage received, hence wage-related contribution paid, by the employee within the respective insurance time period, and the wage received, hence contributions paid, by the average of all insured employees. As a result of this weighting procedure the employee receives for each of his/her period within the work biography a precise figure (1 = average; >1 = under; <1 = over average) which is the outcome of the named relationship. The amount of personal credits in the pension formula is the sum of all insurance periods weighted in the example.

I admit that what I described here is oversimplistic. However, it shows one important element. The old age pension formula is a direct result of the work biography of the insured person. The greater the number of your insured years, and the better your income over time relative to the average, then the higher will be your monthly pension. One can easily recognise the linkage of this formula with the SER paradigm. The formula creates a continuous incentive to perform gainful work – and not only gainful but better than average paid (that is skilled) work. The other side of the coin is that the formula discriminates against 'puzzle' biographies – those with longer periods of non-activity or low pay activity, whatever the reason may be. Do not forget that there are other pension systems which calculate personal credits according to the 'best ten years' (France) or which provide for tax-financed flat-rate or at least minimum pensions (the nordic

European countries). As against those, the German Bismarckian system puts stress on a lifelong continuing achievement principle.

   Within the present debate this structural element is not really put into doubt. On the contrary, the dominant opinion recommends strengthening the equivalence principle because it motivates work and 'protestant work ethics'. Instead, the two points debated most are as follows:

- There is a certain tension inherent in the system of social insurance – the tension between 'social' and 'insurance' (in our example the one between normal and fictitious insurance periods). The modern social state tends to extend the recognition of fictitious times, and hence a wider concept of work (to include more than wage work – for example child or elderly care), and thereby builds incentives for fertility, family life, social cohesion, etc. As against that, the critics of the social state, particularly in times of economic crisis, emphasise the insurance principle and recommend freeing the insurance from 'insurance-alien' charges.[4] This tension has obviously been sharpening in recent years.
- Still more fundamental is the debate over whether this social insurance system has a gender bias and how to cope with it. Obviously, if we compare male and female average biographies we find (if less uniformly than it used to be some decades ago) many more 'puzzle' biographies among the latter and continuous work biographies among the former. The poor in Germany include two female groups – old women and single-caring mothers – due to the fact that the social protection system is oriented toward continuous gainful employment (and hence the SER). This is being perceived more and more as systematic discrimination. Consequently, the claim for recognition of a wider notion of 'work' and a stronger 'decoupling from SER' of certain aspects of social protection often coincide with claims to overcome discrimination within and outside employment.

The other multiplicator of the German old age pensions formula – besides an individual's personal credits – is what I called the *up-to-date old age pensions value* (§ 68 SGB VI). This is the dynamic factor of the formula which links the level of the old age pension not to the contributions paid by the insured person in the past, but rather to the present real net incomes of comparable employees. The dynamic factor was introduced under the Adenauer administration in 1957. The mechanism is too sophisticated to describe here in detail. Let me provide a summary: twenty years ago a worker (credit = 1) has, due to lower real wages, paid lower contributions than we would have paid today. Nevertheless, his credit for that year gets the same value as those paid later. So the system implies a permanent increase in the benefits to be paid in relation to the contributions already paid. This system is called the 'Umlagesystem' (intergenerational levy system – that is, the active population via their contributions finance the pensions of the retired population) which differs from the 'Kapitaldeckungssystem' (capital stock system – that is, the pensions are paid from the capital and the interest as stocked by way of contributions paid in the past).

The financial crisis of the old age insurance associations is due to economic factors (increased unemployment leads toward decreasing contributions) and to demographic factors (increasing life expectancy and decreasing fertility rate lead to an ever increasing shift in the ratio between the active and the retired population). It is not by chance that this leads to new debates about the insurance system. Not only are so-called 'insurance-alien' benefits under scrutiny, the whole system of the 'generation contract' is being challenged. The Sachverständigenrat wants the capital stock system to be seriously reconsidered. Conservative politicians (like Biedenkopf) want the insurance system to be replaced by a tax-financed basic income plus private insurance. The present government proposes to maintain the intergenerational levy system while moderately increasing the contributions, but decreasing the amount of benefits by introducing a 'demographic factor' into the old age pensions formula (BMAS, 1997).

Here again, one can easily demonstrate that what is necessary is not deregulation or privatisation of risks as promoted by some neoclassical analysis, but rather intelligent re-regulation.

Take as another example the *industrial injuries and professional diseases legislation*. Since the Bismarck legislation introducing industrial injuries insurance, there have been two branches of health and safety protection in Germany: the state-run factory inspectorate and the self-monitoring (if mandatory and public-legal) industrial injuries associations (*Berufsgenossenschaften*). These are industry-wide insurance associations of all employers with mandatory membership and risk-related contributions. They have regulatory power over their members regarding insurance, and their own staff and overview capacities on a corporate level, that is self-installed and self-monitored by the insurance provider, rather than on a direct state authority basis.

This system has had many advantages. It has rationalised the conflict over injuries by 'externalising' and 'economising' it. Conflict over an accident was externalised away from the factory to a conflict between worker and Berufsgenossenschaft (the civil responsibility of employers and work mates was, according to §§ 636, 637 Reichsversicherungsordnung, definitively replaced by the contributions paid to the insurance). Proactive health and safety prevention was economised in that the insurance provider developed an interest in lowering the cost of accidents through risk-related insurance tariffs, through a system of setting up strict safety rules, and through a very efficient monitoring system with police-like intervening power.

It is interesting that the work accident insurance system which implies mandatory membership and contributions, a very close network of regulation and controls has never been discussed as a target of deregulation. Employers in general seem to be satisfied with it. Trade unions actively cooperate in it since they got, in 1951, a parity vote in the self-monitoring bodies of the associations. Safety-at-work scholars attribute a high degree of effectiveness to it. The only major challenge currently comes from the European Union which, under the rules concerning free competition, threatens the maintenance of this nationally based system by arguing it is an obstacle to the free movement of goods and services.

Shop floor participation

As was mentioned earlier, the German system implies strong and statutorily reg-ulated (if precisely differentiated) collective representation of labour's interests within the spheres of establishment, enterprise, and labour market. The dense framework of procedural regulation is often mandatory. The Works Councils Act (*Betriebsverfassungsgesetz*) mainly regulates the establishment and forms of participa-tion by the works councils, and the legal means to guarantee participation. Participation is in three forms: information, consultation, and co-determination. In most economic and personnel affairs there are rights of information and con-sultation. By contrast, co-determination covers the field of nearly all 'social issues' (e.g. working time regulation, wage determination methods and holidays).

It might be helpful to demonstrate the role of co-determination in the case where management wants to increase overtime work. Before ordering overtime they have to negotiate with the works council. If the works council does not agree, the employer is not allowed to introduce overtime; managerial prerogative is thus restricted by the works council's co-determination right. Instead the employer has to ask for an arbitration award forwarded by an arbitration board which is com-posed equally of employer's and works council's representatives, plus one so called 'neutral chairman' who has to be appointed with the consent of the two sides. The board's decision is definitive and can only be challenged in the courts inso-far as to check whether the board overstepped its legal discretion. Often, the board has a conciliatory rather than a deciding role bringing the conflicting par-ties to an agreement.

The strong role of the works councils and the highly regulated relationship between management and works councils plays an important role in German industrial relations. Though one has to take into account that works councils exist mainly in medium-sized and large firms, and quite rarely in small ones, they do shape the day-to-day culture in German plants. When, in 1971, the works coun-cils act was improved in favour of the workers' representatives it was at first strongly opposed by employers' representatives, often for political reasons. Today they are accepted in principle as an element of rationalising and channeling con-flict at the shop floor level. Contrary to earlier assumptions that the increased rights of works councils would automatically lead to increased litigation (a 'legal guerilla war') their actual function seems to be different. They seem to be regarded by the parties involved as a sort of background condition for their actions, and although they are not 'applied' in the strict sense, as are statutory provisions, they force the actors to look for rules of 'fairness' and 'common sense' acceptable to their counterparts. That either side can 'threaten' the legal proce-dure of the arbitration board makes it more favourable for both to look for a consensus.

There is possibly not enough empirical evidence to draw far-reaching conclu-sions. But, we know from certain empirical studies that employers widely appre-ciate the works councils system, and that the effectiveness of works councils has increased enormously within the last two decades (Kotthoff, 1981 and 1994).

This is why the present debate on the necessary reform of the works councils system rarely questions the co-determination system as such. Some attack the high costs of social plans awarded by arbitration boards in cases of mass redundancies. More emphasis is given to structural problems which threaten to weaken the effectiveness of the traditional system of interest representation. Lean production and the so-called 'systemic inter-firm integration' tend to weaken centralist firm representation in a double way: by means of intra-firm decentralisation and by means of supra-firm centralisation. Both tendencies require new 'post-fordist' forms of participation (like work groups participation on the one hand and participation 'along logistic chains' on the other). They also challenge the concepts of 'employee' and of the 'establishment' as essential points of reference for labour law and plant representation. Here lies an enourmous need for re-regulation in the near future.

Co-determination on enterprise level

An important element of German industrial relations is what is called '*Mitbestimmung*' (co-determination) in the proper sense. It has to be clearly distinguished from the form of participation executed on establishment level by the works council. Whereas the latter has, as its point of reference, the bulk of technological and labour organisation issues which have to be handled at plant (that is, shop floor or establishment) level, the former is established on the enterprise level and has as a point of reference the economic development of the firm or the group. Enterprise co-determination is nothing other than the fact that employees (and to a certain extent external trade union representatives) have a certain number of seats with full votes in the firm's supervisory board and its committees.[5] Their vote thus concerns the basic economic decisions of the firm. This is why it is important to know the composition of the supervisory board. There are three different forms of enterprise codetermination according to sector and size of the firm:

1   In the *coal mining and steel industries*, since 1951, there has been full parity between capital and labour. That is, shareholders and employees have had equal votes in the supervisory board; the chairman of the board (with the deciding vote) has had to be a neutral party appointed with the consent of both capital and labour; the personnel director (*Arbeitsdirektor – workers' director*) may not be appointed without the consent of the employees' representatives in the board.

2   In *big companies (that is more than 2000 employees)*, since 1976 (and upheld by the Federal Constitutional Court in 1979), there has been near parity between capital and labour. That is, shareholders and employees have had an equal number of seats in the supervisory board; the board has had two chairmen, one from each side, and contrary to the first model the chairman representing capital has the deciding vote; there has to be a personnel director (*Arbeitsdirektor*) who is appointed by the supervisory board in the normal way, without employees' input. Despite this difference with regard to the above, it

is customary that the personnel director is a person who holds the trust of the unions (e.g. an experienced union official).

3   In *all other joint-stock companies* employees have only one-third of the seats in the supervisory board.

In 1990, around 550 companies fell under type 2 co-determination. It is true that there was much political rumour about the Act passed by Parliament in 1976. Employers alleged expropriation, however this was dismissed by the constitutional court. Trade unions decried the 'under-parity', however, they could live with the new model. Various strategies were observed, as some firms – by reducing the number of relevant employees or by changing the legal nature of the firm – tried to escape from coverage under co-determination. But all in all the system seems to be accepted by both sides.

It is interesting that before the 1976 Act was passed, a Commission of Parliamentary Experts under the conservative MB Kurt Biedenkopf had recommended the act with a view to the experiences of the coal and steel industries under 'full parity' co-determination: the Commission stated that co-determination was a very effective lever for the fundamental restructuring of both industries, and that without such a 'social cushion' there would have been many more open conflicts about the radical downsizing and reorganisation process. American observers of German economic co-determination stated that it might be of use to top managers, by giving them useful information about internal problems or the potential of innovation, which otherwise would be lost within the middle ranks of personnel (Smith, 1990). It seems that within the current day-to-day work of the supervisory boards, even the different compositions (and hence shares of votes) of the first two types don't play a significant role. In Germany, supervisory boards are less an institution where the deciding vote matters but an institution which brings about mutual understanding, trust, and thereby consensus. Also, the capital's representatives would prefer to achieve consensus rather than use their majority. Employees' representatives, knowing this, will be prepared to 'moderate' their claims in a way that will be acceptable to capital.

One may wonder why, in an overall situation of globalisation, economic restructuring and upheaval, the political climate around co-determination at both establishment level and enterprise level is relatively calm. Again, keep in mind that none of the relevant political actors in Germany – not even those who are accustomed to the rhetoric of neoclassicalism, deregulation, and privatisation – question these forms of employee participation as such. Many complain, but with only particular and specified claims rather than radical Thatcherite ones. This has to do with something which holds equally for both forms of co-determination, and behind which lies a problem I do not want to hide. Co-determination in the German form/manner necessarily leads to firm-based coalitions between capital and labour. These coalitions are not only a source of cooperation, productiveness and mutual trust, they can also lead to common strategies at the cost of third parties, especially of society in general. Often, employees' representatives share management's views about 'negative external effects' of the firm ('social cost' in the sense of W. F. Kapp) – for example, when preferring overtime to hiring the unemployed, or preferring pollution to cost-intensive environment friendly equipment or, to take an example which happens quite frequently in Germany since the unification, preferring investment in the old Federal Republic to that in the new '*Länder*'. In all these cases, internal consensus is achieved at the expense of actors external to the firm.

The possibility, and in fact existence, of such coalitions may explain many phenomena which at first glance are not comprehensible to an outsider to the German society. It can explain why capital, after at first being politically (ideologically rather than rationally) opposed to the increase of co-determination, has mostly accepted it. It may explain why, on the contrary, they still heavily resist 'externals' (outside experts as well as union officials) having seats on the supervisory boards – because these outsiders threaten to 'internalise' external views. It may explain why at the European level, a first works councils system has recently been achieved, whereas employers' (particularly private employers') resistance to sectorally or European-wide territorially autonomous collective bargaining seems much more difficult to overcome.

Plant- or firm-coalitions between capital and labour may facilitate consensus building and conflict avoidance. But, assessed from the perspective of the sustainable development of society they pose problems. Avoiding negative external effects and promoting positive ones is one of the central issues of contemporary society. Be it the struggle against mass unemployment, or be it the struggle against pollution and global environmental problems – it has, to a large extent, to do with the question of how to 're-internalise' societal interest into the firm's behaviour. There have been numerous proposals – such as establishing an Environment Director in the enterprise or giving society seats and votes on the supervisory board – but there are many unsolved problems. Nevertheless, coping with externalities seems still to be a subject for further reflection on the re-regulation of the plant and the firm.

Collective bargaining

Forms and levels of collective bargaining as well as the contents of collective agreements are among the most disputed areas of contemporary German industrial relations. This has to do with cost but also with the quest for flexibility in the firms. In order to make clear the problems and perspectives I shall first give a sketch of the German legal collective bargaining system, then of the practice of the social partners which developed on that basis.

Collective bargaining is the least statutorily regulated field of German industrial relations.

1   One basic norm in the constitution (article 9 para. 3 *Grundgesetz*) provides for freedom of association. It is the judiciary (constitutional as well as labour courts) who deduce from this basic guarantee the principle of autonomous collective bargaining ('*Tarifautonomie*'), the duty of the state to provide for an

institutional framework for free collective bargaining, and the freedom to take industrial action in order to achieve collective agreements.

2   The Collective Agreements Act (*'Tarifvertragsgesetz'*) contains a purely proce-dural framework for collective bargaining and determines the legal nature of collective agreements. Parties to the collective agreements can be single employers or employers' associations on one side and trade unions on the other. There is no recognition procedure in the case of a plurality of unions. Collective agreements are legally binding – the 'obligatory' part binds the parties to the collective agreement whereas the so called 'normative' part binds all their members (i.e. the individual employers and employees who are members of the respective association or union). As a rule, the agreement has no general effect on non-members (in effect 'ex parte', not 'erga omnes'). Only under very strict conditions and to a very limited extent can their appli-cation be extended to non-members, and only by ministerial decision.

3   Industrial action, though not statutorily mentioned, is allowed for both sides – however, only within the strict limits of what the courts call 'proportionality'. This holds for strikes which are only permitted as '*ultima ratio*'. It holds even more for lock-outs which, at present, are allowed only as a retaliatory weapon and must be proportional to the strike called.

Very roughly, this is nearly all the law says about collective bargaining. The rest is practice. What has developed in Germany as a 'system' of industrial relations hence stems from the social actors, not the law. I see mainly three elements which are worth considering:

1   German trade unions are *unitarian organisations* (*'Einheitsgewerkschaften'*) in that they have neither an exclusive political nor an exclusive religious stance. There, evidently, is a Social Democratic hegemony within the German TU Federation (*'Deutscher Gewerkschaftsbund – DGB'*), but it does not exclude Christian, Communist, or nowadays Green positions. Unitarism also holds in that although all workers within an industry negotiate separately, no particu-lar trades or skills negotiate separately (and hence draw 'demarcation lines' against each other), (*'Ein Betrieb – eine Gewerkschaft'* = 'one plant – one union'). Unitarism is a postwar reaction mainly to the political cleavages which had weakened trade unions against fascism in the interwar period. Though there are some non-DGB unions, they don't have much of an impact on the col-lective bargaining system and they do not create an effective plurality of unions (and hence the need for a procedure of representativeness or recog-nition as it is known in other European and western countries).

2   There is no central bargaining. The *DGB* has a weak role with respect to the branch or sector unions which monopolise collective bargaining. This is why the latter is dominated by *sectorial (industry-wide) bargaining*.[6] On the other hand, sector bargaining is dominant in that the normal wage, working hours, and paid holiday negotiations are not dealt with on the local (plant or enter-prise) level, but on the territorial level. It is at the sectoral level that certain

progress has been achieved (such as six weeks paid sick leave, six weeks paid annual holiday, and the 35-hours week). This progress then was adapted by other sectors and thereby generalised. The key sector in Germany is the metal engineering and electrical sector with its 3 million member *'IG Metall'* as principle social actor. It is not by chance that this sector is where the German collective bargaining system is most challenged by capital.

3   Within the sectors collective bargaining can be characterised as a *dialectic relationship between national and district bargaining*. Only in a few sectors (like the chemical and printing industries) does bargaining take place at national level. In the engineering sector, collective bargaining is coordinated centrally, but performed regionally. This is not a one-sided decision of the unions, but one shared by the employers. This sort of decentralised but sectoral bargaining has contributed to a typical rationalisation of collective bargaining and also of industrial conflict in Germany. The 'normal' strike – don't forget that strikes in Germany are rare – takes place in a typical form. After the breakdown of negotiations, the workers of a very few key plants are called out on strike. The employers will reply with a retaliatory lock-out. They are bound to use this weapon only to a limited extent – 'proportionally' to the extent of the strike. The more the conflict escalates the more the union comes under financial pressure. They have to pay out to their members considerable strike benefits whereas unemployment insurance benefits, after a conservative amendment in 1986, are not paid out to locked-out workers. This reopens the door for new negotiations and agreement.

The collective bargaining system as practised in Germany, with great success over recent decades, had certain preconditions which presently seem to be challenged more than ever before (see in detail Mückenberger, 1995):

• The principle of representation and representativeness – that is, the actors on both sides act on a highly agglomerated level for their members and they are able to bind their members to a decision. Both sides, however, have recently had problems integrating new members with their existing membership due to various differentiations both between enterprise structures and among social milieus. What is thereby in question is whether the employers can continue to effectively speak for 'the industry' and the union for 'the employees'.

• Autonomy of the social partners involved – here increasingly direct and, even more so, indirect state intervention challenges the traditional role of the social partners (think only about the impact the monetary convergence criteria decided upon by the Member States of the European Union at Maastricht has on collective wage bargaining!).

• Collective bargaining used to be a highly professionalised and allegedly a 'neutral' experts' duty. Nowadays, it is becoming increasingly re-politicised.

• The collective agreement has been regarded as a 'socially guiding agreement' – a set of standards beyond the statutory minimum which hinted at the future perspective of social policy as such. This made associations and collective actors attractive for working people. Today collective bargaining is often a zero-sum game of concession bargaining. This weakens the process and makes recruitment still more difficult.

- Traditionally, German trade unions have been regarded as something like an 'agent of the general public interest'. At present, however, they often reveal an ineffectiveness or are prone to promoting particularist interests which, in the long run, causes a sort of legitimation crisis not only of these organisations, but of collective interest representation and organisation as such.

- Collective agreements in Germany (contrary to the United Kingdom) have been regarded as legally binding and hence enforceable agreements. Processes are now under way which challenge even this basic assumption. On the one hand, there are attempts at non-implementation or otherwise avoiding terms of binding agreements (e.g. in the cases of agreements mandatorily limiting working hours, or in cases of the exit of individual employers from the employers' federation which, according to German law, does not liberate them from valid collective agreements). On the other hand, an increasing number of 'agreements' are concluded (e.g. in the chemical industry) in ways which no longer are legally binding, but rather as a 'soft agreement' or a 'letter of intent'.

It is hard to predict how these tendencies will develop. It is evident that a new formula will have to be found governing the relationship between the individual firm and its contractual obligations on the one hand, and the employers' associations and the collective agreements concluded by them on the other. The claim for more flexibility is not only one of capital but also one concerning decentralised participation of the employees (see section on 'Shop floor participation'). What seems to be necessary is a readjustment of new 'floors' within a multi-tiered system: basic statutory guarantees which form something like an 'ordre public social' and are beyond the disposal of the social actors; certain quantitative parameters and qualitative framework provisions fixed by the social partners on sectoral level and leaving space to manoeuvre for the local actors; and decentralised forms of decision-making and participation allowing for local flexibility, innovation, and cooperation. But it is admittedly difficult to develop such ideas as long as the battlefield is mined by shortsighted weapons like deregulation or the mere 'maintenance of rights' claims.

Further perspectives

As was mentioned in the introduction, Germany (like other developed European countries) has to cope with weak growth, mass unemployment, and the consequences of social exclusion. What I wanted to show is that one single way to tackle the current situation does not exist. The search for modernisation is present in all sectors of the social system I discussed. But I also tried to stress that this system contains elements of high cooperativeness and trust which form germs of further productiveness and should therefore be *maintained and at the same time intelligently developed*. I am afraid the appraisal of the market forces school will not be able to cope with this challenge. Regarding this view, I feel affirmed by the fact that even those German politicians who in theory praise the 'free market' in practice are wise enough not to consequently follow their own recipe.

In fact, the crucial question for a society like Germany seems to be: what – if not the mere maintenance of the existing framework and if not its mere deregu-lation – can be *the guiding principles of the intelligent modernisation of the social system?* I think it is inevitable to follow three paths of modernisation. It is true that these three postulates are very rough; they cannot be properly developed here (on some of them see Matthies *et al.*, 1994). Nevertheless, they indicate the direction the intelligent re-regulation of the social regime can take.

- Germany needs an enormous increase in *productiveness and innovation*. This is why a further development of the system of vocational training is necessary, why the learning and communication capacities should be anchored within the employment relationship, and why the encouragement of decentralised responsibility and initiative within plant-level participation and flexible col-lective bargaining structures are paramount. However, in order to make pro-ductiveness and innovation socially viable and sustainable for the ecology, an internalisation of societal needs, or 'social cost', into the production sphere seems desirable.
- At least for the next decade and a half, other strategies to overcome mass unemployment are necessary. Among them, on a European level, a new *redis-tribution of gainful work* seems to be necessary. Such efforts have begun with some success (in the Netherlands and the Nordic countries other than Germany). They have, as a precondition, greater options within the working-time field – be it for further vocational training or be it for caring purposes. Another condition is income support for lower income categories reducing their working-time in favour of the unemployed and a certainty of social pro-tection not strictly linked to the standard employment relationship.
- If one does not believe in a sudden disappearance of unemployment one has, at the same time, to provide for strategies against social exclusion (particularly among young people). There have been frightening developments toward xenophobia and racism among those members of the European populations who face exclusion. Social cohesion, thus, can no longer be taken for granted. It has to be developed. If it is not, the economic recovery of the societies is also no longer secure, because it has to be doubted that a society which can-not guarantee social coherence can have any real chance of developing enhanced productiveness and innovation.

Notes

1 We use the term 'social state' in order to characterise the European continental type of state which: (i) does not confine itself to functions of 'market making' and 'market brak-ing', but also includes the function of 'market correcting'; and (ii) does not restrict the

market correcting function to income redistribution via subsidies and benefits (= the so-called 'welfare state') but also provides for extended social (including public) services and infrastructures (see Esping-Andersen, 1990, 1996).

2 Institut für Weltwirtschaft an der Universität Kiel.

3 Sachverständigenrat zur Begutachtung der gesamtwirtwirtschaftlichen Entwicklung.

4 It is true that social and societal extensions of coverage of the social insurance need not necessarily be financed by insurance, but can also be financed (or re-financed) on a tax basis by the state. However, under the present tendency toward reduction of state debts and public expenditure the recommendation to eliminate insurance-alien benefits quite often imply the elimination of the socially extended benefits themselves.

5 German company law organises joint-stock companies on the basis of dual boards. The supervisory board is elected by the shareholders and the employees according to the ratio as described in the text. They are responsible for the fundamental decisions with respect to the firm's long term economic policy (for example investment, product structure). They also nominate the members of the second board – the board of directors. The latter consists of at least three members: a technical, an economic, and a personnel director. The board of directors takes responsibility for the day-to-day operation of the firm; they are bound to execute the decisions of principle as decided upon by the supervisory board.

6 The most famous exception is the *Volkswagen* enterprise, the biggest German private employer, which is not affiliated with the metal employers' association and hence concludes not sectorial but single employer collective agreements. This is an important background condition for the famous *Volkswagen* agreement from 1993 onward within which a drastic reduction in working time was negotiated in order to protect employment.

References

Bercusson, Brian *et al.* (1996) *Manifest Social Europe*. Brussels: ETUI.

Bundesministerium für Arbeit und Sozialordnung (Hg.) (1997) 'Kommission legt ihre Vorschläge vor', in *Sozialpolitische Informationen*, NT. 2/1997 dating from 6.2.1997.

Esping-Andersen, Gosta (1990) *The Three Worlds of Welfare Capitalism*. Oxford: Polity Press.

Esping-Andersen, Gosta (1996) 'The impasse of labour shedding and familianism in Continental European social policy', in Esping-Andersen (ed.), *Welfare States in Transition*, London: Sage.

Kaspar, Wolfgang (1995) 'Liberating labour. The New Zealand Employment Contracts Act', Kiel: Institut für Weltwirtschaft, Kiel Working Papers No. 694.

Kaspar, Wolfgang (1996) Die Befreiung des Arbeitsmarktes. Neuseeland Wirtschaft im Aufschwung, Gütersloh: Bertelsmann.

Kern (1996a) 'Das vertrackte Problem der Sicherheit: Innovationen im Spannungsfeld zwischen Ressourcenmobilisierung und Risikoaversion', in Fricke (ed.), *Jahrbuch Arbeit und Technik*, Bonn: Dietz.

Kern (1996b) 'German capitalism. How competitive will it be in the future? Conference "The Restructuring of the Economic and Political System in Japan and Europe: Past Legacy and Present Issues"', Milan, May 1996.

Kotthoff, Hermann (1981) *Betriebsräte und betriebliche Herrschaft*. New York: Frankfurt.

Kotthoff, Hermann (1994) Betriebsräte und Bürgerstatus. Wandel und Kontinuität betrieblicher Mitbestimmung, München und Mering.

Marshall, T. H. [1949] (1965) 'Citizenship and social class', in Marshall (ed.), *Class, Citizenship and Social Development*, New York: Anchor.

Matthies, Hildegard *et al.* (1994) *Arbeit 2000. Anforderungen an eine Neugestaltung der Arbeitsverhältnisse*. Reinbek: Rowohlt.

Mückenberger, Ulrich (1986) 'Labour law and industrial relations', in O. Jacobi *et al.* (eds), *Economic Crisis, Trade Unions and the State*, London: Croom Helm Ltd., pp. 236 ff.

Mückenberger, Ulrich (1986) *Die Ausbildungspflicht der Unternehmen nach dem Grundgesetz.* Baden-Baden: Nomos.

Mückenberger, Ulrich (1988) 'Juridification of industrial relations: A German–British comparison', *Comparative Labor Law Journal*, 6(4), 526 ff.

Mückenberger, Ulrich (1993) 'Auf dem Weg zu einem postfordistischen Arbeitsrecht', in W. Müller-Jentsch (ed.), *Konfliktpartnerschaft*, München, pp. 203 ff.

Mückenberger, Ulrich (1995) 'Aktuelle Herausforderungen an das Tarifwesen', in *Kritische Justiz* Vol. 28, pp. 1, 26–44.

Mückenberger, Ulrich, and Simon Deakin (1989) From Deregulation toward a European Floor of Rights, Zeitschrift für ausländisches und internationales Arbeits- und Sozialrecht, Vol. 3, pp. 153–207.

Mückenberger/Offe/Ostner (1989) 'Das staatlich garantierte Grundeinkommen', in Krämer *et al.* (eds), *Festschrift für André Gorz*, Berlin: Rotbuch.

Sachverständigenrat (1996) Sachverständigenrat zur Begutachtung der gesamtwirtschaftlichen Entwicklung. Jahresgutachten 1996/97, Deutscher Bundestag Drucksache 13/6200.

Streeck, Wolfgang (1995) 'From market-making to state-building?' in *Leibfried/Pierson, Europena Social Policy*, Washington: Brookings, pp. 389 ff.

10 Labour 'flexibility' – Securing management's right to manage badly?

Jonathan Michie and Maura Sheehan[1]

Introduction

Frank Wilkinson's classic piece on 'Productive Systems' opens with a warning against the 'increasingly dogmatic reassertion by a growing proportion of economists of the beneficial effects of the invisible hand of market forces'. These reassertions, Wilkinson argues, 'are based not on a careful examination of how economies actually work and have developed but on abstract, a priori reasoning about how they should operate' (Wilkinson, 1983, p. 413). The attempt by the Thatcher Governments in Britain to shift the balance of forces in favour of the market – in other words, in favour of those who have the upper hand in 'free market' processes – was best illustrated, indeed justified, by the 'need to reassert management's right to manage'. The idea was that managers in British firms were constrained by trade unions, by Government regulations and by other institutional arrangements. Given a freer reign – that is, more power – they would do a better job at managing. This begs a number of questions, the most obvious one being whether it is true that the weaker the constraints within which management manages, the better the outcomes? In other words, if managers are given a greater freedom to manage, how will their behaviour change, and will any such change be to the benefit or detriment of the organisations that they manage and the economy more generally?

The above deregulatory argument has been made in particular regarding the need for labour 'flexibility' in order to allow a dynamic and innovative economy. We have attempted to shed light on these issues through two research projects, both still running at the time of writing, which have been investigating what links there are, if any, between on the one hand different approaches by management to so-called 'human resource' practices, including the use of 'flexible' labour, and on the other hand corporate outcomes, and in particular the likelihood or otherwise of firms being innovative, whether in new processes or products.

The 1990 Workplace Industrial Relations Survey (WIRS3)

Labour market deregulation has been seen by the UK's Department of Trade and Industry as playing a key role in the drive for an innovative economy: 'excessive regulation stifles growth, destroys jobs, raises prices and drives companies elsewhere' (DTI, 1995: 18). On the other hand, it has been suggested that the sort of labour market deregulation pursued in Britain during the 1980s and 1990s may risk being detrimental to long-run economic performance by leading to a neglect or undervaluing of assets and processes such as training and innovative activity, which are vital to long-term development and economic progress (Michie and Wilkinson, 1995).

To test these alternative views of how the productive system operates we first analysed the existing data, from the British Workplace Industrial Relations Survey (WIRS). This is a major nationally-funded survey which has been undertaken four times over a twenty-year period.[2] Further details of the latest of these surveys (carried out in 1998) is given in the section on 'Workplace Employment Relations Survey'. However, the issue of innovation was given particular attention in the previous survey, carried out in 1990, and we first therefore used these data to analyse in particular the above argument regarding the need for labour flexibility by firms that are actively innovating. WIRS is the largest interview-based survey of industrial relations practices in the world.[3] The survey was sponsored by the UK Government's Employment Department, the Economic and Social Research Council, the Policy Studies Institute (with funds from the Leverhulme Trust) and the Advisory, Conciliation and Arbitration Service. The 1990 survey was the third (hereafter referred to as WIRS3) and contained information on 2061 establishments with twenty five or more employees in the manufacturing and service industries and the public and private sectors.[4] Describing the survey, Millward (1994) emphasised that:

> ... the surveys cover around 70 per cent of employees in Great Britain. The surveys consist of large, nationally representative samples of workplaces. The design incorporates rigorous statistical sampling and there is no clustering in the sample selection, since this might lead to under-representation of particular types of workplace ... The surveys use role holders as key informants about their workplace. The main respondent in each case is the senior management responsible for personnel or industrial relations matters, broadly defined. Other role-holders (worker representatives and other managers) provide additional information ...
>
> (Millward, 1994: 5)

Michie and Sheehan[5] (1999a) use evidence from WIRS3 to examine how the type of labour demanded by firms and the way in which labour is organized within firms – in other words, the management of human resources and work practices – is correlated with a firms' innovative activities. We investigated the relationship between a firms' human resource management practices on the one hand, and the levels of research and development (R&D) expenditure of those firms and the probability of these firms introducing innovative investment on the other.

Trade union recognition was found to be positively correlated with the probability of the firm innovating. Using evidence from the 1984 WIRS, Machin and

Wadhwani (1991) also found a positive and significant relation between trade unionism on the one hand and investment and the introduction of 'advanced technical change' on the other. Both sets of results are consistent with Daniel's (1987) widely cited finding that unionised establishments were more likely to invest and/or to introduce new technology.

We also found that the use of innovative work practices was positively correlated with the probability of the firm innovating. These innovative work practices were the precise opposite of those encouraged by labour market deregulation, such as the use of short-term contracts, temporary labour and so on. We found that this 'low road' sort of flexibility had no positive correlation whatsoever with the likelihood of innovating. The innovative work practices that were correlated with innovating, far from using 'flexibile' labour in the hire and fire sense, actually included an implicit employment security pledge. Similar results regarding the effect of HRM systems on firm productivity were found by Ichniowski *et al.* (1997).

Using the WIRS3 data, then, we found that the presence of a trade union and the use of innovative work practices were positively correlated with the probability of 'innovating'. In contrast, the use of seasonal, temporary, casual and fixed-term contracts were if anything negatively correlated with the probability of innovating. We are not suggesting that these correlations represent simple, one-way causal processes. Indeed, we found that the labour market flexibility variables were endogenous, thereby implying that the relationships involved were two-way ones. However, our results clearly suggested that promoting what we would characterise as a 'low road' approach to labour market flexibility – in particular encouraging the use of marginal types of employment contracts, for which we tested – is unlikely to be associated with an innovative and dynamic economy.

Worker participation and representation

One problem with the work reported above is that many of the 'progressive' human resource management practices can be used – or misused – in a variety of ways. Quality circles may, for example, allow workers a chance to make suggestions as to how their own work environment could be improved. But if such suggestions are not acted on, then such practices may be worthless. And they may be worse than useless from the employee's point of view if they are simply used by management as a means to continually seek to increase the intensity of work. Similarly, it is in principle better that employees be allowed to make suggestions than not; but when as in some firms there are quotas for suggestions to be made then such schemes may take on an altogether different character. The obvious suggestion would be to scrap the quota for suggestions.

We, therefore, also used WIRS3 to focus explicitly on issues of worker participation and representation. The effect that employee participation and representation has on economic performance at the level of the firm, and nationally, has of course been the subject of economic analysis for some time, having spawned a large number of related literatures.[6] Black and Lynch (1997) find that 'simply introducing high performance workplace practices is not enough to increase establishment productivity'; in line with our findings reported below, they found that increased employee voice was a necessary condition for making such practices actually effective. In their study, almost three-quarters of all establishments had some form of Total Quality Management (TQM) system, but by itself these were not associated with higher productivity. The percentage of workers involved in regular decision-making meetings was, though, positively associated to labour productivity.

In Michie and Sheehan (1999b) we examined not only employee participation and representation mechanisms, including contingent pay schemes, but also included an analysis of the relation between these practices on the one hand and on the other, firstly, flexible job assignment and, secondly, the relation of all this to the firm's innovative activity. We found that for a firm to be innovative:

i   Contingent pay variables were *not* significant;
ii   With increased employee involvement over the previous three years, the sharing of information and consultation with employees about change *did* prove significant;
iii While Joint Consultative Committee (JCC) representation was *not* itself significant, trade union recognition *was* significant; and
iv   An increase in the flexibility of job assignments either through reduced job demarcation and/or a redistribution of tasks amongst manual employees *was* significant.

The likelihood of firms innovating was thus found to be positively correlated with employee representation at work. It may be true that firms can profit in the short term from cost-cutting strategies and work intensification. But over the longer term, it appears likely that developing such participatory and representative mechanisms will prove increasingly important to those firms that wish to compete on the high road of innovation.

The 1998 Workplace Employment Relations Survey (WERS)

The fourth workplace survey – renamed from the Workplace Industrial Relations Survey (WIRS) to the Workplace Employee Relations Survey (WERS) – was undertaken in 1998. Working on the results of this latest survey we found that for private sector firms there was a clear link between the use of more human resource practices and greater employee involvement on the one hand, and positive employee satisfaction and commitment, higher productivity and better financial performance on the other (Guest *et al.*, 2000).[7] Although the results confirmed the positive link between the greater use of human resource practices and a range of outcomes that has been found by other studies on both sides of the Atlantic, the adoption of such practices in the private sector was found to be low. More than half the practices were reported in only 41 per cent of private sector workplaces and in 70 per cent of public sector workplaces. (We return to the reasons for this low take-up in the section on 'Corporate governance'.) We also found that they were more likely to be reported at workplaces where there is a more sophisticated personnel department and a strong trade union presence.

A separate analysis of WERS (Brown *et al.*, 2000) also found that where trade unions are present, employers are more likely to comply with the law regulating employment contracts than they are in the absence of trade union organizations. They are also more likely to improve on those minimum conditions that are required by law.

The WERS asked employees to report their attitudes – on job satisfaction and organizational commitment, on their perceptions of autonomy and discretion, and on the extent of involvement and consultation. Employees were found to display moderate levels of satisfaction and commitment. However, employees reported generally low levels of influence over their work tasks and low levels of consultation by management. WERS suggested that while specific communication practices have no direct association with employee attitudes, an informal climate of involvement and consultation is associated with employee satisfaction and commitment. This reinforces the point made above that it is not whether specific practices are adopted or used that is important, it is *how* they are used, what the *motive* for their use is, and whether their use contributes to a positive climate of involvement and consultation or not, that are the key factors.

HRM and corporate performance

We followed up this analysis of WERS with our own survey. Our aim was to talk with managers responsible for human resource management and also with the Chief Executive Officer (CEO) from the same company. We conducted interviews with 610 managers responsible for human resource management and 462 CEOs from a cross-section of companies in the United Kingdom. The matched pairs were achieved in 237 companies. This is probably the largest company-level survey of this subject to have been undertaken in the United Kingdom to date.[8]

Our analysis of the HR managers' responses indicated a clear association between the number of HR practices adopted and the effectiveness of these practices. Both, in turn, were significantly associated with the HR managers' perceptions of positive employee attitudes and behaviour – which were in turn found to be linked to higher productivity, quality of goods and services and financial results (Guest *et al.*, 2000).

The CEOs' responses indicated a similar set of links except that they gave more emphasis to the effectiveness (i.e. the quality) rather than the number (i.e. the quantity) of human resource practices. The emphasis in our work on the *effectiveness* of practices rather than simply whether they are adopted or not is, we think, an important aspect that deserves to be taken seriously in all such work. Again, this supports the above point that the motivation behind the adoption of practices is the key.

Despite these 'positive' findings, our survey indicated a generally low use of human resource practices. We covered nine areas of HR practice to reflect high commitment/high performance management, namely recruitment and selection, training and development, appraisal, financial flexibility, job design, concern with quality, communication and consultation, employment security, and single status and harmonization. From these areas, we concentrated on a key list of eighteen typical practices. For example, the area of appraisal included two practices: firstly, the percentage of non-managerial employees who have their performance regularly (e.g. quarterly or annually) and formally appraised, and secondly, the percentage of non-managerial employees regularly receiving feedback on job performance from multiple sources (such as line managers, customers and so on).

We found that only one per cent of companies had more than three-quarters of the eighteen measures in place and applying to most workers. Only 26 per cent of companies apply more than half of them. At the other extreme, 20 per cent of organizations make extensive use of less than a quarter of these practices. These results – based on the descriptions and judgements of a large group of senior managers in British industry – support the view that the effective use of a wide range of progressive human resource practices is linked to superior performance. This link includes taking seriously into account employee attitudes and behaviour.

Labour market dynamics and innovation

We undertook a separate survey of firms designed to allow us to examine the following issues in particular:

i   What are the relationships between the various forms of labour market flexibility on the one hand and firms' innovative activities on the other?
ii Are innovating firms more likely to use high performance/innovative work practices?
iii Are there complementarities between practices and, if so, are the firms that use complementary work practices more likely to innovate?
iv How do different aspects of industrial relations affect innovative activities?

This survey was also designed to enable comparisons to be drawn between our results and other studies that examine, to varying degrees, these issues. A further objective of the survey was to extend and test our own previous work reported in the sections on 'Workplace Industrial Relations Survey' and 'Worker participation and representation', which used WIRS3 to examine the relations between HRM practices, labour market flexibility, industrial relations and innovation, and which applied Ichniowski *et al.'s* (1997) methodology of grouping individual work practices into HRM systems. We surveyed a stratified sample of publicly quoted UK manufacturing and service sector firms with more than fifty employees. Interviews were conducted with the Director of Human Resources/Personnel/Employee Relations.[9]

In total, 934 individuals were asked to complete the survey. Of these, 559 declined, nineteen agreed but subsequently failed to complete the interview, and 369 interviews were completed successfully. As a result of missing data, 361 of the total number of responses were usable – a response rate of 39 per cent.

Manufacturing companies were more likely to agree to participate in the survey (with 55 per cent agreeing) compared to service sector companies (with only 24 per cent agreeing). The analysis of firms' innovative behaviour reported in this section was therefore restricted to the 242 manufacturing sector establishments only.[10]

We found a particularly significant relation between product innovation and market share, suggesting a strong relationship between market demand and product innovation (Michie and Sheehan, forthcoming). In relation to our labour flexibility variables, our results indicated that increased *functional* flexibility was significantly positively correlated with all categories of innovation, and in particular with process innovation. High labour turnover was found to be significantly *negatively* correlated with all categories of innovation, and in particular with process innovation. In other words, there appeared to be a strong relation between a high level of functional flexibility and low labour turnover on the one hand, and the probability of introducing a process innovation on the other hand. The use of 'non-traditional' types of contract – temporary, fixed-term, casual or seasonal contracts – was found to be *negatively* correlated with all categories of innovation combined, although not significantly so with product innovation taken alone. The use of part-time employees was found to be negatively correlated with all categories of innovation, significantly so for process innovation.

Labour market deregulation may have 'restored management's right to manage', but it is only some managers who have sought to take advantage of this new-found ease of using 'flexible' labour through part-time and temporary contracts and the like, and these firms have proved to be less innovative than those firms that declined to take such a route. The more innovative firms have been those that have passed up the use of these newly – or at least more readily – available 'flexible' labour practices, resulting from labour market deregulation, and instead have pursued the sort of functional flexibility associated not with short-term and temporary contracts but on the contrary with employment security.

Trade union recognition was found to be *positively* correlated with all categories of innovation, significantly so for the general category of having innovated, and particularly so for product innovation. The difference we find in the significance in the relation between trade unionism on the one hand and either product or process innovation on the other, may reflect the following. We might expect a positive impact from trade unions on product innovation, both proactively through trade unions encouraging management to invest in new product design and models, and also more structurally, by cutting off the 'low road' option of management getting by in the short term with the existing product range through squeezing wage costs. To some extent, the same mechanisms would operate to also encourage process innovation. But process innovation also includes a range of different workplace changes some of which may be quite harmful to, and therefore resisted by, trade union members. The 'process innovation' measure will thus include some developments that would be encouraged by trade unions and others that would be resisted, leading to no overall correlation either way.

We repeated the same sort of exercise as reported in the section on 'WIRS3', of testing for 'bundles' of human resource practices, and found that the use of such bundles of innovative work practices was significantly positively correlated with all categories of innovation, especially process innovation. Firms that incorporated at least one component from each of our HRM policy areas were found to be 34 per cent more likely to innovate compared to firms that used no innovative work practices.

Overall, this survey of firms demonstrated that functionally flexible employees, low labour turnover, the presence of a trade union and the use of progressive work practices are significantly positively correlated with innovation. In contrast, the use of 'flexible' work practices (proxied by contract type) was found to be significantly negatively correlated with overall innovation (and particularly so with process innovation). The use of part-time employees was also negatively correlated with innovation, significantly so for process innovation. This survey of firms thus reinforces our initial results from WIRS3 reported in the sections on 'Workplace Industrial Relations Survey' and 'Worker participation and representation', that there is no evidence whatsoever that the sort of 'flexibility' that results from labour market deregulation leads to a more innovative economy. Far from the creation of such 'flexibility' causing increased innovation, the correlation between the two is found to be negative.

Labour markets and corporate performance

We also used this survey of firms to test for corporate performance more generally. The most common measures of performance in this literature are labour productivity; measures of quality and financial performance; employee turnover; absenteeism; and industrial disputes. Our survey looked at relative financial performance, labour productivity and quality of product (as well as innovation, reported on in the previous section) as indicators of performance outcomes.

The results from analysing the survey returns indicated, in line with the findings for innovation, that 'low road' practices – short-term contracts, a lack of employer commitment to job security, low levels of training and so on – are *negatively* correlated to good corporate performance. In contrast, we found that 'high road' work practices – 'high commitment' organizations or 'transformed' workplaces – were *positively* correlated with good corporate performance.

The coefficient on trade union density from our regression results was negative for financial performance and positive for productivity and product quality (although none of these coefficients proved to be statistically significant). High levels of labour turnover were found to be significantly *negatively* correlated to labour productivity. The percentage of employees on temporary contracts and on fixed-term, casual or seasonal contracts was found to be significantly *negatively* correlated with labour productivity and product quality. The use of part-time employees was found to be significantly negatively correlated to labour productivity. In contrast, the use of fixed-term, casual or seasonal contracts and part-time employees was found to be positively correlated with *financial* performance. Thus, productivity and product quality suffer when firms make greater use of 'flexible' types of employment, although firms still profit from using two of the four types of flexibility, despite the other corporate outcomes being poorer (Michie and Sheehan, 2001).

This link to short-term financial gain may explain the use by some employers of these types of flexible work practices, particularly if under short-term financial pressure. But our results suggest two things. Firstly, following such a course of action is not a 'win win' situation. The gains that the companies can make in short-term profitability are not generated from improved productivity. Rather, they represent a shift to profits, given productivity – a shift, that is, away from employee earnings.

Secondly, while it is thus understandable why firms might resort to such practices, succumbing to such temptation is likely to prove to be self-defeating short-termist behaviour, to the detriment of all the other aspects of corporate performance – productivity, product quality and innovation – on which the firm's financial success itself is ultimately dependent.

Any view of deregulated labour markets creating an innovative and dynamic economy is thus found to be dangerously simplistic. Creating the right sort of flexibility can indeed pay dividends. Allow the wrong sort of flexibility and firms are tempted down a cul-de-sac that allows some short-term pay off by shifting the bargaining power in their favour against a more insecure workforce. But this is the wrong route to go down for improved productivity and competitiveness based on quality and high value added. In short, the sort of labour flexibility that the Government should be encouraging requires investment in people.

The real danger that simple minded policies for labour market deregulation pose is in undermining the confidence of firms to invest in their own workforce, for fear that increased labour turnover may lead to the returns on such investment being lost. Labour deregulation may thus inadvertently lead to a lower level of the sort of labour flexibility that is associated with innovation and good corporate performance. A regulated labour market on the other hand can actually underpin the sort of investment by firms in their own workforce that creates the 'win win' outcome of positive human resource management practices such as high levels of training and involvement, along with improved corporate outcomes in terms of productivity and profitability.

Corporate governance

Given the clear benefits in terms of corporate outcomes from investing in progressive human resource practices, why do more firms not do so? There are no doubt a number of factors, not least is the fact that in the United Kingdom at least, successive Governments have called – and legislated – for greater employee flexibility and have included within this the factors associated with labour market deregulation that lead in precisely the opposite direction, from the sort of investment in progressive human resource practices required. While the survey work reported above finds trade union organizations to be positively correlated with innovation and product quality, labour market deregulation has undermined the ability of trade unions to organize. While progressive human resource practices include employment security pledges, labour market deregulation has pushed in the opposite direction.

In addition, as argued by Sue Konzelmann and Bob Forrant (Ch. 8), corporate governance structures may be biased towards Boards focussing on the short-term costs involved in these progressive human resource practices, and the short-term financial gains that our own survey results did indeed indicate were available via the low-road option, and against a proper appreciation of the potential gains over the longer term from investing in the high road option of high commitment work practices, involving training, consultation, employee participation, employment security pledges and so on.

Interestingly, the UK government has accepted that there are performance benefits to be gained from increasing employee commitment. Tax incentives were introduced in the 2000 Budget to encourage the formation of approved employee shareholder trusts. The idea is that if employees receive shares in the firm, this will increase their commitment to the organization. This initiative needs to be developed, though, along three additional lines.

Firstly, the results reported above demonstrate that what is needed for improved corporate outcomes are not single measures but rather self-reinforcing bundles of measures. Thus, employee share ownership needs to be accompanied by other progressive human resource measures if the desired organizational commitment effects are to be generated.

Secondly, the important factor in influencing outcomes is not whether a certain measure is introduced or not introduced, but rather the way in which it is introduced, the degree of commitment behind it and so on. In the case of employee shareholder trusts, the positive organizational commitment effects that the Government hope will be generated will be more likely to the extent that employees feel that their shareholder trust has an effective voice within the company. For this to happen, these trusts need to be democratised. At present they are a top–down mechanism for rewarding employees in a tax efficient way. The trustees can be appointed by the firm's management and can be removed by the management at any time. The trustees should instead be elected by the employee members of the trust.

This then links, thirdly, to the issue of corporate governance. It has long been acknowledged that corporate governance in the United Kingdom is unsatisfactory. There have been repeated Commissions of enquiry to investigate and report on this. One of the key problems is that the majority shareholders – the financial institutions – show little interest in how the companies that they collectively own are governed. What is needed are institutional shareholders that do have an interest. Democratic employee shareholder trusts could well play just such a role.[11]

Conclusions

This chapter has examined the complex links between labour markets, human resource management, industrial relations and corporate performance. As reported above (sections on 'Workplace Industrial Relation Survey' and 'Worker participation and representation'), we first investigated these issues utilising the existing data sources. This work suggested that the links between what is often broadly referred to as labour 'flexibility' on the one hand, and corporate innovation and performance on the other, depended crucially on the *nature* of this flexibility. Specifically, the sort of 'hire-and-fire' flexibility that firms might be tempted to resort to given a deregulated labour market – particularly if put under short term pressure (by, e.g. an uncompetitive exchange rate) – was found to be negatively correlated with innovative activity. These results led us to want to investigate the issue in greater detail than the existing data sources have hitherto allowed. We therefore designed our own survey questionnaire, albeit attempting to keep this as comparable as possible with previous empirical work in the area (which has mostly been on US data).

We thus undertook a relatively large-scale survey of firms to collect the data necessary to properly test these links between labour market and human resource factors on the one hand, and corporate outcomes on the other. Analysing the data from this survey, our results suggest that policies aimed at increasing labour market 'flexibility' (proxied by contract type and part-time employment), while in some cases having a positive effect on short-term financial performance, invariably have a *negative* effect on labour productivity, product quality and innovation.

Consistent with a growing body of evidence, our results indicate that firms that use 'high commitment' HRM systems perform better than those that do not.[12] This effect was particularly strong in relation to innovation. Moreover, the correlation between performance and work practices was greatest where complementarities amongst practices were greatest. These results, using the data from our own survey which was designed both to test these relations and to be consistent with the work undertaken by others on US data, finds that the results of that US work are consistent with the relationships for firms in Britain, whereby investment in what we have termed 'high road' labour practices do bring a payoff in terms of improved corporate outcomes.

Finally, testing for the effects of competitive pressure on the firms we sampled finds different effects depending on the source of this competition, and in particular on whether it comes from domestic competitors or overseas. This underlines the importance of looking behind general categories – whether they be the degree of competition, or the degree of labour flexibility – to analyse the *qualitative* aspects of such phenomena. The different 'HRM Systems' analysed above all contain practices which might be encouraged through public policy aimed either at explicitly encouraging flexibility or else through a general deregulation of the labour market. This latter approach may reduce a firms' commitment to employment security. But in terms of creating an innovative economy, such an outcome of labour market deregulation would most certainly be creating a low road cul-de-sac. As reported above, firms characterised by such a system are 34 per cent *less* likely to innovate than are firms that follow what we characterise as a 'high road' approach to investing in flexibility.

To return to the question posed at the beginning of this chapter, of whether reducing constraints on management will improve performance, the answer is clearly, 'no – not necessarily'. It all depends on how those constraints influence firm behaviour, and how conversely managers will manage in the absence of such constraints. An early example of a Government introducing legislation to constrain 'management's right to manage' – as it would have been referred to in the 1980s – was the introduction of the Wages Councils in England at the beginning of the twentieth century. Explaining the decision, Winston Churchill did not seek to pretend that this would not act as a constraint on employers – on the contrary, this was its purpose. It was to constrain firms from going down the low road of wage cutting, to prevent, as Churchill explained, the good employer from being undercut by the bad, and the bad by the very worst. Precisely the same constraints are required today, to prevent the good employer being undercut by the bad, not only in terms of wages but also in terms of work practices. The results reported above indicate that constraining managers' right to manage badly – by which we mean taking the short-term option of boosting profits by labour practices which undermine product quality, innovation and productivity – is in the collective long-term interests not only of employees but also of the companies being managed. These necessary constraints can be provided by trade union organisation, by Government legislation, by appropriate corporate governance structures, and perhaps by employee shareholder trusts playing an active role in companies as good corporate citizens.[13] The 1980s' belief that what was needed was labour market deregulation, increased labour flexibility and the 'restoration of management's right to manage' was simply that decade's version of what Wilkinson had warned against as the 'increasingly dogmatic reassertion by a growing proportion of economists of the beneficial effects of the invisible hand of market forces'. The results of the work reported above fully supports the argument in Wilkinson (1983) quoted at the start of this chapter, that these assertions regarding the beneficial effects of the invisible hand of market forces – to which we would add the supposedly beneficial effects of labour market deregulation, labour flexibility and restoring management's right to manage – 'are based not on a careful examination of how economies actually work and have developed but on abstract, a priori reasoning about how they should operate'.

Notes

1 The work reported in this chapter was funded by the Leverhulme Trust (grant F112/AL), the University of London Central Research Fund, and the ESRC's Future of Work Programme (grant L212252040).

2 'There is unanimity among industrial relations specialists that WIRS provides the most authoritative picture of employee–management relations available' (Fernie and Metcalf).

3 See Millward *et al.* (1992) for full details of the third survey and information on the previous WIRSs conducted in 1980 and 1984. See also the special issue of the *British Journal of Industrial Relations*, June 1993.

4 The sampling frame for WIRS3 was the Employment Department's 1987 Census of Employment (CoE). A 'census unit' is an establishment-based measure of individual places of employment at a single address, covering all employees of the identified employer at that address. The CoE file contains data on just over 142,000 establishments and was broadly representative of the population of manufacturing and service sectors, and public and private sector establishments in Britain in 1987. To ensure a high response rate to WIRS, larger establishments were deliberately oversampled but it is

a straightforward matter to make WIRS3 into a nationally representative sample of workplaces in Britain by using a set of weighting factors. Such weights were applied to the data used in our analysis.

5 Maura Sheehan changed her name to Maura Sheehan Quinn in 2001, hence the change in referencing from Michie and Sheehan up to 2000, to Michie and Quinn thereafter.

6 See, for example, the various contributions to Pagano and Rowthorn (1996), and also Winter (1987).

7 This work was funded by the Chartered Institute of Personnel and Development.

8 This work was funded by the ESRC's Future of Work research programme.

9 Where this person was not available, an alternative senior manager was interviewed, namely the Company Chairperson, Managing Director, Chief Executive, Manufacturing Director or Production Director. For 73 companies, the HR person was unable to answer parts of the questionnaire (e.g. some of the questions about performance and innovation). In such cases, the name of the most appropriate person in the company was obtained from the HR person and this person was contacted. Completed questionnaires were obtained for 61 of the 73 companies concerned.

10 This survey was funded by The Leverhulme Trust with co-funding from the University of London Central Research Fund and the Royal Economic Society.

11 This is argued in detail in Michie and Oughton (2001).

12 See, for example, Appelbaum *et al.* (2000) and Baker, T. (1999).

13 'Collective shareholder trusts could signify a shared interest in the long-term success of the organization while at the same time providing a collective voice at Boardroom level for the members of such trusts – namely the employees who are generating wealth for the company.' TUC General Secretary, John Monks, Foreword to Michie and Oughton (2001).

References

Appelbaum, E., Bailey, T., Berg, P. and Kalleberg, A. (2000) *Manufacturing Advantage: Why High-Performance Work Systems Pay Off*. Washington DC: Economic Policy Institute.

Baker, T. (1999) *Doing Well by Doing Good: The Bottom Line on Workplace Practices*. Washington DC: Economic Policy Institute.

Black, S. and Lynch, L. (1997) 'How to compete: the impact of workplace practices and information technology on productivity, National Bureau of Economic Research, Working Paper No. 6120.

Brown, W., Deakin, S., Nash, D., Oxenbridge, S., Pratten, C. and Ryan, P. (2000) 'The future of collectivism in employment', *The Future of Work Bulletin*, Issue 2, Swindon: ESRC.

Daniel, W. (1987) *Workplace Industrial Relations and Technical Change*. London: Frances Pinter and Policy Studies Institute.

Department of Trade and Industry (DTI) (1995) *Competitiveness: Forging Ahead*. London: HMSO.

Fernie, S. and Metcalf, D. (1995) 'Participation, contingent pay, representation and workplace performance: Evidence from Great Britain', *British Journal of Industrial Relations*, 33(2).

Guest, D., Michie, J., Sheehan, M. and Conway, N. (2000) *Employee Relations, HRM and Business Performance: An analysis of the 1998 Workplace Employee Relations Survey*. London: Chartered Institute of Personnel and Development.

Guest, D., Michie, J., Sheehan, M., Conway, N. and Metochi, M. (2000) *Human Resource Management and Performance: First Findings from the Future of Work Study*. London: Chartered Institute of Personnel and Development.

Ichniowski, C., Shaw, K. and Prennushi, G. (1997) 'The effects of human resource management on productivity: a study of steel finishing line', *American Economic Review*, 87(3), 291–313.

Machin, S. and Wadhwani, S. (1991) 'The effects of unions on investment and innovation: Evidence from WIRS', *The Economic Journal*, 101(2).

Michie, J. and Oughton, C. (2001) *Employees Direct: Shareholder Trusts, Business Performance and Corporate Governance*. London: Mutuo.

Michie, J. and Sheehan, M. (1999a) 'HRM practices, R&D expenditure and innovative investment: Evidence from the UK's Workplace Industrial Relations Survey (WIRS)', *Industrial and Corporate Change*, 8(2), 211–34.

Michie, J. and Sheehan, M. (1999b) No innovation without representation? An analysis of participation, representation, R&D and innovation', *Economic Analysis*, 2(2), 85–98.

Michie, J. and Sheehan, M. (2001) 'Labour market flexibility, human resource management and corporate performance', *British Journal of Management*, 12(4), 287–306.

Michie, J. and Sheehan, M. (2003) 'Labour market deregulation, 'Flexibility' and innovation', *Cambridge Journal of Economics*, 27(1).

Michie, J. and Wilkinson, F. (1995) 'Wages, government policy and unemployment', *Review of Political Economy*, 7, 133–49.

Millward, N., Stevens, M., Smart, D. and Hawes, W. (1992) *Workplace Industrial Relations in Transition*. Dartmouth: Aldershot.

Millward, N. (1994) *The New Industrial Relations?* London: Policy Studies Institute.

Pagano, U. and Rowthorn, R. E. (eds) (1996) *Democracy and Efficiency in the Economic Enterprise*. London: Routledge.

Wilkinson, Frank (1983) 'Productive systems', *Cambridge Journal of Economics*, 7(3/4), 413–29.

Winter, S. (1987) 'Knowledge and competence as strategic assets', in Teese, D. (ed.), *The Competitive Challenge: Strategies for Industrial Innovation and Renewal*, Cambridge, MA: Ballinger.

11 The political economy of the minimum wage

Peter Brosnan[1]

Introduction

The last fifty years has seen the development and growth of minimum wage legislation in a wide range of countries. The United Kingdom (1999) and Ireland (2000) are the latest countries to guarantee a minimum level of pay for their employed populations. Just over a hundred countries have ratified International Labour Organisation (ILO) Convention 26 (Convention Concerning the Creation of Minimum Wage-fixing Machinery) since it was adopted in 1928.[2] Despite the widespread ratification of these conventions, minimum wages remain controversial and the international trend is to reduce both the value of statutory minimum wages and their coverage (Standing, 1999).

This chapter examines some of the most important aspects of the political economy of minimum wages.[3] It begins by briefly sketching out the historical development of minimum wage-fixing arrangements. It then examines the case for minimum wages: minimum wages as a tool to reduce inequality, to reduce poverty and to enhance productive systems. The last section considers some difficulties in implementing minimum wage legislation. The debate over alleged disemployment effects is reviewed briefly, as is the relation between minimum wage changes and inflation. The political economy of minimum wages as viewed by employers, trade unions and government are also considered.

Development of minimum wage laws

There have been various forms of minimum wage during the last 4,000 years, but the first of the modern laws providing for minimum wages were adopted in New Zealand in 1894 (Starr, 1981). The early New Zealand legislation provided for a system of dispute resolution which led to awards that set wages and conditions for the category of workers involved in the dispute. The awards applied to all employers, even if they were not a party to the original dispute. Similar systems were set up within a few years in the Australian states, and the principles were enshrined in the Australian Constitution which was adopted in 1901.

Broader legislation was implemented by the state of Massachusetts in 1912. This legislation gave protection to minors and females. Nine other US states followed suit over the next decade, as did most of the Canadian provinces (Russell, 1991).[4] A federal minimum wage was introduced in the United States in 1938, although overage was limited, initially, mainly to firms in heavy industry (Reynolds *et al.*, 1987). The United Kingdom introduced legislation in 1909 to prevent 'sweating', and the Trades Board Acts (1918) provided mechanisms to establish minimum wages in particular occupations. Other European countries introduced minimum wage legislation in the first decades of the twentieth century, mainly to protect homeworkers. France (1915) was the first followed by Norway and Austria (1918) (Starr, 1981). These European experiments, in common with the systems established in New Zealand and Australia guaranteed minimum wages for the workers covered, but fell short of being national systems of minimum wages. Minimum wage laws with broad coverage were implemented much later. New Zealand and Luxembourg each introduced a national minimum wage in 1945, France in 1950, Spain in 1963 and Belgium in 1975.

Although the European countries were notably active in legislating for minimum wages, a remarkable spread of other countries acted to guarantee minimum rates of pay. South American countries, influenced at least in part by papal pronouncements on the rights of working people (Starr, 1981), were among the first. Mexico introduced a statutory minimum wage in 1937 to reflect a guarantee of the 1917 Constitution. Other early legislators include Uruguay (1923), Peru (1916), Cuba (1934) and Brazil (1938).

Today most countries have some form of minimum wage. Asia stands out as the region where minimum wages are less common. India and Sri Lanka, have minimum wage laws which predate independence, while the more industrialised countries such as Japan and Korea adopted appropriate legislation; Japan in 1959 and Korea in 1988.

Within the diversity of international experience with minimum wage arrangements, there are six broad strategies: (a) reliance on collective bargaining but with extensions of collective agreements to other workers (e.g. Germany, Italy); (b) selective intervention with orders that provide for specific legal minima in certain industries or occupations (e.g. Australia, Fiji, Sri Lanka); (c) a statutory national minimum wage with exemption for certain industries or workers (Canada, Korea, United States); (d) a national minimum wage negotiated through collective bargaining but with full, or near full, cover (Belgium, Greece); (e) a statutory national minimum wage with full application (e.g. Brazil, France, Hungary, Luxembourg, Netherlands, New Zealand, Portugal, Spain, United Kingdom, Ireland); (f) a combination of (e) and (b); that is, a statutory minimum wage with full applica-tion which acts as a floor, but additional higher minima in certain industries or occupations (e.g. Kenya, Malta, Mexico, Tanzania, Zambia).

Why minimum wages?

Minimum wages are a direct attempt to combat low pay. The ILO acted within its first decade to adopt a convention on minimum wages (ILO Convention 26 (1928)). The ILO's concern was humanitarian but it was also concerned to prevent social dumping – using low pay to gain a price advantage in international trade. Motives for introducing minimum wages are usually built 'upon three theses: justice, the reduction of poverty and economics' (McMahon, 1991: 312). These three are clearly related and incorporated into the concept of productive systems. To simplify the discussion, the subsections which follow, examine each of these separately. We first look at the case for a minimum wage based on notions of fairness, we then consider the role of a minimum wage in reducing poverty. The third subsection titled 'Minimum wages and productive systems' focuses on the economic aspects, and discusses Wilkinson's (1984) argument that low pay allows the survival of outmoded productive systems; consequently minimum wages have a role to play in encouraging productive systems to be more efficient.

Minimum wages and justice

The recipients of low pay in developed countries appear to be more or less the same whichever country is studied. The low-paid are more likely to be women, young and elderly workers, or part-time workers (on a per-hour basis). They are more likely to be found in retail, distribution, hospitality, agriculture and manufacturing (e.g. Brosnan and Wilkinson, 1989; Rubery, 1995; Buchanan and Watson, 1997). Furthermore, Rubery (1995) suggests the low-paid are also more likely to be found in small firms. Rainnie (1989) also finds this and argues that small business operators take strategic decisions to pay low wages, even though the trade-off may be higher labour turnover. This is so, but low pay does not always result from an employer's inability to pay. Many of the industries where low pay is found are heavily monopolised and owned by transnational companies. This is the case in contract cleaning; it is also true of retailing and catering.

Some economists, following Hicks (1932) would argue that the higher incidence of low pay among these groups is proof of their low productivity. This is clearly a circular argument – low productivity deserves low pay, these people receive low pay, therefore they must have low productivity. A more thorough analysis of what these people do at work reveals a different picture. When job content and the tasks performed are examined, it is found that many of the lowest paid jobs require more skill and carry much more responsibility than many highly paid jobs (Blackburn and Mann, 1979; Craig *et al.*, 1982). In fact, substantial parts of the economy depend on people who are very low-paid. For example some very lucrative professional occupations pay very low wages to female assistants (Brosnan and Wilkinson, 1989).

Low pay is not the just reward for lazy or incompetent workers. It is the product of a social and economic structure which does not allow all workers to compete on equal terms. Some jobs are marked as deserving relatively low pay, while some workers are less preferred by employers, or are in circumstances which prevent them applying for the better jobs. Thus, the privileged categories of worker get access to the well-paid jobs while the unprivileged get access only to what is left – the poorer-paid jobs. The result is that 'workers with … equal skills and abilities are available at widely different prices' (Wilkinson, 1984: 422).

Many of the poorer-paid jobs are those which historically were associated with domestic work or the servant 'classes' – caring, serving, cleaning, cooking or household (or office) management – are afforded low status (Brosnan and Wilkinson, 1988). At the same time, other jobs are designated as 'women's work', or requiring alleged feminine traits (dexterity, patience, caring etc.) and are classified as low skilled and paid accordingly. Amongst the 'male' jobs those which require skills originally used in agriculture, such as gardening, working with animals, road mending and building are also downgraded and paid poorly. Where women perform some of these jobs, for example, working with pets or as an assistant to a veterinary surgeon, the pay may well be even lower still (Brosnan and Wilkinson, 1989).

The jobs which are marked as low-paid are generally filled by people who are, to varying degrees, disadvantaged in the competition for better paid jobs. As Frank Wilkinson (1984) commented 'It is significant that these jobs tend to be filled by women, racial minorities or other "socially disadvantaged" groups' (Wilkinson, 1984: 423). The disadvantage which these groups face is compounded by the difficulties they face in organising for collective bargaining. Their personal circumstances (e.g. the need to care for children) often make it difficult to take part in trade union activity, and the jobs themselves are sometimes structured so that trade union organisation is difficult – jobs which are part-time, in small workplaces, or involving tasks which isolate the workers from each other (e.g. cleaning, driving etc.). Moreover, as Wilkinson (1984) observed in the United Kingdom, it is 'quite usual … to separate such jobs as cleaning, canteen and low-grade clerical work from the main company agreement or for such tasks to be contracted out so that they are lower paid and enjoy less favourable working conditions' (Wilkinson, 1984: 423). Thus, for these low-paid workers, their organisational disadvantages compound their social disadvantages.

The social and economic structure is clearly unjust in that it forces many workers to accept low-paid jobs where their skills are not rewarded. But it is also unjust in that the better paid benefit from the cheap labour of the low-paid. The well-paid benefit from cheaper services where they employ the low-paid directly (e.g. as cleaners). They also benefit if products or services they buy are 'subsidised' by low pay. Thus middle-income households benefit from cheaper restaurant meals, hotel services and the like whose prices are kept down by the low pay of the workers who produce these services. To the extent that the public sector utilises low-paid employees, this delivers a disguised bonus in either lower taxes or a wider range of government services. It is ironic that many of the services consumed by the wealthy are provided by the lowest paid workers.[5]

A minimum wage reduces the extent of low pay and improves the income distribution by truncating the distribution at the level of the minimum wage. Assuming full application and rigorous enforcement, all those earning below the minimum will be brought up to it. Furthermore, those earning at or just above the minimum may also receive increases if their employers have a policy of paying above the minimum. This latter behaviour was observed in the United States when the minimum wage was increased from $3.35 to $3.80 in April 1990. Reviewing the literature on minimum wages and income dispersion, the OECD conclude that 'almost all studies find that minimum wages do lead to a compression of the earnings distribution' (OECD, 1988a: 49) and that countries with higher minima relative to the median have a lower dispersion of earnings (OECD, 1988a).

Introducing a minimum wage does not, by itself, ensure a fairer wage structure. The minimum wage must be enforced, it must be set at a level which ensures that no one is low-paid, and it must be adjusted regularly to take account of changing price levels and movements in other wages. Furthermore, there is no agreed level at which a minimum wage will make wages just. The Council of Europe (1977) suggests the minimum wage be set at 68 per cent of average full-time earnings. Many European countries have failed to attain this level, and few outside Europe would have done so. The OECD (1988b) notes that statutory minima range from '20–33% of the median earnings of full-time workers in the Czech Republic, Japan and Spain to around 60% in Belgium and France'. On the whole, governments and their advisers are timid when it comes to setting minimum wage levels. They are wary of upsetting established differentials, and they tend to believe the disemployment story (discussed below). Nonetheless, provided a minimum wage is set, and set at a reasonable level, it will reduce the extent of wage injustice.

Clearly members of the groups that are most likely to be low-paid will be the principal beneficiaries of a minimum wage or any increase in an established minimum. Thus a realistic minimum would assist governments attain objectives of equal pay for work of equal value. Equal pay for work of equal value would be attained in one stroke for a substantial proportion of women each time the minimum wage is increased. This would not solve the problem of devalued skill content but would remove some of the financial disparity. The gap between the earnings of many other women and their male comparators would be reduced too as those women moved up to the higher minimum. Thus a realistic minimum wage should be an integral part of any campaign for equal pay.

Minimum wages and poverty[6]

A minimum wage is one crucial component of ensuring adequate living standards, and reducing the extent of poverty. It is almost stating the obvious to say that the greater the extent of the low pay problem in a society, the greater the degree of poverty. Nonetheless critics of minimum wages argue that a minimum wage does little to relieve poverty since, on the one hand, most of the poor are not in regular employment (e.g. Johnston and Stark, 1991; Standing, 1999) and on the other hand, some of the lower paid belong to well-off households.

This latter argument defines poverty in terms of households rather than individuals. Clearly, household income is a major factor in determining the consumption levels of individuals, but personal poverty can exist in moderately affluent households. Teenagers, the bulk of the low-paid, do not always receive handouts from their parents, even if the latter are well paid. In any case, if they are forced into this position through low pay, it imposes a financial burden on parents and destroys the independence of working teenagers. A similar argument applies with respect to low-paid women whose husbands are well paid. Despite equal effort in the workplace, the husband is able to make a greater financial contribution to the household and the wife's status and independence is therefore severely diminished. To focus on the income of a person's relatives is to ignore the injustice of not providing an adequate minimum wage. As Rubery (1995) points out, the principle of ' "a fair day's work for a fair day's pay" ... (should) ... apply irrespective of an individual's family circumstances' (Rubery, 1995: 545).

While the dispersion of earnings becomes less after an increase in the minimum wage (Machin and Manning, 1994; Card and Krueger, 1995a; DiNardo *et al.*, 1996), the effect of an increase in minimum wage levels on the distribution of income is less clear cut. Neumark and Wascher (1997) conclude, with respect to the United States, that an increase in the minimum wage has no effect on the incidence of poverty, whereas Card and Krueger (1995a) and Mishel *et al.* (1995) find that it reduces poverty. One reason the US minimum wage is relatively ineffective in reducing poverty is just that it is set so low (Pollin and Luce, 1998). UK research indicated that while a minimum wage would benefit poor households it would not be sufficient to overcome poverty (Sutherland, 1995; Gosling, 1996). Richardson and Harding (1998) reach a similar conclusion with respect to Australia.

In order to overcome the problem of household poverty, many governments have made family income supplements available to families which have adults in employment. These benefits impose high marginal tax rates on recipients because the benefit is abated and eventually withdrawn as their income increases. These benefits catch low-paid workers in the poverty trap – if they improve their gross pay, they barely increase their net income as a result of higher direct taxes and loss of means-tested benefits. The system also provides a disincentive for other family members to join the labour market since they commence work on extremely high marginal tax rates.

To the extent that the state meets a part of the consumption needs of the low-paid out of taxation, it reduces the pressure on employers to pay a reasonable living wage. Any difference between what the worker receives and what the state deems as necessary is made up in transfer payments. The beneficiary of the welfare benefit is not the worker, but their employer who receives an unrecorded subsidy. Indeed, when the social welfare payment is conditional on employment, the minimum wage is the only obstacle to negative wages, that is, workers actually paying employers to give them a job so as to provide access to social welfare (Brosnan and Wilkinson, 1988). Thus the minimum wage has a crucial role in limiting the transfer of social welfare benefits to employers in the guise of low pay.

Much of this may remain hidden from individual workers who struggle to understand the complexities of benefit systems and their interaction with the wage system. To the extent that income becomes separated in the worker's mind from their efforts at work, the effect may be to minimise dissatisfaction with the employer's pay policy. Thus, the subsidies remove the incentive to organise collectively, and they therefore undermine trade unionism making the perpetuation of low pay a stronger probability.

Minimum wages and social welfare are essential complements. While a realistic minimum wage will not overcome poverty among the non-working population, it ensures that no individual worker is forced into poverty due to inadequate pay for their labour. However, unless the minimum wage were set at a very high level, the benefit system remains a necessary component of any policy designed to prevent household poverty. Such policies can only be made effective if they accompanied by a realistic minimum wage.

Minimum wages and productive systems

Firm level

A realistic minimum wage is an essential element in any strategy involving social welfare and labour market policies if that packet is to be both socially equitable and economically efficient. In his original exposition of *Productive systems*, Frank Wilkinson (1984) argues that: 'The ability to take advantage of low pay segments of the labour market adjusts the terms of trade in favour of particular productive systems' (Wilkinson, 1984: 423) and the 'availability of disadvantaged segments in the labour market provides the basis for survival of disadvantaged firms in the product market' (Wilkinson, 1984: 423). A minimum wage, provided it is set at an appropriate level, goes a long way towards altering the terms of trade between different systems, and making it more difficult for disadvantaged firms to rely on disadvantaged labour.

The idea that a minimum wage would pressure disadvantaged firms to become more efficient is not new. It has been a frequent claim of American unions and can be traced back atleast to Webb and Webb (1920). The Webbs observed that a 'Common Rule ... knocks another nail into the coffin of the least intelligent and worst-equipped employers in a trade' (Webb and Webb, 1920: 728–9).

Although low pay may allow badly organised firms, or firms with outdated equipment and methods, to survive and compete, these firms become snared in low productivity traps from which they have little incentive to escape. Their attention becomes concentrated on the very short run and they ignore the need for long-term investment, better production methods and the creation of new and better products or services. When their more efficient competitors adopt advanced technologies or introduce superior products or services, their only hope of survival is to be able to reduce wages further. A minimum wage offers protection to the labour force from this exploitative survival strategy, but it also forces the firm to find other solutions to their lack of competitiveness.

The disadvantaged firms that rely for survival on low pay are mainly in the private sector, but some are in the public sector. Public sector managers who are under pressure to deliver more services on a limited budget are in much the same position as the managers of low-productivity firms. Many of the services provided by central government agencies and local authorities use lowly paid workers in particular roles, for example, non-professionals in the health or education sectors – as a means of reducing costs.

Minimum wages serve a useful purpose in forcing inefficient productive systems to compete on a different basis than wage level. It forces them to invest, to innovate and to become more efficient. These strategies can produce a virtuous circle as the labour force see opportunities in the firm. Morale improves, labour turnover reduces, training becomes more worthwhile for both the employer and employee and this provides a further spur to productivity and innovation. In the public sector, minimum wages have the same effect of forcing managers to find better ways of doing things, and thus producing a more efficient service for the tax-payer.

In highly competitive industries, firms with low profit margins, particularly small firms, cannot increase wages because their competitors would be able to undercut them in the product market. However, a realistic minimum wage forces all firms to pay the minimum and thus takes wages out of competition. The timing of increases is important too. When a minimum wage is being introduced, or is being raised to a realistic level, a helpful strategy is to phase-in the increase in a series of well-publicised steps, such as the Republic of Ireland has done with its new minimum wage.[7] This way the firms affected can plan the adjustment.

The situation is different where the competition is from overseas. Here other government policies may be needed to induce the domestic industry to become more internationally competitive and to support them while they make the transition – policies such as subsidies on technical innovation, assistance with designs or marketing, and tax breaks during the transition period. The latter case highlights the need for the application of international labour standards in all countries, and for international trade and tariff protection to be linked to the exporting countries' implementation of the appropriate ILO conventions.

Economy level

The productive system approach stresses the interrelationship of local and national productive systems (Wilkinson, 1984). Thus the argument sketched above applies at the level of the nation as well as the firm. Countries which permit low wages encourage inefficient firms that are able to use the low pay to compete with more productive nations in the short run. But his strategy has a heavy price. As the high wage countries seek out more advanced labour-saving technologies, the low-wage countries find it more and more difficult to compete on the basis of labour cost, forcing them to reduce wages further. As wages go down, so does consumption; the countries in question are then forced into a downward spiral of low wages, low productivity, low consumption and declining GDP.[8]

A realistic minimum wage has a key role in preventing, or reversing such a trend. Moreover, a realistic minimum has other beneficial effects on the economy. The most immediate would be an increase in domestic consumption. Borooah and Sharpe (1986) have estimated marginal consumption propensities for each quintile using UK data. They determined that quintile Q2, where the low-paid are most likely to be found,[9] had marginal consumption propensities of 1.00, that is to say they would spend all of any increase in income. This contrast with the highest quintile whose propensity to consume was only 0.72. In a later article, Borooah (1988) found that the same quintiles had lower propensities to purchase imported goods. Thus an increase in the minimum wage would increase consumption by more than the increase in the wage bill, and that consumption would be more likely to be consumption of domestic goods and services. Therefore, increasing the minimum wage would add more to domestic demand than an increase in pay at other points in the income distribution.

This increase in consumption would increase employment, and there would be second-round (multiplier) effects as the newly employed spent their income. This would increase consumption and employment further. The extent to which this occurred would depend on the tax system and the pricing behaviour of firms making consumption goods. A less regressive tax system would ensure that an increase in the minimum wage flowed strongly into consumption expenditure.

If firms increased their prices to compensate for the higher wage bill, however, the boost to real consumption, and hence employment, would be less. Nonetheless, any increase in prices is likely to be small. Labour costs are only a small portion of total costs, even in labour intensive industries such as hairdressing. If firms maintain their profit mark-ups and intermediate goods increase in price too (from the effect of the higher minimum wage in other sectors), the increase in final prices should still be less than the increase in labour cost because a portion of final goods are comprised of imports.

The government's accounts are boosted by a higher minimum wage. An immediate benefit is that the higher minimum wage reduces the level of income support paid to the working poor, thus reversing the subsidy previously enjoyed by low-paying employers. The government also receives more income tax, consumption taxes and pays out less in unemployment benefits. In the longer term, the financial benefits to the government sector would be greater as employment continued to expand through the multiplier effect. The improvement in the government's fiscal position makes it more able to help industries which may require assistance in the transition to a higher level of minimum wage, and to better fund government agencies which would also be required to meet the higher minimum wage levels.

It must be stressed that most of the effects described above are fairly modest. Clearly the greater the increase in the minimum, the greater the effects. Also, the lower the subsequent adjustments in prices, the greater the employment increase and the subsequent benefits. While the effects described above are all beneficial, there is a case for staging increases to allow the economy and the component firms to adjust to the more equitable and more efficient regime.

Obstacles to an effective minimum wage

The difficulties in implementing an effective minimum wage mainly boil down to the lack of political will by governments. Governments and their advisers are confused by neoclassical economists who advise against minimum wages. Furthermore, trade unions are sometimes ambivalent and employer groups lobby against minimum wage increases.

The disemployment story

A frequent and confident assertion from neoclassical economists is that a minimum wage increases unemployment (e.g. Stigler, 1946). However, they are never able to explain exactly how this would occur, other than to rely on a two-dimensional diagram with supply and demand curves and an arbitrarily drawn line called the 'Minimum Wage'.

Empirical evidence against this proposition has long been available but has been ignored. As long ago as 1914, C. Smith contributed an article to the *Journal of Political Economy* which investigated the employment effects of Trade Boards which had been established in Ireland and Great Britain. Smith found that while workers' lives were improved by the increase in wages, it did not increase product prices and did not lead to the dismissal of the least productive workers (cited in McMahon, 1991). Many other studies have shown that there is no relationship, or that previously announced relationships are spurious (e.g. Eccles, 1984; Anyadike-Danes and Godley, 1989). These never put the matter to rest as this important piece of neoclassical doctrine 'cannot be wrong' and new data sets, and new econometric specifications are produced which purport to re-establish the status quo. Even so, Richard Freeman (1996), summarising the relevant literature, concludes: 'The debate over the employment effects of the minimum is a debate of values around zero' (Freeman, 1996: 642).

Over the last decade, some neoclassical economists have become less confident of the simple proposition that an increase in the minimum wage will produce an increase in unemployment. In large part, this is due to the work of Card and Krueger who have critiqued previous econometric studies. Card and Krueger (1995a) have argued that these studies, which show an adverse effect on teenage unemployment from an increase in the minimum wage, suffer from a host of problems: omitted variables, endogeneity and inappropriate use of the Kaitz index for the minimum wage in the equations estimated. They also charge authors and editors with 'specification searching' and 'publication bias' that is, authors fishing until they get the 'right' result, and editors and referees only accepting papers which support the conventional wisdom (Card and Krueger, 1995b).

The most interesting part of Card and Krueger's work was their study of fast food restaurants in Pennsylvania and New Jersey before and after New Jersey increased its state minimum wage from $4.25 to $5.05 per hour (Card and Krueger, 1994). Whereas the neoclassical prediction is that employment in these restaurants would decrease, Card and Krueger found it increased. Needless to say, these results raised the ire of other neoclassical economists who had invested careers in the conventional wisdom. Despite the ensuing attacks on Card and Krueger's work (e.g. Hammermesh, 1995; Kennan, 1995), it has stood up to scrutiny. It is not possible to conduct similar studies in other countries because minimum wages elsewhere get adjusted more regularly than they do in the United States.

The Card and Krueger finding is entirely consistent with the analysis in the preceding section. A higher minimum wage increased disposable income for those most likely to spend that income and spend it on local consumption. Thus it is no surprise to find an increase in employment in fast food restaurants – a likely target of expenditure for those benefitting from the increase in pay.

The difficulty with the neoclassical model of the firm is that the real nature of the firm is never clearly stated – other than assumptions about profit maximisation, the slope of its demand curve, and a statement about economies and diseconomies of scale (i.e. that the average cost curve falls then rises).[10] The model as it usually appears gives the impression that a firm expands and contracts according to changes in cost and demand (price). Thus its size increases and decreases much like a balloon as air is forced in or allowed out.

Real firms do not resemble balloons; they are more like a set of blocks. When they contract, one or more blocks disappear. Moreover, if they subsequently expand, the blocks that were lost are not replaced; new ones must be built. This metaphor also applies to the economy. It does not act like a balloon either. As the economy contracts, entire plants or even companies disappear. As the economy expands again, new businesses are created and new plants may also be opened by the surviving firms.

The costs of plant closure, even if the plant subsequently reopens, are considerable. Thus management is not likely to make a decision to close if the chance of survival remains. Within the firm, a similar logic applies. It is costly to lay-off employees and costly to rehire and retrain at a later stage. Thus managers are unlikely to lay-off workers only because of an increase in minimum wage rates.

We have argued before that there are no reasons to believe there would be a significant loss of employment if the minimum wage were increased (Brosnan and Wilkinson, 1988). The beneficiaries of higher minimum wages would only lose their jobs if employers replaced them by other workers (whose wages had not increased) or by capital equipment. In general, low-paid occupations, for example, cleaners, catering staff, sewing machinists, have no close substitutes, or if they do, they are low-paid as well. It is also unlikely that the introduction of a higher minimum wage would lead to a widespread move to replace workers by machines. The important point is that

> jobs are located in technical systems in which labour and its skills are complements to, rather than substitutes for, capital equipment. In these cases, substitution based on relative prices is not feasible and major reorganisations are required to significantly change the ratio of workers to capital equipment. It is unlikely, for example, that fast-food chains or supermarkets would significantly change their methods of operations if the wages of their low-paid employees increased. Moreover, even if employers substituted between grades of workers, or increased the capital intensity of their operation, the overall effect on employment would probably be small because the employment of one grade rises to compensate for the decline in the other.
>
> (Brosnan and Wilkinson, 1988: 31)

The public sector must be regarded as a special case when the disemployment effect is under consideration. Unless public sector employment is to be adversely affected, wage increases would need to be financed by an increase in taxation or in the government deficit. This is of particular significance in policy terms because of the central role assumed in the most recent decades of the fiscal balance in dictating government economic policy. The higher level of public sector pay should be able to be financed easily by the increase in taxation on all wages following an increase in the minimum wage but, nonetheless, the employment effect within the public sector will be determined primarily by the political process.

The most plausible story about the minimum wage causing unemployment is one where an increase in the minimum wage could neither be absorbed within the current cost structure, nor passed on to consumers via higher charges, so that the firm itself would be forced to close. A firm which was forced to close by an increase in the minimum wage is a firm that, in all probability, would have closed sooner rather than later. If the minimum wage forced such an outcome it would allow more efficient firms to capture the business of the defunct firm, and presumably provide better employment opportunities for the workers displaced. Where the firm might be forced to close because it could not compete with cheaper imports, there is a case for government policies of the kind described above to encourage such firms to innovate, and support the firm through that process.

Inflation

Bureaucrats and politicians who oppose minimum wages emphasise potential price increases much less than they emphasise disemployment effects. Yet price increases could well flow from an increase in the minimum wage in certain sectors. Whether prices did increase would depend on several factors: (a) the proportion of wage costs in total costs; (b) the number of workers earning below the new minimum wage; (c) the degree of competition in the product market; and (d) the willingness or ability of competitors to increase their prices.

Clearly, the greater the increase in the minimum, the more workers that will benefit, and the larger the increase will be for each worker affected. A small increase would have a minimal effect on labour costs whereas an increase twice as great would increase average labour costs by a factor many times greater because of larger proportion of workers affected.[11] The size of any increase may also affect pricing decisions. A small increase may be absorbed, while a large increase may induce firms to raise prices. To the extent that increases in the minimum wage were previously publicised and firms adopted more efficient technologies as a result, the efficiency gains could offset any inflationary effects (Hughes, 1976).

Space considerations do not allow an industry-by-industry analysis of the cost implications of increased minima.[12] In any case they would differ between countries. In general, low paying firms in industries where wages were higher would be unlikely to increase their prices; competition with other firms would not make that possible. Where whole industries were low payers, prices may well rise. Where low pay is concentrated on particular occupations within a firm, there could be some increase in price under certain market conditions but any increase is likely to be small.

The other aspect of wage and price increases is the possibility of pay rises for workers whose pay is above the minimum level. In some cases, their employers will give them an increase to maintain margins, or they may be using the minimum wage as a guide to 'community standards' and therefore give an increase to reflect the new 'standard'. The effect of these increases is likely to be negligible because these are the firms that are most likely to absorb the cost of any increase. More widespread wage increases will occur if trade unions make wage demands to restore wage differentials. This could occur, but it is unlikely that low-paid workers would be used as comparators in negotiations. Often low pay occurs because trade unions are not present or are relatively weak. In these industries, it is hard to believe that there would be concerted action to restore differentials. In any case, such claims are likely to be resisted successfully by employers.

The same is true of low-paid occupations in large firms whose

> wages are ... determined by comparison with "the rate for the job" which is fixed in the lowest paid segments of the labour market ... that explains why they *are* low-paid ... It is difficult to see how this situation would be materially affected by increasing the Minimum Wage. Thus ... the knock-on effect from the restoration of differentials disturbed by ... (an increase in the) ... Minimum Wage would be insignificant.
>
> (Brosnan and Wilkinson, 1999: 78)

Trade unions and employers

Although it is usual for employers and trade unions to adopt opposite positions on most industrial issues, this is not always the case when it comes to the minimum wage.

Employers tend to oppose minimum wages in general, and to resist any increase. Trade unions, however also have opposed minimum wage laws, or at least been indifferent to them. This trade union attitude is explained by the commitment to collective bargaining as a means of determining wages, and, in some countries, a trade union distrust of the state.

Where trade unions are relatively strong, and collective bargaining is widespread, unions see little value in a minimum wage. Thus, we find no minimum wage in Sweden, Germany or Norway. Even in countries such as Italy, where unions are much less organised, the extension of bargaining to other workers reduces the demand for a statutory minimum wage. Although Australia has a complex set of industry and occupation minima, a substantial number of Australian workers have no minimum, yet the question of a statutory minimum is rarely raised.

The low-paid are in an unfortunate position. They do not have the strength to organise but, because they are not organised, there is no one who will make the case for a minimum wage. Beyond the indifference to the plight of the low-paid, many trade union officials see a minimum wage as undermining collective bargaining. Union suspicion of minimum wage laws is also linked to a distrust of the state, and in particular, the courts.

American and British unions have long distrusted the state and have therefore resisted minimum wage laws. George Meany, a future president of the American Federation of Labour (AFL), opposed minimum wage laws for men in New York State in the years before Second World War. Another president of the AFL, Samuel Gompers, is even on record as opposing a minimum wage for New York women when it was proposed early in the twentieth century (Rogin, 1962). When Roosevelt proposed a form of minimum wage law, in the 1930s, it was opposed by the AFL on the basis that the minimum wage would soon become the maximum wage (Goulden, 1972).

Wariness of the state has also contributed to the British unions' reticence over a statutory minimum wage. Although the British Trades Union Congress (TUC) has included in its constitution, since 1924, the object of a legal minimum wage for each industry or occupation, when the National Union of Public Employees (NUPE) proposed at the 1986 TUC conference that the next Labour Government should introduce a statutory minimum wage, some delegates objected that it would undermine established differentials and weaken the collective bargaining system (*Guardian*, 4 September 1986). Until the Thatcher era, British trade unions were the main opponents of wages councils (Rubery, 1995). As Rubery (1995) bluntly states: 'The cost of the preference by the trade union movement for voluntarist over other systems of industrial relations has been the tolerance of low pay among the less well-organized groups' (Rubery, 1995: 552).

When trade unions are weaker, a minimum wage is less threatening, even attractive. As an example, New Zealand unions were traditionally indifferent about the statutory minimum wage, and were much more focussed on the awards which provided industrial and occupational minima. After a decade (the 1990s) during which the award system had been abolished, union numbers had reduced and the bargaining system had been severely weakened, New Zealand unions have become more supportive of the statutory minimum wage, which has now been raised to a more realistic level. It has supported collective bargaining by providing a floor upon which better wages can be built.

Government

One reason governments are often reluctant to increase the minimum wage is that treasury departments and other government advisors usually accept the neoclassical disemployment story and caution governments against increasing the minimum wage or at least to hold any increase to a modest level. International agencies come from the same stable and offer the same advice. The World Bank advises governments that minimum wages need to be reduced, while the IMF pressures governments to do precisely that. Standing (1999) highlights the case of Russia, where the IMF threatened to block a loan if the Russian government went ahead with a plan to double the minimum wage, even though the new level would only have been at a fifth of the level needed for bare survival (Standing, 1999: 216).

Legislators generally pay little attention to low pay as either a social or economic issue. Rather than legislate to protect the most vulnerable segments of the labour market, and to ensure that there is a realistic minimum wage, many governments are prepared to allow 'market forces' to determine outcomes. The ensuing unemployment and poverty is then attributed to trade unions, to the personal characteristics of the unemployed themselves, or written off as a 'cost of adjustment'. Governments remain content to use social welfare to moderate the hardship created.

Underlying this attitude is the reality that these policies meet with approval from substantial sections of society. The middle classes resent the idea that their taxes might need to be increased to pay higher wages to those at the bottom of the public sector. They often believe that the low-paid only get what they deserve (cf. Hicks, 1932). Often, at the back of their minds is the realisation that if the minimum wage were set at a more realistic level, they may have to pay more for personal services which they consume disproportionately to the rest of the population. As far as the unemployed and low-paid workers themselves are concerned, they are unlikely to be swinging voters (if they vote at all). Thus conservative parties have no expectation that they could woo their vote, while the left-leaning parties take their vote for granted.

The neglect of the social and economic issues involved in providing adequate wages show up in a host of policies introduced by governments during the 1980s and 1990s. Many of these have been at the urging of the World Bank or the IMF, but they have often been embraced readily by legislatures and recommended strongly by their treasury departments. Five types of policies, implemented in the last two decades have worsened pay at the lower end of the distribution. These policies reduce the degree of regulation in the labour market, reduce the relative power of workers in the labour market, they lower pay or create low-paid jobs or they reduce the real value of the minimum wage.

Policies which reduce the degree of regulation in the labour market

Many countries' governments have 'liberalised' labour markets, reducing the degree of regulation by the state. Furthermore, government departments have been corporatised, giving public sector managers more discretion and weakening the position of public sector unions. At the extreme, government corporations have been sold off. Additionally, many central government and local authority services and functions have been put out to private tender.

Policies which reduce the relative power of workers in the labour market

Governments have allowed unemployment to grow as a deliberate policy choice. At the same time, the unemployed have been increasingly harassed. Out-of-work social security benefits have been reduced, and become harder to access.

Unemployment and other social welfare benefits for teenagers have been made subject to parental means tests, and other benefits have been cut. In these circumstances, many persons wanting full-time jobs are forced to accept part-time employment with its lower pay and frequently with worse conditions.

Policies which lower pay or create low-paid jobs

In addition to the pressure on the unemployed to take low wage jobs, some governments have created 'workfare' schemes where the unemployed are required to 'work for the dole'. Fair relativity as the principle for setting public sector pay has largely been abolished. Pay negotiations in both public and private sectors have become more decentralised. The requirement for government contractors to pay fair wages applies in fewer countries.

Governments have given encouragement to the sectors where low pay and casual employment is most likely to be found. The most obvious of these is tourism. Although it is diffuse, it encompasses passenger transport, the hotel and catering sectors, retailing and entertainment, generally the lowest paying industries. Small business, another site of low pay is encouraged, and sometimes, small businesses have been given special concessions, including exemption from the need to meet labour standards.

Reduction of the real value of the minimum wage

Governments are directly responsible for the minimum wage no matter how it is set. They either determine it directly (e.g. Canada and New Zealand), they set up the authorities that determine the minimum wage 'independently' (e.g. Mexico), or they rely on advice from independent review bodies (e.g. France, Japan, Turkey, United Kingdom). The OECD (1988a) commented that the minimum wage has been allowed to decline in many countries during the 1990s. In fact minimum wages were allowed to decline in earlier periods too. The US minimum wage buys only two-thirds what it did in 1968, and it was not adjusted at all between January 1981 and April 1990. We had commented in an earlier study how the purchasing power of the New Zealand minimum wage had been allowed to decline by almost a half between 1954 and 1984 (Brosnan and Wilkinson, 1989).

The rises and falls in the value of the minimum wage has tended to reflect the political colour of successive governments. For example, the US minimum wage was allowed to decline during the Reagan and Bush administrations and increased by the Clinton administration. The UK minimum wage is a Labour Party initiative which was opposed originally by the Conservative Party.[13] The Australian minima, which are industrially and occupationally specific, have been allowed to decline as the Australian (conservative) government has endeavoured to force workers onto individual contracts or into negotiating directly at their own workplace. Nonetheless, so-called progressive governments have allowed minimum wages to fall in real terms. This reticence on the part of governments means that in some countries, the minimum wage is so low in relation to prevailing wages that it has no impact at all (Standing, 1999).

Inspection and enforcement

A statutory right to a minimum wage is not much use if workers are unaware of their rights, or not able to enforce them. Many workers who are paid below their minimum entitlements are unable to do anything about it. They are reliant on the job for their continuing livelihood, have no trade union or means of effectively challenging their employer, and have few, if any, alternatives for employment. They could report violations to the relevant authority but this presupposes their being aware of their entitlements, having the courage to report their employer, and being able to do so when they may be required to work at the very times the relevant agency is open to receive complaints.

While governments may be prepared to legislate for minimum wages, they are often less inclined to commit resources to inspection and enforcement. Sometimes it is a straightforward fiscal decision. In other cases, governments view the minimum wage legislation as being a statement about what is an appropriate social standard, rather than being something which the state should use its coercive powers to enforce. For their part, employer organisations object to extensive inspection, which they characterise as harassment.[14] Nonetheless, the need for enforcement is growing. As the developed nations de-industrialise, and as more 'flexible' forms of employment are generated, it becomes increasingly difficult to uncover the modern sweat shops which employ workers below the minimum wage.

Conclusion

This chapter has argued that a realistic minimum wage will achieve better pay equity, help reduce poverty and be a stimulus to a more efficient economy. The analysis above has indicated that the strongest effects will be in terms of achieving a fairer pay structure. The introduction of a minimum wage, or an increase in an existing minimum wage, immediately raises workers at the lowest end of the pay distribution to a higher level. A minimum wage is also an essential component in any package of policies designed to reduce household poverty, but it is only a component. It cannot do anything for the poor who are out of the labour force or in the labour force for only a few hours a week. A minimum wage is also an important element in any set of policies designed to make productive systems more efficient. If there is no cheap labour, firms will be less willing to use inefficient processes that were only profitable when staffed by lowly paid employees. Increases in minimum wages also add to domestic demand and further stimulate the national economy.

These benefits of a minimum wage are not guaranteed. Where the minimum is set too low, where the details of minimum entitlements are not well publicised, or where there is a weak regulatory and enforcement system, the benefits will be considerably reduced or even trivial. Reaping the benefits of a minimum wage therefore depends on the state setting the minimum at a realistic level and supporting it with appropriate regulatory machinery.

A minimum wage is only part of the picture. The state needs to provide other supporting policies in the social, economic and industrial relations spheres. In the social sphere there will always be a need for other policies to help those who have limited access to the labour market, or whose circumstances are such that even a realistic minimum wage would not meet all their reasonable needs.

In the economic sphere, a minimum wage needs to be part of a broader industry policy. Where the minimum was raised to a sufficient level that inefficient enterprises become non-viable, the state would need to implement policies to facilitate structural adjustment, and help such firms to invest, to innovate and retrain their labour force. If the enterprises involved were so decrepit that they could not be revitalised, the state would need to provide assistance to the workers who might be displaced so that they could retrain and gain employment in more efficient firms.

A guaranteed minimum wage is an important entitlement, but it is only one of a range which is needed to ensure that employment is fair. Other important entitlement are guarantees of paid holidays, sick pay, maternity leave, limits on the number of hours worked per day and per week, severance pay, protection against unfair dismissal, protection against discrimination and restrictions on the excessive use of casual labour. These can be guaranteed as part of a code of minimum entitlements. It is also crucial that trade unionism be promoted. Without strong unions, and a robust system of collective bargaining, workers would have nothing but their statutory entitlements.

Considerable progress has been made during the twentieth century in achieving minimum wage systems. Minimum wages have evolved over the last half century from piece-meal systems found in a small number of counties, and covering only specific groups of workers to broad systems, covering all the work force in a substantial number of countries. Most countries have some form of minimum wage but few countries have an effective minimum wage system. In many countries, coverage is still not complete, the minimum is set too low or the minimum wage is not enforced. Worse than that, some countries are going backwards by allowing the value of the minimum to decline. Few governments have an adequate minimum wage as a priority objective. Until they do, the problems of low pay will continue. An unjust system is maintained, there is greater personal and household poverty, the state faces increased costs in attempting to modify the degree of poverty, and these problems are compounded by the maintenance of outmoded, inefficient productive systems.

Notes

1 The comments of Robert MacDonald and other colleagues at Griffith University on an earlier draft of this chapter are greatly appreciated.
2 At the time of writing, 101 countries had ratified ILO Convention 26, 52 countries had ratified ILO Convention 99 (Convention Concerning the Creation of Minimum Wage-fixing Machinery in Agriculture (1951)), and 43 countries had ratified ILO Convention 131 (Convention Concerning Minimum Wage-fixing with Special Reference to Developing Countries (1970)).

3 Space limitations prevent discussion of many aspects of minimum wages. The important question of youth minima, which have become increasingly common, is an issue that will have to be put to one side.
4 Russell (1991) makes the important point that while North American governments legislated for *fair* wages for men, they only legislated for *minimum* wages for women.
5 A further injustice of low pay is that where occupational pensions are based on past earnings the low pay will be perpetuated in retirement. While highly paid workers usually receive a substantial pension when they retire, low-paid workers who retire will receive a meagre pension and may be forced to take on further low-paid work in order to make ends meet.
6 It is beyond the scope of this chapter to compare alternative measures of poverty. On this see Viet-Wilson (1998).
7 The Irish minimum wage was introduced in April 2000 at IR£4.40. It increases to IR£4.70 in July 2001 and to IR£5.00 in October 2002.
8 Cahuc and Michel (1996) make a similar argument but they stress the role of human capital development as the key component.
9 The First Quintile (Q1) includes many people who have minimal labour force participation, that is, pensioners etc.
10 This unrealistic assumption is essential to the model as it is usually portrayed. Cost curves are assumed to be smooth, continuous and twice differentiable in order to allow algebraic analysis and to produce certain results, such as marginal cost pricing on which entire branches of neoclassical economics are built.
11 This is illustrated for the United Kingdom by the data in Robson *et al.* (1997).
12 We have presented such an analysis for the United Kingdom and New Zealand elsewhere (Brosnan and Wilkinson, 1988, 1989).
13 Although the Conservative Party claim to no longer oppose the minimum wage, a test will be whether future Conservative governments maintain the real value of the minimum wage or allow it to decline.
14 Recommendation 30 (1928) concerning ILO Convention 26, recommends that a 'sufficient staff of inspectors should be employed ... ascertaining whether the rates in force are ... being paid' (IV(1)).

References

Anyadike-Danes, M. and Godley, W. (1989) 'Real wages and employment: a sceptical view of some recent empirical work', The *Manchester School*, 57(2), 172–87.
Blackburn, R. M. and Mann, M. (1979) *The Working Class in the Labour Market*. London: Macmillan.
Borooah, V. K. and Sharpe, D. R. (1986) 'Aggregate consumption and the distribution of income in the United Kingdom: an econometric analysis', *Economic Journal*, 96(382), 449–66.
Borooah, V. K. (1988) 'Income distribution, consumption patterns and economic outcomes in the United Kingdom', *Contributions to Political Economy*, 7, 49–63.
Brosnan, P. and Wilkinson, F. (1988) 'A national statutory minimum wage and economic efficiency', *Contributions to Political Economy*, 7, 1–48.
Brosnan, P. and Wilkinson, F. (1989) *Low Pay and the Minimum Wage*. Wellington: New Zealand Institute of Industrial Relations Research.
Buchanan, J. and Watson, I. (1997) *A Profile of Low Wage Employees*. Sydney: University of Sydney, Australian Centre for Industrial Relations Research and Training.
Cahuc, P. and Michel, P. (1996) 'Minimum wage unemployment and growth', *European Economic Review*, 40(7), 1463–82.

Card, D. and Krueger, A. (1994) 'Minimum wages and employment: a case study of the fast food industry in New Jersey and Pennsylvania', *American Economic Review*, 84(4), 772–93.

Card, D. and Krueger, A. (1995a) *Myth and Measurement: The New Economics of the Minimum Wage*. Princeton: Princeton University Press.

Card, D. and Krueger, A. (1995b) 'Time series minimum wage studies: a meta-analysis', *American Economic Review*, 85(2), 238–43.

Council of Europe (1977) *Methods of Defining 'Decent' Remuneration*. Strasbourg: Council of Europe.

Craig, C., Rubery, J. and Wilkinson, F. (1982) *Labour Market Structure Industrial Organisation and Low Pay*. Cambridge: Cambridge University Press.

DiNardo, J., Fontin, N. and Lemieux, T. (1996) 'Labor market institutions and the distribution of wages, 1973–1992: a semi-parametric approach', *Econometrica*, 64(5), 1001–44.

Eccles, M. (1984) 'Minimum wage policy in the United States', in Field, F. (ed.), *Policies against Low Pay: An International Perspective*. London: Policy Studies Institute.

Freeman, R. (1996) 'The minimum wage as a redistributive tool', *Economic Journal*, 106, 639–49.

Gosling, A. (1996) 'Minimum wages: possible effects on the distribution of income', *Fiscal Studies*, 17(4), 31–48.

Goulden, J. C. (1972) *Meany: The Unchallenged Strong Man of American Labor*. New York: Atheneum.

Hammermesh, D. (1995) 'Comment', *Industrial and Labor Relation Review*, 48(4), 827–49.

Hicks, J. R. R. (1932) *A Theory of Wages*. London: Macmillan.

Hughes, J. (1976) 'What part can a minimum wage play?', in Field, F. (ed.), *Are Low Wages Inevitable?* Nottingham: Spokesman.

Johnston, P. and Stark, G. (1991) 'The effects of a minimum wage on family incomes', *Fiscal Studies*, 12(3), 88–93.

Kennan, J. (1995) 'The elusive effects of minimum wages', *Journal of Economic Literature*, 33(4), 1949–65.

Machin, S. and Manning, A. (1994) 'The effects of minimum wages on wages dispersion and employment: evidence from the UK wages councils', *Industrial and Labor Relations Review*, 47(2), 319–29.

McMahon, G. V. (1991) *Statutory minimum wage regulation and low pay in the Republic of Ireland*. PhD Thesis, University of Dublin.

Mishel, L., Bernstein, J. and Rassell, E. (1995) *Who Wins with a Higher Minimum Wage?* Washington: Economic Policy Institute.

Neumark, D. and Wascher, W. (1997) *Do Minimum Wages Fight Poverty?* New York: National Bureau of Economic Research.

OECD (1988a) *OECD Employment Outlook*. Paris.

OECD (1988b) *OECD Observer*, 213 (Aug/Sept), 34–6.

Pollin, R. and Luce, S. (1998) *The Living Wage: Building a Fair Economy*. New York: The New Press.

Rainnie, A. (1989) *Industrial Relations in Small Firms*. London: Routledge.

Reynolds, L. G. *et al.* (1987) *Economics of labour*. Englewood Cliffs: Prentice-Hall.

Richardson, S. and Harding, A. (1998) 'Poor workers? The link between low wages, low family income and the tax and transfer systems', *Reshaping the Labour Market: Regulation, Efficiency and Equality in Australia*. Cambridge: Cambridge University press.

Robson, P., Dex, S. and Wilkinson, F. (1997) *The Costs of a Statutory Minimum Wage in Britain*. Cambridge: Judge Institute of Management Studies, University of Cambridge.

Rogin, M. (1962) 'Voluntarism: the political foundations of an anti-political doctrine', *Industrial and Labor Relations Review*, 15(4), 521–35.

Russell, B. (1991) 'A fair or a minimum wage? Women workers, the state and the origins of wage regulation in Western Canada', *Labour/Le Travail*, 28, 59–88.

Rubery, J. (1995) 'The low-paid and the unorganized', in Edwards, P. (ed.), *Industrial Relations: Theory and Practice in Britain*, Oxford: Blackwell.

Standing, G. (1999) *Global Labour Flexibility: Seeking Distributive Justice*. Houndmills: Macmillan.

Starr, G. (1981) *Minimum Wage Fixing*. Geneva: ILO.

Stigler, G. J. (1946) 'The economics of minimum wage legislation', *American Economic Review*, 36(1), 358–65.

Sutherland, H. (1995) 'Minimum wage benefits', *New Economy*, 2(4), 214–19.

Viet-Wilson, J. (1998) *Setting Adequacy Standards*. Bristol: Policy Press.

Webb, S. and Webb, B. (1920) *Industrial Democracy*. London.

Wilkinson, F. (1984) 'Productive systems', *Cambridge Journal of Economics*, 7(3), 413–29.

12 Economic functioning, self-sufficiency and full employment[1]

Roger Tarling and Frank Wilkinson

Introduction

Few economists would disagree that the central object of economic policy should be achieving and sustaining full employment; what they debate is how this can be achieved. Economists have traditionally argued that the labour market cleared; anyone can get a job if they are prepared to accept a market price which declines as the level of employment rises. Keynes identified over-saving as a cause of unemployment and introduced the idea that full employment required government intervention to establish and maintain a sufficiency in effective demand. Persistent inflation in the postwar period led to the re-establishment amongst economists of pre-Keynesian beliefs in a monetary explanation of inflation and a clearing labour market and established the notion of an equilibrium 'natural' level of unemployment at which inflation stabilises. Monetarism rules out a macro-economic intervention route to full employment and directs policy attention towards reform of the supply side of the labour market as the generator of jobs. However, despite seventeen years of continuous labour market deregulation and cutbacks in social welfare to sharpen work incentives, in Britain unemployment, depending on how it is measured, is currently between two to four times higher than it was in the 1970s.[2]

Explanations for this increase vary but the conventional wisdom amongst economists is that the natural rate has shifted. Increases in real (i.e. relative to product prices) raw material prices, capital goods prices, interest rates and exchange rates have been identified as reducing profit rates and thereby lowering the demand for labour. The restoration of profits requires a compensating cut in wages relative to productivity and the refusal of labour to concede this has shifted the natural rate of unemployment upwards. Factors on the supply side of the labour market including asset values, interest rates and social welfare benefits are identified as raising out-of-work income and hence the asking price of labour. High levels of the natural rate of employment are also attributed to trade unions, legal minimum wages, high non-wage labour costs, restrictive labour and employment legislation, population increase, labour saving technical progress, the slow adjustment to external shocks and the effects on the skills and work motivations of the unemployed of long spells of joblessness. Unemployment has therefore been increasingly regarded as resulting from the failure of wages to adjust downward to the falling demand price for labour and/or to the growing unemployability of the increasing proportion of the workforce through lack of skill and/or work motivation. Consequently, even to many economists who would regard themselves as Keynesian, unemployment is seen as voluntary or 'structural' (Phelps, 1992) and not amenable to macro-economic stimuli; diagnoses which lead to such policy recommendations as a determined effort to reduce wages, the introduction of state provided 'citizens income' designed to remove the disincentive effect of the means testing of benefits and the subsidisation of employment by tax relief (Meade, 1995). The requirement is that workers become lower paid and therefore less self sufficient, and/or more dependent on the state.

As opposed to this, this chapter argues that the ability of individuals to function economically so as to achieve and maintain self-sufficiency is critical to the achievement of full employment and a high road to economic growth. Economic functioning however is only in part determined by the individual's own efforts and decisions, the other main factors being embedded in the economic, social and political systems within which the individual is located. These systems structure the incentives, disincentives and barriers which increase or restrict the quality and quantity of economic and social participation of individuals and hence their capacity for self-sufficiency. For example, the segmentation of labour markets, resulting from the exercise of individual and collective power, leads to systematic differences in the valuation of the labour of groups located in the different segments and this reinforces and is reinforced by power inequalities within households and more widely in society.

The chapter further argues that attempts to increase employment by widening the distribution of income and deregulating the labour market have in reality created policy traps which reinforce and exacerbate inequalities and are counterproductive in terms of employment creation. This has put pressure on resources to compensate for the inequalities and to protect the stability of the existing structures. Common sense would recognise that the removal of labour market and other forms of undervaluation to reduce pre-tax income inequality will yield high return in terms of economic and social progress by enabling those currently undervalued to increase their own economic functioning and self-sufficiency. Hence, the chapter argues for a better understanding of what needs to be changed, not only for reasons of social equity and justice but also for the purposes of effective economic policy. Before doing that it is necessary to explain what we mean by economic functioning and self-sufficiency.

Resource endowments, capabilities and economic functioning

Lancaster (1966) maintained that it is the *characteristics* of a product that make it attractive. Sen (1985) argued that characteristics are latent in products and require the appropriate *capabilities* to make them functional. He pointed out (Sen, 1985:10), that it is the physical capabilities of the cyclist which makes functional the transportation characteristic of the bicycle; but then so does the state of the roads, whether the cyclists can afford their own bicycle pump and so on. There are therefore many dimensions to capability and hence to functioning. In this section, the concepts of capability and functioning will be developed within the context of a discussion of the effective mobilisation by individuals of the resources at their disposal as the means of becoming and remaining self-sufficient.

The resource endowments of individuals include their labour power, accumulated assets and entitlements (net of contributions) to private and public transfers.[3] Resource endowments vary widely in both levels and composition between individuals and over an individual's lifetime. For example, the resource endowments of children consist mainly of their claim to intra-household transfers based on their family affiliation and public transfers in the form of child benefits, education, health and other social provisions. In early adult life, the most important part of individuals' resource endowment is usually their labour power and they have probably become net-contributors to the tax/benefit system and possibly to private transfers. The importance of labour power and net contributions to public and private transfers increase with cohabitation and the formation of families but as individuals grow older their net contribution to private transfers can be expected to decline as their children leave the household and when they retire their resource endowments become mainly state transfers, accumulated private assets (including private pension rights) and, possibly, private transfers. There are, however, wide variations between individuals around this stylised lifetime profile of resource endowment related to time spent in education, age at cohabitation and family formation, types of household, participation in the labour market and other socially and economically determined factors.

Given their resource endowments the economic functioning of individuals is determined by what can be described as their capabilities. Capabilities, in the sense used here, depend not only on an individual's personal efficiency and energy but also on the opportunities they have to utilise their resources to the best advantage. The capabilities of individuals in the labour market, for example, depend on employment opportunities and terms and conditions of that employment as well as the effectiveness and intensity of work effort. Capabilities in domestic and other forms of non-market production also have important institutional and organisational dimensions. There are, for example, significant economies of scale in cooking, caring, cleaning and other forms of household production and in the sharing of accommodation, heating and other aspects of communal living. Capabilities also include individuals' knowledge and experience of systems of private and public transfers including, for example, their ability to take advantage of the tax/benefit system by minimising the payment of the former and maximising the receipt of the latter. Together with their resource endowment the capabilities of individuals determine their economic functioning: the flow of income at their disposal and therefore their ability to maintain themselves and accumulate resources.

Economic functioning and the working of labour markets[4]

In conventional economic theory, the initial resource endowments of individuals are taken as given and capabilities are seen as being determined largely by personal qualities. Labour markets are more or less competitive and within them wages reflect the quality of individuals' labour power endowment (their human capital) and their personal efficiency and energy. That these result in a wide dispersion of labour market rewards, some of which may be insufficient to sustain a reasonable standard of life, is a demonstration, it is argued, of how widely dispersed are individual resource endowments and capabilities (Hirsch and Addison, 1986). Within the household, the allocation of members' labour between domestic production and internal transfers are regarded as a consequence of rational choice based on the relative values of individual member's domestic and labour market employment and made by households operating as a single unit. The redistribution of income by the state through a tax and benefit system is recognised as necessary, particularly when the economic functioning of individuals is insufficient to yield some minimum standard of life. But this is qualified by an emphasis on the potential negative incentive effects of lowering the net market income of the tax payer and of raising the non-market income of the benefit recipient.

Conventional economics recognises that although inequalities in resource endowment may exist, these are essentially external to market processes. Therefore, given resource endowments, the economic functioning of individuals is largely determined by how productive they are and how effective market incentives are in mobilising that effort so that wage differences largely reflect relative worth. In contrast to this conventional view, labour market segmentation theorists recognise the importance of relative power in influencing wage differences. In particular, relationships in the labour market are permeated by inequalities of bargaining power, by structural barriers to mobility and by institutionalised discrimination, which together lead to the systematic *undervaluation* of the labour of disadvantaged groups. This focuses attention on the external and internal forces structuring the labour market and how these impact on the capabilities of individuals located in its different segments.

Out-of-market segmentation

Inter-community and inter-family differences in wealth, expectations and information gives individuals variable degrees of access to socialisation, educational and training processes and to job opportunities which enhance the resources and capabilities of the privileged and reduces those of the deprived whatever their inherent qualities. Household organisation also serves to reduce the capabilities of women. Unequally distributed responsibility for domestic labour inhibits the labour market activities of women to extents depending on the collective resource endowment of the household members and the willingness of other members to use their resources (either labour or capital) to provide substitutes for the cooking, cleaning, child care and other domestic services traditionally provided by women. The greater the domestic responsibility of a woman (and hence the greater her transfer to others in her household) the less favourable are her labour market opportunities likely to be. At one extreme, in resource poor households highly dependent on the domestic services of female members (single parent households provide good examples) women will find it extremely difficult to realise their full capability on the labour market whatever skills they might have. At the other extreme, in households with access to ample resources to replace female domestic labour, women members will be strongly placed to exploit fully their labour market assets.

The state represents the third major force differentially influencing the economic functioning of individuals by its labour, industrial and social welfare legislation and by providing child and other forms of care. The growth of the welfare state can be regarded as counteracting social, economic and other disadvantages and therefore breaking down the barriers to effective labour market participation. However, whether individuals can take advantage of education and training to enhance their resource endowment will depend on the willingness and ability of households to support non-economically functioning members and their experience, expectations and information about education, training and labour market opportunities, all of which can expected to discriminate in favour of the resource rich households (Bowles and Gintis, 1976). Moreover, whilst the resource endowment of the better-off can be expected to be enhanced by state education and training provision and social security, the elements of state expenditure to which the worse-off have greatest recourse, work to impair their economic functioning. For example, the capabilities of social welfare recipients are reduced by means-tested benefits which are reduced as incomes rise. This effectively imposes high marginal taxes on the low-income households and ensnares them in the poverty trap (Parker, 1995).

In-market segmentation

Within the labour market professional associations, sectional trade unions and other formal and informal organisations and networks exercise control over entry to particular labour market segments and to training and other forms of in-market advancement restricting access to and the use of human capital. Labour market disadvantages such as sex, race, age, low social status and poor educational achievement are exacerbated by the difficulties such groups experience in forming or joining effective in-market organisations. The hiring, training and labour management policies of firms interrelate with supply side factors in further differentiating job opportunities. Hiring rules adopted by firms rest on signals transmitted by social characteristics (age, sex, race, education and training qualification, dress, deportment etc.) which are only partially objectively based but which are taken to measure the relative worth of job applicants (Spence, 1973). The technical and organisational structure of the firm, the related systems of labour management and collective bargaining (or its absence) structure job opportunities within firms and training and promotion policies regulate the allocation of workers within this internal labour market. Firms with a range of abilities to pay offer widely different levels of wages for comparable jobs so that promotion prospects – in terms of job content and/or pay – exist both within and between firms (Horrell *et al.*, 1989). Successful progression within this job structure enhances the labour market status of individuals whereas redundancy and other involuntary quits, periods out of the labour market for domestic reasons and spells of unemployment have the opposite effect. Thus, job prospects of individuals can be continuously modified from the supply side by their own employment experience and from the demand side by such factors as plant closures, industrial restructuring and changes in hiring and training rules adopted by employers.[5]

The structuring of job opportunities and related differences in the terms and conditions of employment are further reinforced by variations in incidence and effectiveness of collective bargaining and protection afforded by the law. Collective agreements reflect the bargaining power of labour and the ability of firms and industries to pay and so their benefits can vary widely. In some European countries these disadvantages are offset by legally enforceable labour standards. In Britain, however, minimum wage legislation is now non-existent and legally enforceable conditions of employment usually provide a floor of rights significantly below those secured by collective bargaining. Moreover, the employees of small firms, part-timers, workers on temporary and other non-standard contracts and others whose employment status is ambiguous are frequently excluded from the scope of both collective bargaining and protective legislation (Deakin and Morris, 1995).

The general characteristics of labour markets are, therefore, that access to jobs is generally carefully controlled, and the higher the pay and status the more restrictive the rules of entry. Rules of exclusion operate on all groups at all levels and are mutually re-enforcing in the sense that workers in each labour market group, excluded from better jobs, more carefully protect those within their control. However, the ability to exclude others can be expected to decline at successively lower levels in the labour market hierarchy. At the bottom end of the labour market jobs tend to be classified as unskilled whatever their job content, trade unionism is weak or non-existent and the law offers little, if any, protection. As a result, terms and conditions of employment are poor, work is often casualised and non-standard forms of labour contracts are common. Individuals are trapped in this segment by their lack of transferable and/or socially recognised and credentialised skills, by the many forms discrimination takes and by the priority they are obliged to give to domestic and other responsibilities. At this level, jobs tend to be much more open to anyone and therefore regular employees are thrown into competition with students and others who want temporary jobs to top up their income from other sources and who are therefore prepared to accept wages below that necessary for self-sufficiency.

Interaction between internal and external segmentation

There are virtuous and vicious cycles built into the interaction between the resource endowment of individuals, their capabilities and hence their economic functioning. Ample resource endowment creates labour market privilege which enhances capability and economic functioning and increases resource endowment. By contrast, paucity of resource endowment interacts with reduced capabilities in reinforcing poor economic functioning in two separate ways. Lack of resources militates against the development of the human capital of deprived individuals and possibly their personal qualities and hence their capabilities. This defines what might usefully be called the *out-market* undervaluation of the labour of socially deprived individuals. This is compounded by what can be called the *out-market* undervaluation which results from the structuring of labour markets by social, organisational and legal forces which relegates the socially disadvantaged to labour market segments where their capabilities are further reduced because wages are low relative to the real value of labour input.

The segmentation of labour markets and the social and economic deprivation it engenders has significant macro- and micro-economic implications. The *out-market* undervaluation of labour reduces the overall productive potential of an economy whilst *out-market* undervaluation leads to further waste to the extent that it permits the continued existence of outmoded techniques and inefficient managerial practices. *Out-market* undervaluation of labour also leads to a more unequal distribution of income than would be warranted by the distribution of what Marshall called *efficiency* earnings – 'earnings measured with reference to the exertion of ability and efficiency required of the workers' (Marshall, 1947: 549). The beneficiaries of this unequal distribution of income may be either those in receipt of profits or more advantaged groups in the labour market depending on whether, and the extent to which, the cost advantage of employing undervalued labour is passed on to the customer (Marshall, 1947: 549). For example, the availability of undervalued labour is one way by which retail traders and food and drink caterers compete to the price advantage of the customers. In other cases, the redistribution is more direct and here the provision of domestic and other labour services by disadvantaged workers to the more privileged provides an obvious example. This latter resource transfer becomes more indirect but none the less as real when mediated by local and central government and made possible by the low pay of public sector workers. Finally, the unequal degrees of bargaining power of different groups of workers employed by the same firm provide a way by which the relative undervaluation of some workers can benefit others by reducing the conflict between their wage claims and profits. Thus, there is a wide range of direct and indirect ways by which the wage share is distributed unequally in which relative wages, prices and the system of taxation play a part which enhances the resources endowment and capabilities of some and reduces those of others.

The interaction between out-market and in-market segmentation is also a major obstacle to the effectiveness of labour market policies. This double jeopardy strengthens the barrier between unemployment and employment by undermining the ability and willingness of individuals to take up and participate in labour market schemes. It also threatens the effectiveness of even the best-designed measures to secure lasting employment opportunities. The resulting failure of policy initiatives has the additional negative effect of wasting the reserves and resources of the disadvantaged and of nullifying the potential benefits of the resource transfers embodied in the public sector financing of labour market measures. Such outcomes generate disillusionment amongst providers and the provided for and encourages their withdrawal of support and commitment to structures and frameworks for the delivery of active labour market policy whatever their potential value.[6]

Self-sufficiency and power relations

Individuals can be said to be self-sufficient if they can function economically so as to at least sustain throughout their life some minimum customary standard of life. The ability to achieve this objective will depend on both resource endowment and capabilities. It has been argued above that the effectiveness by which labour and material assets can be accumulated and utilised to achieve the customary standard of life will be determined both by the personal qualities of the individual and their relative power in market and non-market activities. Power relations also play an important part in influencing the pattern of contributions to and benefits from private and public transfers. In the traditional family, for example, male dominance structures the flows of income and real service transfers. In the case of public transfers, the importance of power in structuring resource endowment will depend on how the transfers are organised. Where the public welfare system is based on the insurance principle, rights to benefits are established by contributions so that obligations and rights are clearly related. On the other hand, if transfers are made from current taxation, the effective status of the beneficiary is much closer to that of a supplicant dependent on the benevolence of the tax payers expressed through their tolerance to taxation.[7] Therefore transfers out of current taxation are determined more directly by power relationships than transfers resulting from an insurance principle.[8]

In conventional economics, the obstacle to a redistribution of income intended to widen self-sufficiency, either by narrowing wage differentials or increasing transfers, is the risk of a reduction in the overall level of economic performance. By contrast, the recognition of the importance of power inequalities in the market and non-market processes underlying the distribution of income leads to the possibility that a reduction in the undervaluation of labour, a greater equality within households, and a shift to a system of benefits based on the insurance principle can be expected to increase rather than reduce incentives and thereby increase productivity. The important point is that, in a system where differential economic and political power result in the failure of individuals to achieve self-sufficiency, the removal of this disadvantage by a narrowing of the power differentials can be expected to increase the overall economic performance. As a result, the powerful can expect to be compensated at least in part for relinquishing part of the pie as the less powerful begin to function more effectively, as the pie expands and as part of this growth trickles up the income distribution.

Economic theory, economic policy and economic performance

1945–76

The period from the 1930s to the mid-1970s can be viewed as a period when in both economic theory and economic policy there was a recognition of the need for state intervention to improve economic performance at both the micro- and macrolevels by the reduction of inequality. More recently and particularly since the mid 1970s there has been a growing emphasis on the importance of inequality in improving economic performance. A comparison of these two periods should therefore serve to illustrate the dynamic processes as the conditions for economic functioning change.

The experience of unemployment and poverty during the inter-war years and the social accord engendered by the Second World War triggered a revolution in economic theory and policy practice which ushered in a commitment by governments to full employment and the welfare state. In the following three decades, these changes seemed to have been justified by the high rates of economic growth, increasing levels of employment, declining levels of unemployment and a progressive elimination of poverty as a growing proportion of the population of advanced industrial countries became increasingly self-sufficient.

Expanding government expenditure and increased state intervention in the labour market found wide justification amongst economists who encouraged the government to expand education and training in the interest of a larger and better qualified labour force. Better social welfare provision, greater job security and improved labour standards secured by collective bargaining were also welcomed because, it was argued, these measures contributed to human capital formation, facilitated job search and generally increased the efficient utilisation of human resources. Thus economic, social and political pressures combined in the upgrading of the labour force in such a way as to benefit particularly those at the lower levels of the job hierarchy. The position of those who remained trapped, or who were drawn into the lower reaches of the labour market was improved by an extension and strengthening of the regulatory framework to accommodate their needs. The combined effect of high and increasing employment, a consensus across the political spectrum on full employment and the need for a welfare state, and the strengthening of trade union organisation was to reduce the extent of the *in-market* and out-market undervaluation of labour and help redress the power imbalance in state provision. Consequently, the more equal distribution of income, wider educational and training opportunities and more job choice improved the resource endowment and capabilities of hitherto deprived individuals. This improved economic performance by enhancing labour input, underpinned economic progress from the demand side by encouraging the diffusion of new products and thereby raised the customary standard of life and facilitated the labour market upgrading process (Wilkinson, 1988). Thus, both at the level of the individual and the economy, increasing resources and improving capabilities interacted in a virtuous cycle of rising economic performance.

From 1975

From the early 1970s, the cumulative process of economic and social progress has been replaced by a downward cumulative process of increasing inequality and growing poverty. This was precipitated by rising inflation, growing unemployment, progressive de-industrialisation and increasing government expenditure. This burgeoning economic crisis served to discredit the economic and social theories which had directed policy during the Golden Age leading to a re-emergence of pre-Keynesian orthodoxy in economic theory and eventually into economic policy (Wilkinson, 1996). High inflation was attributed to a failure to control the money supply, unemployment to imperfection in the labour markets and over-generous welfare provision and the responsibility for poor industrial performance was laid at the door of organised labour and the erosive effect of high taxation on entrepreneurial initiative. In 1976, under pressure from the oil crisis and the changing conventional wisdom in economic theorising, the British government abandoned its commitment to full employment. Since 1979, control of monetary variables has dominated anti-inflationary policy whilst labour market deregulation and reforms of the benefit system to increase work incentives have been allotted the task of securing full employment.

There can be little doubt that, measured by unemployment levels, these experiments with pre-Keynesian economics have failed. But if, as explained by its apologists, the natural rate of unemployment has shifted because of changes in supply and demand side conditions in the labour market, unemployment is not a good indicator of economic performance. However, other indicators give as little support to the claim that the introduction of monetarist macro-economics or labour market deregulation policies have had their predicted beneficial effect. Between the peak years 1979 and 1990, output per head in manufacturing grew by 3.8 per cent per year but, as manufacturing output increased at less than 1 per cent per year, employment in manufacturing fell at an annual rate in excess of 3 per cent. Investment as a proportion of GDP increased from 17.5 to 19.5 per cent between 1979 and 1990. This was due to a boom in real estate investment. In the distribution and financial sectors, manufacturing investment fell from 3.1 per cent of GDP to 2.6 per cent. The failure of manufacturing output to expand at the same pace as the economy (which grew at 2.2 per cent per year) resulted in a surge of imports, so that Britain became a net importer of manufactured goods for the first time since before the Industrial Revolution. As a consequence of this, the balance of payments on current account deteriorated from a surplus of 1.3 per cent of GDP in 1979 to a deficit of 2.8 per cent of GDP in 1990. The scale of the inflow of capital necessary to sustain the high and growing current account deficit without a collapse of sterling forced up real interest rates. The real short-term interest rate (treasury bill yield adjusted for manufacturing output prices) rose from 2.7 per cent in 1979 to 8.8 per cent in 1990. The only real success of the 1980s was the increase in consumption, which grew in real terms from 57.2 per cent to 63.1 per cent of GDP between 1979 and 1990.

The boom of the late 1980s was brought to an end by a severe credit squeeze. By 1992, GDP was 2.5 per cent below its 1990 level, manufacturing output was

6 per cent lower, manufacturing investment had fallen to 2.2 per cent of GDP, but the balance of payment deficit was still 2.4 per cent of GDP. The economy was stimulated by the British withdrawal from the ERM in September 1992 and the subsequent devaluation and cuts in interest rates. By 1994, GDP was 6 per cent higher than its 1992 level. At very best the latest up-turn in the economy has been weak. Manufacturing output failed to recover its late 1980s peak by 1994 when manufacturing investment was 2 per cent of GDP. Exports responded to the 1992 devaluation, but imports continued to grow strongly, so that the 1994 balance of payments deficit on current account remained as high as 1.6 per cent of GDP. The budget deficit also posed a threat to the recovery. Under the pressure of high levels of unemployment and growing poverty, it proved impossible to contain government expenditure which increased from 39.1 to 43.3 per cent of GDP between 1990 and 1994, with social security spending alone rising from 11.4 to 14.8 per cent of GDP. In early 1995, the supply constraint tightened and price increases in the supply chain began to accelerate. Materials purchased by manufacturing increased in price by 9 per cent between April 1994 and April 1995 and over the same period the prices of metal manufactures, chemicals and man-made fibres, all major industrial inputs, increased by 14, 7.3 and 9.3 per cent respectively. These price increases and the fall in the official unemployment count were interpreted as signalling a future increase in the general price level, and the government increased interest rates. Higher interest charges were added to increasing costs and the increase in output stalled. Interest rates have since been reduced but as yet there are few signs of a recovery in manufacturing and there is nothing to guarantee that if that happens supply shortage induced cost inflation will not take off again.

The implementation of pre-Keynesian macro-economic policies and labour market deregulation (Wilkinson, 1996) have resulted in the re-emergence of mass unemployment of inter-war proportions, a deep restructuring of labour markets away from full-time secure employment and a dramatic increase in inequality of income. Measuring the unemployment consequences of the policy shifts of the 1980s and 1990s raises major problems. Since 1979, no fewer than 30 changes have been made to the way unemployment is officially counted, all but one of which have reduced recorded unemployment. The official definition of unemployment has also been changed from persons registered as unemployed to the current definition of those out of work claiming unemployment benefits of various kinds. Between 1979 and 1993, claimant unemployment increased from around 1 million to 2.8 million. The Unemployment Unit has estimated that on the basis of those registered as unemployed, unemployment increased from around 1.4 million in 1979 to more than 4 million in 1993. These estimates receive support from a study by Wells (1994) which shows a level of unemployment in early 1994 'closer to the Unemployment Unit's total of 4 million than to the official claimant count of under 3 million'.

The record of deregulatory policies is no better, if employment, rather than unemployment, is taken as the measure of success. It is a myth that the policies pursued in the 1980s and the 1990s have led to substantial job growth in comparison to previous decades. Official figures show that by 1983, total employment – a figure which includes employees, the self-employed and members of the armed forces – had fallen by 1.7 million from its 1979 peak. It then recovered slowly, but after 1989 a second intense depression again reduced the number of jobs, to 0.6 million below its 1979 level by the middle of 1993. Employment was also restructured during this period, with a decline in the number of full-time, secure jobs. Between 1979 and 1993, male full-time employment fell by 2.3 million; this was only partly compensated for by an increase of 0.5 million in male part-time jobs. Meanwhile, female employment increased by 1.3 million, although only 196,000 of these jobs were full-time. Overall, in this period, the number of employees fell by 1.7 million and self-employment increased by 1.1 million (0.4 million of whom were part-time). Much of the 'new' self-employment resulted from government incentive schemes for the unemployed, and is very low paid (Joseph Rowntree Foundation, 1995: 53).

As unemployment has grown and employment has become increasingly part-time and/or casual, pay, and more generally income, have become more unequally distributed. Between 1977 and 1992 the average real wages of the bottom 10 per cent of male earners were static; the median or mid-point increase was 27 per cent; while for the top tenth of earners, the average increase was 44 per cent (Goodman and Webb, 1994). During this period, the earnings of non-manual workers rose more quickly than those of manual workers and full-timers' earnings rose more quickly than those of part-time workers. Of the self-employed in 1993, more than 20 per cent had incomes which were below half the average income for all households (Department of Social Security, 1995). The rise in inequality of earnings, together with cuts in social security provision, has contributed to a sharp increase in household poverty. Official sources show that between 1979 and 1993 the lowest decile of households saw no increase in their income before housing costs are taken into account, whereas the highest decile had a rise of 45 per cent. When housing costs are taken into account, the lowest decile had a drop in real income of 17 per cent, compared to an increase of 62 per cent for the highest decile (Department of Social Security, 1995).

The degree of job insecurity and dissatisfaction arising from these developments is not easy to measure. Some part-time jobs are stable and secure, and some individuals may welcome the flexibility offered by part-time work and self-employment. Conversely, many full-time jobs pay very low wages and offer only partial guarantees of continuing employment. The essential question here is how insecurity affects different groups and to what extent it is growing. There is little doubt that an ever-growing number of workers are affected by insecurity. One recent assessment (Coutts and Rowthorn, 1995) is that 13.5 million workers in the British economy are now in a 'primary' sector of the labour force which, on the whole, enjoys secure and well remunerated full-time employment, with a further 6.5 million in an 'intermediate' category of those who, while not having a full-time job, are nevertheless relatively well-paid and secure. This leaves a further 9 million 'disadvantaged' workers without secure or well-paid employment. Of this 9 million, 4.9 million are in employment and 4.1 million are without employment. Thus 'around seventy per cent of the labour force are financially comfortable and rea-sonably secure, while thirty per cent live in either insecurity or comparative poverty' (Coutts and Rowthorn, 1995). This analysis, if anything, errs on the side of caution; it does not seek to assess how many of those in the 'primary' segment, who are apparently secure, perceive their position as being under threat, as more firms use redundancy as a measure of first and not of last resort. The important point is that the ratio of disadvantaged to advantaged has increased over the past fifteen years and continues to do so, and this is undermining the economic func-tioning of the workforce as a whole.

Economic Policy and the four traps

The consequence of the reversal of policy from the mid-1970s has been a grow-ing economic and social polarisation. The rapid increase in the resource endow-ment of households at the top end of the income distribution has combined with improved capabilities as multi-earner households have become the norm and as job opportunities have widened for women. At the bottom end, high unemploy-ment, the disappearance of well-paid male jobs, increased casualisation of work, the growth of part-time work, declining relative pay and cuts in social welfare have served to impede the economic functioning of the relatively poor by reduc-ing their resource endowment and their capabilities. The outcome of policy and the resulting labour market restructuring has sprung four closely interrelated traps: Keynesian unemployment trap, the low wage trap, the fiscal trap and the social deprivation trap.

The Keynesian unemployment trap

The impact of abandoning the full employment objectives in the late 1970s was to increase the involuntary unemployment and lower effective demand. The resulting deep depression in the early 1980s reduced investment in productive industries and impeded its recovery by dampening expectations. This exacerbated the long-term deindustrialisation of the British economy and, as a consequence, the supply side proved incapable of fully responding to the credit induced boom of the 1980s and the resulting trend increase in the propensity to import added to the deflationary bias.[9] The ability of the economy to generate full employment effective demand was further weakened by redistribution of income from the poor, most of whose income is consumed by the rich who save a high proportion of their income and who have a relatively high import propensity. The negative Keynesian employment effects were disguised in the late 1980s by the high levels of speculative real estate investment and debt financed consumer expenditure. But they were revealed and reinforced in the 1990s by the effects of debt over-hang, negative equity, the threat of unemployment and general pessimism on consumer expenditure and by the effects of the 1980s over investment in com-mercial building (the concrete overhang), high real interest rates, and depressed expectation on investment.

The low wage trap

The official supposition is that employers and the economy will respond positively to lower wages and less restrictive employment conditions. But low wage and poor working conditions also offer a means by which firms can compensate for their own weaknesses and shortcomings. The growing availability of undervalued labour allows firms to compensate for organisational and managerial inadequacies, delay the scrapping of obsolete capital equipment and engage in destructive price competition. The absence of wage discipline means that technologically and managerially backward firms can survive, and this helps prevent more progressive firms from expanding their share of the market. The overall effect is a lower average level of productivity and a slower rate of introduction and diffusion of new techniques and products.

More generally, the growing availability of undervalued labour and high unemployment create an environment in which entrepreneurship takes the form of cutting pay, worsening the conditions of employment and the exploitation of low paid labour. This can be expected to crowd-out the 'high road' to competitiveness requiring product and process innovation and a highly skilled, well motivated and co-operative workforce. Competition based on the development of new products has the effect of continuously shifting product market boundaries. If firms fail to respond, they are trapped in declining market niches. Although they may remain viable by cutting labour costs and capturing a larger share of a reduced demand, this can only be a short-term expedient. The long term depends on product-based competition rather than price competition, and this requires an emphasis on research and development, product design and quality. Yet, this strategy is discouraged by low wage competition and its continuous downward pressure on profit margins ruling out long-term considerations, encouraging cost paring which threatens quality standards and discouraging co-operation within and between firms designed to improve performance and foster product and process innovation.

The fiscal trap

The deflationary impact of macro-policy lowers the tax take and increases the social welfare bill while offsetting any incentive tax reductions may have on economic activity and hence the size of the tax base. The use of the tax/benefit system to counter unemployment by subsidising wages risks throwing subsidised labour into competition with unsubsidised labour. This can be expected to drive down wages and increase the incidence of wage subsidy. These Speenhamland effects are already in evidence. In April 1989 there were 285,000 claims for the in-work family credit at a cost of around £7 million per week (around £350 million on an annual basis). By January 1994 family credit had become more generous, the hours conditions had been relaxed, the number of claims for family credit had increased to 521,000 and the annual cost had risen to more than £1 billion (Department of Social Security, 1995). There are further costs to the policy of promoting 'non-standard' forms of work. The proliferation of part-time work at low rates of pay and self-employment means that the direct tax base is being eroded. In construction, which saw a considerable increase in self-employment in the 1980s, both (lawful) tax avoidance and (illegal) tax evasion have become widespread. The resulting loss to government revenues has been estimated at between £2 and £4 billion annually. The tax regime for construction has also contributed to a policy of cut-throat competition based on labour costs which is undermining quality standards and training which is creating serious skill shortages.[10]

The social exclusion trap

Unemployment and the increase in the number of jobs which are low paid, insecure and with poor working conditions has created a widening gap between the increasingly deprived and excluded 'under' class and the affluent 'contentment' class (Galbraith, 1992). But, the boundary between the included and excluded has proved to be by no means permanently fixed. Many of the previously protected white collar and managerial jobs have become increasingly precarious, as large-scale redundancies and casualisation penetrate deeper into the 'primary' employment sectors. Growing poverty and cutbacks in welfare provision have aggravated social trends towards, for example, more single parent families increasing the incidence of destitution in such households. There is also growing evidence of a causal link between, on one side, unemployment, poverty and social exclusion and, on the other, rising crime and declining physical and psychological health. These trends have deepened the vicious cycle of inadequate resources, impaired capabilities and poor economic performance in which a growing number of individuals and households are trapped.

The four traps, economic functioning and self-sufficiency

The Keynesian unemployment, low wage, fiscal and social exclusion traps are mutually reinforcing. The economy is caught in the fiscal trap because of the exchequer cost of the Keynesian unemployment trap and competitive failure due to the low wage trap. Similarly, individuals caught in the Keynesian unemployment trap can be expected to be in the low wage and/or the social exclusion traps. Moreover, unemployability (either actual or imagined by employers) and the lack of education, skill and motivation can be seen as both causes and consequences of being caught in the low wage and social exclusion traps.

The separate and combined effects of the four traps has been to trigger a cumulative downward spiral in the resource endowments and capabilities of individuals and hence their ability to remain self-sufficient. The value of labour power has been eroded by the effect of deindustrialisation and inadequate re-training opportunities whilst capabilities have been devalued by unemployment, the casualisation of work and declining relative pay. The detrimental effects of this on economic functioning are compounded by the growing importance in the resource endowments of poor households of means-tested social welfare benefits, the removal of many young people from the scope of social welfare, the changing sexual composition of employment and the relatively low pay of women. This has changed the pattern of intra-household dependency, increased the burden of sharing within households, exacerbating the trend towards more frequent family breakdown and radically increased the incidence of private inter-household income transfers, obligations which are particularly difficult to enforce. The end of resource sharing with the break-up of households further reduces economic functioning. The capabilities of single parents are reduced by the additional costs of managing small households and the effect of unshared responsibility for child care on labour market activities. The capabilities of young people are severely limited by the absence of a secure domestic base and the resulting poverty rules out the possibility of securing one. The effects of these cumulative downward spirals in economic functioning and self-sufficiency are a large part of the explanation of progressive social and economic degeneration of Britain at both the macro- and micro-levels.

Reversing decline

The single greatest obstacle to adopting policies designed to close the four traps and to reverse the cumulatively economic and social decline is the current conventional economic wisdom and its implementation in policy. This can be called the policy trap: the fifth, and arguably the deepest trap.

The origins of the policy trap

Monetarism and the belief in a causal link between the PSBR and inflation seriously limits the ability of governments to borrow to finance public expenditure. NAIRU, the idea of an inverse causal relationship between levels of unemployment and price inflation, is now so firmly entrenched that central bankers look with deep suspicion at any downward movement of unemployment from any level as signalling potential inflation and the need to increase interest rates.[11] The neo-liberal notion that the relatively rich required higher incomes to provide incentives for investment and entrepreneurship whilst reduced welfare and wages are needed to generate employment for the poor provided the justifications for a more unequal distribution of income and cuts in tax and benefits. The adoption of these views as the conventional economic wisdom lifted responsibility for unemployment and poverty from the government and shifted it to the jobless and the poor. The idea that a more unequal distribution of income is superior on efficiency grounds also formed the basis for an opportunistic alliance between vote seeking political parties offering tax cuts and market deregulation and the rent seeking *contented classes* – special interest groups and voters who stood to benefit from the tax cuts, the availability of low paid labour and the opportunities for profits created by deregulation (Galbraith, 1992). The alliance between the state and the contented classes has been subsequently strengthened by four reinforcing processes. Firstly, the victims of the downward economic and social spiral triggered by policy change have become increasingly alienated from the 'democratic' process so that political exclusion has been added to economic and social exclusion. Secondly, this political exclusion has been progressively reinforced as political parties of the left have abandoned their traditional class allegiances and embraced the new economic and social orthodoxy to compete for the so-called political centre ground. Thirdly, the growing problems of long-term unemployment, poverty, crime and social dislocation over the past two decades have increasingly polarised society and the contented classes have found themselves more and more threatened by the 'dangerous classes'. Fourthly, those promoting the conventional economic wisdom to practitioners have continued to justify their failed predictions by developing theories explaining unemployment, underemployment and poverty in terms of labour market imperfections, welfare state dependency and the low quality and poor motivation of the unemployed, the under-employed and the working poor.[12] By doing so, they have provided continued justification for damaging economic and social policies by the age old expedient of blaming the victim (Ryan, 1971).

It is now virtually impossible for political parties to propose any radical alternatives to those supported by the conventional wisdom. There is general consensus across political parties that the problem of unemployment is a supply side issue to be addressed by training or by such expedients as subsidising jobs; that fiscal and monetary prudence is the essence of macro-economic management; that the welfare state breeds dependency and needs modification to reinforce employment incentives, that labour standards other than a low minimum wage threaten jobs and that union organisations and collective bargaining are outdated forms of labour market institutions. Meanwhile, any party in opposition advocating policies with implications for additional taxation are at grave electoral risk and any party in power contemplating monetary and/or fiscal policies designed to reduce unemployment and alleviate poverty risks opposition from the increasingly independent central bankers and the threat of financial crises in increasingly unregulated capital markets.

Closing the policy trap

As Galbraith (1969) noted when considering the conventional wisdom in social sciences: 'Ideas are inherently conservative. They yield not to the attack of other ideas but to the massive onslaught of circumstance with which they cannot contend' (Galbraith, 1969: 19). The conventional wisdom he had in mind was the pre-Keynesian orthodoxy and the massive onslaught of circumstances was the growing poverty and unemployment of the inter-war years which played no little part in the rise of fascism and the developments leading up to the Second World War. The new conventional wisdom was Keynesianism and welfare state theorising. These ideas were developed to their fullest in the social corporatist states of Europe where increasingly the right to jobs, skills and effective social welfare became recognised as citizen rights and whose governments proved most resistant to the neo-liberal theorising and its regressive consequences. Increasingly, however, they are under the threat of destructive competition from global competitors benefiting from deregulated labour and capital markets and from the effects of the deflationary macro-economic policies, imposed at least partly in response to monetarist inspired Maastricht restrictions on government borrowing. As a result, the core economies of the European Union are beginning to renege on their citizens' economic and social rights and are embarking on the degenerative neo-liberal policy path pioneered by the United States and Britain. Perhaps this will create the 'massive onslaught of circumstances' necessary for a U-turn towards a new conventional wisdom. To be successful, such a development will need to embrace the national and international cohesiveness of the policy development which laid the foundation for the post-1945 revival of Europe.

Closing the Keynesian unemployment, low wage, social exclusion and fiscal traps

Labour standards have a central part to play in reforms of the social security system and making successful policies to increase labour market participation. As currently constituted, the poorest working families have little to gain from higher wages because increases in income are captured by the state by reductions in means-tested benefits. The unemployed are trapped both because the means testing of benefits makes the effective tax rate on their marginal income very high and because job opportunities for the unemployed are generally low paid and unstable. Consequently, although out-of-work benefits are low, they can at least be relied upon whereas that income certainty is sacrificed by participation in segments of the labour market where neither jobs or pay levels are secure (McLaughlin *et al.*, 1989). Improved wage and employment standards would therefore both help lift poor families out of the poverty and unemployment traps and increase the incentive for their members to increase their pay by seeking out better jobs, acquiring training or by other means. Improved wage and employment standards would also contribute to the efficiency of social policy by preventing low paid employment subsidised by social welfare benefits and by ensuring that increased state provision of nursery schools and other measures designed to increase job opportunities result in their beneficiaries enjoying secure well paid jobs rather than providing undervalued labour to low paying employers.

Such reforms are designed to increase the resources and the capabilities of individuals and reduce the risk of poverty and social exclusion. The most efficient way of achieving this at the micro-level is to increase the economic functioning of individuals so that they have more employment generated income. Much has been learned by local action across the European Union about what constitutes good practice in assisting individuals who are long-term unemployed or exposed to social exclusion.[13] However, the requirement is for much greater co-operation and co-ordination between social welfare, state and voluntary organisations helping the disadvantaged, and the labour market organisations responsible for designing and implementing labour market policies directed at assisting individuals. Without this, individuals who are most disadvantaged will not receive the breadth and continuity of assistance essential for raising their capabilities. Therefore, a new consensus is necessary at the national level to ensure that resources from the different areas of policy are available to support the primary objective. But this consensus must include the macro-economic policy makers. Raising the supply potential of the available labour force maybe a necessary but it is not a sufficient condition of full employment. Ultimately, the success of policies aimed at raising the functioning of individuals will depend on the availability of jobs; on dismantling the Keynesian unemployment trap.

This, in turn, will depend on an improvement in competitive performance requiring a closing of the low wage trap by means of an effective system of regulation designed to raise labour standards and to reduce inequality. High and equitable terms and conditions of employment will require employers to improve management, technology and products; encourage them to make better use of their workers by improved training and personnel policy; and create an environment in which workers have the long-term security necessary to benefit from the improved job opportunities. High labour standards also have an important part to play in securing a co-operative work environment, now widely recognised as essential for securing worker co-operation in technical development, product enhancement and continuous quality control. Worker involvement is the key to such development, but this cannot be relied on where workers have no long-term prospects and when there is no assurance that workers' interests will not be summarily sacrificed to those of other stakeholders in the firm, such as shareholders and creditors. The effectiveness of the modern business enterprise depends on providing workers with rights which give them a voice alongside those of other stakeholders. This, along with other aspects of effective labour regulation, requires that workers have independent representation and collective bargaining underpinned by a floor of legal rights to minimum terms and conditions of employment. However, if such policies are to be effective in closing the low wage trap they will need to be supported by measures to ensure the successful redeployment of workers displaced by technical progress and changing consumer demand. This will require effective, universal and equitable social welfare provision; adequate and widely available facilities for retraining and the relocation of workers; the minimisation of barriers to entry into different occupations, a strategy for working time; the provision of high quality child care and effective anti-discrimination policies. Such measures are required to maintain demand in the labour market and to reduce structural unemployment so as to prevent establishment and expansion of disadvantaged social and labour market segments.

The cumulative effects of the policies outlined above will do much to close the fiscal trap (see Kitson *et al.*, 1996). The fiscal benefits of high levels of employment and improved labour market standards are clear. Full employment and a more equal income distribution of income before tax would broaden the tax base, reduce the aggregate social welfare payments and reduce the cost of redistributing income through the expensive tax/benefit network. Good labour market standards would have the added advantage of ensuring that best use was made of government expenditure by removing the risk that any attempt to help the working poor would merely provide wage subsidies for inefficient employers and lead to declining pay levels, increasing employment insecurity, growing poverty and burgeoning social welfare expenditure.

A more permanent measure to close the fiscal trap and remove the cumulative spiral of increasing unemployment, social deprivation and rising budget deficits would be to remove much or all social welfare from the government income and expenditure equation. This could be achieved by a switch away from a social welfare system funded out of current taxation towards mutual insurance schemes by which rights to benefits were established by contributions. For this to be effective, a way would need to be found of ensuring that individuals not active in the labour market – for example, the providers of household services – were credited with contributions. But this broader recognition of what constitutes economic activity would be central to any reforms designed to increase self-sufficiency and economic performance. A major advantage of mutual insurance schemes would be the removal of public transfers from the arena of power politics where the poor are particularly vulnerable. For this to be completely successful would probably require that the responsibility of such a scheme be vested in institutions constitutionally protected from short-term political expediency. To ensure such schemes' viability procedures would be needed by which adjustments could be made to such variables as levels of contributions and benefits, age at retirement to accommodate unpredicted increases in the average length of lifetime and other factors influencing the cost of provision. These schemes would also need to go hand-in-hand with high and relatively stable rates of employment and measures to prevent labour undervaluation to ensure that the actuarial uncertainties of future job loss or low pay did not undermine the validity and viability of the schemes.

Conclusions

It cannot be pretended that this policy transition or its implementation will be easy. There are already examples in Britain of concentrations of social exclusion where two or more generations of households have had no contact with the labour market. Economic functioning for these groups has no meaning. They attract transfers until their eligibility expires or their entitlement is withdrawn, but then the costs of subsequent alienation, crime, ill health and social disruption, replace transfers as a continuing cost on the state and the wider population. Having people outside the systems which maintain and encourage economic functioning is a dead weight on macro-policy – a permanent fiscal trap. Hence a rational view is to make the systems all inclusive.

The micro aspects of integration into full economic functioning fall broadly into two groups: first, the combination of work, welfare and social inclusion, and second the pathways to integration into the core labour market and into self-sufficiency. The constraints on the first stage of integration are the cost burdens of the socially excluded and the difficulties of including the excluded groups into the support structures which are no longer part of their community culture. Recovery for these groups requires raising their capabilities to a level at which they can and will participate and succeed in labour market measures aimed at facilitating economic functioning, but this is expensive and will only be partially self-financing in the short period. Hence, one constraint is the cost burden but another constraint is the difficulty in building a co-operative approach to the socially excluded which involves contributions from a wide variety of state departments and programmes (e.g. labour measures, social welfare, health and education).

Full integration will require continuing support to maintain participation. There are a wide variety of services that need to be provided as a package for individuals, including guidance, counselling, personal problem solving, basic skills, vocational skills, work experience and placements into jobs which have a regular contractual status in the labour market and pay the rate for the job. There are several constraints including the need to establish and reproduce an infrastructure of trainers and providers who have the skills appropriate to delivering the complex assistance required; the need to obtain involvement, commitment and changed attitudes among employers and trade unions to ensure quality employment opportunities; and, full assimilation into the workplace and associated collective bargaining arrangements.

The key to effective micro processes is that the value of participants in programmes is fully recognised and their needs met and that the expectations of outcomes are realistic, both for providers and participants. This requires co-operation between different providers (including the state, local actors, employers and social partners) and between providers and their participants based on a consensus about objectives and a relationship of trust. Overall, policies and structures for welfare, labour market support, health, education, collective bargaining, labour market regulation and social protection need to be complementary and mutually reinforcing. This is the major constraint on how effectively the micro- and macro-economy can be made consistent, because it requires political and social as well as economic consensus and agreement over the rights and responsibilities of all parties. These conditions are constraining and there is potential for significant conflict between the micro and macro requirements. Moving from a situation in which the four traps are operating to one where they have been removed requires careful phasing of changes which show a net gain in economic functioning relative to the absorption of resources at each stage, and which are based on an agreed and accepted change in the balance of power in the labour market and more widely in society.

Notes

1 We are grateful to Oxford University Press for permission to reprint this chapter, which originally appeared in Michie, J. and Grieve Smith, J. (eds), *Employment and Economic Performance*, 1997.
2 For discussion of the evolution of inflation theory in the postwar period see Wilkinson (1996).
3 The most important private transfers are within the household; others include private intra-community income sharing, inter-generational transfers and charities.
4 This section draws heavily on Wilkinson, 1991.

5 For detailed analyses of the dynamic effects of industrial restructuring and changes in hiring, training and other aspects of labour management on the supply and demand side structuring of the labour market see the collection of articles in *Labour and Society*, October, 1988.

6 For a discussion of these effects, see Ergo 2 final report (European Commission/CPC, 1998).

7 The individual usually has the status of tax payers and benefit recipient but not always at the same time. They also may not give equivalent weight to the taxes they pay and the benefits they receive. For example, current tax payers may resist the taxes needed to fund the education for other people despite the fact that they had earlier benefited from education. Moreover, benefit recipients are also taxpayers, but these are more likely to be the indirect taxes which are less politically sensitive if for no other reason they bear down most heavily on the poor.

8 What has been called the fiscal crisis of the state is an example of the taxpayers' exercise of their power.

9 By 1990, the balance of payments on current account was in deficit to the extent of almost 2.8 per cent of GDP; in the same year manufacturing investment was 2.6 per cent of GDP.

10 M. Harvey, *Taxed into Self-Employment: The Unique Case of the UK Construction Industry* (Institute of Employment Rights, 1995).

11 NAIRU thereby becomes a mechanism by which expected inflation is converted into actual unemployment by policy intervention.

12 See, for example, Layard *et al.* (1991), Snower (1994) and Phelps (1992, 1994).

13 See ERGO 1 Final Report.

References

Bowles, S. and Gintis, H. (1976) *Schooling in Capitalist America*. New York: Basic Books.

Coutts, K. and Rowthorn, R. (1995) 'Employment in the United Kingdom: trends and prospects', ESRC Centre for Business Research, University of Cambridge, Working Paper No. 3.

Deakin, S. and Morris, G. S. (1995) *Labour Law*. London: Butterworth.

Department of Social Security (1994) *Social Security Statistics 1993–1994*, tables A1.01, A1.02.

ERGO Programme, Phase One, Final Report, Commission of the European Commission, Director-General for Employment, Industrial Relations and Social Affairs, DG V/A/1, April 1992.

ERGO Programme, Phase Two, Final Report, Commission of the European Commission, Director-General for Employment, Industrial Relations and Social Affairs, DG V/A/1, 1998.

Galbraith, J. K. (1969) *The Affluent Society*. London: Hamish Hamilton.

Galbraith, J. K. (1992) *The Culture of Contentment*. Boston: Houghton Mifflin Company.

Goodman, A. and Webb, S. (1994) 'For richer, for poorer: the changing distribution of income in the UK, 1961–1991', *Fiscal Studies*, 28.

Harvey, M. (1995) *Taxed into Self-Employment: The Unique Case of the UK Construction Industry*, Institute of Employment Rights.

Hirsch, B. T. and Addison, J. T. (1986) *The Economic Analysis of Unions: New Approaches and Evidence*. Boston: Allan and Unwin.

Horrell, S., Rubery, J. and Burchell, B. (1989) 'Unequal jobs or unequal pay?' *Industrial Relations Journal*, 20(3), 176–91.

Joseph Rowntree Foundation, *Inquiry into Income and Wealth, Vol. 2*.

Kitson, M., Michie, J. and Sutherland, H. (1996) *The Fiscal and Distributional Implications of Job Generation*. Cambridge: ESRC Centre for Business Research Working Paper. October 1988.

Lancaster, K. J. (1966) 'A new approach to consumer theory', *Journal of Political Theory*, 43.

Layard, R., Nickell, S. and Jackman, R. (1991) *Unemployment, Macroeconomic Performance and the Labour Market*. Oxford: Oxford University Press.

Marshall, A. (1947) *Principles of Economics*. London: Macmillan, p. 549.

McLaughlin, E., Millar, J. and Cooke, K. (1989) *Work and Welfare Benefits*. Aldershot: Avebury.

Meade, J. E. (1995) Full Employment Regained, University of Cambridge, Department of Applied Economics, Occasional Paper No. 61, Cambridge: Cambridge University Press.

Parker, H. (1995) *Taxes, Benefits and Family Life*. London: Institute for Economic Affairs.

Phelps, E. S. (1992) 'A review of unemployment', *Journal of Economic Literature*, XXX(3), 1476–90.

Ryan, W. (1971) *Blaming the Victim*. New York: Pantheon Books.

Sen, A. (1985) *Commodities and Capabilities*. Amsterdam: North Holland.

Snower, D. J. (1994) 'Converting unemployment benefits into employment subsidies', *American Economic Review*, Papers and Proceedings.

Spence, M. (1973) 'Job market signalling', *Quarterly Journal of Economics*, August, 355–74.

Wells, J. (1994) 'The Missing Million' (Summer), *European Labour Forum*.

Wilkinson, F. (1988) 'Real wages, effective demand and economic development', *Cambridge Journal of Economics*, 7(3–4), 413–29.

Wilkinson, F. (1991) 'The structuring of economic deprivation and social deprivation and the working of the labour market in industrial countries', *Labour and Society*, 16(2).

Wilkinson, F. (1996) 'Changes in the notions of unemployment and what that means for the poor', in P. Arestis, G. Palma and M. Sawyer (eds), Markets, Unemployment and Economic Policy, Essays in Honour of Geoff Harcourt, Vol. 2, London: Routledge.

13 Equal opportunities as a productive factor[1]

Jill Rubery, Jane Humphries, Colette Fagan, Damian Grimshaw and Mark Smith

Equal opportunities has been largely accepted as a socially worthwhile objective, but an objective which is still considered a burden or a constraint on economic growth and development. This view reflects a narrow and short-term economic perspective which tends not only to ignore the interests and well being of the female labour force but also fails to recognise the need to develop new coherent systems of social and economic organisations in the interests of both men and women. Equal opportunities policies go beyond their immediate role to contribute to broader social objectives, including safeguarding social participation and preventing social exclusion. The aim of this chapter is to provide a more in-depth analysis of the potential for equal opportunities to contribute to economic and social well-being, broadly defined.

The European employment strategy, adopted subsequent to the Amsterdam Treaty, has increasingly integrated equal opportunities into the employment approach. In Luxembourg, in 1997, equal opportunities was adopted as one of four employment pillars of the employment guidelines used to construct National Action Plans on employment; subsequently, during the Austrian Presidency of the Council of Ministers, a guideline was added requiring gender mainstreaming through all the employment pillars; and at the Lisbon summit in March 2000, numerical targets were adopted which have relevance to equal opportunities. Specifically, women's employment rate should rise from 51 per cent to 60 per cent as part of a strategy to raise the overall employment rate to 70 per cent by 2010 and member states should improve their childcare facilities in line with best practice in the European Union (EU). Despite these significant political developments in the approach to equal opportunities in employment policy, there are still major gaps in the understanding of the interrelationships between equal opportunities and the dual policy objectives of pursuing an active and productive European economy while maintaining and modernising European social policy. The argument to be made here is that equal opportunities, far from adding an additional constraint or burden, can play an important role in achieving the development of a productive Europe. The notion of equal opportunities, as a productive factor, provides both an underpinning to the case for mainstreaming gender into employment policy and a contribution to the general conceptualisation of social policy as productive and supportive of employment policy.

Broadening the conceptual framework

Conceptualising equal opportunities as a productive factor

The framework for assessing the costs and benefits of policies adopted by economists is traditionally extremely narrow. The conventional depiction of equal opportunities policies is as a form of *consumption* and not as a form of *investment*. As consumption, equal opportunities policies are seen as morally desirable attributes of social and economic life but ones which involve costs. But in so far as equal opportunities policies have effects on the longer run productive capability of individuals, firms, regions and nations, they can be considered investment. At the same time, the objectives of policy can be understood as extending beyond a conventional concern with growth to a broader interest in the quality of life available to citizens. These different perspectives are illustrated in the 2 by 2 matrix shown as Table 13.1.

Under a narrow economist interpretation, the effects of equal opportunities policies are contained in cell 1.1. Equal opportunities policies are thought of as consumption with immediate and palpable costs. These costs feed through a variety of channels to reduce growth. Alternatively, if the objective of economic activity is thought of as broader than growth to include the quality of life, then we move from 1.1 to 1.2. Even though equal opportunities policies are still understood as consumption, they are now allowed to have direct positive effects, again through various channels, on the quality of life. The second column in the matrix

Table 13.1 Alternative economic analyses of equal opportunity policy

	Productivity seen as	
	Growth	Quality of life
Equal opportunities policy seen as		
Consumption	*1.1* Imposes costs on organisations by raising wage costs, restricting working time flexibility, raising training bill, etc. Increases social protection expenditure by increasing family support and services and establishing individualisation of rights.	*1.2* May have positive quality of life effects as expands personal choice; redistributes resources to reduces poverty among women and children; enhances quality of working life by reducing stress and increases rewards from working
Investment	*1.3* Ensures more effective utilisation of human resources and expenditure on education of women; avoids depreciation of investments associated with childcare leave; ensures an appropriate system of securing the reproduction of children.	*1.4* Investment in the development of a new gender contract compatible with new patterns of work life and home life should enhance long-term quality of life for men, women and children and for all varieties of families.

makes explicit the social benefits which stem from policies; here the concern is broadened to take into account the need for social reproduction (Berghman and Fouarge, 1998). Recasting equal opportunities policies as investment shifts us down to the second row of the table. Now even with the narrow focus on growth, equal opportunities policies can be seen as having various potentially positive effects as in 1.3. In 1.4, with the broader perspective on the quality of life and equal opportunities policies thought of as investment, additional positive links are hypothesised. Only by reading equal opportunities policies as *consumption, and only consumption*, and simultaneously holding to a narrow understanding of the objective of economic activity as growth, are we restricted to the negative impacts of policy suggested in 1.1. A broader view and longer time horizon suggest the possibility of significant positive offsets. Unfortunately, conventional analyses have emphasised the narrow economist interpretation of 1.1: this chapter seeks to redress the balance by focusing on a reading of equal opportunities policies as investment and the objective of economic activity as the quality of life.

Countering the view that the status quo is efficient and productive

Recent developments in economic theory have potentially provided the scope for identifying a positive role for equal opportunities policy in promoting economic and social development. The recognition of the existence of missing markets based on information gaps provides scope for the analysis of market failure and inefficient outcomes. Transaction costs theory has incorporated the analysis of social institutions, including the family, into the overall economic framework, thereby providing the opportunity to broaden the analysis to include the private and the public sphere and the organisation of social reproduction alongside that of production. The interest in bargaining theory has implicitly introduced power relations and indeterminacy into the analysis of economic and social relationships. In practice, however, these new theoretical developments have been used as much to defend the status quo as the most efficient outcome unless proved otherwise and not to identify scope for policy intervention. Missing markets are seen as best solved by adding markets and not through policy intervention. Governance structures are regarded as reflecting transactions costs and social preferences and the current institutional arrangements, including, for example, the marriage contract, are considered to be socially optimal. Otherwise, over time, the institutions will be reformed in line with changing tastes and transactions costs. And despite the potential focus on intra as well as inter-household distribution facilitated by bargaining models, economic theory still usually retains the assumption that households take action to maximise household welfare, without reference either to internal distribution or to the potential dissolution of households.

This general tendency to use these approaches to defend not only current economic but also social arrangements is exemplified by Pollak's description of marriage. Complex, continuing relationships are difficult to govern via contracts;

hence agents are said to resort to a more complete form of integration. For Pollak, however, the development of marriage as a social institution is assumed capable of providing an optimum solution to these complex and long-term relationships. Marriage is thus 'flexible enough to allow adaptive, sequential decision making in the face of unfolding events and rigid enough to safeguard each spouse against opportunistic exploitation by the other' (Pollak, 1985: 595). If it were not so, it is argued, agents would stop entering into these contracts.

These approaches can be seen to reflect the predilections of the mainstream to support the status quo and increasingly to bolster this argument by apparently taking into account a wider range of social and institutional arrangements within their framework of analysis. These developments stack the odds against being able to develop an argument for equal opportunities policy within a policy-making community embedded in the mainstream economic approach. Returning to the issue of the marriage contract we can ask the question, does marriage actually offer the same level of protection to each spouse? Even using a transactions costs framework, we can see that specialisation may not benefit women as much as men. If the marriage contract involves an agreement for specialisation and exchange, with women specialising in 'children' on the expectation that men will provide them with support from their earnings in return, problems may arise because of the differential nature of the timing of investment and exchange and the problems of enforcing such contracts in the moral and the legal sense. Opportunistic behaviour by the spouse who has not specialised in marriage-specific capital may lead to termination of the contract or unfavourable contract terms for the spouse who has invested in specialised capital. Women become trapped in marriages by their lack of general capital and may be exploited. Divorce courts can only partly compensate for marital breakdown and women and children clearly suffer economically from divorce much more than men. Poverty among children in single parent households often far outstrips poverty in couple households, particularly in societies where there has been little attempt to introduce policies to support parenting and equal opportunities policies.

But women may, increasingly, take action to protect themselves against these outcomes by, for example, reducing their fertility. Intra-household bargaining may depend to large degree upon external bargaining power and access to independent income; in order to protect their position women may decide that the costs of having children are too great, a tendency indicated by falling fertility rates in many (OECD) countries. Here, we can begin to identify the ways in which change in infrastructure development may change private behaviour within marriage, thereby adding to the social welfare of households and individuals. The extension of state support for childcare is usually regarded as solely a women's issue (Gardiner, 1997: 207) but its provision may change the nature of intra-household bargaining in such a way that it may allow women and men to exercise their actual preferences with respect to childbirth without taking into account the negative impact that childcare in the home may have on long-term household income and indeed intra-household distributional issues.

Identifying specific contributions to a productive society from equal opportunities policy

This example of the marriage contract reveals the different ways in which prevailing social institutions can be interpreted, once the notion is rejected that the status quo is efficient unless otherwise proven. There are three main ways in which we can identify equal opportunities policies as adding potentially to the productivity of the society defined in a broad sense to include social cohesion and coherence and to involve the quality of life.

Enhancing individual opportunities and reducing social risk

The first way in which equal opportunities can make a positive contribution is through enhancing individual opportunities and individual choice and reducing social risk. We have already argued, in the example of the marriage contract, that current social institutions may not provide protection against social risks. Here there are strong arguments that can be made that less specialisation within marriage may help women to establish a more even bargaining power within marriage and reduce the risk of social exclusion and poverty associated with marital breakdown where women currently bear the major burden. However, in order for specialisation to be reduced there needs to be major developments in the social and economic infrastructure to enable households and individuals to break out of the pattern of specialisation. Women in more advantaged positions, possessing high levels of education and/or located in high income households, are already taking such action by remaining in full-time and higher paid positions in the labour market. For those further down the social hierarchy to have similar opportunities, more needs to be done to close the gender pay gap and to provide the infrastructure of childcare and the regulations on working time which are compatible with two-earner households. The single breadwinner household is now in any case facing high long-term risks as more men fail to find or to keep a job paying a wage sufficient to support dependents. A policy to promote economic activity of both partners may therefore benefit both men and women in low income households.

The current government has recognised half of this 'truth' in its policies to promote dual earner households at the bottom of the income distribution through inwork benefits and childcare credits. However, the part of equal opportunities policy which the government has been least willing to address is the gendered nature of labour market organisation, revealed both in pay structures and in working time arrangements. Changing the nature of specialisation in marriage is not possible without action on all these fronts.

Enhancing choice and reducing social risk involves both developing the liberal right to individual choice, not impeded by gender stereotypes and the more radical objective of valuing equally diverse attributes and activities. The former allows individuals and households to make choices over career and domestic arrangements which are not constrained by having to fit the mould of male and female careers and job choices. The latter focuses on whether the current ways in which we value jobs, skills and non-work activities are more reflective of wider power relations than social value. These different approaches have also been labelled the short and the long agenda for equal opportunities (Cockburn, 1991) and can be considered to be mutually compatible rather than competitive; it is unlikely that we can move towards new ways of valuing jobs and activities while we retain the current systems of gender assignment to roles and occupations.

The need to move away from categorisation on the basis of the average behaviour of a subgroup has been brought into sharp perspective by the current debate over the genome project. It is widely recognised that genetic mapping could allow employers and insurance companies to identify groups at risk of particular illnesses and discriminate against them in hiring decisions and provision of insurance. This could create socially disadvantaged and excluded groups deprived of basic citizenship rights. All these dangers apply and have applied to the use of gender stereotypes in job assignment, but the notion that this is discriminatory has not been evident to many policy-makers, as they rationalise the process as reflecting actual real differences between the sexes. Moreover, the integration of women in households with men has served to obscure the social exclusion aspects of the process which only become clear once women need to fend for themselves as lone parents, widows or indeed single and childless women.

Developing human potential

This brings us to the second main way in which equal opportunities can be a productive factor, that is, it allows for human potential to be developed and deployed more effectively, thereby allowing for the possibility of more productive lives for all citizens. This fits with the objectives of the European employment strategy of moving to an active and high productivity economy, achieved through rather than despite a European social policy.

Equal opportunities in education has been more widely accepted than equal opportunities in the labour market and women are, in fact, already participating at an equal and sometimes a higher level than men in education in Europe. However, to the extent that the expansion of education is related to labour market needs there is a fundamental contradiction here in the effectiveness of policies, for those policies which would enable women with medium or high education to remain in the labour market are deemed to be too costly for the economy or tax payer, and yet no such problems are envisaged in funding that education in the first place.

Table 13.2 shows the wide gender gaps in employment rates, even for those with higher education. This suggests that unless we are to retreat from equal opportunities in education the only logic is for governments to establish better policies for keeping at least their higher skilled workers in the labour market. In addition to loss of potential through low participation there is the further problem of underemployment. This applies to the number of hours that women work, particularly where they are confined to short hours part-time jobs to the level of

Table 13.2 Gender differences in employment intensity for higher educated labour (population aged 25–59 with tertiary education)

	Male full-time equivalent employment rate 1995	Female full-time equivalent employment rate	Gender gap in full-time equivalent employment rate
Austria	88.6	75.2	13.4
Belgium	90.8	70.5	20.3
Germany (West)	89.6	67.3	22.3
Germany (East)	85.4	75.8	9.6
Denmark	90.5	74.1	16.4
Spain	83.2	63.7	19.5
Finland	84.1	79.9	4.2
France	88.5	71.2	17.3
Greece	88.5	73.5	15.0
Ireland	90.8	70.7	20.1
Italy	88.1	73.3	14.8
Luxembourg	93.5	72.1	21.4
Netherlands	84.7	55.1	29.6
Portugal	91.6	86.4	5.2
Sweden	85.9	75.5	10.4
UK	89.6	70.1	19.5
E15	88.2	69.8	18.4

Source: European Labour Force Survey 1995. Full-time equivalent rates calculated by treating a part-time job as equivalent to 0.5 of a full-time job.

skills and responsibilities that they are currently allowed to exercise and to the low wages paid in women's jobs which results in low status for the jobs and sometimes in low self-esteem for the employees. Furthermore, women also have more limited opportunities to renew and develop their skills as lifelong learning opportunities tend to be limited to those already in work and in full-time jobs. The European employment strategy is still focused, in part, on creating low wage jobs to provide opportunities for the unemployed; the possibility that there may be sufficient low skilled and low productive jobs does not seem yet to have reached the consciousness of policy-makers. The problem of entrapment of both women and men in low skill and low wage sectors is not addressed as it is assumed that all labour market participants are employed up to the level of their potential. This view persists despite parallel discussion of the impact of gender stereotyping and segregation on effective job choice. Policies to improve opportunities for those already in the labour market could do more to release jobs for the hard to employ while still fulfilling the aim of moving towards a high value economy.

Renewing co-ordination between households, welfare states and labour markets

The third way in which equal opportunity policies can contribute to a productive economy is by allowing a renewed co-ordination between households, welfare state and labour markets. Equal opportunities policies provide the basis for modernising the welfare state through the introduction of new systems of welfare and employment rights more appropriate to match the emerging realities of dual breadwinner households and flexible labour markets. An important part of any modernisation process is the formation of a new gender contract compatible with the changing roles of women and men.

> More women – and also more men – are facing dual and often conflicting labour market and family responsibilities. Ensuring the compatibility of employment and family commitments within individual lives is a major challenge emerging from the process of structural change. Shared family and employment roles will increase the potential labour force, promote a better utilisation of human capital, enhance gender equality, and improve quality of life.
>
> (OECD, 1991: 9)

However, the formation of a new gender and welfare contract will not be automatic; it requires political will and commitment. The rising instability of marriage and associated changes in family structure make traditional assumptions that families are headed by a male breadwinner earning a family wage increasingly unrealistic. Welfare systems were historically founded on assumptions that this was the standard family form. Policy-makers in confronting the issue of how to modernise and develop the welfare system do not have the option of assuming that the world has not changed; women's participation in paid work is rising even in states where there has been little or no public support for the policy and patterns of household and family formation are changing across Europe. There is no chance of a simple return to a single male breadwinner model, nor would such a policy be compatible with the objective of raising the European employment rate. The problem is, however, that in many states there has been little evidence of a systematic consideration of how to adjust to the new realities. While the situation in Europe with respect to family poverty may not be as severe as in the United States, Folbre's analysis of the development in the United States still provides a relevant warning for Europe unless action is taken.

> Both the expansion of markets and the enlargement of state participation in the economy empowered women and youth just enough to destabilise the patriarchal organisation of social reproduction, but not enough to generate a non-patriarchal system that might fairly and efficiently meet the needs of children and other dependants.
>
> (Folbre, 1994: 248)

However, instead of reform of welfare systems being driven by the need to develop a more coherent new approach, the actual changes introduced may be driven by short run cost considerations or may be ideologically motivated, possibly exacerbating the lack of coherence. For example, governments may be promoting the notion of flexible employment while making it increasingly difficult for flexible workers to have access to benefits (Rubery *et al.*, 1998: ch. 4). The promotion of equal opportunities policies has the benefit of forcing policy makers to make the links between labour market organisation, household and welfare systems and social reproduction. The European employment strategy has been increasingly forced to address issues of care arrangements in its strategy of increasing employment participation rates. Much still needs to be done to link together social life and welfare systems with employment objectives, but at least the requirement within the European employment strategy for gender main-streaming in all areas of employment policy provides a basis for beginning that process.

Equal opportunities as a productive factor: empirical evidence

The argument that equal opportunities can be considered a productive factor needs to be developed through the consideration of the specific ways in which an equal opportunities dimension can contribute to a productive economy. In this section, we focus on two areas – promoting a two-earner/two-carer society and desegregating jobs and pay structures – areas where policies to promote greater gender equality can be seen to be both compatible with the European employment strategy and the broader objectives of developing a more cohesive and productive society. Our aim here is to further develop the analytical case while putting some more empirical flesh on the argument, drawing on some secondary sources as well as on some relatively simple primary data analyses.

Promoting a two-earner/two-carer society

It is now widely recognised, and indeed incorporated into European Union targets in the 2000 Lisbon summit, that higher women's employment is the key to higher overall employment rates. Higher employment is the central objective of the European employment strategy, designed to reduce social exclusion and welfare dependency and at the same time to increase the tax base to fund raising welfare demands of an ageing society. Most of the expected growth in the employment rate can be attributed to rising labour market attachment of women. Younger women in all countries are now more educated than their older counterparts and are more likely to see the labour market as a permanent part of their future lives, even when there are children present. This increased labour force attachment of women compensates for the predicted decline in employment rates resulting from a rising share of the working age population aged over fifty, a group currently with relatively low employment rates.

Despite the clear significance of female employment to the overall employment objective, there are many ways in which current policies and institutional arrangements act both to hinder the development of female employment and also to promote a single breadwinner over a dual breadwinner model. Moreover, if women's rising employment is to be compatible with a move towards a more productive society, then measures have to be in place to promote women's involvement in high quality employment and to discourage the development of low paid and marginalised job areas in which women and other groups become trapped. To consider the potential benefits from adopting an equal opportunities perspective both for employment and social welfare objectives we look at the following areas: tax and benefit policy; social security policy and childcare and family policy.

Tax and benefit policy

The European employment strategy has recognised that barriers to women's employment in the form of tax disincentives could act as an impediment to achieving higher female employment rates. In practice, the impact of taxation systems on women's participation rates appears to have declined over recent years as even in countries which have retained strong disincentive effects, such as Germany, women have shown a determination to increase their participation. Under these conditions the taxation question becomes one of gender equity and not one of incentives or disincentives (Gustafson, 1996; Vermeulen *et al.*, 1994; CERC, 1994; Dingledey, 1998). Few countries have used the taxation systems as a positive incentive for female participation; the recent tax reform in the Netherlands which has introduced a small incentive for dual earners remains an exception. However, while tax rates as such do not seem to have a major deterrent effect, a different story may be told about means-tested household benefits as the effective rate of taxation of these benefits is often much higher, sometimes even above 100 per cent. It is these systems which can contribute to social exclusion of whole households and which may reduce the effective choice for women as to whether to work or not.

Despite their more significant impact, EU policies still say relatively little about changing benefit systems to avoid disincentives for women. The OECD (1997a,b), in contrast, has been more explicit in calling for more attention to be paid to the impact of means-testing on incentives for spouses, thereby pointing to the potential inefficiencies of policies of targeting benefits on less well-off households, as these policies may result in barriers to integration for both partners, or for the second partner where the benefits are paid as supplements to the low wage income of one partner. All these disincentive effects are exaggerated, the lower the potential earnings of the second partner, for whether or not to remain on benefits is not a relevant question where the gains from entering the labour market significantly exceed benefit levels. In practice, equal opportunities in wages would provide the most certain way of encouraging the growth of dual-earner societies. Recent trends towards inwork benefits, in for example in the United Kingdom, are introducing or strengthening disincentive effects for at least some categories of households (see Table 13.3 and Blundell and Reed, 1999). These policies are defended as a means of getting households off welfare and into work, but the impact on relatively low income two-earner households, where there are strong disincentives towards the second earner remaining in work are not directly considered. Yet, encouraging withdrawal from the labour market for these women not only raises the tax burden but also encourages discontinuous participation, with subsequent

Table 13.3 Estimates of the impact of Working Families Tax Credit on Employment Rates (1998 budget figures for WFTC rates)

	Gregg et al. (1999)		Blundell et al. (1998)		Paull et al. (1999)	
	Estimated increase in employment (thousands)	Estimated increase in employment rate	Estimated increase in employment (thousands)	Estimated increase in employment rate	Estimated increase in employment (thousands)	Estimated increase in employment rate
Single parents	+28,600	+1.85	+34,000	+2.20	+24,700	+1.60
Married women, partner not working	+14,610	+1.75	+11,000	+1.32		
Married women, partner working	−29,050	−0.83	−20,000	−0.57		
Married men, partner not working	+16,820	+0.48	+13,000	+0.37		
Married men, partner working	+1,790	+0.05	−10,500	−0.30		
Total	+32,770		+27,500			

Source: Blundell and Reed (1999).

loss of skills and future social protection for the women in question. An equal opportunities perspective would not only consider the impact at a household and cross sectional level but also identify these potential long-term costs of reintroducing relatively penal rates of marginal taxation. Similar arguments can be made with respect to the structure of childcare costs, as we discuss further below.

Social security contributions and social protection

A further aspect of women's employment experience relates to their involvement in low wage and part-time jobs, often referred to as marginal jobs. Systems which promote marginal part-time jobs through the exclusion of these jobs from social security contributions may be considered to be promoting both gender inequality and inefficient cross-subsidisation between those employers whose workers are integrated in the social security system and those who avoid these costs by concentrating employment in jobs below the thresholds for social protection. Some governments even present policies which allow exemptions from social security contributions for lower paid workers as promoting equal opportunities as such schemes tend to increase the employment of women; yet the counterpart of this promotion is the development of incentives to create gender-specific jobs at the margin of the labour market. Bettio *et al.* (1998) have argued that it might be possible instead to reduce employer and employee hourly social security contributions on hours between 26 and 32 a week but constant on either side of this hours band, thereby providing an incentive to employ people to work for these hours (Bettio *et al.*, 1998). If combined with a progressive and individualised tax system even more incentives would be provided for both members of the household to work these hours rather than one specialising in long hours and the other in short hours of work combined with domestic tasks, a policy which might reduce the specialisation in marriage associated with high social risks for women. A scheme such as this was introduced in France under the 'Loi Robien' but here the legislation encouraged hours reductions to between 16 and 32 hours. This law was introduced in 1996 to tackle high levels of unemployment in France by encouraging reduced working hours to create or protect jobs.

In 1996, a smaller share of the European labour force was found within the 26–32 hours band than the share found at either extreme of the distribution: for example 11 per cent of female employees and 3 per cent of male employees worked between 26 and 32 hours compared to 10 per cent of women working 15 hours or less and 23 per cent of male employees working more than 40 hours a week. A redistribution of work away from the extremes the impact could be to raise both the employment rate and the share of the workforce making social security contributions. For example, even if the working hours of only half of the employees working marginal hours (less than 15) and half of those working long hours (more than 40) were regrouped into jobs lasting 26 to 32 hours band, there would be a net increase in the number of employees in employment in all countries except the Netherlands, and at the EU level the employment rate would rise by 4 per cent (see Figure 13.1). The favourable effect is due to the higher

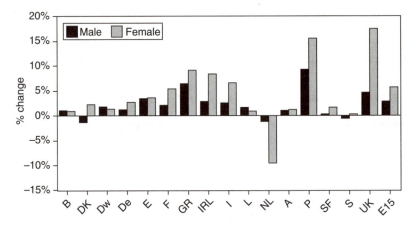

Figure 13.1 Percentage change in employees in employment, after redistribution of hours, 1996.

Source: European Labour Force Survey 1996.

Note: See text for details of redistribution.

quantity of working hours concentrated in long rather than marginal jobs, and the net fall in the Netherlands thus occurs because in this country the high share of short part-time jobs is not compensated by many long hour jobs. The impact of such a redistributive policy could also be to open up segregated parts of the labour market to both men and women, so that the shorter full-time hours in male-type jobs would be more open to women and the longer part-time jobs would be more open to men. Even if we assume that the redistributed hours provide opportunities for men and women in proportion to their current share of total employees within each member state, the impact at the EU level would be to raise the employment rate for women by 5.7 per cent and for men by 2.8 per cent. Women's employment would rise in all countries except the Netherlands and by over 15 per cent in Portugal and the United Kingdom. Such calculations do not include any adjustment for associated productivity gains from an hours reduction and the inevitable reorganisation of working arrangements that would occur in many cases. Nevertheless, this calculation does suggest that the employment effects across the EU as a whole could be large and beneficial, with women working longer hours, men working shorter hours and a smaller part of the labour market subject to gender segregation based on working hours.

Childcare and family policy

Policies towards the family in many countries remain based around the notion of a male breadwinner and a non-working spouse, despite the empirical evidence which has shown a sustained trend decline in the traditional nuclear family.

The failure of policy-makers to catch up with the changing patterns of work and family life may in part be associated with the attempts by mainstream economists to rationalise the breadwinner model as an efficient form of division of labour reflecting comparative advantage (Becker, 1981). This traditional division of labour has, however, in part at least, reflected the societal context in which the household is located. Under conditions where women obtain a lower return to working than men, this feeds back into, and reinforces, the household division of labour. In turn, women's actual or expected domestic responsibilities contribute to the maintenance of sex-segregated employment patterns (Humphries and Rubery, 1995; Rubery *et al.*, 1996). The mutual conditioning between activity in the labour market and the home maintains the 'gender order' (Connell, 1987). From this societal perspective, policies which weaken the existing 'male bread-winner' gender division of labour in households and address the persistence of gender segregation within labour markets can be argued to yield efficiency gains as well as equity gains on a number of criteria at the macroeconomic, firm and household level. This provides a much wider basis for policy intervention to change the nature of constraints which shape women's and men's decisions and actions in the labour market and in their domestic lives than that provided by the narrow explanation of gender differences offered by neo-classical economics.

It is with the onset of motherhood that women's employment rates start to fall below those of men's. At the same time, there is a marked national variation in the extent to which motherhood triggers labour market exits or a reduction in working hours. From a lifetime perspective, labour market exits to raise children are inefficient for the women involved and their households. Such interruptions frequently lead to a loss of occupational status upon labour market re-entry (Dex, 1987; McRae, 1991), producing a negative impact on women's future earnings and pensions. Policies which enable women to maintain a labour market profile of continuous employment when raising children create the necessary conditions for women to maximise their career potential and their lifetime earnings. Waldfogel (1993) has estimated that where UK or American women are able to take advantage of maternity leave provision and return to the same job with the same employer they are able to reduce the gender pay gap by 43 per cent in the United States and by 37 per cent in the United Kingdom. Household efficiency might be maximised by both parents putting time into paid work and child-rearing, rather than one parent 'over-specialising' in unpaid work (Owen, 1987). This is because the sharp depreciation in the returns to employment associated with a labour market quit coexist with a diminishing rate of return to the amount of time invested in employment by a continuous worker.

Joshi and Davies (1992) estimated that in the United Kingdom, women in the 1980s lost over 50 per cent of lifetime earnings as a result of quitting the labour market to have children, this loss composed in almost equal parts of lost years of work, reduced hours after returning to work and lower hourly earnings as a result of quits. Table 13.4 compares the result for mothers in the United Kingdom to the losses faced by German, French and Swedish mothers, based on estimates of earnings profiles in each of the four countries. German mothers also face losses

Table 13.4 Effects of bearing two children on employment and earnings

Loss factor	France	Germany	Great Britain	Sweden
Lost years				
All years	0.0	−10.0	−8.0	−2.0
Full-time years	0.0	−16.0	−22.0	−15.0
Part-time years	0.0	6.0	14.0	13.0
Full-time equivalent years	0.0	−12.9	−15.9	−4.8
Lost earnings (as % of childless earnings)	1.0	48.6	57.4	16.1
Components of lost earnings (as % of total)				
Due to lost years	0.0	60.1	32.1	30.7
Due to lost hours	0.0	17.6	33.3	45.7
Due to lower pay	100.0	22.4	34.5	23.6

Source: Joshi and Davies, 1992: table 3.

Note: Probability of participation fixed at 0.85 at age 20. The base case is a woman worker who has no children and is continuously employed until age 60. Years of work and costs are measured from ages 25–59 inclusive.

of close to 50 per cent mainly due to spending even more whole years out of the labour force. Swedish mothers, in contrast, only face losses of 16 per cent, with the main cause here being that the large number of years that Swedish women tend to work part-time after childbirth. In France, however, the costs of childbirth appear almost zero as mothers only take maternity leave and return to full-time work. In a similar exercise the same authors (Joshi and Davies, 1993) have calculated the impact on British women of access to the same childcare facilities as apply in Germany (kindergarten at age 3), in France (readily available childcare and full-time work) and Sweden (childcare combined with long part-time work). The estimated impact is only to reduce the 57 per cent cost to 56 per cent with the German childcare provision, to 24 per cent under the Swedish system but to only 8 per cent under the French system.

Few households are in a position to make this type of calculation of foregone household life-time income arising from employment interruptions in a context where there is little public help for childcare. Individuals have to make narrower, short-term calculations as they are unwilling or unable to enter into debt to fund childcare in anticipation of future higher earnings; individual households are thus unlikely to substitute for social provision even when they are made aware of the longer term costs. For example, evidence from the United Kingdom indicates that the usual consideration is the immediate financial one of the net return to women's employment once childcare costs have been set against her net earnings. This net return is an important influence on the decision about whether to return to employment after the exhaustion of maternity leave (Brannen and Moss, 1991; McRae, 1991). Recent data suggest that the risk of employment interruption is being increasingly recognised by women but particularly by higher skilled women.

The impact of children on estimated lifetime earnings varies from £250,000 for a low-skilled mother of two to £20,000 for a high-skilled mother of two (Rake, 2000). These variations reflect differences in the participation patterns of skilled and less skilled women, with the more skilled taking actions which may seem expensive in the short term, such as paying for childcare, but which protect their earnings over the longer term.

Thus, where there is a lack of public policies to enable mothers to reconcile employment with childcare responsibilities, the private solutions that households find may be sub-optimal in the long run particularly for less skilled women with lower potential salaries to cover the costs of childcare. If market failures persist in connection with maternal employment, then the economy may become locked into an enduring sub-optimality (Bruegel and Perrons, 1995). Policy intervention would not just produce efficiency gains for households, but would also address market failures arising from employers' behaviour and in turn produce aggregate gains for the economy. The immediate costs of women's employment interruptions for employers are the loss of experienced staff; the longer term global cost is the underdevelopment of women's contribution to the formal economy. Although employers may introduce measures to retain or recruit mothers of young children through 'family friendly' policies to reduce turnover costs, reliance upon voluntary employer provision is risky. First, employers making provision may face disproportionate costs if they attract more than the normal share of applicants likely to make use of the family friendly options. Furthermore, these policies may be curtailed in times of recession (Dickens, 1994). For example, the Midland Bank famously committed itself to establishing 300 workplace nurseries at a time of tight labour markets in Britain in the late 1980s but stopped its programme when the number reached 100 and the problems of retention had subsided. This cyclical interest in equal opportunities prevents a long-term market-led expansion of family policies and contributes to future potential skills shortages when the economy picks up. In contrast, economy-wide measures would spread the costs more evenly across employers and increase the overall female labour supply (Holtermann, 1995).

The efficiency gains from supporting mothers to remain in employment can also be considered in relation to the impact of such policies on the coherence and rationality of the pattern of income distribution over the life cycle (Anxo *et al.*, 1999). Where having children leads to employment interruptions and loss of income there are both costs to the households concerned and distortions in the labour market caused by the pressure on young men, in particular, to find jobs offering 'family wages' and/or extensive overtime opportunities. The pressure on household income caused by employment interruption is increasing as women's earnings now play a more important role in initial household formation and in the household budgets of young childless couples. There are also costs of not promoting equal opportunities that may be hidden, non-monetised or indeed borne by people not included in policy evaluations, such as children. There is widespread evidence, for example, that women undertake a double burden when they enter the labour market, which leads to considerable time pressure and stress

(Gershuny *et al.*, 1994; Hochschild, 1997; Sullivan, 1997). These problems may be exacerbated when parents are under pressure to work highly variable hours, including during evenings and weekends. Research in the United Kingdom suggests that it is the number and scheduling of hours worked by parents, rather than employment itself, which impacts on the quality of leisure and family time. Negative impacts arise when fathers are largely absent from family life due to working excessively long hours, or where work schedules prevent couples from having common periods of leisure and relaxation (Ferri and Smith, 1996; Sullivan, 1996). These time pressures on the quality of family life cannot be easily resolved at the microlevel through parents changing their participation patterns because of the long-term costs of either moving out of the labour market altogether or switching to part-time hours, particularly in labour markets where there is no right to reduce hours when responsible for a young child.

Efficiency and productivity implications of desegregating job and pay structures

Gender segregation is a persistent feature of European labour markets, even though women hold a growing proportion of jobs and spend a larger proportion of their working years in the labour market than in earlier periods this century (Rubery and Fagan, 1993; Anker, 1998; Rubery *et al.*, 1999). Labour markets can be regarded as having interlocking gender and occupational hierarchies, so that at each level of skill or qualification women are located in a lower-paid or lower-status position than men (Gottschall, 1995). Where women have gained entry into male-dominated professional jobs it has often been associated with a downgrading of the status of the profession, or the concentration of women in the less prestigious sub-specialisms of the profession (Crompton and Sanderson, 1990; Reskin and Roos, 1990). There are even fewer signs of jobs becoming less segregated in intermediate and lower-level occupations: clerical work is now female-dominated in most member states; most manual production and transport jobs are still done by men and most low-skill service jobs are done by women. Women who work part-time are even more segregated from male workers than women in full-time jobs, and are concentrated in an even narrower range of sectors and occupations (Rubery and Fagan, 1993; Fagan and Rubery, 1996).

Sex segregated employment patterns may be mobilised implicitly or explicitly with processes of employment restructuring, possibly leading to re-segregation around a new employment configuration. Alternatively, segregation may inhibit processes of labour market adjustment where there are borders which prevent one sex from moving into the labour market of the other. The main beneficiaries of the existence of segregation are those employers who can draw upon pools of cheap female labour and some male workers who manage to retain a monopoly over better-paid job areas. The costs of segregation are borne directly by women, but the channelling of women into certain jobs is also a cost to society, for women's skills are frequently under-used. One of the central features of the gender pay gap, is its association with sex segregation by occupation, industry and workplace

(Rubery, 1992; Millward and Woodland, 1995; OECD, 1998). Research into occupational gender segregation reveals considerable constraints on women's occupational choice, arising not only from the socialisation of women in the education and family system, but also from employer recruitment practices and the shaping of organisational and work cultures (Collinson *et al.*, 1990; Reskin and Roos, 1990). These constraints on labour market choice disturb the efficiency of the allocation of labour within the labour market. Even where there is an apparent matching of employment patterns to revealed preferences in the form of job applications, this does not necessarily imply efficiency. Individual women may not be able to exercise their preferences to train in and pursue careers in job areas where they expect to encounter discriminatory employers, or exclusion by male co-workers through hostility or excessively masculine work environments. Similarly men may find it difficult to consider work in a largely female environment, particularly where gender segregation is reinforced by low wages and part-time working hours. These constraints may create rigid labour markets such that, for example, the male unemployed may feel excluded from many of the new job growth areas.

Gender segregation is not only a symptom of gender inequality but also a process that facilitates the production and reproduction of gender inequality. Male-dominated and female-dominated occupations provide a basis for continuing to differentiate the terms and conditions on which men and women are employed. Hence the problem of segregation involves both the under-utilization of women's full potential and skills and the under-valuation of the jobs that women do. Women's lower pay fuels an inefficient sexual division of labour inside and outside the labour market by constraining the matrix of choices faced by both men and women. Individual households are unable to change the gender division of labour between paid and unpaid work without severe economic penalties if they live in a society in which earnings and job opportunities in the labour market are linked to gender. Progress towards gender equality in the division of labour inside and outside the labour market is therefore dependent upon policies to narrow the gender pay gap.

However, the gender pay gap is not simply a story of sex segregation and the 'underemployment' of women relative to their potential. As Figure 13.2 reveals, there are wide variations in the gender pay gap across countries and these variations are not systematically related to the pattern of occupational segregation. The structure of occupational earnings is not systematically related to skills and may also reflect gender discrimination. This finding applies to both regulated and decentralised systems of pay determination: under the former, pay structures may reflect relative collective bargaining strength, while under the latter there is increased scope for employer discretion, allowing sex bias to unhinge the link between pay and skills (Bevan and Thompson, 1992; Rubery, 1994, 1995). The undervaluation of 'women's work' may also generate a vicious cycle of underinvestment in skills leading to even greater inequality in earnings over the life cycle (Schömann and Becker, 1995; Tuijnman and Schömann, 1996).

Once the lack of correspondence between the pay and the skill structure is recognised, it is possible to make an argument that greater gender equality can be

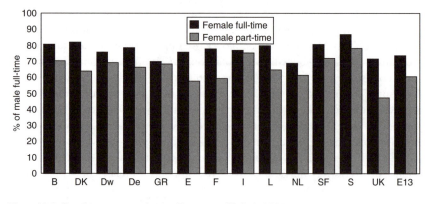

Figure 13.2 Gender wage gap in the European Union, 1995.

Source: Structure of Earnings Survey (Applica, 1998).

Note: Hourly data excluding overtime payments.

pursued not only as a goal in its own right, but also as an integral component of the productive capability of economy and society. In models of mainstream economics, the sexual division of labour reflects the efficient outcome of a set of free choices over entry into occupations which, in turn, reflect individuals' given preferences, initial endowments and rates of time preference. If the relative pay of occupations where women predominate is found to be low, then – following Adam Smith's theory of compensating differentials – this must be explained by a strong preference among women to work in these occupations (Humphries, 1995), a preference related according to the 'New Household Economics' literature by expected patterns of labour market participation over the life cycle. These notions have been critiqued and rejected on both theoretical and empirical grounds. For example, women are more likely to invest less in education due to expectations of lower pay, not due to expected employment over the life cycle (Blinder, 1973; Beller, 1982; England, 1982). Empirical evidence showing pay deteriorating as women enter an occupation (such as bank cashiers, clerical work and school teachers – Kessler-Harris, 1990; Reskin and Roos, 1990) suggests that pay levels are a reflection of gender segregation rather than an independent variable in occupational choice.

Advocates of equal opportunities have been at the forefront of dismantling the supposed determinate relationship between pay and skills. Evidence of the gendered valuation of skills (Phillips and Taylor, 1980; Armstrong, 1982; Horrell *et al.*, 1990) and the undervaluation of jobs performed by women (Sorensen, 1984; Acker, 1989; Blum, 1991; Rubery, 1992) provides further proof of the inefficient biases inherent in the labour market. Differences in male and female earnings also reflect, in part, the historical legacy of undervaluation of work done by women twinned with the association of men's work with a 'family wage'. Studies of the economic dependency of married women on their partners show that the resources of the male partner continue to have the single most important impact on the couple's life chances, although there is steady movement towards a more equal contribution from the wife to the household's financial position (Sørensen and McLanahan, 1987; Davies and Joshi, 1995; Ward *et al.*, 1996; van Berkel and Dirk de Graaf, 1998). Women's disadvantaged position in the labour market is thus reinforced by economic dependency in the household, reflecting the linkage between low rates of pay for female-dominated occupations and women's specialisation in domestic labour (Bruegel and Perrons, 1995). Neo-classical economists acknowledge the persistence of sex discrimination but argue that this must reflect a 'market failure'. Their policy recommendation is thus to encourage greater labour market flexibility, but in practice flexibility enhances employer discretion over pay practices, a discretion which is likely to lead to an exacerbation of sex discrimination and a widening of the gender pay gap (Rubery, 1995, 1997).

Indeed, a policy to close the gender pay gap needs to be pursued through strategies to upgrade and protect the pay of women, not through the deregulation and downgrading of the male labour market. In the United Kingdom, the gender pay ratio among manual workers has improved over recent years, but at the cost of a fall in male average earnings, representing the apparent demise of the family wage. Equalisation through levelling down has had the perverse effect of a withdrawal of low-skilled married couples from the labour market, since the uncertain prospects of new non-standard forms of employment and the lack of publicly-funded childcare support make it difficult for dual-earner couples to meet reproduction costs (McLaughlin, 1991; Gregg and Wadsworth, 1995). In an innovative assessment of the changing nature of the employment structure and welfare system in the United Kingdom over the 1980s, McLaughlin (1995) argues that there has been a growth in 'highly commodified forms of employment' where the low wage does not meet short-term maintenance costs and neither employer nor employee contributes to long-term costs of social reproduction (pension, healthcare etc.). The new inwork benefit system in the United Kingdom reinforces this subsidy effect, but involves the state as well as 'good' employers. The new national minimum wage is set at too low a level to provide for subsistence needs, so that the new inwork benefit systems are likely both to lead to long-term increased financial burdens on the state and to a situation where men and women may increasingly work alongside each other earning the same wage from the employer, but with the male worker more likely to be in receipt of top up earnings from the state. Far from deregulation leading to labour market flexibility, it has resulted in a new form of labour market rigidity resulting in high levels of subsidy from the state and new forms of segmentation.

If gender pay inequality is underpinned by income subsidies between firms, allowing low performing firms to free-ride on high-paying, high-performing firms and on the tax payer, then the reduction in the gender pay gap is an important component in attempts to improve efficiency among firms. Policies to reduce the gender pay gap thus include the targeting of rigidities in industry structure caused by cross-firm subsidies, by improving the efficient performance of high-paying firms and pushing low-paying firms out of the market (Craig *et al.*, 1982; Brosnan and Wilkinson, 1988; Deakin and Wilkinson, 1991). Also, labour market opportunities for the unemployed and inactive could be enhanced through changes in the welfare system in recognition of the rise of non-standard forms of employment and dual-earner households (Atkinson and Micklewright, 1991; McLaughlin, 1991; Grimshaw and Rubery, 1997).

The promotion of equal opportunities in access to work and equal pay can be an active component in the transformation of wages, employment and work organisation. A number of studies show that pursuit of equal pay as part of a collective bargaining agenda may act as a significant catalyst or force for wide-ranging changes (Feldberg, 1992; Gilbert and Secker, 1995; IDS, 1997). For example, moves to harmonise pay and conditions of manual and non-manual employees in UK local government were largely inspired by equal pay considerations. (IDS, 1997). This harmonisation provides an opportunity, which may or may not be grasped, to move towards more innovative forms of work organisation which breach the traditional manual/non-manual divide within local government. As an integral feature of the collective bargaining agenda, the pursuit of equal opportunities may also have positive implications for a wide range of issues around union activity and recruitment (Hege, 1997; Leisink, 1997), employment structure and work organisation (Bercusson and Dickens, 1996). In a recent study of equal opportunities and collective bargaining in Europe, it is argued that this linkage is an important lever in the modernisation of collective bargaining to facilitate union renewal and to enhance the legitimacy of joint regulation by social partners (Dickens, 1998).

> This (linkage) could take bargaining into areas of personnel policy which in many countries have not been subject to joint regulation, and will involve making links between the domestic and employment spheres, between working life, community life and domestic life … Women's different concerns and priorities provide a catalyst for challenging and enlarging definitions of collective bargaining and of union issues.
>
> (Dickens, 1998: 42)

One spin-off from the inclusion of equal opportunities as a pillar of the European employment policy could be a broadening of the employment agenda, both within national governments and among the social partners.

Conclusions

Two main arguments can be made for equal opportunities to be considered as a productive factor. Firstly, it provides an essential perspective for economic and social policymaking. Changing patterns of gender relations have been at the centre of the restructuring of the employment and social system which is leading to calls from policy-makers and economists for the modernisation and reorganisation of labour market and social welfare institutions. The equal opportunities dimension must be incorporated into the process of reform and change if the result is to be a more coherent relationship between institutional arrangements and the aspirations and behaviour of women and men.

The introduction of this perspective can be seen as productive in three different but interrelated ways: it can improve efficiency and realism in the policy-making process by forcing policy-makers to recognise that the old models of male breadwinner households and dependent wives can no longer be used as the basis for employment and social policymaking; second, it can enhance the quality of lives for both men and women, and for children; and third, it can contribute to the development of European comparative advantage by ensuring more effective development and deployment of human potential. Above all, an equal opportunities perspective should encourage a more holistic and coherent approach to policy, providing some protection against piecemeal and ad hoc responses to pressures for short-term adaptation and quick fixes. Attention to equal opportunities can not only enhance coherence but also improve the likelihood of meeting European employment objectives such as higher employment rates and lower social exclusion. A prime example of that incoherence which detracts from employment performance can be found in the apparent willingness of states to invest in the advanced education of women but their failure to provide the opportunities for women to use their talents and skills effectively in the labour market through the development of equal opportunities policies. Similarly, policies to upgrade the position of women in the labour market could provide a more effective means of solving the apparent problem of a shortage of jobs for the low skilled unemployed by releasing more of the less skilled jobs which women currently occupy.

This final example brings us to the second main argument for equal opportunities as a productive factor, that is, that it can increase flexibility and decrease individual and social risk. What we mean by flexibility here is the opposite of some common interpretations of the term; instead of flexibility interpreted as the concentration of social and economic risk on a marginalised peripheral group, we interpret flexibility here as an enhancement of the capacities and adaptability of all individuals, both men and women. One of the main ways in which equal opportunities would increase flexibility is by reducing specialisation within marriage, thereby reducing the concentration of the risk of marriage breakdown on the female partner. By enabling both men and women to share in wage work and in domestic work we enhance both the quality of lives and provide the flexibility to adapt to changes over the life cycle, in care responsibilities and in labour market opportunities. Within the labour market equal opportunities could also increase flexibility and reduce risk, by reducing gender segregation based around rigid job divisions, wage inequalities and working time differentiation. Policies to promote the erosion of these divisions involve the upgrading of the pay, training and career opportunities in women's jobs and the development of working time policies to discourage both very long and very short working hours. Such changes could provide the opportunity for new and innovative forms of work organisation, for the development of more fulfilling and rewarding careers, particularly in services, and at the same time enhance the opportunities to move from unemployment into work by expanding opportunities for both men and women to move into a wider range of jobs in the labour market. It is time that gender segregation and the gendered organisation of work is recognised to be a fundamental constraint on the development of a flexible and cohesive society.

These two arguments for equal opportunities to be regarded as a productive factor also provide the theoretical and practical underpinning for the policy of mainstreaming gender within European employment policy. Without the introduction of gender equality at the heart of the employment policy strategy, Europe will fail to make the fundamental adjustments necessary to its employment and welfare systems to bring about a new employment order compatible with the needs of both social justice and economic efficiency.

Notes

1 This chapter is based on a study undertaken in January 1999 for the Policy and Perspective Group, DV5 European Commission as part of their programme of work on social policy as a productive factor. We are grateful for the support of the EC; however, the views expressed are those of the authors alone.

References

Acker, J. (1989) *Doing Comparable Worth: Gender, Class and Pay Equity*. Philadelphia: Temple University Press.

Anker, R. (1998) *Gender and Jobs*. ILO: Geneva.

Anxo, D., Flood, L., and Rubery, J. (1999) *Household income distribution, working time patterns, tax and transfer systems: an international comparison*. Centre for European Labour Market Studies, Department of Economics, University of Göteborg, Sweden and Graue Reihe, Institut Arbeit und Technik, Gelsenkirchen, mimeographed.

Armstrong, P. (1982) 'If it's only women it doesn't matter so much,' in West, J. (ed.), *Work, Women and the Labour Market*, London: Routledge and Kegan Paul.

Atkinson, A. B. and Micklewright, J. (1991) 'Unemployment compensation and labour market transitions: a critical review,' *Journal of Economic Literature*, 29, 1679–727.

Becker, G. (1981) *A Treatise on the Family*. Cambridge, MA: Harvard University.

Beller, A. (1982) 'Occupational segregation by sex: determinants and changes.' *Journal of Human Resources*, 17(3), 371–92.

Bercusson, B. and Dickens, L. (1996) *Equal Opportunities and Collective Bargaining in Europe: Defining the Issues*, European Foundation for the Improvement of Living and Working Conditions, Luxembourg: Office for Official Publications of the European Communities.

Berghman, J. and Fouarge, D. (1998) 'Social Protection as a Productive Factor: Collecting Evidence of Trends and Cases in the EU', *European Commission Directorate-General V*, Policy and Perspective Group.

Bettio, F., Del Bono, E., and Smith, M. (1998) *Working Time Patterns in the European Union: Policies and Innovations*. A Report for the European Commission's Equal Opportunity Unit, DG-V.

Bevan, S. and Thompson, M. (1992) *Merit Pay, Performance Appraisal and Attitudes to Women's Work*. Institute of Manpower Studies, Report No. 234, for the Equal Opportunities Commission.

Blinder, Alan S. (1973) 'Wage discrimination: reduced form and structural estimates', *Journal of Human Resources*, 8, 436–55.

Blundell, R. and Reed, H. (1999) *The Employment Effects of Working Families Tax Credit*. Institute for Fiscal Studies Briefing Notes 6/99.

Blundell, R., Duncan, A., McCrae, J., and Meghir, C. (1998) 'The labour market impact of working families tax credit', Institute for Fiscal Studies Report to the Bank of England Monetary Policy Committee, December.

Blum, L. M. (1991) *Between Feminism and Labour: The Significance of the Comparable Worth Movement*. Berkeley: University of California Press.

Brannen, J. and Moss, P. (1991) *Managing Mothers: Dual Earner Households after Maternity Leave*. London: Unwin Hyman.

Brosnan, P. and Wilkinson, F. (1988) 'A national statutory minimum wage and economic efficiency', *Contributions to Political Economy*, 7, 1–48.

Bruegel, I. and Perrons, D. (1995) 'Where do the costs of unequal treatment for women fall? An analysis of the incidence of the costs of unequal pay and sex discrimination in the UK', in Humphries, J. and Rubery, J. (eds), *The Economics of Equal Opportunities*, Equal Opportunities Commission, Manchester. 155–174.

CERC (1994) *Social Welfare and Economic Activity of Women in Europe*. V/2184/94-EN, Brussels: European Commission.

Cockburn, C. (1991) *In the Way of Women: Men's Resistance to Sex Equality in Organisations*. London: Macmillan.

Collinson, D. L., Knights, D., and Collinson, M. (1990) *Managing to Discriminate*. London: Routledge.

Connell, R. W. (1987) *Gender and Power*. Cambridge: Polity Press.

Craig, C., Rubery, J., Tarling, R., and Wilkinson, F. (1982) *Labour Market Structure, Industrial Organisation and Low Pay*. Cambridge: Cambridge University Press.

Crompton, R. and Sanderson, K. (1990) *Gendered Jobs and Social Change*. London: Unwin Hyman.

Davis, H. and Joshi, H. (1995) 'Social and family security in the redress of unequal opportunities', in Humphries, J. and Rubery, J. (eds), *The Economics of Equal Opportunities*, Equal Opportunities Commission, Manchester, 203–18.

Deakin, S. and Wilkinson, F. (1991) *The Economics of Employment Rights*. The Institute of Employment Rights, London.

Dex, S. (1987) *Women's Occupational Mobility: A Lifetime Perspective*. London: Macmillan.

Dickens, L. (1994) 'The business case for women's equality: Is the carrot better than the stick?' *Employee Relations*, 16, 5–17.

Dickens, L. (1998) *Equal Opportunities and Collective Bargaining in Europe: Illuminating the Process*. European Foundation for the Improvement of Living and Working Conditions, Luxembourg: Office for Official Publications of the European Communities.

Dingledey, I. (1998) *Work, the Family and the Tax and Social Security System: The Rewards and Penalties of Various Patterns of Household Economic Activity and Working Time*. Wissenschaftzentrum Nordrhein-Westfalen, Institut Arbeit und Technik.

England, P. (1982) 'The failure of human capital to explain occupational sex segregation', *Journal of Human Resources*, 17(3), 358–70.

Fagan, C. and Rubery, J. (1996) 'The salience of the part-time divide in the European Union', *European Sociological Review*, 12(3), 227–50.

Feldberg, R. L. (1992) 'Comparable worth and nurses in the USA', in Kahn, P. and Meehan, E. (eds), *Equal Value/Comparable Worth in the UK and the USA*, London: Macmillan Press.

Ferri, E. and Smith, K. (1996) *Parenting in the 1990s*. London: Family Policy Studies Centre.

Folbre, N. (1994) *Who Pays for the Kids: Gender and the Structures of Constraint.* London: Routledge.

Gardiner, J. (1997) *Gender, Care and Economics.* London: Macmillan.

Gershuny, J., Godwin, M., and Jones, S. (1994) 'The domestic labour revolution: a process of lagged adaptation' in Anderson, M., Bechhofer, F., and Gershuny, J. (eds), *The Social and Political Economy of the Household*, Oxford: Oxford University Press.

Gilbert, K. and Secker, J. (1995) 'Generating equality? Equal pay, decentralisation and the electricity supply industry,' *British Journal of Industrial Relations*, 33(2), 191–207.

Gottschall, K. (1995) 'Geschlechterverhältnis und Arbeitsmarktsegregation' in Becker-Smith, R. and Knapp, G. A. (eds), *Das Geschlechterverhältnis als Gegenstand der Sozialwissenschaften*, Frankfurt on the Main/New York: Campus Verlag.

Gregg, P. and Wadsworth, J. (1995) 'Gender, households and access to employment,' in Humphries, J. and Rubery, J. (eds), *The Economics of Equal Opportunities*, Equal Opportunities Commission, Manchester.

Gregg, P., Johnson, P., and Reed, H. (1999) 'Entering work and the British tax and benefit system', Institute for Fiscal Studies, March.

Grimshaw, D. and Rubery, J. (1997) 'Workforce heterogeneity and unemployment benefits: the need for policy reassessment in the European Union,' *Journal of European Social Policy*, 7(4), 291–318.

Gustaffson, S. (1996) 'Tax regimes and labour market performance,' in Schmid, G., O'Reilly, J. and Schömann, K. (eds), *International Handbook of Labour Market Policy and Evaluation*, Cheltenham: Edward Elgar.

Hege, A. (1997) 'Trade unions in crisis: a European renaissance?' *Transfer*, 3(3), 498–514.

Hochschild, A. R. (1997) *The Time Bind.* New York: Metropolitan Books.

Holtermann, S. (1995) 'The costs and benefits to British employers of measures to promote equality of opportunity', in Humphries, J. and Rubery, J. (eds), *The Economics of Equal Opportunities*, Equal Opportunities Commission, Manchester 137–154.

Horrell, S., Rubery, J., and Burchell, B. (1990) 'Gender and skills,' *Work, Employment and Society*, 4(2), 189–216.

Humphries, J. (ed.) (1995) *Gender and Economics.* Cheltenham: Edward Elgar.

Humphries, J. and Rubery, J. (eds) (1995) *The Economic of Equal Opportunities*, Manchester: Equal Opportunities Commission.

IDS (1997) 'Local government "single status" deal,' *IDS Report*, Incomes Data Services 743, August.

Joshi, H. and Davies, H. (1992) 'Mothers' human capital and childcare in Britain,' *National Institute Economic Review*, November, 50–62.

Joshi, H. and Davies, H. (1993) 'Day care in Europe and mothers' foregone earnings,' *International Labour Review*, 132(6), 561–79.

Kessler-Harris, A. (1990) *A Woman's Wage: Historical Meaning and Social Consequences.* Lexington, Kentucky: The University Press of Kentucky.

Leisink, P. (1997) 'New union constituencies call for differentiated agendas and democratic participation,' *Transfer*, 3(3), 534–50.

McLaughlin, E. (1991) 'Work and welfare benefits: social security, employment and unemployment in the 1990s', *Journal of Social Policy*, 20(4), 485–508.

McLaughlin, E. (1995) 'Gender and egalitarianism in the British welfare state,' in Humphries, J. and Rubery, J. (eds), *The Economics of Equal Opportunities*, Equal Opportunities Commission, Manchester.

McRae, S. (1991) *Maternity Rights in Britain: The Experience of Women and Employers.* London: Policy Studies Institute.

Millward, N. and Woodland, S. (1995) 'Gender segregation and male/female wage differences', in Humphries, J. and Rubery, J. (eds), *The Economics of Equal Opportunities*, Equal Opportunities Commission, Manchester.

OECD (1991) *Shaping Structural Change: The Role of Women*. Paris: Report of the High Level Group of Experts.

OECD (1997a) *Employment Outlook*. Paris: OECD.

OECD (1997b) *Labour Market Policies: New Challenges – Policies for Low-Paid Workers and Unskilled Job Seekers*. Directorate for Education, Employment, Labour and Social Affairs.

OECD (1998) *The Future of Female-Dominated Occupations*. Paris: OECD.

Owen, S. (1987) 'Household production and economic efficiency: Arguments for and against domestic specialisation' *Work, Employment and Society*, 1(2), 157–78.

Paull, G., Walker, I., and Zhu, Y. (1999) 'Child support reform: some analysis of the 1999 White Paper', Institute for Fiscal Studies, October.

Phillips, A. and Taylor, B. (1980) 'Sex and skill: Notes towards a feminist economics,' *Feminist Review*, 6, 79–88.

Pollack, R. A. (1985) 'A transactions cost approach to families and households', *Journal of Economic Literature*, XXIII(2), 581–608.

Rake, K. (ed.) (2000) *Women's Incomes over the Lifetime*. Cabinet Office.

Reskin, B. F. and Roos, P. A. (1990) *Job Queues, Gender Queues: Explaining Women's Inroads into Male Occupations*. Philadelphia: Temple University Press.

Rubery, J. (1992) *Economics of Equal Value*, Equal Opportunities Commission's Research Discussion Series 3. Manchester: Equal Opportunities Commission.

Rubery, J. (1994) 'Decentralisation and individualisation: the implications for equal pay,' *Economies et Sociétés*, 18, 79–97.

Rubery, J. (1995) 'Performance-related pay and the prospects for gender pay equity,' *Journal of Management Studies*, 32(5).

Rubery, J. (1997) 'Wages and the labour market,' *British Journal of Industrial Relations*, 35(3), 337–66.

Rubery, J. and Fagan, C. (1993) *Occupational Segregation of Women and Men in the European Community*. Social Europe Supplement 3/93. Luxembourg: Office for Official Publications of the European Communities.

Rubery, J., Fagan, C., and Maier, F. (1996) 'Occupational segregation, discrimination and equal opportunity' in Schmid, G., O'Reilly, J. and Schömann, K. (eds), *International Handbook of Labour Market Policy and Evaluation*, Cheltenham: Edward Elgar.

Rubery, J., Smith, M., Fagan, C., and Grimshaw (1998) *Women and European Employment*. Routledge: London.

Rubery, J., Smith, M., and Fagan, C. (1999) *Women's Employment in Europe: Trends and prospects*. London: Routledge.

Schömann, K. and Becker, R. (1995) 'Participation in further education over the life-course: a longitudinal study of three birth cohorts in the Federal Republic of Germany,' *European Sociological Review*, 11(2), 1–22, 187–208.

Sorensen, E. (1984) 'Equal pay for comparable worth: a policy for eliminating the undervaluation of women's work,' *Journal of Economic Issues*, 18(2).

Sørensen, A. and McLanahan, S. (1987) 'Married women's economic dependency, 1940–1980', *American Journal of Sociology*, 93, 659–87.

Sullivan, O. (1996) 'Time co-ordination, the domestic division of labour and affective relations: Time use and the enjoyment of activities within couples,' *Sociology*, 30(1), 79–100.

Sullivan, O. (1997) 'Time waits for no (wo)man: An investigation of the gendered experience of domestic time', *Work, Employment and Society*, 31(2), 221–40.

Tuijnman, A. J. and Schömann, K. (1996) 'Life-long learning and skill formation,' in Schmid, G., O'Reilly, J. and Schömann, K. (eds), *International Handbook of Labour Market Policy and Evaluation*, Cheltenham: Edward Elgar.

Van Berkel, M. and Dirk De Graaf, N. (1998) 'Married women's economic dependency in the Netherlands, 1979–1991,' *British Journal of Sociology*, 49(1), 97–117.

Vermeulen, H., Dex, S., Callan, T., Dankmeyer, B., Gustafsson, S., Lausten, M., Smith, N., Schmaus, G., and Vlasblom, D. (1994) *Tax Systems and Married Women's Labour Force Participation: A Seven Country Comparison*. ESRC Research Centre on Micro-Social Change in Britain Working Paper, University of Essex, UK.

Waldfogel, J. (1993) *The Family Gap for Young Women in the US and the UK: Can Maternity Leave Make a Difference?* Kennedy School of Government, Harvard University.

Ward, C., Dale, A., and Joshi, H. (1996) 'Combining employment and child-care: An escape from dependence?' *Journal of Social Policy*, 25(2), 223–47.

14 Decent work as a development objective

Gerry Rodgers[1]

The first part of this chapter reviews current debates about labour standards and international trade. It is useful to start by revisiting these rather narrowly based debates, because one is drawn to the conclusion that a broader framework of the relationships between work, employment and development is a better guide for policy. It is argued here that decent work offers such a broader framework, and one which can capture both social and economic goals of development. To illustrate this, the chapter first reviews how development objectives have changed over time, and then discusses the concept of decent work and its value as an objective in different development situations. It treats a couple of troublesome issues in a little more detail – first, whether there are trade-offs between the quantity of employment and how decent that employment is, and second, the relevance of decent work in the informal economy. The chapter concludes by returning to the international scenario, suggesting that the goal of decent work can guide action at the global level.

Introduction

There is presently a great deal of interest in and controversy over the role that labour standards (and other social and environmental standards) should play in the international economy. This is not a new debate – it was one of the reasons for the creation of the International Labour Organization (ILO) more than eighty years ago. But it has come to the fore again in recent years.

This issue reemerged in the Uruguay Round of trade negotiations and in the creation of the World Trade Organization, and in particular in the first WTO Ministerial meeting in Singapore in 1996. The question was whether the WTO should deal with trade and labour standards. In the end that meeting reaffirmed the ILO's authority as the competent body to set and deal with these standards. The issue continues to be raised and debated, however, in one form or another, as diverse views persist. Many developing countries strongly oppose any hint of linkage between trade and labour standards, which they consider a disguised form of protectionism. Prime Minister Mahathir of Malaysia expressed this view strongly when he wrote, in 1994, that 'it is not charity but fear of competition' that causes workers and governments in industrialized countries to take an interest in working conditions in newly industrializing countries (Mahathir, 1994). The failure of the WTO meeting in Seattle to launch a new round of trade negotiations can in part be traced to the lack of agreement on this matter.

There are several different debates here, and although they are intertwined it is important to try to distinguish them. There is the question of how to create a level playing field for international trade; the means to promote human rights; and the relationship between trade and development.

First, the question of the level playing field. Underlying the international trading system is a set of rules intended to prevent countries from gaining an unfair advantage in trade. The case is often made that these rules should include certain labour and other social standards, on the argument that they affect the costs of production and so make goods produced in countries with lower standards more competitive in world markets, causing jobs to be lost and wages reduced in countries with high social standards. The phrase 'social dumping' is often used. Attention nowadays is concentrated on the 'core', enabling labour standards concerned with freedom of association and collective bargaining, with discrimination and forced labour, and with child labour, which were singled out by the World Summit on Social Development in 1995 as the social floor of the global economy. Of course, the idea of a level playing field is by no means limited to labour standards. Many developing countries argue that the cards are stacked against them in international trade because of the concentration of knowledge and infrastructure, and financial and technological capability in the North, so that an overall concept of fairness would have to deal with these inequalities as well.

The second debate is about rights. There is a strengthening global movement concerned with the promotion and protection of a wide range of human rights, among which workers' rights form an important subset. The concern with rights is a constant one in the international community, but there are periods when it receives more attention, and that has been the case over the last decade. One reason may be the end of the Cold War, as the terms of international debate have moved away from ideological confrontation. Another reason is globalization, which along with new communications technologies has led to an increased flow of information about abuses and denials of rights, which were previously hidden behind national borders. And a third reason is the increasing scope and organization of civil society, which has developed new capabilities for advocacy and protest, which can be seen in the streets from Seattle in 1999 to Nice in 2000 and Genoa in 2001. This renewed concern with rights has impinged on the debate about trade, in that trade sanctions have been seen by some as a way of promoting and advancing rights in countries which deny them. But this is a debate which follows a different logic from that of fair trade.

The third debate is about trade and development. Two points are particularly relevant here. First, access to the global economy is now generally regarded as a necessary condition for growth and development, and trade as a critical element in strategies to raise employment and incomes. Differences in labour costs are a source of comparative advantage, which contributes to export growth and economic development, and so should not be artificially reduced. Second, development policies need to handle the adverse consequences, for workers and their families, of integration in the global economy. Under globalization, open markets create opportunities, but they also create insecurities, new winners and new losers. Social and labour policies are required to handle these outcomes. These two issues are different, but they support a common conclusion, that labour (and other social) policies need to be seen as part of a coherent development strategy, in which the response to global opportunities depends on an integrated view of economic and social objectives.

To accommodate these three debates we need to take a broader approach which imposes coherence on these different goals and different perspectives. Ultimately the development agenda has to incorporate rights, as it must also build in goals of employment, income and security. In this process, trade is one of the sources of growth and employment, and its expansion depends on agreement about the level playing field, so these different elements are interconnected. They need to be integrated within a framework in which they are mutually reinforcing.

The ILO's decent work approach, which covers a critical part of the economic and social policy agenda, can play a strategic role in building such a framework.

Decent work defined

Before continuing, a brief explanation is required of this notion of decent work, where this expression comes from, and what it refers to.

When you ask people what they feel is important, what they aspire to, they talk about employment and security for themselves and their families, the ability to provide their children with education and opportunities in life, health and other care when needed, a voice in their community and their working environment, their rights at work and person respected. The expression of these goals will be different if you are an agricultural labourer in Bihar or a high-tech worker in Silicon Valley, but there is a common underlying idea, that people have aspirations which cut across and bring together these different domains. In a recent World Bank publication, *Voices of the Poor*, it is commented that 'the poor view well-being holistically'. Actually, that is not only true for the poor. People at all levels of living have broad and complex goals which they see as in an integrated way, in which work and income and security are almost always central elements. In his first report to the ILO Conference after taking office as Director General of ILO in 1999, Juan Somavia summed up this set of goals in the term 'decent work' (ILO, 1999).

In English, the word decent has quite a specific meaning. If you say, I have a decent job, a decent income, it is a positive expression – the job or income is good, it meets your expectations and those of your community, but it is not exaggerated – it falls within the reasonable aspirations of reasonable people. It's a word which does not always translate well – in other languages the concept is not exactly the same, and 'decent' may be interpreted in a particular narrow sense as the opposite of 'indecent', and given a moral connotation. But this is not the main usage in English, instead, the word is used to capture the combination of suffi-ciency and desirability.

And the word 'work' is used because it is wider than employment or a job. Work includes not only wage employment, but also self-employment and home-working. It includes the wide range of activities in the informal economy. It also extends to domestic activities like cooking and cleaning which most people regard as work. In other words, decent work doesn't refer only to, say, wage employment in large firms. It reflects a broader notion of participation in the economy and the community.

This paper develops the argument that decent work, rather than just employ-ment or income, should be a basic goal of development, and one that is equally valid in low income and high income situations.

The evolution of development objectives

In order to consider decent work as a development objective, let us first briefly review the historical context. Development objectives reflect political, cultural, social and economic perceptions, and these change over time. In the 1950s and 1960s the dominant goals of development were expressed in terms of *industrial-ization and modernization*. In dualistic economies, the growth of the modern indus-trial sector would provide the motor for development, absorbing labour supply from traditional and rural sectors.

By the 1970s, attention had turned to *employment and inequality*. It was perceived that economic growth and trickle-down alone would not suffice to overcome problems of poverty and unemployment. Employment was seen in a mainly instrumental sense: that is to say, although work was also an objective in its own right, its main purpose was to generate both production and income, as a means of distributing the benefits of development more widely. This led to the ILO's basic needs strategy, which was an attempt to reorient development towards sat-isfying the basic needs of the population as a whole through policies on both sup-ply and demand sides. Basic needs went beyond income and employment to encompass public goods and participation.

In the 1980s, faced with persistent economic crisis and structural problems of low growth in the world economy, development goals were made subordinate to *structural adjustment*. A return to growth, it was argued, depended on fiscal ortho-doxy, market reforms and investment in human capital. By 1990, the World Bank's World Development Report would make the case that such policies, com-bined with social safety-nets where needed, provided the route to poverty allevia-tion (World Bank, 1990).

But by the early 1990s, there was widespread concern about the slow pace of overall economic and social progress. The first UNDP *Human Development Report*, which was also published in 1990, reflected the concern that the true *human goals of development* were being neglected. A series of United Nations global conferences took the debate further: environment in Rio in 1992; human rights in Vienna in 1993; population and development in Cairo in 1994. The process culminated in the two major conferences of 1995, the Fourth World Conference on Women in Beijing, which moved gender equality up the priority list, and the World Summit for Social Development in Copenhagen.

These conferences were a massive mobilization of the global community, including many heads of state and other leaders from both governments and non-governmental organizations. What they had in common was that they put people back on the radar screen. These conferences declared that production, growth and development were not ends in themselves: they have to meet the needs of people, for rights and justice, for participation and equity, for environment, for social integration, for employment. Each of these conferences identified a range of concrete actions, and addressed recommendations to the leaders of the world about how social and economic goals should be addressed together. For instance, the 1995 Social Summit identified ten commitments, ranging from employment to gender equality to the critical needs of African development.

As was already mentioned, one of the more striking features of this process has been an increased emphasis on rights as intrinsic to the development agenda. The 2000 *Human Development Report* stresses the interaction between human rights and human development. 'Human development and human rights are close enough in motivation and concern to be compatible and congruous, and they are different enough in strategy and design to supplement each other fruitfully. A more integrated approach can thus bring significant rewards, and facilitate in practical ways the shared attempts to advance the dignity, well-being and freedom of individuals in general' (UNDP, 2000). There is also a growing perception that the State is only one of the actors – development is something which people do, rather than something which is done for them, and rights have to be claimed and defended – leading to much more stress on organization, participation and representation. The World Bank's 2000 *World Development Report* also goes some way down this road by identifying empowerment, along with opportunity and security, as a route to poverty reduction (World Bank, 2000).

This does not imply that a more narrowly economistic conception of development has disappeared. On the contrary, it continues to dominate perceptions and policy making in many quarters. Success still measured by economic growth, and financial goals still take precedence over social ones. Economic actors continue to be driven by economic goals. In other words, the expanding concern with human development has not yet given rise to a perspective which adequately integrates economic and social objectives.

Perhaps the person who has contributed most to bridging this divide in recent years is Amartya Sen. In his book, *Development as Freedom*, he argues for a conception of development which essentially consists of the expanding of freedoms, which embrace political, social and economic goals. Development also involves the removal of 'unfreedoms' such as poverty, lack of access to public infrastructure or the denial of civil rights. It consists essentially of the expansion of the capabilities of people to achieve goals that they value.

These freedoms, in Sen's vision, have a threefold relationship with development: first, as goals in their own right (constitutive); second, because they contribute to the achievement of other valued goals such as security or social integration (instrumental); and third, in the definition and building of consensus around social needs, values and priorities (constructive).

This interaction between freedoms and development is an important aspect of the rationale for decent work as a development goal. Decent work brings together different types of freedoms, using Sen's terminology – workers' rights, income security, employment opportunities. These are goals in their own right, but taken together they are more than the sum of the parts. Both social and economic factors are involved, and the decent work approach attempts to bring them together and to set them within a coherent framework.

The content of decent work

Let me now elaborate on the notion of decent work. As I said a moment ago, this perspective aims to capture the key aspects of work which are important for people. There are four main dimensions:

- work and employment itself
- rights at work
- security
- representation and dialogue

The first dimension concerns work itself. Almost everyone works in one way or another, although much of this work may not be adequately recognized or rewarded. There are questions of both quantity and quality. People need to have enough work, notably as a source of income. There are some 160 million people in the world today who are unemployed, according to ILO estimates. But it is not enough to have work; we also have to take into account the content of this work and the conditions under which it is performed. This may radically affect its contribution to the personal goals of the workers concerned. The employment goal is best expressed as adequate opportunities for productive and meaningful work, in decent conditions – that means we have to take into account working time and work intensity, the need for a living income, the possibilities for personal development, the opportunities to use one's capabilities. It includes formal and informal work, in the home, in the factory, in the street. It includes women and men – much work by women, especially in the home, is undervalued or invisible. Women are better educated and hold more jobs world-wide than ever before. But they are heavily over-represented in precarious jobs, and they rarely break through the so-called 'glass ceiling' separating them from top-level management and professional positions (ILO, 1997). Decent work may also mean not working too much or the possibility of retirement. Within the concept of decent work there is a broader notion of the place of work in life – so freedom from excessive work is an objective as well.

The second dimension concerns basic rights at work. These have been expressed in the ILO's core labour standards: freedom of association, freedom from discrimination, freedom from forced labour, freedom from child labour. Of course, which rights are considered to be basic has varied historically – these rights would not have received universal acceptance 100 years ago, when few women had the vote and colonial systems were built on principles of unequal treatment. But the unanimous acceptance of these rights in the 1995 Social Summit gives them global scope today. Some people argue that they do not go far enough – that there should be a basic right to a living wage, for instance, or a safe workplace. These are issues on which debate should continue, but the choice of these four domains reflects their character as basic enabling rights, which means that they provide a base on which other rights and capabilities can be built. Many other vital rights are very desirable goals, but are dependent on the availability of resources within particular systems of production and distribution.

The third dimension concerns security. Much work is insecure, either because it is irregular or temporary, because income varies, because it is physically risky or generates vulnerability to disease, or in other ways. Security is a powerful need, and it can be achieved in a variety of ways – through formal social insurance systems which provide for contingencies such as illness, unemployment or old age; through informal mechanisms of solidarity and sharing; through investment in workplace safety; and through labour market institutions and policies which protect workers against fluctuations in employment – legislation or collective agreements to discourage layoffs, for instance, or training systems which offer routes back into the labour market. The effectiveness of these systems varies widely, and ILO estimates suggest that only twenty per cent of the worlds' workers have adequate social protection.

And the fourth dimension concerns representation and dialogue. The ways in which people's voices can be heard are a crucial aspect of decent work. For workers, the classic route to representation and dialogue is through trade union organization, but if decent work is to include work beyond wage labour, it must also encompass other forms of organization, at the community level, for instance, or of the self-employed. The organization of employers is equally important. The institutional framework within which these voices are heard – the framework for collective bargaining or for local level decision-making, for instance – determines to a large extent whether common goals can be identified and agreements reached. It is through social dialogue that widespread support for the other three dimensions of decent work may be built. But as a recent ILO report on this issue shows, there remain major gaps in social dialogue around the world (ILO, 2000c).

Each of these four dimensions of decent work has its own characteristics, but they are closely interconnected. They contribute jointly to societal goals such as social integration, poverty eradication and personal fulfilment. Take social integration. It is clear that work contributes to integration, but only if it is performed under the right conditions – without discrimination, not forced, in an environment in which collective goals reflect the views of those concerned. With respect to poverty eradication, the immediate goal may be some combination of security and adequate employment, but rights and representation are needed to achieve them.

Each of the dimensions of decent work – work, rights, security and dialogue – identifies goals which are valid in their own right. But in addition, progress in any one dimension of decent work may reinforce progress in other dimensions. In some cases this is obvious – higher levels of employment contribute directly to greater security – but in many other cases the relationship is more subtle and often contested.

A couple of examples will illustrate this. The first concerns the impact of security on levels of employment. This is a complex relationship. It is sometimes said that too much security is bad for employment – that people with greater security of employment and income put less effort into their work and so are less productive, so that – indirectly – greater security reduces output and employment. But in reality the empirical evidence is mixed. High levels of security, for instance in some public sector enterprises, may make adjustment or innovation difficult, and so adversely affect economic performance. But countries such as Sweden which have maintained high levels of employment security, or countries such as the Netherlands which have maintained high levels of income security, have also performed well in terms of employment. There is no sign that legislation to increase employment security in Chile or Korea in the 1990s had adverse effects on employment. On the contrary, when the Asian financial crisis struck, it could be seen that the mechanisms for security were too weak, so that the crisis had unnecessarily large effects on unemployment, incomes and poverty. In another aspect of security, safety at work, the evidence is still clearer. Greater levels of safety contribute enormously to productivity. Most enterprises invest too little in such forms of security, partly because they only capture a part of the benefits, which are shared with workers and with society at large.

The second example concerns the contribution of freedom of association and collective bargaining to economic performance, development and – indirectly – employment. It is often argued that this relationship is negative, because collective organization increases inequality by creating insiders and outsiders, because it impedes technological change, or because it drives wages above market clearing level. This view is frequent among neoclassical economists, and has influenced the policies of the World Bank, but it is also found in more structuralist writings, for example, Singh and Zammit (2000).

However, a recent ILO paper reviewed the evidence on this issue systematically (ILO, 2000b), covering both macro-economic and enterprise level relationships. It concluded that 'freedom of association and … collective bargaining … are not a barrier to economic performance'. While there are many factors involved, dialogue and trust help to promote adherence to common goals by employers and workers, or ensure that the views of different actors are understood, or provide a stable social environment which is conducive to investment and innovation. Of course this is not always true, and adversarial relations are common. But the essential point is that under the right institutional arrangements in labour and product markets, there is a great deal of potential for synergy between the social and economic goals underlying decent work.

This is in fact a general consideration – the different dimensions of decent work are mutually reinforcing, but the institutional conditions have to be right. That is something decent work shares with other development goals. Institution-building is an essential part of a decent work strategy, as it is an essential part of development.

Decent work in different development situations

How can this concept be applied in the extremely varied levels and processes of development? Is there a uniform level of decent work, to which everyone can aspire, or does it vary in time and space? And if so, how do we decide what is decent?

There are two important points here. The first is that decent work has a floor, but no ceiling. The second is that above the floor, what is seen as decent embodies universal rights and principles, but reflects the values and possibilities of each society. In that sense it provides a moving target, a goal which evolves as the possibilities of societies also evolve, so the threshold advances with economic and social progress.

First, let us consider the floor. As mentioned above, the global community has recognized the ILO's core labour standards as the floor of the global economy. Nevertheless, the idea that these standards can benefit agricultural labourers or other poor workers in low income countries is often attacked, on the grounds that people in poverty just need income and employment, and that basic rights are not relevant. But this view is misplaced. Poverty is not just a question of income, but also of rights and capabilities. For example, in parts of India agricultural labourers are vulnerable to bonded labour; their rights to organization are widely contested; and women and girls are subject to widespread discrimination. Similar examples can be found in other countries. Where these denials can be overcome, living conditions are systematically improved. The social floor is as relevant in these situations as it is in the Fourth World of large cities of Europe and North America, where the problem may be the trafficking of migrants or the exclusion of the homeless.

What else belongs in the floor? An important value is universality – that decent work should be for everyone. All those who work have rights at work. This includes the goal of gender equality (ILO, 2000a). Some would argue against universality on the grounds of infeasibility – that rights are meaningless without the means or the agents to enforce them, and for many workers in informal or domestic environments that unfortunately describes their situation. But Sen (2000) makes a powerful case in favour of universality, regardless of whether the institutions for enforcement are in place – only if it is always an explicit aim can it ultimately be achieved.

Others argue for the inclusion of a wider range of rights in a social floor – for instance, rights such as the right to work, and the right to just and favourable remuneration, both of which are included in the Universal Declaration of Human Rights. These are issues which can be debated. They go beyond enabling rights to goals which require economic resources. Clearly what constitutes just and favourable remuneration will depend on the possibilities of each society. A case can be made that a much wider social floor should be specified, and that all should have the responsibility to help ensure that it is respected; it is an idea with strong appeal. But there is no general international agreement on the level of such a floor, and such ideas do not yet have the strong global backing that exists for the enabling rights and principles of the core labour standards.

Second, above the floor the notion of decent work provides a framework for continuous progress on the basis of common principles. It is not a strait-jacket – on the contrary, the goals depend on each society's values, priorities and possibilities, which may change over time. Not long ago, there was widespread agreement that night work for women should be prohibited – today, there is much less support for this idea, in many parts of the world, as concepts of gender equality have changed. Many of the elements of decent work, such as levels of economic security or the quality of employment, are development goals for which targets can rise with economic possibilities. In this process the ILO's standards system provides powerful support to help lock in advances on all dimensions of decent work, offering benchmarks which can guide progress, and against which progress can be measured.

Some examples can illustrate this point. What might be the goals in terms of security at work in different circumstances? For agricultural labourers in Bihar, living without reserves on casual daily employment, the priority may be protection against flood or drought, which dramatically affects the stability of income. Work is also often carried on in extremely unhealthy or unhygienic conditions, and accident rates are high. These workers are largely unorganized, and so cannot easily defend their interests. These conditions define priorities for policy, in terms of ensuring basic security and eliminating major risks.

In a middle income country, say Chile, the goals may be more specific and targeted. Export sectors – fishing, forestry, mining – face economic pressures in competitive international markets which may make safety a secondary consideration in the enterprises concerned. It is necessary to develop codes of conduct and methods of production which counter this tendency. Small firms do not have the resources or are not subject to inspections, and so create less secure jobs than large firms. A substantial minority of the population achieves adequate levels of security, but exclusion and deprivation is all the greater among those who fall outside the mainstream policy net.

At high income levels, attention may shift to stress and similar disorders. (These are present at lower income levels, prominently so in Chile, but receive less priority.) Policies may aim at reducing identifiable physical risks to insignificance, and the 'precautionary principle' may come into play, in which protection is extended to areas where there may be risks but evidence on their magnitude is lacking. Most high income societies also suffer from gaps in social security coverage or have precarious segments in their labour markets which generate intense exclusions among disadvantaged groups – illegal migrants or the illiterate, for instance – and these too may be a major policy concern.

The content of a decent work agenda, then, will vary across economic and developmental situations. These examples concern security, but examples can also be given for employment, rights or social dialogue. In each society, targets and benchmarks will be different, but the overall framework and its underlying principles will be similar. Taken together, they have the potential to offer a coherent development agenda.

The link between achieving decent work and eliminating poverty is particularly worth exploring further. The poverty threshold, like a decent work target, depends on the social and economic resources of societies, and so has a relative component. As a result the official poverty line in the United States is much higher than in India. The word 'decent', too, involves some notion of the normal standards of society. Lack of decent work therefore has something common with concepts of deprivation or exclusion, both of which are concerned with social and economic situations which do not meet social standards. The work on relative and multiple deprivation by, for instance, Peter Townsend in London, looks at why some people fail to achieve the standards – in work, in levels of living, in access to public services, in education, etc. – which correspond to the normal conditions of participation in the society concerned. This provides a rich seam of thinking which is entirely relevant to the analysis of decent work.

The issue was summed up in an ILO review of action against poverty in 1995: 'The ILO concern with social justice leads naturally to a stress on rights and standards: rights, as the basis for participation by labour in society; standards, as a means to express those rights. With respect to poverty, the prevailing philosophy can be expressed as a right to inclusion, in the sense of participation, protection, access to decent jobs and decent incomes. But the fulfilment of this right depends on economic preconditions, and to meet these preconditions it is necessary to build up the capacities of labour and of the corresponding systems of production. Thus, the achievement of rights involves the development of both economic and social capability.'

Some specific concerns

While many aspects of decent work need more analysis, two among them are particularly important in development debates: first, is there a trade-off between employment creation and how decent that employment is? And second, what is the relevance of decent work in the informal economy?

Trade-offs

One common reaction to the notion of decent work takes the form, 'in the process of development the immediate need is work and income, let us worry about how decent it is later'.

There are two points here. The first is whether the relative priority of different dimensions of decent work varies with the level of income or development. For instance, might employment be more important than security at low income levels, and security more important than employment at high income levels? The second is whether progress in one aspect of decent work may be at the cost of progress in another.

With respect to the first point, no doubt if you are starving, any work is better than none. But in reality, people have aspirations at all levels of living that are wider than that. People on the edge of starvation still demand dignity and respect. As Bruton and Fairris (1999) point out, safety, rights and other aspects of decent work are valued by workers as much at low incomes as at higher ones. No doubt the weight given to different dimensions of work will change as overall living standards rise. But it is a misconception to think that the qualitative aspects of decent work only enter the equation once a certain standard of living has been reached.

On the second aspect, in a purely theoretical sense, unless the different dimensions of decent work are perfect complements, there must at some level be a tradeoff between them. Improving conditions of work, for instance, has a cost. If that cost is not absorbed by higher productivity, there will be a negative effect on employment in a normal labour market. This is another strand of the argument that work should come first, and decent work later.

However, as we have just seen, there is evidence that progress in rights, in security, in conditions of work and in social dialogue will often have a positive impact on employment and productivity if the institutional conditions are right. Ultimately this is an empirical question, and it is one on which information is quite patchy – it is an important area for future research, because it conditions the setting of particular decent work targets, and determines policy priorities if they are to be achieved.

There is another powerful argument which is relevant here: path dependency. Unless the institutions and rules which generate decent work are built into low income environments, it becomes difficult to introduce them when incomes rise. That is the way child labour at the age of ten or twelve becomes normal, undermining any hope for those children to develop capabilities for a better life. That is the way gender discrimination or bonded labour get embedded in production systems. It is only too easy for these inequalities and deprivations to become part of everyday perceptions and patterns of behaviour. And the result is to multiply the difficulties of achieving social objectives which are built around universality and equality.

Inequality, informality and decent work

Another common argument which needs to be considered is that a focus on decent work is biased towards relatively well protected and higher income groups in the formal sector. This is a widespread criticism of formal labour standards, and of the action of trade unions and employer organizations. Singh and Zammit (2000), for instance, argue that 'the texts of these conventions [ILO Conventions 87 and 98 on freedom of association and collective bargaining] reflect the needs and institutions of advanced countries at a particular moment in time' … 'human rights defined and interpreted in terms of these two core conventions are destined only for a small part of the working population, benefitting mainly those who are already relatively privileged'.

But this is a misreading. Freedom of association is as important in the informal economy as it is in the formal, although it may take different forms. It is a basic freedom, in Sen's sense, one which also permits other freedoms to be attained. The real issue is how to extend these rights to all segments of the labour market, not to limit their application.

This problem is essentially one of agency. In the absence of formal organization, and given the relative ineffectiveness of state intervention, the extension to the informal economy of the goal of decent work cannot depend on the mechanisms of State regulation which are applied elsewhere. Ways are needed to increase capabilities and strengthen voice, to generate and transfer resources and change incentives. This may involve new forms of action by existing actors, but also requires support to new actors and new institutions. Many trade unions have recognized the challenge and are trying to extend their capabilities to informal workers, while organizations which are active among informal sector workers, such as SEWA, have demonstrated that a great deal can be achieved.

It is important to recognize that the informal 'sector', as it is often called, is not a sector in the sense of a separable economic activity. Much informal production is closely linked with the formal economy. Bidi production in parts of India is a good example. The tobacco and tendu leaf required for its production are purchased on a large scale (in the case of tendu leaf, through government auction) by a formal sector company. These inputs are distributed through intermediaries who arrange the actual bidi rolling by large numbers of homeworkers, mainly women and children. This part of the production system is highly informal. Bidis are then collected by the intermediaries, and packaged and traded by the formal enterprise. In this production process, both formal and informal elements are present, and different rules and labour conditions apply in different parts of the production system.

Bidi production is a particularly clear example, but it is not exceptional. The formal and informal economies are closely intertwined. If we think of the informal economy as a separate sector, there is a risk that we will concentrate our attention on sectoral solutions which neglect the reality of economic integration. But the resources for decent work policies in the informal economy, both financial and organizational, may be found in the formal segment of the same production system.

This argument can also be applied to employment conditions, security and other dimensions of decent work. Informal work often reflects the deliberate avoidance of social standards, especially unregistered employment in formal enterprises. But even in the informal economy, better protected employment may well pay for itself through higher productivity. A careful and progressive choice of standards can also help reduce the incentives for avoidance of regulation. New instruments to provide security in informal environments, such as micro-insurance, may also be more effective than traditional policies. In other words, the goal of decent work can guide policy choices in the informal economy too.

There are surely many groups of workers in the informal economy for whom decent work is a very distant goal. Nevertheless, the broader objective of decent work can still provide a framework which helps specify priority actions and reachable targets, and helps identify agents who can promote these goals. But it would be a mistake to underestimate the challenge. It is in the informal economy that the goal of universality faces its severest test.

Decent work as an objective of the international community at the global level

The notion of decent work, as presented here, offers an integrated approach to social and economic goals, involving the promotion of rights, employment, security and social dialogue. That is not only a national policy agenda. Many of the factors which need to be tackled lie in the international and global economy – trade, capital flows, cross-border production systems. So promoting decent work also means changing the way the global economy works, if its benefits are to reach more people. Decent work is not only a development objective at the national level, but also a guiding principle for the global economy.

Notes

1 This chapter is based on the V. V. Giri Memorial Lecture given to the 42nd Annual Meeting of the Indian Society of Labour Economics, Jabalpur, Madhya Pradesh, 10 December 2000. It is reprinted from the *Indian Journal of Labour Economics*, 44(1), Jan–March 2001, with permission, with minor changes and corrections. The author works for the International Labour Organization in Geneva. Views expressed in this chapter are personal and are not necessarily shared by the ILO.

References

Ahmad, E., Dreze, J. and Sen, A. K. (1991) *Social Security in Developing Countries*. Oxford: OUP.

Bardhan, P. (2000) 'Social justice in the global economy', ILO Social Policy Lectures, University of the Western Cape, South Africa.

Bobbio, N. (1996) *The Age of Rights*. Oxford: Policy Press.

Breman, J., Das, A. and Agarwal, R. (2000) *Down and Out: Labouring Under Global Capitalism*. Delhi: OUP.

Bruton, H. and Fairris, D. (1999) 'Work and development', *International Labour Review*, 138(1), 5–30.

Giri, V. V. [1958] (1993) Presidential lecture delivered to the 1958 founding ISLE conference', in Papola, T. S., Ghose, P. P. and Sharma, A. (eds), *Labour, Employment and Industrial Relations in India*, Delhi: B.R. Publishing Corporation.

Giri, V. V. (1969) 'National regeneration problems and prospects', Address to the Administrative Staff College of India, 6–7 December 1969.

ILO (1997) *Breaking Through the Glass Ceiling: Women in Management*. Geneva: ILO.

ILO (1998) *Chile: Crecimiento, Empleo y el Desafío de la Justicia Social*. Santiago: OIT.

ILO (1999) 'Decent work', Report of the Director General to the 1999 International Labour Conference, Geneva.

ILO (2000a) *Decent Work for Women*. Geneva: ILO.

ILO (2000b) 'Organization, bargaining and dialogue for development in a globalizing world', Working Party on the Social Dimension of Globalization, GB.279/WP/SDG/2, Geneva.

ILO (2000c) 'Your voice at work', Global report under the Follow-up to the ILO Declaration on Fundamental Principles and Rights at Work, Geneva.

Lamy, P. (2000) 'Challenges confronting the world trade system today', First annual lecture, European Foreign Affairs Review, Brussels, 8 November 2000.

Lund, C. (1998) 'Development and rights: tempering universalism and relativism', *The European Journal of Development Research*, 10(2), 1–6.

Narayan, D., Chambers, R., Shah, M. K. and Petesch, P. (2000) *Voices of the Poor: Crying Out for Change*. New York: OUP for the World Bank.

Nussbaum, M. (1999) 'Women and equality: the capabilities approach', *International Labour Review*, 138(3), 227–45.

Mahalanobis, P. C. [1959] (1993) 'Labour problems in a mixed economy' presidential address delivered to the 1959 ISLE conference', in Papola, T. S., Ghose, P. P. and Sharma, A. (eds), *Labour, Employment and Industrial Relations in India*, Delhi: B.R. Publishing Corporation.

Mahathir bin Mohamad (1994) 'Workers' rights in the developing countries', in *Visions of the Future of Social Justice*, Geneva: ILO.

Rodgers, G. (ed.) (1995) *The Poverty Agenda and the ILO: Issues for Research and Action*. Geneva: International Institute for Labour Studies.

Rodgers, G., Gore, C. and de Figueiredo J. B. (eds) (1995) *Social Exclusion: Rhetoric, Reality, Responses*. Geneva: International Institute for Labour Studies.

Sen, A. (1999) *Development as Freedom*. Oxford: Oxford University Press.

Sen, A. (2000) 'Work and rights', *International Labour Review*, 139(2), 119–28.

Singh, A. and Zammit, A. (2000) *The Global Labour Standards Controversy: Critical Issues for Developing Countries*. Geneva: The South Centre.

UNDP (2000) *Human Development Report 2000*. New York: OUP.

Weeks, J. (1999) 'Wages, employment and workers' rights in Latin America, 1970–98', *International Labour Review*, 138(2), 151–69.

World Bank (1990) *World Development Report, 1990: Poverty*. Washington, DC, New York: Oxford University Press.

World Bank (2000) *World Development Report, 2000/01: Attacking Poverty*. New York: OUP.

Index

ability to pay model 104
Adam Smith 15
Adams, W. 106
Addison, J. T. 216
advertising 52
Alberts, R. C. 51
'American exceptionalism' 110
American individualism 124
anticipated productivity gains 126
anti-discrimination policies 231
anti-union strategy 112
Appelbaum, E. 22, 26, 132
arms-length market relations 26
asset specificity 18
asymmetric power relations 47–8, 51–4;
    transformation of 53
asymmetries of information 74
Atiyah, P. S. 19
'atomistic' market 57
'atypical workers' 164
Auer, P. 132

Bachmann, R. 31, 36
bankruptcies 43
bargaining power 104–5, 109–10, 116,
    122–3, 216, 240; inequalities of 216
Baritz, L. 23, 25
barriers to entry 231
basic rights at work 268
Batt, R. 22, 26, 132
Bechmann, R. 29
Berk, G. 17
Best, M. H. 26, 32, 44
Biggs, A. 20–1
Blackburn, S. 62, 66
Black, S. 180
Blair, M. 131, 134
blue-collar workers 140
Blyton, P. 22

boundary-less work 147
boundary spanners 60, 67–70
'bounded rationality' 78
branding 52
Brosnan, P. 195
Brown, C. 132
Brown, J. S. 72
brown-outs 43
Bruton, H. 274
Burchell, B. 29, 35
buyer–customer relations 31
'buyer-driven' supply chain 49

calculative trust 64
capabilities 74, 83, 214–15, 220–1;
    economic notion 74; a kind of
    freedom 83
capitalist power; misuse of 35
capital markets 26, 230
Card, D. 201
casual workers 30
Chandler, A. D. 16, 135
childcare 248–52
client firms 68–70
Coase, R. H. 15, 76, 80, 135
Coase theorem 80
Cockburn, C. 241
co-determination 33, 168–71
cohabitation 215
collective bargaining 7, 21, 31, 86, 124,
    160–1, 171–4, 193, 195, 204, 218,
    221, 231, 256, 264, 270; rationalisation
    of 173
collective representation 74
collective trust 31
collective voice 32
Collins, D. 52
commodification of labour 43
communities of practice 60, 67, 69–72

competence trust 29
competition 40, 42, 45, 47, 49–51, 55,
  226; changing forms of 51–5;
  channelling of 49, 51; as instituted
  economic process 42, 45–51; norms and
  formal institutions of 50; price-cutting
  forms of 47; product-based 226; scales
  of 50; units of 49
competitive processes: institutionalisation
  of 45
competitive unionism 110–11, 122–3
consumption 237
contented classes 228
continual cost cutting 153
contract settlement patterns 109
'contractual' trust 29, 61, 72
'convention of trust' 87
coordinated bargaining 112
Cormier, D. 105
corporate governance 26, 130, 132, 186–7
corporate liberalism 17
corporate performance: HRM and 182
corporate restructuring 130–1, 133–4
cost cutting approach 152
cost-plus contracting 107
craft-based system 164
Craypo, C. 104, 106
'creative' work systems 6, 129, 131–2,
  137–8, 141, 144, 148, 150–1, 153
Crosby, J. 148
cultural individualism 124

Deakin, S. 16, 74, 218
decentralised participation 174
decent work 263, 265–6, 268, 271; as a
  development objective 266–8; in
  different development situations 271–3;
  framework 8
'degenerative competition' 53
de-industrialization 6, 112, 222, 227
Dei Ottati, G. 31–2
deregulated labour 230
deregulation 6, 112, 114–15, 126, 228;
  effects on industry earnings 126
deregulatory approach 1
destructive market pressures 138, 141
destructive markets 6
Dex, S. 249
dialogue 269
discrimination against pregnant workers 83
discrimination against women 163
'double shift' of employment 94
dual breadwinner households 243
dual-earner households 256

Duguid, P. 72
dynamic efficiency 137

Eaton, A. 132
economic functioning: and the working of
  labour markets 216
economic laws 1
economic man 15, 17, 22, 33–4
economic reconstruction 75
economic reduction 64
economic uncertainty 29, 138
effective minimum wage: obstacles 200
efficiency earnings 219
efficiency wage 18
Elkin, A. J. 98
embeddedness 42–4
employee involvement 140
employer ability to pay 105
employment: 'flexible' types of 185;
  legislation 213; protection 159;
  relationship 30, 87
encapsulated trust 62–5
endowments 80
equal opportunities 236–7, 241, 244–5,
  251, 256; in employment policy 236;
  policies 236, 242; as a productive
  factor 237; in wages 245
European labour markets 47
European Monetary Union (EMU) 159
European Survey on Working
  Condition 93

Fairris, D. 274
family policy 248–52
'family wage' 254
female domestic labour 217
female employment 224
female labour force 236
female manual workers 92
financial restructuring 133
firm specific skills 133
fiscal disincentives 8
fiscal trap 226
flexible work assignments 26
flexible work organizations 140
forced labour 264
formula bargaining 112–14
fragmentation of the workforce 163
freedom of association 264, 270, 275
freedom of contract 15
'free' labour market 84
friendship-based trust 64
Fulconis, F. 49
functional flexibility 140

Galbraith, J. K. 25, 227–8
Gardiner, J. 239
gender equality 271
gender pay gap 255
gender relations: changing patterns of 256
gender segregation 252–3
General Electric 147–9
'General Health Questionnaire'
   (GHQ) 92
global competition state 159
global corporations 152
'globalisation' 26, 140, 159
good faith bargaining 150
'goodwill' trust 29, 61, 72
Gottschall, K. 252
government deregulation 104, 107
Granovetter, M. 42–3
Green, F. 90
Gross, J. A. 122
Guest, D. 22

Hansen, F. 139
Hard HRM 22
Hardin, R. 61–2
Harris, L. 98
Harrison, B. 140
Harvey, M. 40
Hayek, F. 27, 76
health care benefits 114
hierarchical management 26
high performance practices 140
high wage firms 152
'hire-and-fire' flexibility 188
Hirsch, B. T. 216
Hodgson, G. 76
Hollway, W. 19–23, 25
Holtermann, S. 251
hostile takeovers 16
hourly employees 133
household wealth 139
Hoxie, R. F. 20
HRM practices 26
'humanisation of work' 85–6
human potential 241–2
human relations 23; management 2,
   18, 20–2
'human resource management' (HRM) 22
Humphries, J. 249

Ichino, A. 84
Ichino, P. 84
impact of security: on levels of
   employment 270
incentive pay schemes 26

incentive pay systems 137
income dispersion 195
income inequality 139
'incremental innovation' 164
inductive trust 64, 66
Industrial Democracy Project 22
industrial oligopoly 106–7
industrial relations 159
industrial restructuring 6, 112, 234
industry 20, 274; human factor in 20
inequality of earnings 224
inequality of income 223
inflation 139, 203
informal economy 275–6
information asymmetry 18
'information transmission systems' 77
in-market segmentation 217
'Instituted Economic Process' 3, 40–5
institutional barriers 106, 122–3
institutional capability 84–5
institutional change 3
institutional environment 4
institutional foundations 29; for
   trust 29–33
institutional framework 150–1;
   capitalist 151
institutional investors 145–52
institutionalised discrimination 216
institutional power 36
intergenerational levy system 167
inter-organisational trust 60, 67–71
intra-household bargaining 239
investment 237

Jefferys, J. B. 52
job insecurity: and pressure 92
Job Insecurity and Work Intensification
   Survey (JIWIS) 89
job intensification: distribution 91

Kanban system 71
Karasek, R. A. 93
Kaspar, W. 160
Kaufman, L. 119
Kern 163
Keynesian economics 56
Keynesianism 10
Keynesian unemployment trap 225, 231
Kiel Institute of World Economics 160
Kirzner, I. 16
Kochan, T. 132, 140
Konzelmann, S. 24
Kotthoff, H. 168
Krueger, A. 201

labor cost differentials 114
labor–management relationships 150
labour: deregulation 186; 'flexibility' 178
labour management 18, 22, 217; and
   collective bargaining 217; inter-personal
   skills in 22; policies 217; and power
   18–23
labour market 26, 75, 185–8, 206, 213–14,
   221, 223; balance of power in the 26;
   and corporate performance 185–6;
   deregulation 180, 184, 213, 222–3;
   flexibility 75, 189; imperfections 229;
   regulation in the 206; restructuring 223,
   225; state intervention in the 221
labour market exits 249
labour mobility 32
labour regulation 74
labour saving technical progress 213
Lancaster, K. J. 214
Lane, C. 29, 31
Lave, J. 70, 72
'laws of the market' 1
Lazonick, W. 137
'leap-frogging' 116
legal minimum wages 213
level playing field 264–5
Levine, D. 132
Lewis, D. 77
liberal economics 15
life-time earnings: impact of children
   on 251
Livet, P. 61
'Loi Robien' 247
Lorenz, E. 60, 68
low wage trap 226
Luhmann, N. 29
Lynch, L. 180

Maastricht restrictions: on government
   borrowing 230
management theorists 27
managerial authority 18
managerial employees 133; long-term
   employment contracts with 133
'managerial prerogative' 82
manual workers 92
Manufacturer Brand productive
   system 51, 55
manufacturing investment 223
marginal jobs 247–8
market: barriers 123; competition 3–4;
   liberalization 1, 6; and power 14–17
'market perfecting' 76
market pressures: destructive 151

market-correcting rules 74
marriage: as a social institution 239
'marriage bar' norm 83
marriage contract 240
marriage specific capital 239
Marshall, A. 15–16, 219
Marshall, T. H. 164
Marxist economics 17
Marx, K. 25
Master and Servant Laws 18
McDermott, R. 70
McGuire, P. 43
McKersie, R. B. 24
McMahon, G. V. 194
McRae, S. 249
Meade, J. E. 214
means-tested benefits 217, 230
mergers 16
Michie, J. 181
Miller, P. 21
minimum 'fair wage' 82
minimum wages 192–7, 199, 201,
   207–10; and justice 194; laws 84, 192,
   205; political economy of the 192;
   and poverty 196–8; and productive
   systems 198–200; real value of the
   207–8; realistic 199; for women 210
minimum wage legislation 218
mobility: structural barriers to 216
modern capitalism: development of 130
monopoly profits 16
'moral contracts' (*contrats moraux*) 68
Morris, G. S. 218
Mückenberger, U. 162
Murray, H. 22
mutual dependence 12, 14, 47–8, 54;
   in economics 14–26
mutual gains enterprises 140
mutual interests 11–12; and institutions
   12–13; in productive systems 11–12

National Mediation Board
   (NMB) 116
national minimum wage 255
National Union of Public Employees
   (NUPE) 205
negative externalities 16
neoclassical economics 2–3
neo-liberal macroeconomic policies 26
neo-liberal revival 10
'neo-Polanyans' 56
new competition 26
'new economy' stocks 152
new institutional economics 76

New Zealand Employment Contracts Act
   1991 160
Nissen, B. 104
'no-frills, economy flight' 115
non-gainful work 163
non-wage labour costs 213
Nordstöm, K. 99
norm-based trust 66
nuclear family 248

O'Brien, D. P. 16
Odagiri, H. 135
old age pension system 165
oligopolistic control 106
open-ended commitments 29
operational efficiency 137
'opportunism' 87
Ortega, R. 56
orthodox economists 17
Osterman, P. 132, 140
O'Sullivan, M. 137, 139
out-market undervaluation: of labour 219
out-of-market segmentation 216–17
out-of-work income 213
over-saving: cause of employment 213

Parker, H. 217
partnership (*partenariat*) 23–4, 68–9
partnership system 70–1
part-time workers: low-paid 194
path dependence 78, 86
pattern settlements 114
pay levels 254; reflection of gender
   segregation 254
pay structures 252
Penrose, E. 135
'Percentage Utilisation of Labour' 90
performance bargaining 113
personal trust 31
Persson, B. 33
Pettit, B. 66
Pettit, P. 61
Phelps, E. S. 214
'pluralistic' industrial relations 24
Polanyi, K. 41–3
policy traps 214, 228
Pollack, R. A. 239
Pollard, S. 18
poverty trap 217
power asymmetries 12, 48–9
pregnancy protection laws 84
pre-tax income inequality 214
primitive traits: essential for
   production 27

'principle of need' 165
private transfers 215, 233
privatisation 170
process innovation 184
productive efficiency 107
productive systems 4, 1–14, 136;
   coevolution 4; and creative work
   systems 136; evolution 13–14;
   restructuring 131–3
'productive systems' approach 1–3, 5, 7–9,
   40–2, 89, 130, 136
product market competition 52–3, 106
profit sharing 137; schemes 129
property rules 77
'protestant work ethics' 166
psychological contract 28
public transfers 215
purchasing agent 68

Railway Labor Act (RLA) 115
redistribution 80–1; of income 216, 220
reducing social risk 240
regulatory competition 85
Reich, M. 132
relation-specific skills 83
relative power 11–12, 14; in economics
   14–26; and institutions 12–13;
   in productive systems 11–12
relevant work force 108–9; organizing
   108–9
removal of 'unfreedoms' 267
representation 269
'residual claimants' 130, 133
resource allocations 74
resource endowments 214–16, 219–21,
   225, 227; of individuals 218
restrictive labour 213
retailing 120
Reynaud, B. 61
Richardsonian notions: of
   complementarity 48; of dissimilar
   capabilities 48
Ridderstråle, J. 99
Roe, M. 78
Rosch, P. J. 98
Rose, N. 21
Rowntree, S. 21
Rubery, J. 205, 249, 255
Ryan, W. 229

Sabel, C. 28
Sako, M. 29, 31, 61
Salais, R. 74
Schumpeter, J. 16

scientific management 18–20, 25, 34; and human relations 25; of work 18–19
Scott, R. V. 119
security 269
self-interest-based trust: in organisations 66
self-sufficiency: and power relations 220
Sen, A. 74, 82–3, 214–15
Sewell, G. 24
sex-segregated employment patterns 249
Sheehan, M. 181
shop floor participation 161, 168–9
short-run cost cutting 135
single parent households 239
skilled labour 160
Slater, R. 147
Slinger, G. 16, 21
Smith 170
Smithfield Tool 141–2
Snyder, W. 70
social citizenship 5
social deprivation trap 225
'social dumping' 264
social equity 214
social exclusion 8, 240, 245; trap 227
social insurance 164–6; system of 7, 164–7
'socially disadvantaged' groups 195
social market economy 159
sociological reduction 64
social protection 247
social relations of production 11, 136
social rights 74, 82, 85; and the market 74; as institutionalised capabilities 82–4
social security contributions 247
social uncertainty 29, 138
social welfare benefits 213
social welfare payment 197
soft HRM 22
Solow, R. 82
spatial limitation rule 106–7
Spence, M. 217
spontaneous order 78, 80–1; regulation and efficiency 78–80
Standard Contract Terms Act 31
'Standard Employment Relationship' (SER) 160, 162
Standing, G. 207
Starr, G. 192–3
state expenditure 217
'step-by-step' rule 68
stock market restructuring 131, 133
stock markets 151
Strasser, S. 52
strawberry market 57

Streeck, W. 159
stress 97; and lost productivity 97–101
'stress prevention' 98
sub-contracting practices 71
subcontractors 69–70
subsidisation of employment: by tax relief 214
Sugden, R. 80
Supermarket brand manufacturers 54
Supermarket Brand productive system 51, 55
Supiot, A. 74
supplier migration 151; program 149

takeovers 16
tax-financial basic income 167
technical relations of production 11, 136
Tedlow, R. S. 52
tertiarisation: of the economy 163
the market 76; as a spontaneous order 76
tolerance of mistakes 99
Tony Blair 24
Total Quality Management (TQM) system 24, 181
trade-offs 273–4
trade unions 204; and employers 204–5
traditional social state 159
transactions costs 4, 16, 74–7, 135; framework 239; theory 238
Trist, E. 22
trust 64; in organisations 64–7
Turnbull, P. 22
Turner, L. 132
two-earner/two-carer society 244–5
Tyson, L. 132

'underemployment' of women 253
unemployment 139
union bargaining power: in the US 104
United Steelworkers of America (USWA) 144

Vance, S. S. 119
vocational training 7, 160–2; 'dual system' of 7, 160–2
Voos, P. 132

wage depression 139
wage–effort relationship 5
wage injustice 196
wage payment systems 19
wage solidarity 32
wage substituting benefits 160
Wal-Mart 119–21, 124–6, 154

Walton, R. E. 24
Warneryd, K. 77
Warr, P. 93
Webb, B. 75
Webb, S. 75
Weber, M. 45
welfare state 5, 86, 217, 221
welfare state dependency 229
welfare systems 243
Wenger, E. 70, 72
white-collar workers 92
white-collar workforce 147
Wilkinson, B. 24
Wilkinson, F. 18, 29, 41, 74, 194–5, 198, 221, 223
Williamson, O. E. 16, 63–4, 135
women's employment 245; barriers to 245
women's employment interruptions 251

women's work 195
Wood, S. 24
work accident insurance system 167
work biography 163
worker participation 180–1
'worker stakeholders' 120
work intensification 89–92, 101
work organisation 17; and power 17–23
work practices 129
work systems 28–33, 131
Workplace Employment Relations Survey (WERS) 181
Workplace Industrial Relations Survey (WIRS3) 178
workplace pressures 96–8
work-related complaints 94
work-related illness 100
works councils system 168, 171

Also available from Routledge:

Democracy, Citizenship and the Global City
Edited by Engin F. Isin
Hb: 0415216672
Pb: 0415216680

The Market or the Public Domain
Edited by Daniel Drache
Hb: 0415254698
Pb: 0415254701

Microeconomic Policy
Solomon I. Cohen
Hb: 0415236002
Pb: 0415236010

Regulation Theory
Robert Boyer, Yves Saillard
Hb: 0415237211
Pb: 041523722X

Reclaiming Evolution
Howard J. Sherman, William M. Dugger
Hb: 0415232635
Pb: 0415232643

Information and ordering details
For price availability and ordering visit our website
www.tandf.co.uk
Alternatively our books are available from all good bookshops